SHARING THE
SAME BOWL

SHARING THE SAME BOWL

A Socioeconomic History
of Women and Class
in Accra, Ghana

Claire C. Robertson

INDIANA UNIVERSITY PRESS
Bloomington

Copy produced at the Douglas M. Goode Digital Systems Laboratory, Indiana University.

Library of Congress Cataloging in Publication Data

Robertson, Claire C., 1944-
        Sharing the Same Bowl

        Bibliography: p.
        1. Women--Ghana--Accra--Economic conditions.
2. Women--Ghana--Accra--Social conditions. 3. Women--
Ghana--Accra--Case studies. 4. Social classes--Accra--
Ghana. 5. Ga (African people) I. Title.
HQ1816.Z8A277 1983   305.4'2'09667   83-48112
ISBN 0-253-35205-3
1 2 3 4 5 88 87 86 85 84

To my mothers,
for their patience and trust

CONTENTS

TABLES

FIGURES

PLATES

ACKNOWLEDGMENTS

This study could never have been undertaken and completed without the help of many people in many parts of the world. My primary debt is, of course, to my husband, Edward Robertson, not only for his patience throughout the exigencies of the research and preparation of the manuscript, but also for taking primary responsibility for the computerization of the data. His help and support was invaluable in all stages of the work. I am also greatly indebted to Ethel Richardson for patient preparation of the final manuscript and to John Hollingsworth of the Indiana University Cartographic Laboratory for the maps and figures.

In Ghana my greatest debt is to the hundreds of cooperative survey respondents, many of whom became friends. Among them, the late Madame Rebecca Osekua Afful was outstanding as my Ghanaian mother. Her patience, humor, and cooperation widened my knowledge of Central Accra at every point; she is sorely missed. For information about Ga customs I owe my greatest debt to the Ga Maŋtsɛ, Nii Amugi II, and Mr. A. A. Amartey of the Bureau of Ghana Languages. My research assistants, Ms. Klokai Colley, Ms. Mary Bortey, and Mr. Daoud Yemoh, were indispensable, dependable, and invaluable in translating interviews or carrying out further archival searches. Mrs. Rose Danso-Nyarko, Mrs. Faustina Wereko, and Mr. Ben Alordeh provided needed support services under difficult circumstances. At the University of Ghana Drs. N. O. Addo, Victor Nyanteng, and Kwaku Nukunya, and Mrs. Phyllis Nyanteng gave superlative help and advice at various points. Dr. DeGraft-Johnson and Mr. Colecraft of the Central Bureau of Statistics were extremely helpful in making census materials available.

For their help with conceptualizing portions of the manuscript I am greatly indebted to Jan Vansina, Philip Curtin, Aidan Southall, Beverly Houghton, Dorothy D. Vellenga, Jean Robinson, Margaret Strobel, Bonnie Kettel, Ake Blomquist, and others. Lastly, without post-doctoral grants from the Social Science Research Council/American Council of Learned Societies, and the Ford Foundation, the research would not have been completed. Their support, both monetary and moral, was much appreciated.

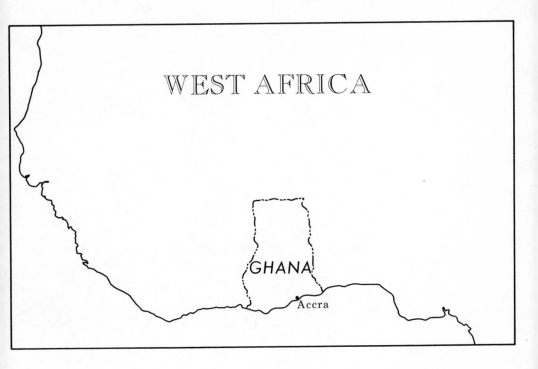

PROLOGUE

At Accra the ancient surf pounds the dusty beach. A rusting hulk, long since pillaged of valuables, lies grounded, disintegrating into the foam. The rough deep surf kills some who live by it, and eats its persistent way into the African continent. Behind the beach is an old settlement teeming with young life. Long ago people of many colors bought and sold each other here. Now more subtle forms of oppression place a heavy burden on the women, who care for the weak, the young, the old, and the childless. With scarves binding their hair, long cloths enclosing babies on their backs, and cheerful desperation, they frequent the markets and streets selling a few tomatoes or fish.

My name is Dei. I live in this house with my cousins and my grandchildren. I am about fifty-eight years old, though I cannot be sure, having not been to school. I am a widow with two grown children (one died). I grew up in this house with my mother. We sold tomatoes. She took care of me until I had to take care of her; she lived to be very old indeed. She arranged my marriage, but I grew to love my husband. He always provided for the children. I was happy compared to many people. However, he died young, leaving me to support the children, much to my grief. I did not want to remarry so that some man might give me trouble, my marriage was so pleasant. Then I had to find a more lucrative trade, so I took up selling drinks. The fact that I toiled and managed to give two children an education (and that they behaved themselves and finished school) gives me immense satisfaction. Now I cannot get the drinks and have stopped; I look to them for help. I regret very much that I did not put something by which could have yielded income now. Perhaps if I had planned carefully I could have both cared for the children and saved for the future. Of course, then I saw things differently. Now time has passed and cannot be brought back. I must be satisfied with my situation because no other possibility exists.

Like the sea, they endure as the foundation on which much depends. Unlike the sea, they seldom overcome; the obstacles are too great and embedded too deeply.

I

WOMEN AND

SOCIOECONOMIC CHANGE

Improving our analysis of women and class formation is necessary to refine our perceptions of social structures, the impact of colonialism, and the organization of African production. This study of a long-settled urban population, the Ga of Central Accra, Ghana, will explore change in women's access to the means of production through analysis of shifting socioeconomic structure in the late nineteenth and twentieth centuries. In examining changes in the organization of trade, residence, marriage, inheritance, fertility, education, and support of dependents, a pattern emerges of increased autonomy for women but decreasing power through lack of access to resources. An important determinant of the direction of these changes is Ga participation in the shift from a corporate kin to a capitalist mode of production, creating a basic change in the nature of women's subordination.

The focus of this study is the oldest neighborhood in Accra, Ussher Town in Central Accra, and the least educated people in it, the Ga women. While we will make excursions to the suburb of Kaneshie, it is in Central Accra that the issue rests. Is it becoming a ghetto of people who have few options for getting out, and few rights if they stay put?

As a coastal people living in an area which became the terminus for one of the main trade routes to the coast, the Ga experienced long and intensive contact with Europeans and other Africans. They have been fixed in the area where they are now, from the Densu River to the Chemmu lagoon and north to the Akwapim hills, for more than a thousand years.[1] Although their original capital until 1680 was inland at Ayawaso, about twenty miles northwest of Accra, they were participants in the trade in European goods well before that date, starting in the fifteenth century.[2] They have probably been urbanized to some extent from the time of Ayawaso, founded in the

---

[1]P. Ozanne, "Notes on the Early Historical Archaeology of Accra," *Transactions of the Historical Society of Ghana* VI (1962): 66; A. A. Amartey, *Omanye Aba* (Accra: Bureau of Ghana Languages, 1969), pp. 11-12, gives a Ga king list which goes back to 1483.

[2]K. B. Dickson, *A Historical Geography of Ghana* (London: Cambridge University Press, 1969), p. 68.

late sixteenth century, to the present. They are a relatively small group of
people, who formed only 2.5% of the total population of Ghana in 1960, and
they are concentrated in Accra (15% of the Ga in Ghana lived in *Central
Accra* in 1960).[3]

Because of their relatively early, intensive, and positive contact with
Europeans, it has often been assumed that they have been "westernized" to
a considerable extent. Certainly their exposure to European trade and education might lead some to expect their adoption of "western" marriage customs or language. Until the nineteenth century their contacts with Europeans were primarily economic as intermediaries in the trade with Asante.
But from the 1820s on, western education was supplied by missionaries in
constantly increasing amounts, especially for boys, so that as early as 1872
Ga men were requesting the government to provide improved and expanded
education in English.[4] Nevertheless, as most people who have studied the
Ga would agree, they are not "westernized" to any great extent.[5] In fact,
developing a model to deal with women and class formation, and change in
general among Central Accra Ga required discarding a number of concepts
which turned out to be irrelevant in this African context because they grew
out of western experience. Before discussing that model it is necessary to
clean up the debris from a number of ideas which have obscured rather than
illuminated historical processes of socioeconomic change in Africa.

Sterile Models I: Inevitable Westernization

Dichotomous models for socioeconomic change have had strong popularity with Africanist social scientists. One of the least valuable of these which,
no matter how many times it is batted down, seems always to bob up again,
is the use of the traditional-modern dichotomy to describe socioeconomic
change. It is ahistorical because change is continuous in all societies, making
it impossible to fix on one (usually apocryphal) point as "traditional" and
another as "modern" (which is the goal to be achieved). In practice, the
model chosen for "modern" is usually Euro-American, so that the term
"westernization" is used constantly, with all of its false implications that the

---

[3]M. Kilson, "Urban Tribesmen: Social Continuity and Change Among the Ga in Accra,
Ghana," Ph.D. diss. Harvard University (1966), p. 20.

[4]Ghana National Archives, Administrative Papers 1/12/3, petition from the residents of
James and Ussher Towns to the Acting Administrator of the Gold Coast, October 21, 1872.
Subsequent references to these archival papers will bear the prefixes SCT, SNA, or ADM, ac-
cording to their series.

[5]*Accra City Handbook* (Accra City Council Public Relations Section, 1977), p. 7, states:

The people of Accra have a proud and unique tradition which has bound them
together as a community. The influence of British colonial administration and
Christian missionaries had little or no effect on the traditions of the Ga people.
For, although a greater [*sic*] number of people became Christians and were
trained in mission schools yet the traditional values of African society, ways of
life and customs had been and still are, jealously preserved in the city.

rest of the world will infallibly become more western (whatever that means) in its socioeconomic forms.[6] Thus a dilemma is created wherein "modern" is impossible to achieve because Euro-American conditions keep changing, not to mention the fact that no other societies duplicate exactly the factors which determined the direction of change in western societies. A corollary of this approach identifies the "westernized" elite as the most important group to study on the assumption that where they lead others will follow as wealth increases with development.[7] But the evidence so far proves neither assumption to be valid. Not all Third World countries have profited from development; development has not in general distributed income more equally to help more people imitate the elites; and Third World elites do not necessarily copy western elites in most respects. More recently scholars have shifted their attention to studying activities more characteristic of the masses. This study falls into the latter category.

Sterile Models Ia: The informal sector and women's domestic work

Another dual division commonly used, dividing the economy into the formal and informal sectors for purposes of analysis, accomplishes much of the same thing as the traditional-modern dichotomy, with which in fact the sectors are sometimes equated. It begs the question of the direction in which a society is moving, and measures all progress on a scale where success is defined by how far the population of a country has been absorbed into capital-intensive, large-scale enterprises. Again we find the western model

---

[6]R. Clignet, *Many Wives, Many Powers* (Evanston: Northwestern University Press, 1970), pp. 281-98; J. C. Caldwell, *Population Growth and Family Change in Africa* (Canberra: Australian National University Press, 1968), p. 5; J. C. Caldwell, *The Socio-Economic Explanation of High Fertility*, Monograph No. 1, Australian National University Changing African Family Project Series (Canberra: Australian National University, 1976), p. 108; D. I. Pool, "Social Change and Interest in Family Planning in Ghana: An Exploratory Analysis," *Canadian Journal of African Studies* IV, no. 2 (1970): 207; W. J. Goode, *World Revolution and Family Patterns* (New York: Free Press of Glencoe, 1963), p. 1. The U.S. government's *Ghana Handbook* states it most succinctly, "Family life in urban areas approximates Western behavior in varying degrees, depending on the family's position between traditional and modern influence" (p. 126). Others who have launched vigorous attacks on the concepts of westernization and modernization are: L. Bossen, "Women in modernizing societies," *American Ethnologist* II, no. 4 (1975): 598; C. Oppong, "Joint Conjugal Roles and 'Extended Families': A Preliminary Note on a Mode of Classifying Conjugal Family Relationships," *Journal of Comparative Family Studies* II, no. 2 (Autumn 1971): 180; S. Mintz, "Men, Women and Trade," *Comparative Studies in Society and History* XIII (1971): 267; G. Jahoda, "Supernatural beliefs and changing cognitive structures among Ghanaian university students," *Journal of Cross-Cultural Psychology* I, no. 2 (1972): 117-18.

[7]Caldwell, *Population Growth*, pp. 41, 184.

[8]Ironically enough, Caldwell, who commits this fault in the realm of social analysis, nevertheless condemns it when committed by economists; "there is no point in carrying out an economic analysis if the researcher substitutes his own society's economic ends," *The Socio-Economic Explanation*, p. 76.

achieving prominence as the preferred goal of economic change.[8]

The definitions of the informal sector used preclude any meaningful analysis of the situation for women, in particular. For instance, women's activities are usually lumped into the informal sector, which is assumed to be characterized by underemployment, labor intensity, low productivity, and lack of capital formation.[9] One economist described it as including, "not only the spectrum of modern trade and services but to a much greater extent, the unenumerated, unorganized, marginal activities of petty trade and services . . . carried on by the underemployed at a subsistence level and thus in reality representing an extension into the urban areas of the traditional rural-subsistence economy."[10] In fact, the whole "informal sector," which often employs over 70% of the labor force in developing countries, is usually ignored in econometrics because it is thought to be unmeasurable. The resultant statistics which are used in economic planning are correspondingly weak and insignificant as measurements of performance. While recent studies have shown that enterprises included in the informal sector because of their small size are often well-organized, efficient, and profit-making,[11] there has neither been wide recognition of the need to question the derivation of the categories, nor large efforts to measure the economic input of small enterprises for inclusion in the gross national product.[12] Nor has there been much effort to study those enterprises conducted mainly by women.[13]

In fact, women's work is sometimes automatically defined as domestic labor without further examination. Engels, although he had studied the

---

[9]K. Hart, "Informal Income Opportunities and Urban Employment in Ghana," *Journal of Modern African Studies* XI, no. 1 (1973): 68-69, is one of the few to question the definitions and pose the question of how much capital may be generated in the "informal" sector, as well as what linkages exist between the sectors. W. F. Steel, *Small-Scale Employment and Production in Developing Countries, Evidence from Ghana* (New York: Praeger, 1977), p. 14, made the assumption of no capital formation in the "informal" sector, although he later questioned it (personal communication). M. P. Miracle, D. S. Miracle and L. Cohen, in "Informal Savings Mobilization in Africa," *Economic Development and Cultural Change* XXVIII, no. 4 (July 1980): 720, showed that "[unlike in] most versions of the dual economy model with its 'subsistence' sector . . . [assumed by] planners and policy makers . . ., not only is there typically a capital market in the informal sector but . . . a great diversity of institutions operate within it, with enormous intracountry and intraprovince variations being manifest in some instances. . . ."

[10]Paul Bairoch quoted in G. Schneider et al., "The Volta Region and Accra: Urbanisation, Migration and Employment in Ghana," International Labour Office Urbanisation and Employment Programme Working Paper (Geneva: 1978), p. 72.

[11]Schneider et al., "The Volta Region and Accra," p. 73; Steel, *Small-Scale Employment*; F. C. Child, "Small Scale Rural Industry in Kenya," University of California-Los Angeles, African Studies Center Occasional Paper No. 17 (1977); C. Liedholm and E. Chuta, "The Economics of Rural and Urban Small-Scale Industries in Sierra Leone," Michigan State University Department of Agricultural Economics, African Rural Economy Paper No. 14 (1976).

[12]It would be very difficult and perhaps unreliable to extrapolate from the many studies of small-scale industries, for instance, to the macro-level of a whole economy.

[13]In 1978 Liedholm found that women in Honduras, much to that government's astonishment, owned and operated 70% of the rural small-scale industries, personal communication, Feb. 1980.

terrible conditions for women workers in English factories, still committed this error.[14] Domestic labor in this context is considered to be outside of the capitalist mode and without productive value. In estimating GNP, economists generally ignore the manifestly productive non-salaried labor of women as housewives and traders, which drastically impairs their analysis.[15] Thus a woman who works eighteen hours a day trading and childrearing may be classified as underemployed (!) because there are many other women selling the same commodity.[16] We do not have enough data to make such assumptions. Nor has it been proved that labor intensity is always bad. In fact, one could probably make a good case proving that the government bureaucracy, that mainstay of the "formal" sector, is often labor-intensive.

Why then should it be assumed that the instant wages are paid surplus value and/or efficiency is created? In fact, sometimes certain work is classified as unproductive and in the "informal" sector *because* it is done by women. The use of vocabulary reflects this. Thus, women are traders; men are entrepreneurs or small businessmen.[17] Mintz noted a *Time* magazine article which exaggerated such assumptions; "while it lauded the commercial zeal of the market women of Latin America, [it] almost entirely ignored the economic and political significance of their activities and ideology, and dwelt instead on their picturesqueness and doubtful morals."[18] The absurdity of the situation becomes patent when one considers the seamstress who may work at home alone, or for another seamstress with two or three apprentices, or in a factory. Only the third alternative would be classified as highly productive because it is in the "modern" sector, according to the dual economy analysis.[19] Many development planners prefer dealing with *un*employment (instead of *under*employment) where people (mostly literate men, because those counted are usually registered at employment agencies) do nothing,

---

[14] *The Woman Question, Selections from the Writings of Marx, Engels, Lenin and Stalin* (N.Y.: International Publishers, 1951), p. 40.

[15] P. Smith, "Domestic Labour and Marx's Theory of Value," in *Feminism and Materialism*, p. 199; K. Ewusi, "Women in Occupations in Ghana," paper presented at Seminar on Women and Development, Ghana National Council on Women and Development (NCWD), Accra (Sept. 1978). Likewise, L. G. Reynolds, in *Economics: A General Introduction* (New York: Irwin, 1973), p. 676, calculated the ratio of farm workers to arable land including only men in dealing with developing countries, when we know that much agricultural labor is done by women!

[16] W. R. Armstrong and T. G. McGee, "Revolutionary change and the Third World city: A theory of urban involution," *Civilisations* XVIII, no. 3 (1968): 360.

[17] R. Reiter, "Introduction," in *Toward an Anthropology of Women*, ed. R. Reiter (N.Y.: Monthly Review Press, 1975), p. 12; S. Leith-Ross, *African Women* (New York: Praeger, 1965), p. 21. Thus, R. Genoud, *Nationalism and Economic Development in Ghana* (New York: Praeger, 1969), p. 18, "The share, as well as the type of activity of women in this sector, show that the tertiary sector in Ghana is not modern and perhaps partly parasitic. . . ."

[18] S. Mintz, "Peasant Market Places and Economic Development in Latin America," Vanderbilt University Graduate Center for Latin American Studies Occasional Paper No. 4 (July 1964), p. 6.

[19] J. Bryson, "Women and Economic Development in Cameroon," USAID report (Jan. 1979), p. 88; Reiter, "Introduction," p. 12.

since they cannot find wage-paying jobs in the "formal" sector.[20]

Another strand of thinking in the Marxist mode sees the informal sector as an unfortunate and inevitable product of capitalism. Because those who are in the informal sector are often self-employed, they are not a wage-earning proletariat in the orthodox sense of the term. Thus, some theorists prefer to ignore, or merely deplore, the existence of the informal sector because, by absorbing excess labor, they feel it inhibits the development of revolutionary class consciousness.[21] For different reasons, then, theorists and development planners of various persuasions often push capital-intensive industrialization as a necessary prerequisite for development using the faulty assumptions underlying the traditional-modern, or informal-formal labor sectors approaches. This is unfortunate, as well as unrealistic, since there is much potential in the informal sector that might be utilized to the profit of everyone in creating development from below, which would incorporate women in an ongoing regenerative process.

We can do better, but doing better requires an inclusion of considera-tion of the roles of women at the most basic level. Weeks made an excellent beginning in rethinking some of the assumptions which exclude women. He reminds us that the "indigenous, innovative, adaptive and dynamic responses" of African entrepreneurs to the growth of world trade in the eighteenth and nineteenth centuries were then stifled by colonialism, which legislated against them and in favor of European-controlled large firms. This forced the small entrepreneurs into what came to be called the "traditional" sector. Thus, belonging to the informal sector was a consequence of lack of access to state power and the absence of tariff protection.[22] He did not men-tion, however, that women as the chief entrepreneurs and laborers in many places were the main sufferers under these policies, since new forms of employment were opened up for men but usually not for women. It seems wisest, then, to follow Weeks' advice and base one's analysis on access to resources or economic power, rather than on an artificial dichotomy which, in effect, blesses the continuation of development policies which benefit the rich and penalize the poor, including most women.[23]

Doing better has therefore required rethinking our assumptions. There is no great rift between the self-employed and those who earn wages, but

---

[20]Mintz, "Peasant Market Places," p. 7; S. Schiavo-Campo and H. Singer, *Perspectives of Economic Development* (Boston: Houghton-Mifflin, 1970), pp. 50-51.

[21]R. Sandbrook and J. Arn, *The Labouring Poor and Urban Class Formation: The Case of Greater Accra,* McGill University Centre for Developing Area Studies Occasional Mono-graph Series No. 12 (1977), p. 7; Armstrong and McGee, "Revolutionary change," p. 354; T. G. McGee, *The Urbanisation Process in the Third World* (London: G. Bell and Sons Ltd., 1971), p 65; P. Bartle, "Modernization and the Decline in Women's Status: An Exam-ple from a Matrilineal Akan Community," paper presented at NCWD Seminar on Women and Development, Accra (Sept. 1978), p. 17.

[22]J. Weeks, "Employment and the Growth of Towns," in *The Population Factor in African Studies,* ed. R. P. Moss and R. J. A. Rathbone (London: University of London Press, 1975), pp. 148-52.

[23]Weeks, "Employment," p. 154; "To him who hath shall be given" is Cairncross' First Law of Development; Schiavo-Campo and Singer, *Perspectives,* p. 78.

rather many people pursue multiple occupations of both types. Consequently, there are frequent capital transfers between the supposedly separate sectors. In both people operate on the same principles, maximizing efficiency and profits where possible. In certain contexts becoming more efficient may necessitate more labor intensity. In such cases we are not talking about increasing individual productivity, but rather increasing overall productivity and profitability in the most efficient manner. When we divide up the economy for purposes of analysis, the terms primary, secondary and tertiary sectors, referring respectively to agriculture, manufacturing, and services seem most useful. No assumptions are made concerning relative efficiency of the sectors.

Similarly, the boundary between productive and reproductive labor is redrawn, using the Althusserian concept of reproduction of the relations of production. Reproduction is divided into social reproduction, reproduction of the labor force, and biological reproduction. All three functions are primarily performed by women, who socialize the children, perform necessary services for the workers, such as laundry and cooking, and bear the children. When these services are unpaid, as they usually are, they increase the surplus value of the workers' wages by subsidizing them. Such free services both allow the employers to pay their workers less, and free a greater proportion of the workers' wages for savings, investment, or discretionary spending. Women therefore provide "that portion of labor performed in commodity production which is unpaid and goes to profits for capitalist accumulation or consumption." By doing so, women add to surplus value.[24] But not all Marxist thought is of equal value.

Sterile Models II: Marxist ethnocentrism

Developing a new model for women and class formation required not only discarding some concepts but also modifying others. The most relevant theories of socioeconomic change here come out of Marxist thought, but with some modifications. Engels developed most thoroughly an effort to relate social and economic forms taking the position of women into account in *The Origin of the Family, Private Property and the State* (1891).[25] His description of the evolution of social (marital) forms and economy embodies a kind of positivism and also a great deal of ethnocentrism.

> For the period of savagery, group marriage; for barbarism, pairing marriage; for civilization, monogamy, supplemented by adultery and prostitution. Between pairing marriage and monogamy intervenes a period in the

---

[24]J. Gardiner, "Women's Domestic Labor," in *Capitalist Patriarchy and the Case for Socialist Feminism*, ed. Z. Eisenstein (N.Y.: Monthly Review Press, 1979), p. 182. An excellent discussion of these points is in Michèle Barrett, *Women's Oppression Today, Problems in Marxist Feminist Analysis* (London: Verso, 1980), pp. 16-21.

[25]*The Woman Question*, p. 40. Marx and Lenin tended to see women as victims, while Stalin saw them as faceless workers.

upper stage of barbarism when men have female slaves at their command
and polygamy is practiced.

He saw the highest stage, monogamy, as having arisen from the concentration of wealth among individuals, that is, from the development of private
property. Men's and women's work was complementary before private property existed, and therefore of equal social significance, giving women an
equal role in decisionmaking. People owned tools, which would probably be
passed on to persons of the same sex, not necessarily their own children.
This property did not fall into the category of what he saw as private property, which was only goods with *productive potential*. As the latter
developed, women's labor in the household lost social value and became
private. As a result she lost adult status as her productive and reproductive
functions came to be used for the enrichment of her male relatives or husband, who were the social producers. Hence "[i]n the family, [the husband]
is the bourgeois; the wife is the proletariat."[26] Women's consequent legal
inequality was thus connected to their lack of economic power, and "the first
condition for the liberation of the wife is to bring the whole female sex back
into public industry [which will] in turn demand the abolition of the monogamous family as the economic unit of society."[27]

The first problem with Engels' formulation is that it assumed that,
because men's and women's work was complementary, it was recognized as
being of equal value and gave women power in decisionmaking. His study of
the Iroquois understandably led him in this direction, and many studies show
a direct link between economic power and political influence. However, the
assumption is fallacious because economic value does not necessarily determine social worth. Women's necessary economic functions both inside and
outside the home have long been undervalued, partly because of the whole
concatenation of magico-religious thought which declared women to be pol-
luting agents unfit to participate in public decisions.[28] Engels' failure to
take into account the ideology concerning women's inferiority then weakens
his proposed remedy of having women work outside the home. In many
societies, as with the Ga, most women have always worked outside the home
but have still been considered by men to be inferior and consequently
blocked from having authority over men. Engels also assumed that women's
"private" labor would be for the use of a male head of household, bringing
us to the women-as-adjuncts-of-men error. Engels and others have

---

[26]F. Engels, *The Origin of the Family, Private Property and the State* (N.Y.: Pathfinder
Press, 1978), p. 81.

[27]*The Woman Question*, pp. 67, 40. In a modern restatement of this theory, Heleieth
Saffioti wrote, "This high rate of female participation in the labor force of the socialist nations is responsible for the improvement as time goes on, in women's position relative to
men's, on a world scale." "Women, Mode of Production, and Social Formations," *Latin
American Perspectives* IV, nos. 1-2 (Winter/Spring 1977): 34.

[28]J. Delaney, M. J. Lupton, E. Toth, *The Curse, A Cultural History of Menstruation*
(New York: E. P. Dutton and Co., Inc., 1976), chapter 4; Neuma Aguiar, "The Impact of
Industrialization on Women's Work Roles in Northeast Brazil," in *Sex and Class in Latin
America*, ed. J. Nash and H. Safa (New York: Praeger, 1976), pp. 120-24.

commonly assumed community of property in marriage and therefore assigned women's class position according to that of their nearest male relations, even while distinguishing the differential rewards for men's and women's labor. It is at this point, then, that we must embark on an attempt to reformulate the relationship of gender and class formation, while acknowledging that in looking at the economic functions of women, early Marxist thought pioneered a meaningful way to grasp the question.

Women and Class Formation

This study attempts to define some of the relationships between women and class formation. A number of questions need to be raised on this subject, many of which have been previously ignored because a woman's class position has been assumed to be identical to that of a male having authority over her, whether that be father, brother, or most commonly, husband. Aside from the obviously flawed assumption that there is always a male with authority over any given woman, the women-as-adjuncts-of-men error has gravely impaired consideration of women's class position, even in cases where most women are in direct economic subordination to men. In fact, discussions of class often contain not only the assumption that women have the same socioeconomic status as their husbands, but also that a western-type nuclear family is a given, and that women only determine their own status when they are unmarried.[29] In Euro-American situations this may be a valid assumption under certain circumstances--but even then it ignores male-female power relations within the situation where a woman takes her social status from that of her husband. What if, as in many cases, she has limited or no access to the economic resources of her husband and no external source of income or power? If a sizeable number of wives are in that situation we cannot say that they have the same economic status as their husbands and subsume them into the same class. They do not have the same relationship to the means of production, but a relationship mediated by that of their husbands.[30] Also, we cannot ignore the differential rewards for, and nature of, women's economic activities outside the home when determining economic status.[31]

---

[29] J. Acker, "Women and Social Stratification: A Case of Intellectual Sexism," *American Journal of Sociology* LXXVIII, no. 4 (Jan. 1973): 937; J. Gardiner, "Women in the Labour Process and Class Structure," in *Class and Class Structure*, ed. A. Hunt (London: Lawrence and Wishart, 1977), p. 162; and H. Saffioti, *Women in Class Society*, trans. M. Vale (New York: Monthly Review Press, 1978). All have excellent discussions of these points.

[30] For a discussion of western husbands' mediation of their wives' class position see Barrett, *Women's Oppression*, pp. 13-15.

[31] E. O. Wright and L. Perrone, in "Marxist Class Categories and Income Inequality," *American Sociological Review* XLII (1977): 38, took the healthy step of using gender as an independent factor in assessing American class positions and income, assuming that every individual counts equally. In their results gender rather than race was the strongest deter-

When considering other cultures automatically classifying women's socioeconomic status with that of their husbands is even less permissible without verification drawn from the society in question. We cannot assume that a social structure common to portions of the western bourgeoisie is universal. In many African societies, at least, the facts that women may own and control their own property, and that spouses are neither coresident nor practice community of property make the assumption untenable. We need, then, to consider the following set of questions concerning the relationship of women to class formation.

1. What is the relationship of gender stratification, or the subordination of women (if present), to class formation?

2. Is there some point at which gender stratification becomes class formation along gender lines?

3. What is the relationship between the sexual division of labor and the mode of production? How has this changed over time?[32]

4. How are changes in women's class position related to changes in the sexual division of labor, modes of production, and class formation in general?

I will attempt to answer these for this case, but we must also seek wider answers for these questions in order to decolonize our thinking about women and class, as well as reformulate concepts of class formation in general.

Class is defined here as referring to a group of people having the same relationship to the means of production. Such a definition should ideally include some political and ideological content.[33] The ideology of gender has been used not only to assign economic roles, but also to define political and religious roles. In this monograph, however, I will not deal with this problem since I will be chiefly concerned with economic roles, especially as they are articulated within family structures. Using the above definition, one can see that the categories of gender and class approach unity in the case of Ga and other women now in Ghana. These women can be considered as belonging to separate classes or class fractions, since their relationship to the means of production differs substantially from most men's through differential access

---

minant of pay differentials, with the biggest gap existing between white males and females. Black males were closer to white males than to either female group, with white females lowest on the scale of all four groups.

[32]I do not find it productive to assume, as Karen Sacks does in *Sisters and Wives* (Westport, Conn.: Greenwood Press, 1979), p. 73, that "Gender underlies but is not synonymous with either men's or women's relations to the means of production." Gender identity can, in fact, structure one's relationship to the means of production in some cases. The clearest one is that of Zapotec neuterized men who are brought up to be weavers/embroiderers. Anya Royce, personal communication.

[33]S. Katz, in *Marxism, Africa and Social Class: A Critique of Relevant Theories*, McGill University Centre for Developing Area Studies Occasional Monograph Series No. 14 (1980), pp. 79-80, emphasized that Marx acknowledged the determinant role of the political and ideological, as well as the economic, in creating social classes.

to resources such as land, labor, and education.[34] But this has not always been the case. The means of production themselves have changed, along with the relationship of the sexes to them. But before we can construct a model to illustrate this change, we need to consider briefly the relationship between family structure and class formation.

A number of arguments have been made in the past to deny the possibility of class formation in Africa by emphasizing the corporate solidarity of kin groups.[35] According to these arguments, which are another manifestation of the women-as-adjuncts-of-men error, class formation is impossible where family/lineage loyalties are such that economic inequalities are avoided. In fact, these arguments are used by the dominant classes to mask the reality of class formation and consolidation of privilege.[36] Jewsiewicki has put forth three analytical principles which illustrate problems with making an opposition between class and kin structures: (1) a dominant group which is consolidating itself as a class may use the ideology of kinship as a tool to arrest formation of other classes (or, I would add, their class consciousness); (2) the absence of a legal notion of private property does not prevent unequal appropriation of surplus production whose legitimation accompanies class formation; and (3) a general market in goods and services is not required for the crystallization of social inequality into class structure, although such a market is required so that social relations become monetized.[37] In any case, in the Ga example both a legal notion of private property and a general market for goods and services have existed for at least several centuries.

In fact, there is no necessary opposition between the existence of corporate kin groups and class formation. Kinship structure is used in many societies to allocate power over resources, and that structure may entail systematically depriving certain groups of resources. In precolonial Africa kinship structures often played an integral role in determining the nature and extent of slave labor exploitation, for instance. The usual underprivileged groups in corporate kin groupings were young people and women. But males more often had the opportunity as they aged to assume power over

---

[34]N. Poulantzas, in *Political Power and Social Classes*, trans. T. O'Hagan (London: New Left Books, 1973), p. 38, says that class fractions "coincide with important economic differentiations and, as such, can even take on an important role as social forces, a role relatively distinct from that of the other fractions of their class." In a review article of American women and stratification literature Acker makes a similar argument: "[t]he situation of women within the class structure is precisely their situation within the sex structure . . . the two structures are identical for women." J. Acker, "Women and Stratification: A Review of Recent Literature," *Contemporary Sociology* IX (Jan. 1980): 25-35.

[35]One of the best summaries of these arguments is in Katz, *Marxism*, chapter I.

[36]A good example is Mobutu's *authenticité* campaign in Zaïre. See F. Wilson, "Reinventing the Past and Circumscribing the Future: *Authenticité* and the Negative Image of Women's Work in Zaïre," in *Women and Work in Africa*, ed. E. Bay (Boulder, Co., 1982), pp. 153-70.

[37]B. Jewsiewicki, "Lineage Mode of Production: Social Inequalities in Equatorial Central Africa," in *Modes of Production in Africa: The Precolonial Era*, ed. D. Crummey and C. C. Stewart (Beverly Hills, Calif.: Sage Publications, 1978), p. 94.

resources, whereas women remained underprivileged whatever their age--
often permanently. Advancing age, however, normally mitigated subordination for free women. While the addition of educational opportunities helped
to undermine the authority of the elders and increase that of young men, it
did not perform the same function for many women. Neither equality or
eventual equity should be assumed when dealing with societies with strong
corporate kin groups.[38] Getting rid of the opposition between kinship structures and class formation then allows us to question the usual sharp distinction between precapitalist and capitalist social formations. Certainly in
Africa the boundaries are not distinct. This study will show, furthermore,
that residential groupings can be more important than corporate lineage
structures in determining the allocation of resources among family members.

Having established that women must be considered independently of
men in discussing class formation, we can then develop a model for women
and class formation which attempts to describe change during the late
nineteenth and twentieth centuries in Accra. The wider implications of this
model and its explanatory functions, will be left for discussion in the conclusion.

From Age to Gender: A Chronology of Changing Hierarchical Structure

It has long been accepted that a fundamental difference between
nineteenth century sub-Saharan Africa and Europe lay in the basis of wealth.
In Europe the private ownership of land constituted the basis of wealth
which was then transmuted into the private ownership of factories and other
means of production. In precolonial Africa land was mostly communally
owned and plentiful. Draught animals were not used often, and therefore
did not substitute for human labor. Control of labor consequently constituted the basis of wealth and means of production, and determined the
amount of surplus generated to create wealth. In this situation the Marxist
distinction between the private and social use of labor (only in the latter
were wages paid and therefore surplus value created) becomes tenuous
because slaves and family workers were not paid wages by their owners, but
their labor had much surplus value, freeing their mistresses and masters for
more profitable work. In the substantially monetized economy of the
nineteenth century Gold Coast, those with strong control over labor could
convert surplus labor into capital for investment in building houses or
expanding businesses.

Women in this situation were not as disadvantaged as they became
later, when the basis of wealth shifted to become privately owned land and

---

[38]Sacks, *Sisters*, pp. 194-97, is an example drawn from feminist literature rather than
that of African nationalists/socialists, where the existence of corporate kin groups in a society is presumed to further "sisterly," and therefore more egalitarian, relations of production.

businesses. This evolution was complex and involved changes in labor recruitment patterns. It was not a change from "primitive egalitarianism" to complex capitalism--rather the nature of the hierarchy changed. Three stages can be discerned from before 1860 to the present, which involved the transition from a corporate kin to a capitalist mode of production. A corporate kin mode of production is defined as the cooperation of kin in a hierarchical labor-intensive organization of production.[39] The boundaries between the stages are not fixed but permeable as one mode of production succeeds another in dominance.[40]

During the nineteenth century until about 1860, Ga labor recruitment for both men and women was primarily through two closely related, but sexually segregated, structures. In both older people had authority over people of the same sex who were junior, either by age and relationship, or by socioeconomic status, like slaves and pawns. The male structure, however, had authority over the female one. Men had more power to recruit women through patrilineal structure and ideology than women did to recruit men. For example, a woman was expected to work on her husband's farm, but not vice versa.[41] Men's and women's economic functions were separate but complementary. Two examples would be the fishing complex, where men caught and women processed and sold the fish, and the sexual division of labor in farming (men cleared, women planted, and so on). Women more often had to rely on purchased labor for help. Not only in Accra but in most of sub-Saharan Africa, most slaves were women. Whether they were legally owned by women or men, their labor was chiefly used by other women because of the sexual division of labor.[42] Sometimes the only way a woman could recruit male labor was through having male slaves or employees under her.

This labor recruitment system was not egalitarian, but contributed to a great deal of socioeconomic differentiation within Ga society. There were wealthy traders and chiefs, usually men, some skilled artisans like goldsmiths, self-employed fishermen, farmers of both sexes, women traders, many apprentices of both sexes, both related and unrelated to their masters and mistresses, and lowest on the scale, pawns and slaves, usually female. Senior men had most authority within the hierarchy, but senior women had

---

[39] I have chosen to use Sacks' term, *Sisters*, pp. 73-74, rather than that of either C. Meillassoux, *L'Esclavage en Afrique Précoloniale* (Paris: François Maspero, 1975), or P.-P. Rey, "The Lineage Mode of Production," *Critique of Anthropology* I, no. 3 (spring 1975): 27-80, whose "lineage mode of production" describes a similar phenomenon. In this case the women's kin groups involved in cooperative production were not organized according to patrifiliation, even though the Ga trace descent patrilineally.

[40] Saffioti, "Women," p. 30, "[H]istorically a mode of production is not realized in a pure form but mingled with a variety of work relations which belong to other modes of production."

[41] M. J. Field, *The Social Organisation of the Ga People* (London: Crown Agents, 1940), p. 64.

[42] C. Robertson and M. Klein, "The Role of Women in African Slave Systems," in *Women and Slavery in Africa*, ed. C. Robertson and M. Klein (Madison: University of Wisconsin Press, 1983). When the sexual division of labor broke down under slavery it was usually because men were doing women's work, rather than vice versa.

a good deal of autonomy expressed by those post-menopausal women who had some political authority in patrilineage affairs, and also complete domination over junior females. The relative autonomy of the sexes reduced the friction between them in that competition took place within the separate hierarchies, although occasionally a portion of the female hierarchy might be mobilized to assert or maintain a position against the male one. Into this category fall the various mechanisms of ridicule used by women against men to maintain or modify social norms pertaining to women, noted in various parts of Africa and present among the Ga.[43]

This hierarchical organization of labor recruitment and control prevailed in much of sub-Saharan Africa in various forms and can be offered as one explanation for the technological lag whereby neither the plow nor the wheel were adopted, even though some African societies had early contact with other societies which used them. Simply stated, the laborers, the subordinate members of the hierarchy, did not get a significantly greater share of the fruits of their labor if they increased their production, so they had little incentive (or capital) to do so.[44] Given a situation with plentiful land and scarce labor, one might suppose that the elders would wish to increase production by importing technology, just as Americans did to replace slave labor. But this solution was less attractive in a situation where the land was not private property and political power rested not only on economic status, but also on numbers of clients and followers. There was little benefit to be gained by eliminating labor intensity in this situation, either for the workers or the elders. Rather than an egalitarian "African" mode of production suggested by Coquery-Vidrovitch, then,[45] I would suggest a hierarchical corporate kin mode of production in which age played a primary role in assigning position. This organization is not exclusively African, but also has relevance for many other societies enduring long periods without technological change to raise individual productivity.

---

[43]A Cameroonian example of this phenomenon is given by Bryson, "Women," p. 26. The Aba Riots, or Igbo Women's War, was an effort by the female hierarchy to maintain its position against colonial encroachment. See also S. G. Rogers' "Anti-Colonial Protest in Africa: A Female Strategy Reconsidered," *Heresies* III, no. 1 (1980): 22-25.

[44]This explanation can also be given for feudal Europe's technological backwardness in a similar situation of contact with technological improvements. The serfs had no incentive and little capital to make innovations.

[45]C. Coquery-Vidrovitch, "The Political Economy of the African Peasantry and Modes of Production," in *The Political Economy of Contemporary Africa*, ed. P. C. W. Gutkind and I. Wallerstein (Beverly Hills, Calif.: Sage Publications, 1976), pp. 102-4. She suggested that under an "African mode of production," each family was a self-sufficient unit and the egalitarian land tenure system hindered economic progress because it forbade concentration of wealth and power, and also social differentiation into classes. However, Magubane and others have noted the unequal nature of many precolonial African societies, which were certainly not producing only for subsistence. Bernard Magubane, "The Evolution of the Class Structure in Africa," in *Political Economy*, ed. Gutkind and Wallerstein, p. 174: "The absence of private property in land, which has enamored many African socialists, did not mean that Africa prior to the incorporation into the world capitalist system was an eldorado [*sic*] of egalitarianism." He noted that class divisions expressed themselves in property relations, such as the ownership of large herds.

In the third quarter of the nineteenth century, the mode of production began to shift, but the changes affected the sexes differently. From about 1860 to 1952 there was a shift from a corporate kin to a capitalist mode of production for many Ga men, in which they played the role of wage earners working for expatriate administrators and businessmen. Their necessity for, and capabilities of, recruiting labor through the lineage system diminished greatly. Meanwhile, the female hierarchy remained the chief mechanism for women to secure labor, because women were still involved in labor-intensive activities. This divergence contributed greatly to a segregation of male and female labor. Colonialism, officially imposed in 1874, reduced the power of the male elders by stripping them of much of their political power, while the women elders turned their attention to the increased trading opportunities for middlewomen. These helped their assertion of independence from the male elders.[46]

Cross-sexual labor recruitment virtually stopped because of the different education and skills obtained by men and women, and the reduction in farming. Men were trained in vocational schools or their apprenticeship system for skilled trades such as carpentry and masonry, or at European-type schools to become clerks and petty administrators. The moving of the Colony's capital to Accra in 1877 created a higher demand for literate skills and provided employment for many Ga men. In fact, so many men were clerically trained by 1889 that there was an oversupply on the labor market in Accra with a consequent drop in wages.[47] In 1902 Governor Nathan complained that no Ga unskilled male laborers could be found so that he was forced to hire women.[48] This was but the beginning of a major shift in the mode of production, which was heightened by the increasing economic importance of cash crops, mainly farmed by men. In Accra fishing and farming lost importance, making labor intensity less common.

At the same time land was being converted to private ownership in Accra and becoming valuable. The patrilineage elders used their authority to convert their wealth from labor control to control of resources like land. But the women's authority structure was ignored by the colonialists and lost whatever political power it had had. However, it gained in economic power through expansion of the trading system. Successful traders increased their independence, but with a heightened dependence on trading for their support. Women got out of farming and production in general, in favor of

---

[46]For an analogous case see D. F. Bryceson and M. Mbilinyi, "The Changing Role of Tanzanian Women in Production: From Peasants to Proletarians," paper, 1978. "[T]he lineage relations of production, the basis of control over women in precapitalist social formations, was being destroyed by the process of capital penetration partly through the active agency of the colonial state" (p. 18).

[47]R. Szereszewski, *Structural Changes in the Economy of Ghana 1891-1911* (London: Weidenfeld and Nicolson, 1965), p. 8; C. C. Reindorf, *The History of The Gold Coast and Asante* (ca. 1890; reprint ed., Accra: Ghana Universities Press, 1966), p. 320. Girls' schools mainly concentrated on home economics type of instruction, and were far less numerous, in any case. ADM 5/3/7, Report . . . on Economic Agriculture (1889), pp. 153-54.

[48]SNA 11/1772, *Palaver Book*, pp. 100-101, interview between Gov. Nathan and Ga Maŋtsɛ Nii Tackie Tawia, April 17, 1902.

marketing. The importation of European goods made local production less important, in any case, while the increasing size of Accra made middle-women functions more vital.

The importance of women's trading during this period, and its contribution to women's autonomy can be held responsible for many of the views that "modernization" and colonialism raised the status of women. For women like these the power of the male elders to control women's lives was severely impaired. The seeds of its reduction were planted in the previous period, but also existed in the cultural institutions whereby women could act for themselves in economic transactions and possessed separate property in marriage. They also declared their independence in progressively arranging more of their own marriages. This intermediate period, which mainly coincided with that of high colonialism in the Gold Coast Colony, also saw further steps in undermining the female authority structure by weakening the autonomy of the women's trade and their power to recruit labor. Within the period a number of stages can be identified, which will be elaborated upon later.

In the third period, from about 1952 on, these weaknesses eventually came to the fore and served to at least partially reintegrate the sexes into a unitary social structure, but with a male-dominated capitalist hierarchy in charge. In this hierarchy the new knowledge gained through formal education made more difference in achieving authority than the wisdom of age. The means of production for everyone became land and physical assets. Capitalism penetrated farther through the increased influence of multinational corporations, who opened branch stores inland, thus coopting Ga women's role in long-distance trade. Political power shifted to Ghanaian men, beginning with self-rule in 1952, and being completed at independence in 1957. After the boom of the 1950s and early 1960s, trade declined along with the rest of the economy. Neo-colonialism affected it adversely; efforts to achieve socialism failed. Ghanaian men found women's economic autonomy threatening, and repressive legislation aimed at traders began in the 1960s.[49]

Success in trade came to depend on superior access to influential men rather than skills nurtured in the female apprenticeship system. The apprenticeship system itself was undermined by the women sending their daughters to school after World War II. This move to diversify their options instead helped young women to question the authority of female elders. The increasing independence of young women was manifested in their arranging their own marriages. Increasingly, women's networks bore the major share of the dependency burden; economic independence from their men was bought dearly. Capital accumulated under male control. The problem became how to gain access to that capital, but retain autonomy. Informal

---

[49]C. Obbo, in *African Women, Their Struggle for Economic Independence* (London: Zed Press, 1980), p. 48, describes an analogous situation in Uganda: "Men feared that financial independence might give their women ideas of independence in other areas, namely sexual independence."

long- or short-term liaisons with men became an approved method because women could retain autonomy over their lives. For the highly educated, formal marriage to an elite man seemed to offer security in exchange for loss of autonomy. Worst off were the poor but respectable women whose marriages and occupations lacked security, but who chose not to submit in such an overt way to the new male-dominated hierarchy. They are the focus of this study, and the ultimate victims of Ghana's absorption into the world capitalist system. Gender, rather than age, has become the primary social characteristic determining access to resources, indicating a basic change in the nature of women's subordination.

* * * * *

We have, then, three periods. In the first, the nineteenth century up until about 1860, women were subordinate but with some autonomy and authority within a corporate kin mode of production where the sexes cooperated. In the second, which coincided with colonialism, women attained increased autonomy with the expansion of trading activities accompanied by increased penetration of capitalism in rural areas. The movement out of production into distribution weakened the corporate kin mode of production, although the expansion of distributive activities masked the weakness. In the third period there was a further erosion of the corporate kin mode of production as it was undermined by the capitalist one, which was manifested in loss of autonomy and decreasing scale of businesses for the women. These periods will be analyzed here, not in chronological order, but in terms of changes in the access to resources of women in the various spheres of their lives. Beginning with an essential survey of changes in the local economy, I will then describe women's inferior access to land and their struggles to achieve autonomy through the lineage system by utilizing flexible inheritance and residence patterns. Shifts in the organization and conditions of women's trades are then considered, showing a decline in their viability and options. Their access to education and extended kin resources will subsequently be discussed in the context of residential segregation by economic status. The strength of female networks is also considered, with emphasis on the impact of formal education on the apprenticeship system and access to capital. The penultimate chapter describes some of the results and/or manifestations of class formation that can be seen in changes in the marriage system and the dependency burden. By piecing together the chronology of changes in all of these aspects a picture emerges of deprivation for women which they ironically furthered at times in attempting to shore up their position.

By delving into most aspects of these women's lives one can paint a composite picture of the socioeconomics of a segment of urban society, not only the women. While the Gold Coast/Ghana economy has experienced fluctuations during the twentieth century, more recent changes have made life especially hard for the small traders. They are in the majority and the focus of this study. Because their work is so intimately tied to economic conditions in the whole of Ghana, and because of their vital roles as bulk-breakers and suppliers of goods to outlying areas, they can be viewed as a barometer of economic change; change in their economic situation has implications for change all across the society. Damaging them will imperil the socioeconomic health of all of Ghanaian society, which fact Ghana governments persistently ignore in their anxiety to find scapegoats for economic ills. For, these women are not alone, but intimately connected to the men and to the world at large in ways that many of us would like to forget. Let them not be forgotten.

> Lo, a certain time is coming;
> When the world was created, it was not like this that the world was created
> A certain civilization is coming,
> Oshwila, a certain civilization is coming,
> Grandfather's world, it was not like this that the world was created,
> A certain civilization is coming,
> Oshwila, a certain civilization is coming.
>
> *Kple* song sung by Ga spirit mediums[50]

Methodology

Quantitative Sources--The Samples

It is permissible to study any particular segment of a society as long as the researcher builds into the results a consideration of the possible biases involved. If all researchers were precise in describing their methodology, it would be evident that some studies present the men's reality as being the group's reality by interviewing men only. Sometimes the separation of men's and women's spheres in a society means that the sex of the researcher determines those who can be most fruitfully interviewed. The Ga are such a case. In some cases the fact that researchers were males who partook of narrow ideas about women's proper functions made male bias inevitable.[51] With the Ga I am particularly fortunate to have available ethnographic data collected primarily by women, such as Field, Kilson, and Azu. This does not mean, however, that I am now justified in imposing female bias. Rather, we should all strive for a balancing of interests wherein sex is an important *stated*

---

[50]M. Kilson, *Kpele Lala* (Cambridge: Harvard University Press, 1971), p. 133.

[51]Reiter, "Introduction," p. 12. In studying Nigerian women, Leith-Ross, *African Women*, p. 21, commented,

Even with the highest degree of trained discernment, it is difficult for a male investigator to get an accurate impression of what goes on in a woman's mind when it is revealed to him by another man; and with all possible goodwill, it is difficult for that man not to be biased by tradition, vanity, or self-importance. He will probably, and often unconsciously, make out that the woman is of little account, that her whole life is in his hands, that she has no will, no means, no property, no power, nor organization nor means of redress. . . .

variable.

While my original goal was to study women, I did not confine my surveys to women only. The conditions under which I was interviewing, however, made that bias stronger. In 1971-72 I interviewed in Central Accra daily in the mornings from about 8 A.M. to 1 P.M.; in 1977-78 I worked in both Kaneshie and Central Accra daily from about 8:30 A.M. to 4:30 P.M. Only occasionally when required by an informant would I interview at night. A result of this practice was a bias toward interviewing women, who were far more likely to work in the home.[52] The men were at offices or businesses in many cases. Thus, in the original large survey of 1971-72, out of 252 senior persons in compounds, 238 were women. The men included were often retired. Likewise, in 1977-78 in Kaneshie, while the proportion was not as striking because of the different nature of the population, more women than men were interviewed, and also in Central Accra among retired persons. However, in 1978 with the schoolgirls, market girls, market women, and women in their forties, the purposes of the surveys excluded men. Let us consider more specifically, then, the data base for this study.

During sixteen months in 1971-72 and six months in 1977-78 I devoted approximately three-quarters of my time to conducting a total of nine small surveys. In 1971-72 my research assistant and I began by conducting a preliminary survey of approximately 250 compounds in one part of Ussher Town. Figure I-1 gives the locale surveyed in both 1971-72 and 1977-78. In the original survey information was gathered from one person in the compound--usually the head--concerning occupation and residence, and those of their spouse(s), children, parents, grandparents, and great-grandparents. The person's education and voluntary association membership were recorded, as well as the relationship of the other adults living in the compound to the respondent. A diagram of the compound was made. The method employed in selecting compounds was to go into each compound along a street or alley within a block and ask to speak to the head. If no one was there or the person was uncooperative we proceeded to the next compound. A few compounds inhabited only by non-Ga were also omitted, thus assuring only the inclusion of long-urbanized people. The 1971-72 survey yielded direct or indirect information from 252 heads, or younger volunteers, concerning some 2,900 persons. These results, as well as those from subsequent surveys, were computerized.

After completing the original survey, I selected from that sample a smaller group of women ranging in age from thirty-eight to ninety-eight to be intensively interviewed. The criteria for selection included length of residence in Accra, whether or not the informant followed the same trade as her mother and grandmother did, and intelligence and cooperativeness of the informant. I tried to obtain an equal number of informants in each age group, and a fairly wide distribution of occupations. In the end, seventy-two women were interviewed in a survey covering work, marital, and residential histories. I attempted here not only to gather vital statistics, but also to get

---

[52]However, there are more women than men in Central Accra.

Figure I-I Ussher Town — Locale of Surveys

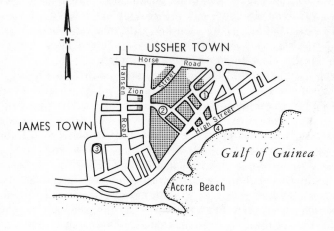

▨ Area of surveys

① Salaga Market

② Bukom Square

③ James Town I Middle School

④ Ussher Fort

an idea about women's attitudes concerning the topics under discussion. The information was usually gleaned from an individual in two to four interviews lasting an hour each on successive days. If there were any glaring contradictions or omissions we visited the person again later to rectify the problem. The interviews were conducted in Ga, my research assistant translating when necessary. As a cross check the recordings of the interviews were translated by other assistants and the translations compared with my notes. Although a set group of questions on each topic was asked each individual in order to get comparable information, digressions were encouraged and yielded much valuable information. The final procedure with this group of women was the choice of eight of the best ones in terms of cooperativeness and quality of memory to be further interviewed. These eight women were asked to tell us the stories of their lives in their own terms. In order to give a more vivid impression of the quality of the lives of these women I have included four of these life histories as portraits here. Quotations from life history and survey informants are in italics in the body of this work. I have also used symbols drawn from linguistics to indicate Ga pronunciation: ɔ is pronounced "aw," ʃ indicates "sh," η is approximately equivalent to "ng" and ε is a short "e."

These surveys yielded diachronic information, not only from the women's own accounts of the past, but also from comparing age cohorts within the survey to see if changing work, residential, or marital patterns could be discerned. If the sample size of a cohort was small (under 20), I usually took the combined results of several cohorts. Although the choice of subjects in the smaller survey (number = 72) was nonrandom in the statistical sense, the information still has some validity on several grounds. I cannot say that the data absolutely prove anything statistically, but on the grounds of internal consistency, confirmation by knowledge gained independently of the surveys, and occasionally, intuition, there are some results which are too strong to ignore.

The surveys conducted in 1977-78 have more statistical validity. From information gained in 1971-72, I decided to use the survey method to examine further three main aspects: (1) the economic and social relationships between Ga inhabitants of Kaneshie and Central Accra; (2) the impact of formal education on informal education, in this case, the market girls' apprenticeship system; and (3) marital and fertility patterns among Central Accra women in their forties. This last survey added another younger age cohort for purposes of comparison to the small 1971-72 survey.

Accordingly, I began by surveying every other house in three different sections of Kaneshie: Old Kaneshie, the area built by the colonial government to house earthquake victims in 1940; another housing estate built by the Ghana government around 1960 named Awudome Estates, plus a portion of the adjoining Kaneshie Estates; and New Kaneshie, an area in North Kaneshie of mixed estate and owner-constructed houses dating from the 1970s. Figure I-2 gives the locale of the original survey. We administered 280 short questionnaires concerning ethnicity, occupation, houseownership, and residential grouping, approximately two-thirds in English and the rest in

Figure I-2 Kaneshie — locale of surveys

Ga. When a Ga resident was interviewed a further section was included concerning origins, residential history, and the residence, age, education, and occupations of ancestors, siblings, and offspring. From among the 67 Ga respondents with Central Accra origins 45 households were chosen, on the basis of willingness to cooperate, for further interviewing about their social and financial connections with Central Accra. The original intention was to have a larger sample, but we had overestimated the proportion of Ga in Kaneshie, and time did not allow further short surveying to recruit more people. This was, incidentally, the only time a problem was encountered in recruiting informants in either 1971-72 or 1977-78. The long questionnaire was time-consuming and some people did not want to be bothered, understandably enough.

The rest of the 1977-78 survey work was done in Central Accra. To supplement the data on economic dependency and fertility, I conducted two surveys, one of 101 older Ga retired persons of both sexes and one of 101 Ga women in their forties. The retired people were selected randomly, one from every other compound in the same area covered in 1971-72. As a result, four or five of the people from the 1971-72 large survey were again interviewed, but this time asked in detail about their sources of support. The women in their forties, selected randomly in the same manner, were asked about fertility, contraception, marital history, and financial support. There was no overlap in personnel from 1971-72 in that survey.

The other Central Accra surveys were mainly aimed at testing the impact of formal education on the informal market apprenticeship system. This posed a problem, since there was no way in a synchronic study of testing, for instance, the comparative success in business of girls who had gone through the two systems, which I soon discovered were not mutually exclusive in any case. I decided to test the marketing knowledge of market and schoolgirls, using a sample of market women as a control. The sample size for each group was 40 to 42. The schoolgirls were drawn from Form 1 classes (approximately equivalent to seventh grade in American schools) at two James Town public middle schools; they ranged in age from 12 to 16. The middle schools were chosen because they mostly serve Central Accra and are probably typical of their sort. The market girls were chosen and interviewed in and around the immediate vicinity of Salaga Market. The girls were asked about trading experience and knowledge, family background, and contraception. The Salaga Market women were asked about trading experience and knowledge only. Every third trader inside and outside the market was interviewed in Ga, with my research assistant translating when necessary. The level of cooperation in all three surveys was quite good, especially since it took approximately an hour to interview one respondent.

To facilitate cooperation in the Central Accra surveys which occupied more than half an hour of the respondent's time, a small gratuity was given upon completion of the interviewing. The amount was calculated to make them feel that they were not being exploited for their good nature, but also to depress a desire to do it solely for profit. This was also done in Old

Kaneshie when appropriate with people in the small sample. In wealthier households, however, this offer would have been insulting and was not made.

Qualitative Sources

Using participant observation, oral, and written materials I attempted to develop an appreciation of the ambience and history of the two areas, Central Accra, in particular. The oral sources were quite varied: spirit mediums, social workers, a judge, elders and chiefs, taxi drivers, and government officers of various sorts. Among them Nii Amugi II, the present titular head of the Ga, or Ga Maŋtsɛ, A. A. Amartey, head of the Ga section of the Ghana Bureau of Languages, S. K. Afful of the Central Revenue Department, Alhaji Mohamed Makwei Laryea, and N. A. Ammah were most informative. The written sources included travelers' accounts, anthropologists, Ga writings, novels, and archival and court records. Among the anthropologists the works of Field, Kilson, Azu (Mills-Odoi), and Pogucki gave a more than adequate background on social organization and religion. Travelers' accounts are extensive, going back at least to Pieter de Marees in the sixteenth century. Among the works written by first-language Ga speakers are the oral traditions recorded by the Reverend Carl Reindorf in the late nineteenth century, which are invaluable. Numerous lawyers have written on Ga property and inheritance customs, among them A. B. Quartey-Papafio and Nii Amaa Ollennu. Quartey-Papafio, Bruce-Myers, and A. A. Amartey have published studies of Ga social customs and organization.

The National Archives of Ghana proved an excellent quarry for information of all sorts. Accra is especially well documented in archival materials and censuses. The Colonial Reports published by the British Colonial Office paid particular attention to conditions in its administrative capital. Unfortunately for my purposes, the Accra District Court Records yielded much less information than was hoped, because the Ga were not in the habit of taking domestic cases to court. They rather settled them at home or in the local chief's court. Also, the information given in many cases was not sufficient to be of any value. The incompleteness of the records for some years prevented their being of any statistical use. Because of time limitations, I examined most years from 1875 to 1900, and only one out of every five years thereafter (1905, 1910, etc.). I also was able to use some Ga court records in the possession of Nii Amugi II. The Ga Maŋtsɛ's records were extremely valuable but too limited in chronological scope to be of any statistical use in showing change over time, since only a series from the 1920s and early 1930s was available.

Quantitative Versus Qualitative Data--Bias

In this study the problem of the proper relationship between quantitative and qualitative data kept cropping up. As a historian I have a bias toward giving priority to qualitative data, but my training in anthropology, sociology, demography, and economics would not permit satisfaction with only qualitative evidence. Thus, I made a pragmatic compromise, using more conventional historical data for the oldest background, and more survey data for the current situation. In many cases there were both kinds of data--from statistical comparison of age cohorts and observations by other sources. I generally discounted 1971-72 statistical indicators not supported by other evidence. Conversely, if there was no statistical evidence for a quantifiable phenomenon mentioned in other sources, I discounted it. Inevitably, many grey areas remained, which were most aptly filled by material from oral interviews with selected informants. When oral information contrasted with survey results, I rechecked both and then attempted to find a coherent explanation for the discrepancy if it still stood. In fact, sometimes the contradictions were most illuminating in showing the distance between socioeconomic theory and practice. It was then fruitful to ask appropriate informants for an explanation for a discrepancy. If none could be found, I filed the quantitative data under subjects for further thought.

Another bias I began with I was forced to change. Before starting the fieldwork I was not particularly interested in economics, causal or otherwise. But by the time I had tried an initial pre-survey in 1971-72, the overweening importance of trading activities in pervading every aspect of the women's lives made a consideration of economics imperative. And when the time came to analyze the data in depth, the most cogent explanations often were economic ones. I started out to work with women; I ended by working with traders.[53]

---

[53]*Every* woman in the initial large survey had traded at some time in her life.

II

THE HISTORICAL CONTEXT:

ACCRA AND ECONOMIC CHANGE

Accra Until the Twentieth Century

The oldest area of settlement in Accra is Ussher Town, also called Asere. At its center is Bukom Square, a large dusty bare spot surrounded by houses which sprawl in many directions. Some have two stories, but most are one-story affairs composed of an original house which might have been swish (baked mud and sand), or rebuilt in cinder block, with numerous additions made at various times out of various materials. Most houses surround a courtyard, the whole complex being called a compound. The area is redolent of the many activities, such as fishsmoking and cooking, carried on by women in the courtyards of the compounds. Salaga Market, the main market serving the area, is two blocks down the street.[1]

In 1845 Horatio Bridge, an American ship captain and friend of Nathaniel Hawthorne, visited Accra and wrote, "My impressions of Accra are more favorable than of any other place which I have yet seen in Africa." He then went on to describe the generally open aspect of the savanna area around it, with the forest (the Akwapim scarp) in the distance to the north above the plains. The wealth of the town caused him to say, "Accra is the land of plenty in Africa. Beef, mutton, turkeys and chickens abound; and its supply of European necessaries and luxuries is unequalled." His host, James Bannerman, conducted a trade with the interior which brought people two or three hundred miles to see him.[2] Bridge found, then, a cosmopolitan place whose origins must be sought earlier, for by the nineteenth century Accra had a population of between ten and twenty thousand, and extensive interior

---

[1]This market was named after the famous market at Salaga in the interior, where many northern traders came to carry on their business.

[2]H. Bridge *Journal of an African Cruiser* (1845; reprint ed., London: Dawsons of Pall Mall, 1968), pp. 141-42.

and exterior connections.[3] In fact, Accra at that point was already of considerable antiquity.

Accra developed not from one center, but from a series of contiguous settlements formed at different times beginning in the fifteenth century by different peoples. Now the original settlements have grown into a continuous whole, but they preserve in their customs traces of their different origins. Asere, Abola and Gbese are supposed to be the oldest and most Ga of the quarters. Otublohum was originally settled by Akwamu and Denkyera. These four together make up what is called Ussher Town, the area the Dutch claimed as their jurisdiction in the seventeenth century. The other three quarters, Alata or Ŋlɛʃi, Sempe, and Akaŋmadze are supposed to be of more recent origin. Alata was settled by Nigerian workers imported to build a European fort. The last three are commonly referred to as James Town, which was the area of British jurisdiction in Accra. Of these quarters, Asere is by far the largest in population and area and the locus of much of this study. All seven make up what is now known as Central Accra,[4] and all have chiefs called maŋtsɛ mei (plural of maŋtsɛ, literally "father of the country or area").

The growth of Accra was stimulated by the arrival of the Europeans. The Portuguese built a small fort at Accra in 1482. In the seventeenth century the English, Dutch, Swedes and Danes followed suit and established their spheres of interest.[5] The internal situation on the Gold Coast also contributed strongly to its development. In 1677 the Akwamu destroyed "Great Accra" or Ayawaso, and in 1680 "Little Accra" or Ussher Town. This dealt a severe blow to what Barbot had described as a "pretty handsome and commodious market town well govern'd and much resorted to." By 1700, however, it seems to have recovered and even expanded with the addition of the refugees from Ayawaso. From that time on it became the capital of the Ga state, whose organization was much influenced by the Akwamu and the Fanti.[6] After being tributary to the Akwamu until 1730, it was independent, except for a brief subjection to the Asante state at the beginning of the nineteenth century, until the British declared the Gold Coast a Crown Colony in 1874. Before that the British had exercised considerable influence by establishing informal protectorates on the Gold Coast, first by the Company of Merchants Trading to Africa, and then by the Crown. In Accra their influence was moderated by competition with the Dutch, who, however,

---

[3]H. Debrunner, "The Church of Christ at Accra before 1917," MS in Basel Mission Papers, Ghana National Archives, EC 7/19 (n.d.), p. 7. M. Johnson, "Census, Map and Guesstimates," in *African Historical Demography* (Edinburgh: Centre of African Studies, 1977), pp. 282-83, has done the most thorough historical estimates of Accra's population.

[4]K. B. Dickson, *A Historical Geography of Ghana* (London: Cambridge University Press, 1969), p. 50; M. Manoukian, *Akan and Ga-Adangme Peoples*, ed. D. Forde, Ethnographic Survey of Africa, West Africa, Part I (London: International African Institute, 1950), p. 67; F. E. K. Amoah, "Accra: A Study of the Development of a West African City," M.S. thesis, Institute of African Studies, University of Ghana (1964), p. 19.

[5]Dickson, *Historical Geography*, p. 45; Amoah, "Accra," p. 16.

[6]Dickson, *Historical Geography*, pp. 50, 68; K. Y. Daaku, *Trade and Politics on the Gold*

sold their fort at Accra to the British in 1868. In 1877 the British transferred the administrative headquarters of the Gold Coast from Cape Coast to Accra.

By the beginning of the twentieth century, then, the Ga had been under official British rule for about thirty years, with a much longer period preceding that of strong interference by Europeans in local affairs. So reduced was the political power of the Ga in the 1870s that at one point the Ga Maŋtsε was sent into exile for being refractory. Mary Kingsley summed up the position of the Ga Maŋtsε acutely in 1877.

> Tackie is a spare old man, with a subdued manner. His sovereign rights are acknowledged by the government so far as to hold him more or less responsible for any iniquity committed by his people; and as the government do not allow him to execute or flagellate the said people, earthly pomp is rather a hollow thing to Tackie.[7]

Because of their position economically and politically, the Ga had strong contacts with many other peoples over a long period of time. This resulted in much intermarriage, especially in Accra, where for a long time the Ga were thought to be matrilineal by the colonial authorities because there were so many Fanti lineages from further west along the coast. *There is no such thing as a pure Ga*, I was told repeatedly. Some prominent Ga lineages started out as no such thing. The Bannerman family, for instance, was founded by a Scots father and an Asante mother in the early nineteenth century.[8] Also, in the process of lateral migration along the West African coast, some families of Brazilian, Sierra Leonean, and Nigerian origins settled in Accra and became Ga. Entering the twentieth century, then, we find a people who had already been exposed to strong European influence in politics and who were open to outside influences within West Africa, having intermarried for generations with other peoples. They also, however, maintained a strong and distinct cultural identity and language.

Economic History of Accra Until the Twentieth Century

Beginning very early, the coastal area in which Accra is situated was a center of trade and agriculture. Before the arrival of the Portuguese late in the fifteenth century, Accra was probably participating in a lateral coastal trade.[9] The coastal plain around Accra, which is much drier than most of the West African coast, lends itself very well to the raising of livestock; men

---

Coast 1600-1720 (Oxford: Clarendon Press, 1970), p. 154.

[7]M. H. Kingsley, *Travels in West Africa* (1897; reprint ed., New York: Barnes and Noble, Inc., 1965), p. 30.

[8]Bridge, *Journal*, pp. IX, 141; R. Sanjek, "Cognitive maps of the ethnic domain in urban Ghana: reflections on variability and change," *American Ethnologist* IV, no. 4 (Nov. 1977): 615.

[9]B. Belasco, *The Entrepreneur as Culture Hero, Preadaptations in Nigerian Economic Development* (N.Y.: Bergin/Praeger, 1980), p. 74.

in Accra raised pigs. People also boiled sea water to get salt which they traded inland along with fish. Millet, or maize (if it was present) might have been traded both ways, as no other coastal area was so suited to its cultivation.[10] The coming of the Europeans added more commodities to the repertoire of the Ga traders. Their aptitude for trade caused de Marees to remark in 1600 that "the Accra people are a crafty and subtle people, and the subtillest of all that Coast, both for traffique and otherwise."[11]

By the middle of the seventeenth century Accra was the major center for the gold trade on the West African coast. The Ga were raising cattle for sale and taking European goods, salt, and fish to the interior to exchange for gold and slaves. At this time the main market was at Abonse, about twenty miles inland. The Ga were the intermediaries between the Europeans and the peoples inland and did not allow inland traders to come down to the coast.[12] By the mid-eighteenth century Reindorf reported that "the king [of Accra] and many of his people had grown rich" from the slave trade.[13] The increasing wealth of Accra stimulated the Akwamu, and later the Asante, to wish to control it. For Accra not only received trade from Asante, but also from Salaga and the eastern trade routes.

Accra's prosperity continued until the nineteenth century when the Asante wars occasionally made the inland trade routes insecure. This, combined with the British efforts to stop the slave trade, reduced its prosperity somewhat in the first half of the nineteenth century. Ivory and gold dust were the principal commodities traded then, in exchange for gunpowder, rum, and cloth.[14] The trade in cattle, fish, and maize was still being pursued, with the addition of palm oil. The slave trade continued, although somewhat reduced. Around 1810 Accra had eight stone houses, a respectable number at that time.[15] Duncan's description of the trade in Accra in 1847 is similar, but he went on to note that some of the African merchants had been

---

[10]M. D. B. Kilson, *Kpele Lala* (Cambridge: Harvard University Press, 1971), p. 182; Dickson, *Historical Geography*, pp. 86, 98; M. Nathan, "The Gold Coast at the End of the Seventeenth Century Under the Danes and the Dutch," *Journal of the African Society* IV, no. 13 (Oct. 1904): 28. Wilks and Fage were convinced of the existence of a lateral coastal trade prior to the arrival of the Portuguese; P. Ozanne, "Notes on the Later Prehistory of Accra," *Journal of the Historical Society of Nigeria* III (1964): 23. Ozanne concurred with archaeological evidence, pp. 19-20.

[11]P. de Marees, "A description and Historicall Declaration of the Golden Kingdome of Guinea . . .," in *Purchas His Pilgrimes*, trans. G. A. Dantisc, ed. Samuel Purchas (1600; reprint ed., New York: AMS Press Inc., 1965, VI: 262. He also specifically mentioned women traders.

[12]Amoah, "Accra," pp. 32, 35; I. Quaye, "The Ga and Their Neighbors 1600-1742," Ph.D. diss. University of Ghana (1972), pp. 33-34, 80.

[13]C. C. Reindorf, *The History of the Gold Coast and Asante* (ca. 1890; reprint ed., Accra: Ghana Universities Press, 1966), p. 73.

[14]J. Dawson cited in G. E. Metcalf, *Great Britain and Ghana: Documents of Ghana History, 1807-1857* (London: Thomas Nelson and Sons Ltd., 1964), p. 29.

[15]K. B. Dickson, "The Evolution of Seaports in Ghana, 1800-1928," *Annals of the Association of American Geographers* LV, no. 1 (March 1965): 104.

educated in England and possessed large houses.[16] However, until cocoa began to be exported in large quantities in the next century, Accra was neither as large nor as wealthy a port as Cape Coast.[17]

In the second half of the nineteenth century further economic differentiation among the Accra population becomes evident. A number of wealthy Ga merchants became involved in agricultural enterprises. Africanus Horton noted in 1868 that many prominent Ga merchants owned coffee plantations in the bush.[18] These were forerunners of the extensive Ga involvement in cocoa farming which started in about the 1890s. Coincident with this trend was an important shift in the occupations of many Ga men. Until the second half of the nineteenth century most men were farmers or fishermen; traders and chiefs were in the minority forming the wealthy elite. The chiefs in Accra had very early learned to use their positions to become wealthy merchants on their own. They and some of the prominent mulatto, Sierra Leonean, and Brazilian families were among the wealthy in nineteenth century Accra. The men in these families often possessed high educational qualifications which helped them to get ahead in the European trade. Below them were the artisans, mostly goldsmiths, until the intervention of the Basel Mission Society changed the situation in the third quarter of the nineteenth century. In 1857 the B.M.S. opened a workshop in Osu near Accra, and later one in Accra, to teach skills such as carpentry, masonry, coopering and shoemaking, thus adding greatly to the small pool of European-type skilled laborers.[19] This effect was heightened by Ga men incorporating the teaching of these skills into their own apprenticeship system. The girls, however, were taught sewing.[20] The men's new skills took immediate effect, earning mention to the British Parliament's Select Committee on Africa.[21]

Such was the impact of the new skills that by the 1870s Accra had become the principal source of skilled labor on the West African coast, a situation which lasted through World War I.[22] Traveling along the coast to work fit into a tradition which went back at least to the sixteenth century. De Marees noted in 1600 that the men frequently went on trips as far afield as São Tome or Angola.[23] Many workers subsequently went to Nigeria, the

---

[16] J. Duncan, *Travels in Western Africa in 1845 and 1846* (London: Richard Bentley, 1847), I: 85.

[17] Great Britain, *Gold Coast Annual Colonial Reports, 1896-1920* (hereafter referred to as *Annual Colonial Report*); Dickson, "Evolution," p. 105.

[18] J. A. Horton, *West African Countries and Peoples* (1868; reprint ed., Edinburgh: University Press, 1969), p. 133.

[19] R. Szereszewski, *Structural Changes in the Economy of Ghana 1891-1911* (London: Weidenfeld and Nicolson, 1965), p. 8.

[20] Reindorf, *History*, p. 222.

[21] *Minutes of the Select Committee on Africa* (West Coast), June 12, 1865, 315, testimony of W. A. Ross being questioned by C. B. Adderley, Chairman.

[22] Szereszewski, *Structural Changes*, p. 9.

[23] De Marees, "Description," p. 272.

Cameroons, and the Congo, and some went westward to Liberia.[24] In the 1890s the demand was particularly strong, causing missionaries to complain that their congregations were diminished, while the government lamented the scarcity of labor.[25] In 1897 an attempt by the government to limit or abolish recruitment for the Congo in Accra was met by instant vociferous opposition: a demonstration and a petition from the residents of Accra to the Secretary of State for the Colonies. They pointed out that if the government would pay better wages, more people would stay, and that the laborers returning from the Congo had brought back with them a much needed extra source of income.[26]

By 1902, when the government complained to the Ga Maŋtsɛ that it could not find men carriers in Accra, he replied that there were no Ga laborers any more, only skilled workmen.[27] Later, when the demand from abroad diminished, the paradoxical situation arose that the Ga Maŋtsɛ could complain of unemployment, while the Governor pleaded for day laborers to do agricultural and sanitary work so they would not have to import Kru and Northerners to do it.[28]

The other development in late nineteenth century Accra which furthered social differentiation and helped create a shortage of male unskilled labor was that increased educational opportunities gave Ga men a great advantage in seeking civil service jobs. Although the Fanti were first in the field, the shift of the capital to Accra gave Ga men better access to government jobs after 1877 (until 1905 the civil service examination was held only at Accra).[29] But by 1889 it was reported that young educated men "now flood the clerical market and have almost reduced the rate of wages below the means of living."[30] Thus from about 1860 to 1900 occupational options changed for Ga men, in particular, but the women were not given the same opportunities. In 1902 when Governor Nathan wanted porters he could not find any men, but he could get women.[31]

Along with a taste for foreign food and luxury items, the Ga migrant laborers brought back cocoa, which revolutionized the economy of the Gold Coast. In 1878 a blacksmith from Osu named Tetteh Quashie brought back

[24]M. Kilson, "Variations in Ga Culture in Central Accra," *Ghana Journal of Sociology* III, no. 1 (Feb. 1967): 33.

[25]Debrunner, p. 22. SNA 11/1374, Letter from Elder, Dempster and Co. to R. Cowan McKinnon, May 11, 1894; *Annual Colonial Report* (1892), p. 18.

[26]Great Britain, Public Record Office, Papers of the Secretary of State for the Colonies, 96/298/ petition May 31, 1897, p. 11. Part of their grievances stemmed from the fact that the government had broken a strike of sanitary laborers by importing Kru scabs, thus lowering wages.

[27]SNA 11/1773, *Palaver Book*, pp. 100-101, interview April 17, 1902.

[28]SNA 11/1089, interview October 17, 1923.

[29]*Annual Colonial Report* (1905), p. 27.

[30]ADM 5/3/7, Report . . . on Economic Agriculture (1889), pp. 153-154. See below Chapter V for a brief history of early formal education in Accra.

[31]SNA 11/1772, *Palaver Book*, pp. 100-101, interview between Governor Nathan and Ga Maŋtsɛ Nii Tackie Tawia, April 17, 1902.

some cocoa pods from Fernando Po and set up a nursery. His efforts were furthered by Governor William Brandford Griffith, who set up an experimental farm at Aburi to supply seedlings to farmers after 1886. By 1900 rapid expansion of its cultivation had taken place and planters were constructing bush paths for rolling the casks to market.[32] By 1910 cocoa was the Gold Coast's largest export.[33]

The spectacular development of the cocoa industry in Ghana has been chronicled elsewhere, but the part played by Accra in it needs to be emphasized. The first area to come under intensive cocoa cultivation was the Akwapim hills immediately to the north of Accra. From the beginning the Ga played an extremely important role in its expansion. Some of the wealthier men became what Polly Hill called "creditor-farmers" or "farmer-financiers", using a sort of tenant-farming system.[34] Others became cocoa buyers, or small farmers. The wealth from cocoa poured into Accra and became the main foundation for its growth in the twentieth century. The other major change, then, at the end of the nineteenth century, was that the whole economy of Ghana moved toward a dependence on one crop which, though profitable at the time, was to become disastrous later.[35]

Accra in the Twentieth Century: Growth

From 1890 to 1919 the people of Accra experienced a number of vicissitudes which caused its population to fluctuate widely: a famine, a devastating fire in 1894, an earthquake in 1906, the bubonic plague in 1908, and the influenza epidemic of 1918-19. It was thus not until after World War I that the spectacular growth of Accra started, changing it from a Ga-dominated town of about 20,000 persons into an urban complex of almost one million in 1980. The World Wars can be used as benchmarks which roughly define changes taking place in the town and in people's lives.

The interwar period saw the initiation of the radical changes which came about after World War II. Accra's population grew from 38,000 in 1921 to 60,000 in 1931, and to 135,000 in 1948. Until World II Ga

----

[32]F. Agbodeka, *Ghana in the Twentieth Century* (Accra: Ghana Universities Press, 1972), pp. 30-33.

[33]P. Hill, *The Migrant Cocoa-Farmers of Southern Ghana* (Cambridge: University Press, 1963), p. 172.

[34]Hill, *Migrant Cocoa-Farmers*, p. 186.

[35]Szereszewski, *Structural Changes*, p. 9, stated:
    an economy geared to the industrial world came into being largely during [1891 to 1901], as a result of a change in the pattern of utilization of the store of wealth of the territory, the resources of the forest belt. This change was stimulated by the foreign elements on the coast—but was made possible by the rapid expansion of new patterns of economic activity in the indigenous sphere. The fact that almost all the population of the coastal strip and the forest belt of the Gold Coast had long standing experience of commercial activities, i.e. of the exchange of goods and services, and a large proportion had contact with or at least a notion of European goods, was one of the keys to that development.

outnumbered others in the population, but in the 1920s men began out-
numbering women as a symptom of the steadily increasing proportion of
migrants in the population.[36] The 1920s and 1930s saw the initial growth of
suburbs, which after World War II gradually dwarfed Central Accra in population and importance. A severe earthquake in 1939 destroyed much of Central Accra, giving an added impetus for some to move to the suburbs. A
housing estate was built at Kaneshie to accommodate people from Asere, a
badly affected area. The government's rehousing program was sidetracked
by the war, however, and most people had to make do with rebuilding their
old homes. Throughout these years the tendency was for those who could
afford it to build houses in the newer areas and move out of Central Accra, a
physical expression of the increasing socioeconomic differentiation among the
population.

The interwar period also saw the first major changes in transportation
which helped make Accra the major Gold Coast port. In the period before
World War I the initial development of roads into the interior and the beginning of the railroad to Kumasi took place. But it was only after World War
I that the real revolution in transportation hit Accra. The introduction of
the light Ford truck and the extension of roads greatly increased road transport to the interior.[37] Whereas in 1919 the Gold Coast had 1,200 miles of
motorable roads, by 1923 it had 3,200, and the cost of lorry transportation
was halved by the introduction of blacktopping. In 1923 the Accra-Kumasi
railroad was completed.[38] In 1934 Reynolds reported that the railway connection to Akim had "practically killed" head porterage and rolling cocoa
casks to market.[39] Within Accra the use of mule transport stopped after
1925, and municipal bus service started in 1927.[40] From 1910 to 1942 Accra
was the largest port in the Gold Coast for the export of cocoa, and it was
also the largest center for the import of foreign goods from 1918 to 1936.[41]
Thus, it was the major center of surface transportation in the Gold Coast in
the interwar years.

The population growth of these years was aided by the increased provision of European-type health care facilities, as well as by an awakened concern of the colonial officials for sanitary conditions, especially in Central
Accra. The first hospital, Korle Bu, was opened in 1923, and the Accra
Maternity Hospital and Princess Marie Louise Hospital for children followed
shortly thereafter. By 1938 some 35,000 outpatients were treated yearly at
the three hospitals.[42] The effects of this change were particularly noticeable
in the infant mortality rate. From 1930 to 1960 Ghanaian life expectancy

[36] Gold Coast Census, 1921, 1931, 1948.

[37] Dickson, "Evolution," p. 110.

[38] Annual Colonial Report (1923-24), pp. 15, 42; P. R. Gould. The Development of the
Transportation Pattern in Ghana (Evanston: Northwestern University Press, 1960), p. 66.

[39] A. J. Reynolds, African Passage (London: Frederick Muller Ltd., 1934), p. 141.

[40] Annual Colonial Report (1924-25), p. 57; Amoah, "Accra," p. 74.

[41] Annual Colonial Reports (1920-36); Dickson, "Evolution," p. 111.

[42] Annual Colonial Reports (1884-1938).

rose from 30 to 45 years.[43] People began to get accustomed to using hospitals.

Sanitary conditions in Central Accra appalled many European observers. The overcrowding and lack of sewage facilities made it an ideal breeding ground for epidemics. Starting at the end of the nineteenth century the British took rudimentary sanitary measures, such as building public latrines, sewage ditches, and providing safe drinking water. These improvements were welcomed by many Accra people, although they objected to the water rate. It was the campaigns against mosquitoes, fishsmoking and pigbreeding in Accra, as well as the occasional arbitrary behavior of the sanitary inspectors, which earned them the lasting opprobrium of the inhabitants.[44] The sanitary inspectors became the personification of the colonial government for many inhabitants of Central Accra. In some years hundreds and even thousands of women were prosecuted for having standing water or filth in the compound. So many women came up before the District Court for sanitary offenses that the routine "he" referring to the accused in the court records was eventually changed to a routine "she."[45]

Other improvements in Accra, such as installing street lights, opening cemeteries, and making and paving streets, began in the late nineteenth century. In 1904 the construction of the Accra waterworks began at Weija; they were in operation in 1914, which eliminated many problems.[46] People had depended on rainwater from rooftop storage tanks, or water drawn from polluted wells. Both water supplies dried up in frequent droughts. Water was sometimes sold for as much as 6 d. a gallon before World War I.[47] The sanitary public water system remedied the situation until recently. Also, by 1930 electricity was becoming common in homes in Accra.[48] The interwar period, then, saw significant improvements in the provision of amenities which raised the standards of living and of health care.

World War II itself changed the nature of Accra. It brought the beginning of a large flood of immigration and an even more cosmopolitan atmosphere to Accra. In 1942 the headquarters of British West African military operations was established at Accra. The Americans also installed themselves there, along with an important airbase. Providing food and services for these people made this period a prosperous one for some of the local traders.

---

[43] J. North, M. Fuchs-Carsch, J. Bryson and S. Blumenfeld, *Women in National Development in Ghana*, U.S. Agency for International Development, Women in Development Office report (Department of State, April 1975), p. 70.

[44] SNA 11/294 (1908). Fist fights and legal cases resulted from their actions on occasion.

[45] SCT 17/4/30 ff.; SCT 17/5/63.

[46] F. Agbodeka, *Ghana in the Twentieth Century* (Accra: Ghana Universities Press, 1972), p. 44.

[47] R. R. Kuczynski, *Demographic Survey of the British Colonial Empire* (London: Oxford University Press, 1948), p. 478. Accra's annual rainfall averages around 27 inches.

[48] Amoah, "Accra," p. 66; Dickson, *Historical Geography*, p. 259.

But the 1950s were the most prosperous era the country had ever had. A great building boom filled in much of the area that is now Accra. The population more than doubled between 1948 and 1960 to become 388,000.[49] The foundation of all of this prosperity was, of course, high cocoa prices. Here it is necessary to backtrack a bit chronologically in order to examine the evolution of the Ghanaian economy, upon which so much of this story depends.

The Gold Coast Economy from 1900 to 1952

In 1952 the Gold Coast attained self-government with Kwame Nkrumah as prime minister. The time from 1900 to 1952 can be considered the high colonial period for Ghana, when British economic policy largely determined its fate and set the terms of future weaknesses. The period before World War I (1914-18) saw the collapse of both government-owned and foreign-controlled agriculture on the Gold Coast because of unwillingness to make capital investment. At the same time the trans-Saharan caravan trade, which had one of its main termini in the northern Gold Coast, was mainly destroyed by extortionate British-imposed toll collectors. Likewise, large European-controlled firms with superior resources at their command drove most of their smaller African competitors out of business, and then lowered the prices they would pay for local commodities. Thus, one of the first attempts by European companies to lower the price of cocoa came in 1904-05. Nonetheless, the first cocoa boom was responsible for financing much of the improved transport, government railroads and private roads and paths built mainly with communal labor.[50]

Cocoa exports remedied the deficit which had worried the British government, but the effects of World War I were not beneficial. War recruitment and the 1918 influenza caused shortages of skilled labor.[51] The cost of living indices (Table II-1) show that the first startling rise in prices and wages came after World War I. The introduction of paper money after the war exacerbated the situation, since the market women often refused to take it. People hoarded gold and silver.[52] In 1924, the *maŋtsɛmei* complained to the government that the lorries and the railroad had cut into the mule transport trade carting cocoa, that no one would buy houses put up for sale, that school leavers could not find work, that the Prison Department had quit buying kenkey (the Ga staple food) from the women, and that European

---

[49] *Ghana Census* (1960).

[50] Agbodeka, *Ghana*, pp. 29-35, 37-39.

[51] N. A. Cox-George, *Studies in Finance and Development: The Gold Coast (Ghana) Experience 1914-1950* (London: Dennis Dobson, 1973), p. 62.

[52] SNA 11/1088, welcoming speech of Ga Maŋtsɛ and *maŋtsɛmei* to Governor Guggisberg, Nov. 28, 1919.

Table II-1. Cost of Living Indices for Accra, 1901-78.[a]

Year	Retail food price index[b]	Index - all commodities	Salaried wage index	Real wage index[c]
1901	100	100		100
1903			100	100
1911	111			105
1913			117	105
1921	157			115
1923			180	115
1931	103			154
1933			159	154
1938	108			
1939		45		
1946		122	152	107
1948	141	141		107
1951	262[d]			
1952		216[e]	312	128
1954	243	214	312	128
1960	277	231		
1964	339	303	356	105
1966	543	399	401	74
1968	451	408	416[f]	92
1970	586	485	458	78
1974	873	811	721[g]	83
1975	1,074			
1976	1,825			
1977(July)	4,314[h]			
1978(April)	10,063[i]			

[a]See Appendix A for a full explanation of the derivation of the figures in Table II-1, and of the changes in the use and value of currency in Gold Coast/Ghana over the twentieth century.

[b]K. Ewusi,"Changing Patterns of Household Expenditure in Ghana," paper presented at the Conference on Innovation in African Economic History, Legon, Dec. 1975, p. 25; "The Determinants of Price Fluctuations in Ghana," ISSER Discussion Paper No. 2, Dec. 1977, p. 13, noted that local food prices have been the greatest factor in driving up the Accra consumer price index; they are given the most weight.

[c]Calculated using food price index only.

[d]For local food prices only, extrapolated from Seers and Ross, Report, p. 23.

[e]1939-52 extrapolated from Ewusi, "Determinants," p. 35.

[f]1968 and 1970 were calculated using wages of public sector construction workers, monthly and daily rated workers, with the respective weights of 8, 6, and 3.

[g]1974 was extrapolated from the Economic Survey of Ghana for public sector workers in establishments employing more than 10 employees in that year, and covers all of Ghana. Many of these are concentrated in Accra, however. The original figure of 656 was adjusted in accordance within a ratio derived from the 1968 and 1970 comparable figures.

[h]1970-77 extrapolated from Ewusi, "Determinants," pp. 10-11, and Ewusi, office wall, ISSER, Univ. of Ghana, 1978.

[i]1975-78 based only on prices of local foods.

cocoa contractors were replacing African cocoa buyers as middlemen.[53] The Gold Coast was caught up in what Lewis called the great tropical depression of 1913 to 1950, and the record cocoa crop of 1920 did not help. The prices of primary products slid with relation to manufactured goods.[54] Shortages of imported goods caused prices to go up during World War I and they stayed up until the late 1920s.

Nonetheless, under the aegis of Governor Guggisberg in the 1920s, some attention was paid to the development of education and transport in the Gold Coast. In 1928 the first deep water port, Takoradi, was opened. Until 1943 the financing of development came entirely through indirect taxes (mainly duties on imports and exports) and private investment, in line with the British policy of having colonies pay their own way. The main concentration was on the extraction of resources, so that by 1950 the Gold Coast was the second largest supplier of manganese in the world, with the timber and diamond industries also supplying a respectable amount.[55]

Toward the end of the 1920s the economy was looking a bit better, but the world depression of the 1930s caused renewed deterioration. In the 1930s, although the Gold Coast exported more than it imported, the amount of exports and imports went down drastically. Public works virtually halted, causing unemployment. In 1931 the Annual Report stated that, "while . . . the standard of living has not been noticeably affected by the general depression, the amount of money in circulation and the buried resources of the family unit have shrunk below the pre-war level."[56] The government tried to remedy the situation by putting smaller denomination coins into circulation, which they thought would reduce the cost of living.[57] Cocoa holdups by producers seeking higher prices occurred periodically throughout the 1930s and further reduced the amount of cocoa exported. In 1931 swollen shoot disease appeared in the Eastern Region and started its deadly progression, which has by now seriously impaired Ghana's cocoa production. It caused the center of cocoa cultivation to move further westward, which ultimately meant that more cocoa was exported from Takoradi than Accra. Its unfortunate coincidence with the depression in the Gold Coast only worsened the situation. Salaried wage earners were, however, relatively well off in this period. Their wages did not fall nearly as much as food prices did, which is reflected in the 1938 cost of food given in Table II-1. By this time a significant number of Ga men earned salaries. It was not until the mid-1960s that inflation caused a reversal of the trend, and wages no longer kept substantially ahead of price hikes.

---

[53]SNA 11/889, *Report on the Objections against the application of the Municipal Corporations Ordinance, 1924 to . . . Accra* (Gold Coast: Government Printer, 1925), p. 4. Kenkey is an anglicized version of the Portuguese word for the Ga staple food, called *kɔmi* in Ga.

[54]W. A. Lewis, ed., *Tropical Development 1880-1913* (London: George Allen and Unwin Ltd., 1970), p. 33.

[55]Cox-George, *Studies*, pp. 80, 97, 23, 60.

[56]*Annual Colonial Report* (1931), p. 44; (1933), p. 65.

[57]SNA 11/1510, memo from Secretary of State for the Colonies, March 13, 1933.

The cost of living started rising during World War II. From 1939 to the end of 1941 prices went up by 51% within the Gold Coast as a whole, but wages went down.[58] During World War II farmers produced less since they could not get imported goods and sometimes could not export what they did produce, which only drove prices higher.[59] It was partly inflation which caused the 1948 riots in Accra. In 1952 Seers and Ross in their report on the Gold Coast economy termed it "fragile" and pointed to many weaknesses which the development of the next decade would only disguise. They found: no checks to inflationary spending, which was exacerbated by light taxes, low inventories of goods, and an inelastic supply of local foodstuffs; much delay in imports; difficulties in transport; ineffective price controls; foreign exchange earnings from only one source, cocoa, whose prices varied radically from year to year and season to season; low productivity caused partially by a high incidence of disease and poor diet; shortage of skilled labor; and little use by the general public of savings institutions, which meant there was no capital market. They saw inflation as the most basic problem, one contributing factor being the over-issuing of British West African currency in 1947-50. They attributed the large increases in food prices of 1949 to 1951 to lack of incentives being given to farmers to increase productivity.[60] Like most pre-1970 analysts, they failed to note that agricultural inputs were mainly to men doing cash-cropping, rather than to women doing most of the food production. Also, women farmers' lack of access to capital reduced their productivity by creating problems with making improvements and indebtedness to the women wholesaler-collectors.

With regard to the urban situation, Seers and Ross noted housing shortages caused by the increased influx of rural migrants, and persistent high unemployment, particularly among unskilled laborers and those whom they considered to be marginally qualified for clerical positions.[61] Going into the period of greatest prosperity, then, there was evidence of underlying weaknesses which the policies of subsequent years only worsened.

[58]W. Birmingham, "An Index of Real Wages of the Unskilled Labourer in Accra, 1939-59," *Economic Bulletin of Ghana* IV, no. 3 (March 1960): 3-4; ADM 5/3/4, *Report on the Inquiry into the Cost of Living in the Gold Coast held in January, 1942* (Accra: Gold Coast Government Printer, 1942), p. 5.

[59]E. J. Berg, "Real Income Trends in West Africa," in *Economic Transition in Africa*, ed. M. H. Herskovits and M. Harwitz (Evanston: Northwestern University Press, 1964), p. 212.

[60]D. Seers and C. R. Ross, *Report on Financial and Physical Problems of Development in the Gold Coast* (Accra: Office of the Government Statistician, July 1952), pp. 1-5, 96, 101-02, 105, 53, 77.

[61]Seers and Ross, *Report*, p. 29.

Ghana's Economy, 1953 to 1983

[Our goals are] the total abolition of unemployment, malnutrition and illiteracy, and the creation of conditions where all our people can enjoy good health, proper housing, where our children can have the best of educational facilities and where every citizen has the fullest opportunities to develop and use his skills and talents. In addition to these national benefits, it is my earnest hope that what we achieve here in Ghana will serve as an example and an inspiration to our sister countries throughout Africa.

Kwame Nkrumah, 1962[62]

Economic development in the late 1940s and early 1950s seemed to support the rosy future predicted by President Nkrumah. A boom caused by high cocoa prices and exports built up foreign reserves. Cocoa farmers profited the most at first, and their spending on imported consumer goods exacerbated inflationary tendencies.[63] Prices and wages rose. From 1954 to 1960 imports of foodstuffs almost doubled in value. At the same time in Accra expenditure patterns showed more money being spent on services and rent in proportion to food.[64] Per capita income in Ghana went steadily up. This period of unparalleled prosperity peaked around the time of independence in 1957. Because of it, Adelman and Morris, using statistics covering 1957 to 1962, classified Ghana as being at an intermediate level of development, as opposed to the lower level obtaining in other sub-Saharan African countries.[65] Nkrumah was not the only one misled by the economic indicators, but the structure was only superficially stable.[66]

One result was the reckless spending of reserves by the Nkrumah government on projects promoting import substitution and industrialization. The former resulted in a number of not very profitable final-stage assembly plants, Moskvitch cars being one example. Such endeavors wasted foreign exchange in buying parts and did not provide substantial savings to the consumer because of the high assembly cost in Ghana. Some of the industrialization projects were useful, such as the building of the Volta Dam and the Tema complex (a deep water port near Accra.) But there were also some useless ones, such as the construction of a gigantic cocoa storage bin at

---

[62]Cox-George, *Studies*, p. 210.

[63]Seers and Ross, *Report*, pp. 19, 25; Cox-George, *Studies*, p. 156.

[64]R. Szereszewski, "Patterns of Consumption," in *A Study of Contemporary Ghana*, ed. W. Birmingham et al. (London: George Allen and Unwin Ltd., 1966), I: 114.

[65]I. Adelman and C. T. Morris, *Society, Politics and Economic Development* (Baltimore: Johns Hopkins Press, 1967), p. 203.

[66]Cox-George, *Studies*, p. 211, who wrote his work in 1961, made the same mistake, which makes bitter reading in retrospect.

Ghana will be catapulted into the orbit of economic maturity in the "seventies" and if the world price of cocoa is stabilized and if its characteristic good luck continues to attend the country, the GDP will come out with a spectacular big bulge in the middle "seventies" if not earlier and the standard of life with it.

Tema, too big and too weak to be of use.[67] Such expenditures brought a gradual diminishing of foreign exchange in 1957-58, and then rapid loss in 1959-61, with the accumulation of foreign debts.[68] By 1961 Ghana's sterling reserves were two-fifths of the 1955 total; there was a tenfold increase in the public debt from 1958 to 1964.[69]

While the government spent its resources on capital-intensive development projects and neglected agriculture, the private sector invested in building and construction, rather than expansion of businesses or other avenues which would generate more growth.[70] Because of the cocoa boom and the accumulated reserves the economy could tolerate all of this for a relatively short period; from 1956 to 1962 the average yearly growth in the gross domestic product hovered around 5%. But in the mid-1960s the situation changed for the worse, and the weaknesses of these policies became evident immediately in the fall in GDP growth to only 1.4% per annum from 1962 to 1968.[71]

The problem was not only the slump in cocoa prices, but also increasing corruption in government, which was facilitated by the state takeover of some industries. In a kind of reverse Midas effect, everything Nkrumah and his cohorts touched was bled for funds, tarnished by corruption, and ultimately left to stagnate in a welter of nepotistic Convention People's Party bureaucrats.[72] Import licensing and price controls were imposed to try to halt inflation and restrict the soaring demand for imported goods, but these did more to provide new avenues for corruption than to remedy the situation. Deficit financing was resorted to increasingly and by 1966 foreign debt had grown into a monster which devoured almost half of the GDP.[73] Agriculture remained the stepchild of development, with productivity at the same level from 1960 to 1965, while the rural consumer price index was usually higher than the urban one. Exports were not diversified with cocoa still

[67]Some have questioned the utility of the Volta Dam since it put a large proportion of Ghana's arable farmland under water and helped to spread river blindness, while electricity sales to neighboring countries have not fulfilled expectations and the equipment is beginning to break down.

[68]J. C. Leith, *Foreign Trade Regimes and Economic Development: Ghana* (New York: National Bureau of Economic Research, 1974), pp. 4-5, 48, 80.

[69]A. J. Killick, "The Monetary Effects of Recent Budgets in Ghana," in *Readings in the Applied Economics of Africa*, ed. E. H. Whetham and J. I. Currie (Cambridge: Cambridge University Press, 1967), II: 97, 113.

[70]R. Genoud, *National and Economic Development in Ghana* (New York: Praeger, 1969), p. 145. P. Marris and A. Somerset, in *The African Entrepreneur* (New York: Africana Publishing Corporation, 1972), give a good description of the constraints on African entrepreneurs that restrict their choice of investments.

[71]K. Ewusi, "West African Economies—Some Basic Economic Problems," University of Ghana Institute of Statistical, Social and Economic Research (ISSER), Technical Publications Series No. 25, 1971, p. 50; Genoud, *National and Economic Development*, p. 142.

[72]C. C. Robertson, review of *Ghana's First Republic* by Trevor Jones, *International Journal of African Historical Studies* XI, no. 3 (Fall 1978): 525.

[73]Leith, *Foreign Trade*, p. 5; K. Ewusi, "The Determinants of Price Fluctuation in Ghana," ISSER Discussion Paper 2 (Dec. 1977), p. 2.

supplying an overwhelming percentage of Ghana's foreign exchange. After 1965 even cocoa production went down because of low world prices and lack of extension services, imported sprays, and fertilizers to improve yield. Swollen shoot disease control measures virtually stopped.[74]

The micro-level effects of these macro-level changes were disastrous. Prices continued to rise but wages leveled off a bit. In Accra local food prices between 1961 and 1965 rose by 93%, imported food prices by 55%, while the wages of workers in large establishments rose by only 20%.[75] Per capita real income in Ghana actually fell from 1962 to 1965, and unemployment tripled from 1960 to 1967 to become 12% of the labor force.[76] According to Ewusi, income distribution between 1956 and 1968 became more unequal, with the richest 10% of the population gaining proportionately more than the poorest 10% percent.[77]

The problems showed up critically in the supply of imports. Periodic shortages of foreign exchange made chronic scarcities of imported goods inevitable. While consumer goods formed over half of Ghana's imports in 1959, they sank to only a third in 1965.[78] Meanwhile Ghanaians increasingly depended on imports to supply not only luxuries but also basic food needs. In fact, some imports like sardines had become essential in order to provide adequate protein for the population, whose growth had by then exceeded food supplies for some time. From 1955 to 1968 there was a 96.4% increase in the amount of food imported, which also reflected the reduction in cultivated acreage of food staples.[79]

It is not surprising, then, that the manifold shortages in Accra in 1965-66 were a strong factor in the overthrow of Nkrumah by a military coup. His charisma submerged by economic woes, he left behind a nation gutted of reserves, and an example of government for the benefit of the few in the name of the many. The damage wrought was incalculable. The pattern he set has not substantially been altered by subsequent governments, although less glamour has accompanied their corruption.

---

[74]Ghana, Central Bureau of Statistics, *Economic Survey*, 1969-71, p. 10; Ewusi, "West African Economies," pp. 55-56.

[75]E. Reusse and R. M. Lawson, "The Effect of Economic Development on Metropolitan Food Marketing: a Case Study of Food Retail Trade in Accra," *East African Journal of Rural Development* II, no. 1 (1969): 36.

[76]N. O. Addo, "Urbanization, Population, and Employment in Ghana" in *Population Growth and Economic Development in Africa*, ed. S. H. Ominde and C. N. Ejiogu (London: Heineman, 1972), p. 249; J. M. Due, in "Development Without Growth—The Case of Ghana in the 1960s?" *Economic Bulletin of Ghana* III (1973): 4, has estimated that per capita income in Ghana fell by 5% per annum from 1960 to 1968.

[77]K. Ewusi, *Economic Inequality in Ghana* (Accra: New Times Corporation, 1977), pp. 71-72.

[78]N. Ahmad, *Deficit Financing, Inflation and Capital Formation: The Ghanaian Experience, 1960-65* (Munich: Weltform Verlag, 1970), pp. 112, 91.

[79]R. Orraca-Tetteh, *Effects of Rapid Population Trends for Policy Measures in West Africa*, Ghana Population Studies No. 3 (1971), pp. 59-60.

From 1967 to 1983: The Slide

The manifest economic problems of Nkrumah's last years made it evident that drastic measures were needed to shore up the economy, but the succeeding governments attempted cosmetic measures only.[80] Military rule was succeeded by civilian rule, military rule again, civilian rule, and then military rule again at the end of 1981. The chief policies attempted were ineffectual price controls, currency manipulation, and debt rescheduling or repudiation; there was no rearrangement of priorities. The Acheampong military government was in power when most of this research was done and had the longest tenure in office (1972-78) of any government since Nkrumah. It soon exceeded its predecessors in its skill at draining public funds into private pockets. In 1978 it became known that the cocoa crop had been sold for the next two years, but no one seemed to know where the money had gone. The currency was still grossly overvalued, making imports cheap and discouraging exports.

A flourishing black market grew up; the gross inflation gave the impression that the government was printing money at whim. It was; from 1971 to 1977 the average rate of increase in the money supply was 80%.[81] Table II-1 shows what was happening under an inflation rate that has been variously estimated at 30% to 50% per annum.[82] The tragedy of these years made even the late Nkrumah years halcyon in retrospect. In 1979 the World Bank found it necessary to revise Ghana's annual per capita income *down* from $450 to $380, as cocoa production reached a record low.[83] Ghana went from supplying a third of the world's cocoa to less than a fifth; the lands were overworked and no new suitable lands could be found.[84] While I could not get wage data to supply a 1978 real wage index figure, a guesstimate would make the decline in purchasing power for average people about eighty percent between 1974 and 1978. So far, neither the Akuffo, Limann nor the Rawlings governments of 1978-83 have done anything effective to help the situation, a reality where even basic medicines and staples are unavailable unless one farms or can afford trips abroad to replenish supplies. The 1983 influx of refugees from Nigeria only produced catastrophe from disaster. In a time of world hardship, Ghanaians also suffer the penalty of economic mismanagement with no clear remedies evident. In 1974 an economist commented, "by the late 1960s the accumulated assortment of [policy] instruments, acting in uncertain ways on a variety of targets, made the effective

---

[80]For a more detailed analysis of the Ankrah through the Acheampong years, see Leith, *Foreign Trade.*

[81]B. Beckman, "Ghana, 1951-78: the Agrarian Basis of the Post-Colonial State," in *Introduction to Rural Development in Tropical Africa*, ed. J. Heyer et al. (N.Y.: St. Martin's, 1981), p. 155.

[82]Ewusi, "Determinants," pp. 8, 38.

[83]*New York Times*, October 10, 1979, p. 1.

[84]Beckman, "Ghana," p. 157.

formulation of economic policy an incredibly difficult and complex task."[85] I would add, it is also a thankless one which many Ghanaians with appropriate skills have fled for the easier living abroad.

In fact, in 1983 all of the weaknesses described by Seers and Ross still existed in the Ghanaian economy with the added problems of: (1) no remaining sterling reserves, (2) deficit-financing by governments since the early 1960s with an excessive expansion of money supply by the banking system, (3) high cost of industrial production due to underutilization and inefficiency, (4) falling food production, (5) high population growth, (6) imported inflation (the high cost of oil, for instance), (7) a huge jump in unemployment with an oversupply of clerically trained workers but continuing lack of technicians,[86] and, most important, (8) the increased poverty and desperation of the low income workers who make up most of the population.

Central Accra in the Late Twentieth Century: Decay

The results of socioeconomic residential differentiation and impoverishment of lower income workers are evident in Central Accra. Most of the profits of "development" have been spent elsewhere, such as installing improved amenities in the wealthier suburbs. Because there is a charge for public latrines, they are not often used. Chamber pots substitute for the almost universal lack of flush toilets. The plot of Marshall's novel, *Bukom*, centers around a retired Ga civil servant's ambition to build a flush toilet for the compound, an effort which required much sacrifice from everyone.[87] Out of sixty-eight compounds in the small survey in 1972 only five, or 7%, percent possessed piped water. Most people still get their water from public standpipes, of which there is usually one per block, making lines inevitable. Because of overpopulation, breakdown of equipment, and drought, the water supply is sometimes erratic, causing hoarding.[88] This tendency was institutionalized by the Acheampong government, which in 1975 declared its intention to close down the public standpipes, forcing those who could afford it to have their own pipes installed, and those who could not, to buy water from them. In 1979 there was a period of two weeks when no water was available in all of Accra. In 1972 38% of the compounds had electricity, compared to 56% of 202 compounds in 1978. The usual one bulb compared unfavorably to the completely electrified suburbs, although favorably to many rural areas.

Economic differentiation is also evident in that the brunt of Accra's phenomenal population growth, up to 564,000 in 1970, has been borne by

---

[85]Leith, *Foreign Trade*, p. 161.

[86]Ewusi, "Determinants," pp. 24-26; Addo, "Urbanization," pp. 249-50.

[87]B. Marshall, *Bukom* (London: Longman's, 1979).

[88]*Accra Daily Graphic*, March 14, 1951, p. 7.

already densely populated areas like Ussher Town.[89] The statement of this
anonymous Ghanaian in 1955 is only one in a long line of opinions from both
European and indigenous sources which condemned Ussher Town as a slum.

> [Ussher Town and James Town] present the worst spectacle in the whole
> city of Accra. The buildings are squalid ramshakles [sic] with hardly any
> ventilation. Added to this is the fact that the areas are overpopulated. In
> some of the so-called homes as many as 12 people sleep in a room measur-
> ing less than ten feet square. These eye-sores must be removed before In-
> dependence Day if we are to retain any respect in the eyes of foreign visi-
> tors.[90]

Instead, a fence was built along the main street to hide what was perceived
as sordid reality from foreign visitors.

Anonymous actually understated the density of population in Ussher
Town. In 1891 the average number of persons per house was already
12.02.[91] In 1919 a medical report claimed, "Shortage of housing accommodation is a sinister feature of most coast towns at present. Evacuation of dila-
pidated buildings and prosecutions for overcrowding are unjustifiable in the
absence of reasonable accommodation elsewhere." In 1931 the population
density for Accra District was 223 persons per square mile, and presumably
much higher for Central Accra.[92] In 1958 Ussher Town had the highest density of population in Accra with over three hundred persons per square
acre.[93] In 1970 the density was 26.02 persons per room,[94] while in new elite
residential areas building codes have been followed and houses spaced well
apart. The density in Ridge, an old exclusive area, is no greater now than
before. The squalor which may mistakenly have been attributed by outsiders to Central Accra in the past is now becoming a reality.

* * * * *

We can sum up the economic evolution of Accra, then, according to the
three periods in the original model presented in Chapter I. In the precolonial
era up to about 1860, there was steadily increasing commerce and linkages
with various European powers, which entailed the thorough monetization of
the coastal economy. The indigenous corporate kin mode of production,
however, adapted to increased opportunities profitably, without damage to
its structure. Within the second, mostly colonial, period several stages can

[89]*Ghana Census* 1970, II: 202-03. I am indebted to Mr. Colecraft of the Central Bureau
of Statistics and Dr. DeGraft-Johnson of ISSER at the University of Ghana, formerly of the
Central Bureau of Statistics, for allowing me to use unreleased 1970 census materials. The
Accra Plan of the Ghana Ministry of Housing put out in 1958 projected an upper limit for
Accra's population in *1978* of 337,000, showing the lack of provision for such growth. Gha-
na, Ministry of Housing, *Accra Plan* (Accra: Government Printers, 1958), p. 118.

[90]*Accra Daily Graphic*, August 3, 1955, p. 5, letter to the editor.

[91]*Gold Coast Census*, 1891.

[92]Kuczynski, *Demographic Survey*, pp. 478, 420.

[93]*Accra Plan*, p. 41.

[94]*Ghana Census* 1970.

be discerned. From 1860 to about 1910 the Ga male corporate kin mode of production was substantially modified to include more skilled laborers, while men in increasing numbers moved outside it entirely to take advantage of formal educational opportunities. Meanwhile, the corporate kin mode of production remained intact for the women. The economy in general was being transformed by increasing cash crop production and extractive activities furthered by the colonial regime.

The next stage, the interwar period, marked the first substantial changes for women because of the advent of better transportation. The increasing importance of cash crops helped the conversion to a dependence on imported goods, which were one manifestation of the increased penetration of capital. By the late 1930s the Gold Coast was no longer self-sufficient in food production, and a typical colonial economy had fully developed.[95] After World War II the Gold Coast was moving toward independence and even greater dependence on foreign capital. Nkrumah's "African Socialism" did not succeed in removing economic power from the multinational corporations, although it did aid in the entrenchment in power of a multiethnic bureaucratic bourgeoisie in Ghana. It also established a few large factories and helped to discourage local entrepreneurs by nationalizing their businesses (if successful and large), while competition from the multinationals undermined them. Development projects often relied on outside advice rather than indigenous expertise and failed to respond to local requirements.[96] Government corruption and lack of knowledge allowed ill-conceived, impractical or poorly executed development projects to proceed. Concentration on capital-intensive development to the neglect of agriculture and small business, along with inflation and other problems, harmed an economy now in dire straits. The results for Accra were evident in a sprawl of expensive suburban housing which contrasts sharply with the increasingly crowded slums like Ussher Town and Nima, a physical expression of class differentiation.

---

[95]B. Grier, "Underdevelopment, Modes of Production, and the State in Colonial Ghana," *African Studies Review* XXIV, no. 1 (Mar. 1981): 40-42. Grier also said (p. 22), "[t]he overall impact of the colonial period in Ghana was not only the structural blocking of any capitalist transformation but an internal disarticulation and reintegration of the precapitalist mode of production into the world system in the interests of European capitalism."

[96]R. M. Lawson, in *The Changing Economy of the Lower Volta 1954-67* (N.Y.: Oxford University Press, 1972), p. 79, gives one example in a State Farms Corporation project which used Eastern bloc equipment and management, and paid no attention to the knowledge and needs of local farmers around Battor in the Eastern Region. The project failed, and its history is duplicated in many others which used aid from Western governments and private sources.

III

THE SOCIAL CONTEXT:

FEMALE STRATEGIES

IN A MALE-DOMINATED SYSTEM

The Ga have patrilineages in which men wield most of the authority. Women in this situation have therefore been motivated to exploit flexible rules concerning inheritance and residence to achieve a measure of autonomy and authority. This chapter explores how they have accomplished this, while giving a brief introduction to Ga social organization: change and continuity in their affiliation, inheritance and residential patterns. We shall see here that women's inferior access to the resource of real estate in the old inheritance system carried over when land ownership was privatized to contribute significantly to making most women members of an underclass.

Affiliation

The Ga overwhelmingly trace descent patrilineally.[1] The sociopolitical structure of Central Accra and the Ga villages rests upon this fact. The original seven quarters of Accra each have their own chiefs, who are usually heads of influential Ga patrilineages possessing land rights within that quarter. The patrilineages also have priests and priestesses who mediate relations with the ancestors and the family gods. Any Ga person can usually tell an inquirer the clan (we) or major lineage from which he or she comes, and often, even if they have never lived in Central Accra, they will know ultimately from which quarter that clan came.[2] Surnames are often derived

---

[1] In the 1971-72 large sample of 223 women, only 13, or 6%, said that they belonged to the major lineage of their mothers. Of these, five were either products of intermarriage with matrilineal peoples or illegitimate unions. This left eight cases of Ga matrifiliation, some of which came from immigrant Akan families, often of chiefly origin where they retained matrilinearity. Ivor Wilks discusses the results of patrilineal-matrilineal intermarriage in one family of *maŋtsɛmei* in "Akwamu and Otublohum: An Eighteenth Century Akan Marriage Arrangement," *Africa* XXIX (1959): 391-404. In the past some confusion existed concerning Ga descent due to the colonial authorities' assumption that matrilinearity predominated in Accra as it did at Cape Coast, the first capital.

[2] A list of the quarters with their component clans, and the family names of the clans can be found in A. A. Amartey, *Omanye Aba* (Accra: Bureau of Ghana Languages, 1969).

from clan names. At Hↄmↄwↄ, the yearly harvest festival in August or September (depending on the clan), all clan members are supposed to come to Accra to their houses of origin (adebↄʃia, literally "ancestors' house") to celebrate with a reunion. Before the Ga became so widely dispersed, this meant that the people in the villages around Accra came back to visit for the duration of the festival, bringing with them gifts of food. The Ga villages around Accra are affiliated with various quarters according to their founder's affiliation.[3] The maŋtsɛmei of the quarters therefore have authority over the land and inhabitants of these villages, who regard Accra as their place of origin and permanent home.[4]

While Ga clan affiliation is usually traced patrilineally, there are exceptions within the patrilineal system caused by the father not claiming the child. At the naming, or outdooring ceremony, eight days after the birth of the child, the father gives it a family name, usually patrilineally in accordance with sex, order of birth, and alternate generations.[5] Each clan has its own set of names. Since the custom of giving surnames developed later than that of giving family names, a typical genealogy might look like Figure III-1.

Figure III-I

Hypothetical genealogy of a Ga lineage — Ayite, founder

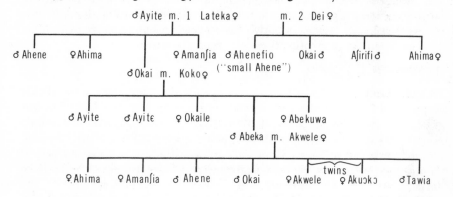

In accordance with Fox's usage, I am using clan to refer to a person's we or major patrilineage, and lineage for minor patrilineage here. R. Fox, *Kinship and Marriage* (London: Penguin Books, 1967), p. 50.

[3]The 1911 *Census of the Gold Coast* listed the Accra villages under the quarters to which they belong.

[4]Osu (Christiansborg), Labadi, Nungwa, and Teshie are also considered to be places of origin and have attendant villages.

[5]For further elaboration on the Ga outdooring ceremony, or *kpodziemↄ*, see Y. Manteko, *Outdooring in Accra* (Accra, 1967), African Studies Institute Pamphlet Collection, University of Ghana.

Confusion is avoided by giving people nicknames, such as "Ahenefio." Twins have a particular set of names given by sex and order of birth, and also the children born after twins, no matter in what clan they occur. Terms of reference and address go by generation also, since all persons of the same sex belonging to the same generation are considered to bear a similar relationship to any given person. For example, a woman's mother's mother's sister or her father's mother's sister are called *Naa* by her, just as her paternal and maternal grandmothers are. Thus, from a person's name alone another Ga person can immediately tell his or her clan (and therefore quarter) affiliation, gender, and birth order with respect to full siblings. What will not be immediately evident, however, is the identity of his or her biological father. In most cases it will be the namer, but not always.

By giving the child a name a man assumes responsibility as social father. If the man said to be the genitor of the child by the mother refuses to name it, someone else usually performs that function, the father's father, the mother's father, or its stepfather.[6] As long as some male accepts and names the child it will bear no stigma and be considered legitimate. The masculine symbolism within the lineage system is expressed in the fact that any child, regardless of sex, must have a *male* sponsor to be considered legitimate. However, if no male accepts responsibility, the child perforce will belong to its mother's lineage, usually her father's patrilineage. But the child will not possess fixed patrilineal inheritance rights in it because of being considered illegitimate. Both mother and child bear a stigma if this happens, although less so recently. This phenomenon is rare since children and the capability of creating them are generally prized.[7]

Inheritance

Although patrifiliation can be considered a norm in Ga society, inheritance rights are not transmitted unilaterally, perhaps because they are subject to manipulation for economic ends. For instance, women's very lack of authority, ideologically and practically, within the patrilineages gave them an incentive to expand their authority where they could--economically. The result is a flexible situation difficult to describe using one term, in which certain property and rights are passed from mother to daughter, other property and rights from father to son, and some things cognatically, without regard to sex. The residential system, to be discussed in the next section, can be considered as cause and effect in this development.

Before discussing property rights, it is necessary to understand general concepts of Ga property ownership. The highest priests, the Nai, Sakumɔ, and Kɔle Wulɔmei, had the original authority to permit land to be taken up and used. As representatives of the original Guan inhabitants, they were the

---

[6] *James Town Maŋtsɛ's Judgment Book*, pp. 338-42 (case 1932).

[7] For further discussion of Ga concepts about legitimacy and illegitimacy see M. J. Field, *The Social Organisation of the Ga People* (London: Crown Agents, 1940), p. 23.

ritual owners of the land. But there is no indication that having once given permission to a lineage to use land, that they could arbitrarily remove the rights of the lineage to that land. Pogucki studied the subject intensively, and found that people originally had only usufructuary, not proprietary, rights to land.[8] However, it may have become private property, once allocated.

Now virtually all land in Central Accra is private property before the law. It may belong to an individual or to a lineage as a corporation, or be in dispute, but once ownership is established (sometimes by long and costly litigation) the owner can rent, sell, or work the land at will (subject, of course, to the whims of the Ghana government).[9] How long this state of affairs has persisted is unclear. Pogucki stated that "dealings in land for valuable considerations appear to have been known for a very long period, perhaps even at the time of the establishment of the European forts."[10]

In the seventeenth and eighteenth centuries, as the political heads of the Ga state became more powerful, they could, on occasion, install and remove priests. In some cases they assumed the power to allocate land.[11] The conflict between priests and chiefs over land rights surfaced in the twentieth century in windy legal battles over monetary compensation for land required by the government. Land sales became a large source of income for Ga lineages, mantsɛmei, priests, and other individuals, mainly men.[12] The stakes were high in this game; land value per acre went from about £800 in 1903 to £30,000 in 1954 in Central Accra.[13] Why did the men especially profit? Because the authority to manipulate land ownership belongs mainly to male lineage elders of the Central Accra clans. The women heads of households almost universally stated that it was impossible for them to have any say in the sale or improvement of their residences, and that the men would have to decide on such action. Only exceptionally does a woman become an influential elder.

Even without sale, the income from lineage property may also go predominantly to men. This income (usually rents) is divided into shares with the largest portion going to the senior members of the lineage. An attempt is usually made to keep the property together, although as a last

---

[8]R. J. H. Pogucki, *Report on Land Tenure in Customary Law of the Non-Akan Areas of the Gold Coast Colony Part II: Ga* (1954; reprint ed., Accra: Lands Department, 1968), pp. 36-37, 32; C. C. Reindorf, *The History of the Gold Coast and Asante* (ca. 1890; reprint ed., Accra: Ghana Universities Press, 1966), p. 107; SCT 2/6/17, *High Court Judgment Book*, pp. 341-46 (case April 16, 1932).

[9]Ghana, Ministry of Housing, *Accra Plan* (Accra: Government Printers, 1958), p. 75. "Particularly in the central portions [of Accra] there is much land which is in individual ownership and in which interests very much akin to freehold exist. This land is freely sold or leased." However, there was no registration of titles to land at that time.

[10]Pogucki, *Report*, p. 32.

[11]Reindorf, *History*, pp. 13, 102, 109.

[12]SCT 2/6/18, *High Court Judgment Book*, pp. 1-167 (case May 31, 1951); SCT 2/6/2, *High Court Judgment Book*, pp. 312-17 (case Dec. 8, 1908).

[13]*Annual Colonial Reports* (1903), p. 23, (1925-26), p. 33; Pogucki, *Report*, p. 18.

resort land might be sold to raise money to pay group debts, maintain the family house, erect a new building, or pay for education or medical expenses.[14] Rarely, the property-owing corporation of the lineage may be dissolved because the elders decide to sell all of the property. In one lineage this happened because the members were dispersed and some of the wealthier male members wanted more authority over the property, while others had little interest in it. The wealthier interested members bought out the others and became the sole owners of portions of the old lineage property. Also, lineage property may gradually dwindle in size and importance as a result of members having been given portions of land to build on or farm, which then become their personal property.[15] In this way lineage property may become rather than a corporate interest, "an entitlement from which each in due time can claim his portion," producing what Marris and Somerset called an "enabling attitude" favorable to entrepreneurs.[16]

While the male elders or the wealthier male members of the lineage usually have most of the authority to dispose of lineage property, occasionally a woman is allowed to take part in these decisions. A respected older woman may become an elder by agreement of the other elders; her standing would be enhanced if she had become wealthy through trade. If she is the oldest member of a patrilineage she may even become its head by election of the elders, age taking precedence over gender. This is called ∫uonɔ famɔ, "sitting on the lap."[17] Only postmenopausal women are eligible to be elder or head, however, because of the association of ideas of pollution with menstruous women.[18] Women are usually only allowed authority over other women. This may be reinforced by the women's own desire to have some authority; the men will not respect them, so they *stay with other women.* In the lineage organization this is shown by the separation of men and women, with authority over the women being delegated by the elders to the oldest or most respected woman or a council of women, subject, of course, to the ultimate authority of the male elders.[19] In lineage decisions, then, women are almost always subordinate to men, which means that the use of lineage property will probably be more to the advantage of men than women. In getting collateral for loans or land for building a house, women must usually rely on their own efforts.

---

[14]Field, *Social Organisation*, p. 45; Pogucki, *Report*, p. 58.

[15]Mills-Odoi found in Labadi that wealthier members of Ga major lineages were sometimes more influential than the elders in determining the disposition of lineage property. D. G. Mills-Odoi, "The La Family and Social Change," Master's thesis Institute of African Studies, University of Ghana (1967), pp. 107, 104. This has now been published as a book under her married name: Gladys Azu, *The Ga Family and Social Change* (Leiden: Afrika Studie Centrum, 1974).

[16]P. Marris and A. Somerset, *The African Entrepreneur* (New York: Africana Publishing Corp., 1972), p. 148.

[17]Interview with Nii Amugi II, Ga Maŋtsɛ, December 16, 1971.

[18]Field, *Social Organisation*, p. 6.

[19]Mills-Odoi, "La Family," p. 16; M. D. Kilson, "Urban Tribesmen: Social Continuity and Change Among the Ga in Accra, Ghana," Ph.D. diss. Harvard University (1966), p. 37.

Underlying these separate gender hierarchies is an ideological separation between the sexes and hierarchical ranking of the sexes in Ga society which is almost insurmountable. Kilson described it as a "basic antagonism between, and radical separation of the sexes in Ga society."[20] The subordination of women to men in the symbolic realm is reinforced by strong social conditioning. To be male is associated with right (as opposed to left), good, straight, and rational, whereas female entails left, bad, crooked, and irrational.[21] Men take precedence over women at all life cycle rituals (except female puberty rites) and male deities are superior to female ones. As a symbol of the reversed order of things (chaos) men and women dress in opposite sex clothing at one stage of the Hɔmɔwɔ celebrations.[22] Boys and girls are encouraged to play in separate groups at different games and are expected to behave differently at a younger age than in many societies.[23] A result of male supremacy in cosmological and lineage systems is that women in general have less understanding of Ga customs and are less able to interpret Ga culture. The women would refer to the men for details on lineage histories and Ga customs. Many women perform lineage rituals, but fewer women than men understand them.[24] Even Ga spirit mediums are surprisingly ignorant of certain traditions. Thus, contrary to the usual situation, the more educated men are the stronger transmitters of Ga culture, while the mostly illiterate women in Central Accra are less knowledgeable about old customs and less interested in them.

Women, then, have less of a vested interest in maintaining the lineage system than men do, which is expressed in their lack of concern about Central Accra property and their desire to acquire suburban land and houses. Their attention is focused on self-acquired property, whose control is facilitated by the use of verbal or written wills, and by the system of reciprocal obligations which is supposed to operate between a person and his or her potential heirs. An heir can be disqualified from obtaining rights to lineage or self-acquired property because of failure to fulfill these obligations, the primary one being paying for the funeral of the deceased. By taking advantage of these conditions both men and women have been able to inherit property which theoretically should have gone elsewhere. The women, in particular, can profit from the situation by endowing their heirs with their self-acquired property and thus escape the disabilities imposed by male dominance in lineage property rights.

It is possible that both men and women are more interested in developing self-acquired, rather than lineage property, but for the women the advantages are greater. In 1911 Hutton-Mills, a Gold Coast member of the

[20]Kilson, "Urban Tribesmen," p. 60.

[21]M. D. Kilson, "The Ga Naming Rite," *Anthropos* 63/64 (1968-69): 906.

[22]Kilson, "Urban Tribesmen," pp. 119, 127n., 137.

[23]Mills-Odoi, "La Family," p. 77; Barrington Kaye, *Bringing Up Children in Ghana* (London: George Allen and Unwin, Ltd., 1962), p. 130.

[24]M. D. Kilson, "Variations in Ga Culture in Central Accra," *Ghana Journal of Sociology* III, no. 1 (Feb. 1967): 46, 50.

Legislative Council, stated:

> The chief reason for the unsightly condition of Accra is to be ascribed to
> the family property system, since the natives have now recognized the ad-
> vantages in individual property and do not care to spend their money on
> the improvement of family property, since they are precluded from dispos-
> ing of it during their lifetime or by will without the concurrence of all
> members of the family.[25]

A common practice is to live in Central Accra rent-free and rent out a house
built in the suburbs, putting money for repairs only into the latter.[26] The
woman who said, *this house is not mine, so I do not care what is done to it,*
was typical in my experience. The situation is exacerbated by the residential system, whereby most women live in their mothers', rather than their
fathers', compounds, which means that they do not have ownership rights in
the compound where they are living. If none of the inhabitants are owners,
no improvements are made, and repairs are done only in a piecemeal fashion.
Even if they do possess ownership rights they must defer decisions to the
male authorities, who might live elsewhere and do nothing.

Lineage and self-acquired property are manipulated quite differently,
and people generally take advantage of that fact. Theoretically, the lineage
elders even control the reallocation of a person's room in the lineage house
after his or her death. In practice, however, whoever has the strongest
presumptive interest in that room, usually a man or woman's oldest child or
sibling of the same sex, will live there unless the elders are strongly opposed
to it. If, as often happens, his or her logical successors have all moved out of
Central Accra, any person who has rights to live there and wishes to do so
may move in, unless those in authority strongly object to his or her character or sex. The deceased's share of lineage income goes not to his or her suc-
cessor in the room, but back into the pool to be redistributed. The size of
the share a person receives is roughly determined first by generation, and
then by age within that generation, and then by character. Men receive
more than women, but it is not clear whether a junior male member would
get more than a senior female member. The allocation of shares is at the
discretion of the elders, and all factors are supposed to be taken into
account.

While it is mostly lineage property which comes under the authority of
the elders, a person's self-acquired property may also do so in cases of intes-
tacy. These would normally be the elders of his or her minimal lineage, but
their decision might be appealed first to those of the maximal lineage, then
to the *maŋtsɛ* of the appropriate quarter, and ultimately to the Ga Maŋtsɛ or
the Accra District Courts. The elders would probably allocate a person's
property differently than the person would in a will. They are more likely to
be influenced by considerations of how well the potential heirs fulfilled their
funeral obligations to the deceased, and of rights determined by generation

---

[25]ADM 4/1/9, *Legislative Council Minutes*, Nov. 6, 1911, p. 18.

[26]E. Eames and J. G. Goode, in *Urban Poverty in a Cross-Cultural Context* (New York:
The Free Press, 1973), p. 201, have noted this phenomenon elsewhere.

and age. The latter are more important, but the former sometimes play a significant role in their decision. Funerals are the most important occasion for display and can be quite costly. The expenses are usually split among all those who feel they have obligations toward the deceased person or his or her family. A husband who failed to pay most of the funeral expenses for his wife sometimes forfeited claim to the children.[27] A person who bore most of the funeral expenses (except a spouse) is entitled to receive most of the deceased's property, as was the case for a woman I knew who paid for her father's funeral. In another example a man sued his brother's children because he had paid all of his brother's funeral expenses and inherited nothing.[28] In another case a woman paid the funeral expenses for a relative of her debtor, hoping to be repaid the debt thereby. She then sued the family for not having done so. She won, and was repaid both the debt and the funeral expenses.[29]

Actually, funeral obligations are only one part of the reciprocal duties which ought to be performed between relatives. How well a person fulfilled all of these obligations may well determine how much the elders decide to give him or her of the estate of the deceased. Because of this phenomenon, Field stated in 1940 that the Ga have:

no rigid laws of inheritance as a European understands codified law . . . People receive what they are deemed to deserve. A next of kin who is unanimously voted a thoroughly worthless character may be disinherited entirely: a distant relative who has lived with the deceased and been a prop and comfort to him may receive something approaching a son's portion . . . Nobody has a right to make any demands on the grounds of such-and-such a kinship relation.

The obligation of reciprocity is very strong, especially between parents and children; the elders will definitely take fulfillment of those obligations into consideration when dividing up an estate. As one woman said, *Those who have done the work should get the reward. For instance, if a man builds a house with the help of his children, they and not his sister's children should inherit.* This situation obviously permits a lot of flexibility.

Reciprocity factors aside, Field stated that when the elders bestowed a deceased man's self-acquired property, the largest shares went first to his younger brothers in order of age, and then to the oldest male in the generation of his sons and his brother's sons, while an analogous pattern prevailed with women and their sisters and daughters. The heirs in that order supervised a person's real property, which was usually kept intact, and distributed shares of the income to the other heirs in accordance with seniority based on generation and age. A man's daughters were supposed to receive smaller shares of his estate than his sons, and a woman's children equal shares of her

---

[27]Field, *Social Organisation*, pp. 55-56. The situation seldom arose because of the high divorce rate and the disparity in age between most husbands and wives, which meant that husbands generally died before their wives.

[28]SCT 2/6/5, p. 116, *High Court Judgment Book* (case June 14, 1915).

[29]*Ga Maŋtsɛ's Civil Court Record* (1922-24), p. 355 (case 1923).

estate regardless of sex.[30] Pogucki, Allott, and Elias-- writing later and not always distinguishing between testamentary and intestate disposition--stated that a person's children inherit his or her self-acquired property, receiving equal shares regardless of sex, with the eldest acting as administrator of the immovable property. If a man has a number of wives the property is first split equally by number of wives before being divided among the children.[31] Women's disability in terms of the lineage distribution of personal property, then, can vary from being negligible to extensive. It becomes clearer in looking at Table III-1, which shows that most of the valuable assets of women in the 1971-72 small survey were self-acquired.

One result of this disability is the women's increasing predilection for making either verbal (*samanso*) or written wills which remove from the elders the power to allocate personal property. Property disposed of by will usually goes to the individual's children according to his or her preference. More people are tending to make written wills, even if they are illiterate. In the small 1971-72 survey only 30% of the women in their sixties or over had made or were planning to make written wills, as opposed to 62% of the women in their forties and fifties. The making of written wills in favor of offspring precludes much interference by siblings or other relatives of the deceased in an effort to get shares of the estate.

Another device which consolidates the children's rights are gifts *inter vivos* (between living persons) of self-acquired property. Women were particularly likely to employ the latter method so that their children would not

Table III-1.
Women's Property Ownership by Mode of Acquisition, 1971-72.[a]

Method of Acquisition	Percent of Women Owning:			
	House/ Room	Unimproved Land/Farm	Jewelry	Canoe/ Net
Self-acquired	24	31	35	4
Inherited	4	20	18	0

[a]Based on information from 71 women. These figures may be too low, since people are wary of disclosing their assets for fear of government intervention to collect taxes, or importunate relatives.

---

[30]Field, *Social Organisation*, pp. 43-46.

[31]This practice corresponds to the "house-property" complex within patrilineal societies described in J. Goody and J. Buckley, "Inheritance and Women's Labour in Africa," *Africa* XLVIII, no. 2 (April 1973): 114. Pogucki, *Report*, pp. 73-74; A. N. Allott, "A Note on the Ga Law of Succession," *Bull. of the London School of Oriental and African Studies* XV, part I (1953): 168-69; T. O. Elias, *Ghana and Sierra Leone: The Development of Their Laws and Constitutions* (London: Stevens and Sons Ltd., 1962), pp. 162-63. This analysis is also supported by an important case not previously cited which came before the James Town Maŋtsɛ: *James Town Maŋtsɛ's Judgment Book*, pp. 378-80 (case 1933).

have to endure much litigation in the effort to probate the will. Given that a woman's financial identity was often inextricably tied to that of her daughter(s) because they were in business together, it only makes sense that a house built with the profits from that business would go to her daughters during her lifetime. In fact, economic cooperation between mothers and daughters has created a tendency for women to leave self-acquired property to their daughters only in fulfilling their reciprocal obligations. One woman said disgustedly that she was going to leave all of her things to one of her daughters because *my other children do not help me. They do nothing for me, so I shall leave her everything I have.* Another woman said that she was leaving everything, including a house, to her daughters, not her sons, because her husband would take care of the boys, so she had to provide for the girls. In the court records it was not uncommon to find daughters inheriting houses, in particular, from their mothers, even over their mother's sisters' rights.[32] In the 1971-72 small survey 52% of the women were planning to leave their personal property to their children regardless of sex, while 34% were going to leave it to their daughters only, and 13% to their sons only. The 34% contrasts with the 10% who had inherited their mothers' property in families where the fathers' property had gone to sons only. Mother-daughter, father-son devolution of self-acquired property may be an increasing phenomenon, then,[33] although cognatic patterns of passing self-acquired property to one's children were still more common. Out of seventeen cases where women had inherited real property (houses or land), five had gotten it from their mothers or mother's mothers, but nine received it from their fathers, father's fathers, or father's sisters.

One possible definition of property rights (or power) is that they equal the amount of control a person has over goods and services. In considering control over goods, i.e., property, within the Ga lineage system here, it has been shown that the subordinate position of women within the lineage system may have given them an impetus to invest their resources in self-acquired property, whose disposition is more amenable to their control. This is part of a larger trend within Ga society towards the individualization of property control, but women have more incentive than men to further the

---

[32]SCT 17/4/2, pp. 153-54 (case 1875); *James Town Maŋtsɛ's Judgment Book*, p. 132 (case April 12, 1924). SCT 2/6/31, *High Court Judgment Book*, p. 382 (case October 17, 1957).

[33]Goody calls this practice, where property is passed between members of the same sex, "homogeneous transmission" of property, and claims that it is very common in West Africa. J. Goody, *Comparative Studies in Kinship* (Stanford: Stanford University Press, 1969), p. 77. In this interpretation I differ from both Quartey-Papafio and Kilson, who (writing respectively in 1910 and 1968) claimed that inheritance patterns go primarily by sex, that is, sons inherit from fathers and daughters from mothers. In fact, there is no doubt that certain titles have always been passed in that manner, but the normative pattern of inheritance of self-acquired property is still cognatic, to children of both sexes. A. B. Quartey-Papafio, "Law of Succession Among the Akras or the Ga Tribes Proper of the Gold Coast," *Journal of the African Society* X, no. 37 (Oct. 1910): 64-65; Kilson, "Ga Naming Rite," p. 905; Interview with Naa Mannye, January 19, 1972; M. J. Field, *Religion and Medicine of the Ga People* (Accra: Presbyterian Book Depot, 1937), p. 201.

process.

Nevertheless, for both men and women there is a tendency for individual self-acquired property to become patrilineage property.[34] There were numerous houses in Ussher Town that were built on lineage or purchased land by an individual who during his or her lifetime was considered to be the owner of the house. After the owner's death they passed to his or her children and their children, progressively belonging to wider kinship groups. In this progression the property became subject to the same male-dominated lineage structure as other patrilineage property. So, while the original owner may have been a woman, the property might not have been passed along a female line, but rather reverted to a cognatic pattern. There were women, however, who as eldest daughters had inherited houses from their mothers, who had gotten the houses from their mothers. Mother-daughter succession to real property did sometimes persist for several generations (four was the most recorded).

In the end there is no way that a Ga woman can ensure the prosperous future of her female offspring, since entail of estates seems to be unknown. Most women must rely on self-acquired property for their own prosperity, as Table III-1 shows. In the acquisition of property, however, the other aspect of property rights mentioned above, control of people's services, is also vital, and can be identified with that control of labor which we called the means of production. In the next section the utility of the Ga residential system in promoting this control for women will be considered.

Residence and the Life Cycle

Residential patterns result from the processes of cyclical and evolutionary change taking place within a group. Cyclical change happens because individuals within the group make decisions about where to live based on different needs at different points in their life cycle. The cumulative effect of these decisions creates a pattern of development within a household that is the developmental cycle of the domestic group.[35] The concept of residence reflecting choices based mainly on cyclical needs is valuable, but one must also consider evolutionary change caused by choices made because of socioeconomic change within a society. Residential patterns still express individual choices made on the basis of needs at various points in the life cycle, but those needs have been changed by events within the society.

One process within Ga society which changed and is changing people's residential choices was the creation of a large and significant class of literate and skilled workers in Accra. One result of this development, which mostly

---

[34]Pogucki, *Report*, p. 80; P. Hill, *The Migrant Cocoa-farmers of Southern Ghana* (Cambridge: University Press, 1963), p. 131.

[35]J. Goody, ed., *The Development Cycle in Domestic Groups* (Cambridge: University Press, 1962); Paul Bohannan, *Social Anthropology* (New York: Holt, Rinehart, and Winston, 1965), pp. 361-62.

excluded women, was an increasing separation of the sexes in Ga society expressed at the residential level. This segregation was accentuated by the change from rural to urban occupations (until the interwar period, many Ga who lived in Accra still farmed the surrounding area). For some Ga men the change was a dual one, from rural to urban to suburban, while for more Ga women it was simply from rural to urban in their trading activities. Here these changes will be documented, including changes within the women's life cycles which have caused them to modify their residential choices.

If one follows Goodenough's advice and classifies residential systems on the basis of the most important social relationship emphasized in the residential pattern, rather than where married couples live,[36] in Ussher Town in the 1970s the dominant relationship expressed in the residential system was the mother-daughter one. There were more women than men, and these women usually lived with their female matrilateral relatives.[37] There were three main types of residential groupings, the most common being a multigenerational compound inhabited by a group of matrilaterally related persons. Next in frequency were compounds containing siblings or half-siblings and their offspring, and then came multigenerational compounds inhabited by patrilaterally related groups of people. Figure III-2 shows a typical example of each type. Table III-2 gives the percentages of male and female respondents in the large 1971-72 survey living in each type of situation.

The men were most likely to live in sibling or patrilaterally related predominantly male groupings. To perpetuate this situation boys are supposed to be sent to their fathers some time between the ages of six and twelve. The father's compound could be as much as several miles away from that of the mother, in Central Accra or even in the suburbs, if the father had left his lineage compound. The women's houses are called *yeiamli* and the men's *hiiamli*, which are in theory patrilineal residences segregated by sex. There might have been a temporary shift of residence for a woman because of marriage, but that was not important enough to warrant defining the whole system by that characteristic.

Table III-2.
Residential Type Participation According to Sex, 1971-72.[a]

Percent of:	Matrilateral	Sibling	Patrilateral	Other	Total
Women	60.7	21.0	9.8	8.5	100.0
Men	12.5	41.7	33.3	12.5	100.0

[a]Sample size is 238.

---

[36]W. H. Goodenough, "Residence Rules," in *Marriage, Family and Residence*, ed. Paul Bohannan and John Middleton (Garden City, New York: Natural History Press, 1968), pp. 306, 318.

[37]In 1960 women were 58% of the Ga population of Ussher and James Towns. Kilson, "Urban Tribesmen," p. 26.

Figure III-2 Typical Compounds in Central Accra,
with relationship of inhabitants to head *

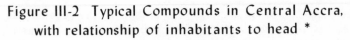

Matrilateral

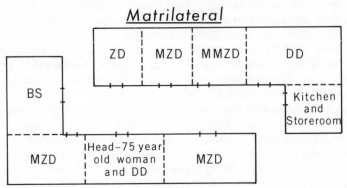

Sibling

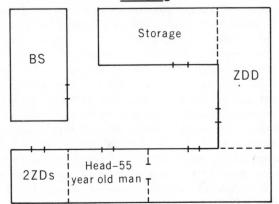

Patrilateral

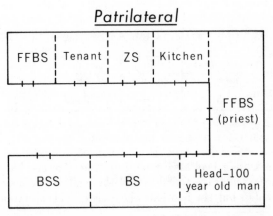

Children not included, only heads of family unit occupying each room.

The high proportion of sibling type groupings is a result of the tradition of Ga men building their own houses and then leaving them to their children of both sexes. Some of this type of compound have come to be inhabited by matrilateral groupings if the brothers in turn move out and start their own households. The sisters are more likely to stay and leave their residential rights in the compound to their daughters. Most of the persons subsumed under "other" were living with their own children only or alone. Again, because men were more likely to form new households, they showed a higher percentage in that category.

The reasons behind the residential choices of women in the 1971-72 small survey fall into three main categories. Fifty-nine percent attributed their living arrangements to patterns of authority and their residential and/or property rights within the compound, 45% to social relations and matters of habit, and 14% to reasons having to do with their work. These reasons could be positive or negative; that is, whether a person liked or disliked the living arrangement, the reason was given equal weight. In approaching the residential system, then, these categories seem valid and will be considered in order of importance, the last being reserved for later discussion, along with other aspects of the impact of trading on women's lives.

Patterns of Authority and Residential Rights

One of the most frequently cited reasons for liking or disliking a given residential arrangement was the degree to which the informant felt that she had authority within the compound. In general, if a woman was the oldest resident of a women's compound she was happy with the arrangement because it allowed her to dispose things according to her preferences. The female hierarchy was most evident in the residential system. The duties of the head of the house were to allocate rooms, settle disputes, see that repairs were made, and collect and dispose of rents from tenants. Her position allowed her to demand help from other residents for maintenance and utility costs. She could also request, and usually receive, more help in personal matters than other compound residents. While this authority was probably a perpetual feature of the residential system, the changes within the system may be increasing its scope.

In general, authority over the compound has been removed from those who should ideally have it, the male members of the owning patrilineage. In theory, the rights to live in a compound are supposed to be passed patrilineally, as is its ownership.[38] In practice, residential rights have come to be passed patrilaterally for men and matrilaterally for women. So, one often found a *yeiamli* where the women all belonged to different patrilineages, because they took their clan affiliations from their fathers, but none of them belonged to the patrilineage which owned the land or the house. Perhaps a female ancestor did; but she had long since died. This situation occasionally

---

[38]Mills-Odoi, "La Family," p. 30.

arose from a woman having built a house on patrilineal land. The house was then considered to be hers and she usually lived there with her female matrilateral relatives and children.[39] In this way the authority of the male members of the patrilineage over the residents of that compound had considerably weakened. It had become difficult for them to tell the head, a woman only distantly related to them, to carry out decisions that they made. Occasionally, the male members of a patrilineage who owned a *yeiamli* would delegate a female member to go live in the house to supervise it for them, but this was rare. However, the women generally did not question the men's authority in these matters, and presumably would have submitted peaceably to eviction if they had no ownership rights in a compound.

This matrilateral transmission of women's residential rights was well established, and can be seen as a factor in reinforcing matriarchal authority. In the small 1971-72 survey 70% of the women had residential rights where they were living inherited through their mothers, and 30% through their fathers. In the large 1971-72 sample of 238 people, 73% of the women were living in houses where their mothers and/or their mothers' relatives lived, and 23% of the men. Sixty-nine percent of the men lived in their fathers' or fathers' relatives' house, but only 19% of the women. More men than women had taken up on cognatically-inherited residential rights. Some respondents even denied a woman's right to live in her father's house, such as this woman. *In our society this has been the situation from time immemorial: the boy can come to the mother's home but not live there and the girl can go to the father's home but not live there.* Most women living in their father's houses did so because of cross-cousin marriage if it was a lineage house; they had inherited residential rights from their mothers also. Sometimes they were spirit mediums for patrilineal gods or goddesses, or living in their paternal grandmother's room in a *yeiamli*. Otherwise, women lived in houses their fathers built (i.e., self-acquired property) through cognatic inheritance or because their fathers had given houses built on their mothers' patrilineal land to their mothers. Several women who had none of these reasons and were living in their fathers' *wekuʃia* (lineage house) for convenience purposes felt themselves to be in an anomalous position with no rights there. In effect, it was not so much that women were deprived of residential rights, as it was that their rights were defined more narrowly than the men's, just as their inheritance rights were.

Men also tended to have more authority in the compounds. Table III-3, based on the results of the 1971-72 large survey, shows that more men were heads of women's compounds than vice versa, and that more men than women were heads of compounds containing adults of both sexes, despite the fact that in total numbers more women than men were heads of compounds. In no case was a woman head of a compound containing only other male adults. The high percentage of male heads of mixed gender compounds was partly accounted for by older women having moved into places vacated by men in a former *hiiamli*. Kilson noted that in such cases some rooms were

---

[39]Kilson, "Urban Tribesmen," p. 67.

**Table III-3. Sex Composition of Compound Population
According to Sex of Head, 1971-72.[a]**

Other Adult	Sex of Head of Compound:	
Inhabitants of Compound	Female	Male
Women Only, %	47.7	3.9
Men Only, %	0.0	19.2
Both Sexes, %	52.3	76.9
Total %	100.0	100.0

[a]These figures include 242 individuals, each living in a different compound, and do not take into account the sex of adult tenants in the compound.

becoming reserved for the use of one sex, rather than having separate sections for the sexes.[40] The women heads of mixed compounds usually had authority over men younger than they were, their adult sons or siblings' sons. So, while women were sometimes gaining more authority because of abdication of responsibility on the part of the men, the men who stayed still wielded proportionately more power than the women did.

Symptomatic of men's superior position within the compound and the lineage was the greater amount of space allotted to them. A typical men's compound was likely to be cleaner and less crowded than a women's compound. Because women often conducted business in their homes and therefore had bulky equipment and smelly ingredients lying around, a women's courtyard was more crowded. Also, the women had the small children with them, who contributed liberally to the noise and confusion in some courtyards. The women's compounds which were both peaceful and scrupulously neat and clean tended to be inhabited by childless women or those whose children lived elsewhere. Sometimes the men rationalized the separation of the sexes by saying that they did not like all the noise and bother of living with food preparation and children.[41] A man felt that he was entitled to a room of his own and he usually had one. A typical situation existed in one compound, where a woman shared her room with two grown daughters, while each of her four teenage sons had a room of his own. In a court case a woman who shared her room with her two sisters and three of their grown daughters, plus a newborn grandchild, wanted the use of another room in the compound for her 22 year old son, because the roof of his room leaked.[42] Partly this had to do with the incest taboo which says that related adult men and women should not sleep in the same room, but it is worthwhile noting that it was usually the women who crowded together to provide a room for a male, rather than vice versa.

---

[40]Kilson, "Urban Tribesmen," p. 66.

[41]Mills-Odoi, "La Family," p. 25.

[42]SCT 17/4/88, pp. 156-57 (case July 20, 1955).

In terms of residential rights, then, we find that most people had a choice of places to live based on rights inherited from different sides of the family. Women, however, had more limited rights than men, and were not usually willing to assert rights to their father's lineage houses, whereas men often stayed in their mothers' houses. Nevertheless, a woman might still have had considerable flexibility in her choice of residence. One toothless old blind woman was typical in this respect.

Naa Ahima[43] spent most of her days at the house of her sons, which was built by her husband on his patrilineal land, and in which she had inherited a life estate entitling her to a share of the rents. She slept at her mother's sister's house, however, in which she had inherited a share. Any time left over was spent at her mother's *wekufia*. All of these houses were within about a mile of one another, over which she had to be led by a young relative.

Authority was strengthened by ownership rights, and this woman accordingly spent most of her time where she had the most proprietary rights. In that respect she was an exception, however. Most women did not have the option of living where they owned a share in the property. Some 27% of the 1971-72 small sample expressed discontent with their present residence but said that they had nowhere else to go; they were clustered in the younger age groups, where accession to authority within the compound had not alleviated the disadvantages of living in Central Accra. Their aspirations focused on moving to the suburbs.

A possible increase in authority for women has come from the exodus of wealthy and influential men, in particular, to the suburbs. In this process the men are following a Ga tradition of lineage segmentation, whereby the younger men sometimes set up new households which used to be adjacent to their lineage compounds, but now must be elsewhere because of scarcity of building space in Central Accra. On leaving Central Accra many men lost interest in lineage property and as a consequence became absentee heads, exercising no functions. Often when asked who was the head of a particular compound, a woman head would think for some time and then dredge up a vague memory of, for example, a mother's brother's son's son who lived somewhere in a suburb, but was never seen in Central Accra and obviously wielded no authority. In the large 1971-72 survey 52% of the houses were built by men and 35.5% by women, but in 12.5% of the cases people did not know who had built them. In those cases (and in cases where women built the houses) it was usually women who exercised authority within the compounds, the original owners having abdicated responsibility.

Because so many men are leaving, the number of Ga female-headed households in Ussher Town has been going up. In 1958 Acquah found that 59% of the heads of households in Ussher Town were female, while in 1965 Kilson's survey showed 78% with female heads.[44] The 1971-72 small survey

---

[43]To preserve anonymity, I have substituted similar names.

[44]I. Acquah, *Accra Survey* (London: University of London Press, Ltd., 1958), p. 38; Kilson, "Urban Tribesmen," pp. 101n., 96.

showed 73% of the compounds with resident female heads. So, succession to headship was more frequent for women in Central Accra, while establishment of new household units was more likely for men.[45] Older women were gaining more authority, but the shift of interest away from Central Accra on the part of wealthier men and women and young people made that authority a prize not coveted by many. If the men were to take a renewed interest in Central Accra they would have no problem regaining their position, since the women mostly acknowledged their superior rights. The main struggle for fame and fortune is going on elsewhere.

Social Factors in Choice of Residence: the Life Cycle

Forty-five percent of the women in the 1971-72 small survey gave reasons having to do with social relations and matters of habit for their residential choice. One reason for the importance of this type of answer was their age; the women were mostly in their forties and over, so they had had more than half a lifetime to develop roots in the area in which they had lived most of their lives. They were often heads of households and so had a vested interest in their compounds. Indeed, the residential stability of the Ga population of Central Accra was one of its most striking features. Over 85% of the people in the large 1971-72 survey were born in Central Accra, and another 10% elsewhere in Accra or in a Ga village.[46] It is no wonder, then, that many women gave their reason for staying in Central Accra as some equivalent of, *I was born here, and I will die here.*

Both the longevity of individual tenure in Central Accra and their sense of ancestral belonging contributed to people's commitment to living there. In the large 1971-72 survey, for 66% of the subjects all of the immediate ancestors on both sides as far back as they could remember came from Central Accra. Not only were they from Central Accra, but usually from Ussher Town and often from the same quarter as the respondent. Some women felt very strongly that they should remain in their ancestral houses to ensure that communication with their ancestors was maintained. This was particularly true of spirit mediums, for whom it was part of their ritual duties, but also other women occasionally claimed to be afraid of the wrath of the ancestors if they were to leave. In this respect Naa Abla's answer was typical:

> *I am the deputy of all those who have died so I will never leave here until I die, even if I have built many houses elsewhere. . . . Every year I cook* kpekple,[47] *so if I leave this place and there is no one to do it, the spirits [of the ancestors] will come and kill me. They left me to take care of the house.*

---

[45]Kilson, "Urban Tribesmen," p. 93.

[46]Kilson noted that in Ussher Town in 1965, 73% of the heads of household had lived in the same house for 11 years or more, and 87% of the women had lived in the same house all of their lives. Ninety-one percent of the sample was born in Central Accra. All of these percentages were higher than comparable figures for James Town and Korle Woko, two areas where extensive rebuilding had taken place. Kilson, "Urban Tribesmen," pp. 95, 22.

[47]The food prepared for Hɔmɔwɔ when greetings are sent to the ancestors.

They see me while I cannot see them. So, it is not good for me to leave this place.

While statistically the population of Central Accra appears to be remarkably stable, a closer examination shows that this is in a framework of mobility within a circumscribed area. The question, "have you lived in this house all of your life?" elicited a positive answer in most cases, not because a person was always physically present in that house, but because she regarded it as her permanent home. We saw in the previous section that many people have rights to live in various places within Central Accra according to their preferences. However, many people also spent time in Ga villages, or even elsewhere in Ghana and abroad. A woman might have been sent as a girl to help her mother's sister who was living temporarily in Nsawam, some 25 miles from Accra, come back to her mother in Accra, married and gone with her husband on transfer upcountry or abroad, gone back to her mother upon returning, gone upcountry again as a partner in the fish trade, and come back to Accra again for her old age. In spite of all this mobility, she probably spent most of her life in Accra.

The demands of the life cycle which cause changes of residence are both social and economic. During her childhood a woman lived mainly where her mother did, unless she was sent to help a relative or fostered out to someone else. Thus, in most cases girls had little choice about where they lived. It did happen, however, that a strong-minded girl decided to live with someone other than her mother, such as the woman who as a girl attached herself to her father's sister's household, which she found more to her liking. As she got older a woman's power of choosing her residence increased, but did not become fully recognized by the society until she was married with children. At that point she might have had a choice about whether or not to live with her husband, if the husband requested it. Most of the women in the small sample in their fifties and over had lived with their husbands, usually early in the marriage in a Ga village, where they helped with the farming or by fishselling. The village houses were regarded as temporary dwellings, and usually contained only a man and one wife, and their children. This neolocal pattern is duplicated in the living arrangements of Ga couples who live in the Accra suburbs.

If a woman lived in Central Accra she almost invariably lived with her female relatives; if she lived elsewhere she was probably with her husband when established in one place for any length of time (discounting trading trips). Before World War II if she lived with her husband elsewhere, it would probably have been in a Ga village. Now it would most likely be in a suburb. There were exceptions, of course, before World War II and now in the pattern of conjugal living being associated with neolocality, usually at a distance. In the 1971-72 large survey only 1.3% of the women were living with their husbands,[48] but mostly not in neolocal situations, while another

---

[48]To my knowledge only two couples were encountered in the large 1971-72 survey. In one case the man's wife was living with him in his *wekuʃia,* and in another case, next door in the *yeiamli* of his *wekuʃia.* However, it was often difficult to determine who was married

1.8% were living with their spouses' relatives. In general, this was an unpopular situation, as the statistics show. In the small 1971-72 survey, opinion was unanimous that women do not like to live with their husbands in the husband's *wekuſia*, usually because of potential conflicts with the husbands' relatives and lack of authority. Most were agreeable to the idea of living neolocally with the husband, however; 50 out of 70 women in the small survey had done so at some point in their lives.

Conjugal living is associated with neolocality, which usually had the connotations of relative wealth and higher status, making it an ideal for some women. In comparing three areas in Central Accra, Ussher Town, James Town, and Korle Woko (Riponsville, a newer area), Kilson found that the proportion of coresident spouses varied directly with that of persons having middle class (white collar) occupations, and inversely with the ethnic homogeneity, longevity, and stability of the population.[49] Another factor responsible for this phenomenon was the antiquity of the housing; more rebuilding had been done in James Town than Ussher Town due to the earthquake, and Korle Woko was a government housing estate established in the 1920s. New construction allowed more neolocal situations to develop.

The high status associations of living in the suburbs made it a desirable goal for many people. The women in the 1971-72 small survey reflected this aspiration. The commitment of the younger women, in particular, to staying in Central Accra was markedly less than that of the older women. This was indicated by whether or not they wanted their children to stay there. A majority of those in their sixties and over did, while it was the opposite with the younger women. Also, there was a steady diminution by age group in the number of women who wanted to build or rebuild houses in Central Accra. Over a third of the oldest (eighties and nineties age group) said they would like to, while none of the women in their forties and thirties desired it. Some of this change in attitude, of course, was merely an indication of where different women were in the life cycle, but it cannot all be accounted for in that way. Some of the younger women were concerned because they felt that Central Accra was a bad place to bring up young children. However, poverty usually prevented them from implementing their desire to move, *unless* they went to live with their husbands. Most of the younger women stayed in Central Accra. In the large 1971-72 sample, among the children of 249 subjects, 63% of the surviving daughters were still in Central Accra, as opposed to 42% of the sons. Thirty-eight percent of the sons were living in the suburbs, compared to 25% of the daughters. The difference between the sons and daughters who were aged in their thirties, when a man would be setting up his independent establishment, or a woman would be most likely to live with her husband, was more striking; 56% of the sons were in the

---

to whom, as Field noted (*Social Organisation*, p. 8), since women did not adopt their husbands' surnames and only went to their husbands at night.

[49]Kilson, "Urban Tribesmen," pp. 65-66. The proportions of coresident spouses were as follows: Ussher Town—men 13%, women 11%; James Town—men 31%, women 18%; Korle Woko—men 47%, women 42%.

suburbs, as opposed to 30% of the daughters.

Although women generally approved of neolocality, they were not willing to commit themselves to it permanently. Sixty-nine percent of the women in the 1971-72 small survey preferred living apart from their husbands, and this preference did not change significantly by age group (5% were undecided and 26% preferred conjugal residence). Many women appreciated the freedom associated with living apart from their husbands. One woman who was divorced by her first husband because of her (assumed) infidelity said, *If you live together with your husband you feel ill at ease; it is better when you go and see him occasionally.* Because of the high divorce rate, living with a husband was viewed as a temporary arrangement. Women felt they had more security of tenure with their own relatives. They did not like the husbands' supervising their social and economic activities, an inevitable result of assumed male supremacy.

Separate residences for spouses were a particularly advantageous arrangement for the women when a man had more than one wife. A wife usually went to the husband at night when he requested it. She cooked his food for him during the day and either sent it to him via the children or took it herself. If a man had more than one wife they were supposed to take turns coming to him on a weekly or monthly basis, with time out for childbirth, of course. The wife who was sleeping with the husband cooked for him. If a woman for some reason could not cook for her husband when she was supposed to, a female relative often substituted for her. Likewise, female relatives might have concealed extramarital affairs in some cases.[50] So, while some women wanted the higher status and more commodious living offered by the suburbs, they at the same time were not willing to sacrifice the benefits of nonconjugal living, especially if their husbands had other wives living with them.

Marriage, then, was not an important determinant of residential choice; only two of the 72 women in the 1971-72 small survey had taken their husbands' residence into consideration in making that choice. Most of the women had lived with their husbands at some point, but usually only for short periods of time early in the marriage. When the husband moved back to Accra the wife returned to her mother's house.

When a woman was in her twenties and thirties one of the most appealing aspects of living with her female relatives was having their help in watching children too large to take to market, but too small to send to school or to help. With the gradual reduction of the children's dependence as they got older, she was freer to decide where to live on the basis of her own convenience, but at the same time the approach of old age gave her a heightened need for security. She was more likely to stay in the compound with her matrilateral relatives, where her rights were most secure and her authority the greatest. Some benefits an older woman derived from this arrangement were the services of: small children for running errands, women of various ages as business partners, and able-bodied women to care for her

---

[50]Field, *Social Organisation*, p. 7.

when she was sick and conduct business transactions for her by proxy. Because she had spent most of her life there, she was surrounded not only by relatives, but also by friends, and did not want to uproot herself and break her old connections. When she got too feeble to work she expected support from her children, food from her daughters and money from her sons. She was more likely to get it from her daughters if she was staying with them. So, while younger women preferred living in Accra for reasons such as being able to get everything they wanted, the excitement of the city, its modern conveniences, and its being fashionable, the older women referred more often to factors concerning connections with relatives and habit.

*   *   *   *   *

We have seen that residential patterns in Central Accra, while they do not conform to Ga methods of tracing clan affiliation, fit nicely with the emergent inheritance patterns. In fact, they are mutually interactive, linked together by the support patterns which will be considered in more detail later. Residential, inheritance, and support patterns had tendencies toward bilaterality, mirroring the differentiated male and female hierarchies among Central Accra Ga. But the female hierarchy is increasingly associated with poverty, as is living in Central Accra, so that this evidence of female autonomy does not also prove an increase in female authority with the society as a whole.[51] It rather shows an attempt by women to maximize their scarce resources.

However, women's strategies to maximize their access to labor by coresidence with other women, which served as a compensation for limited access to real estate, had the effect of perhaps decreasing further that access. Because coresidence often helped determine inheritance rights, the fact that most women stayed with their mothers not on their lineage property, undoubtedly helped to deprive them of property. Logically enough then, women concentrated on self-acquired property. In a similar manner, women's own actions in practicing cognatic devolution of property tended to dissipate female resources. We will see later that women's paying for their sons' education performed a similar function.

The inheritance and residential patterns of Central Accra Ga women, then, show that their survival has been based on mother-daughter economic and social cooperation. In the absence of other viable options their future survival will depend on the continuing strength of this relationship, the foundation of female networks. In order to test that strength I will first examine change in the organization of women's trade in Chapter IV, and then the impact of formal education in Chapter V.

---

[51]It is important not to mistake economic autonomy from men for economic power, as C. Dinan does in studying a sample of 65 Accra elite single women, "Pragmatists or Feminists? The Professional 'Single' Women of Accra, Ghana," *Cahiers d'Etudes Africaines* 65, XVII, no. 1 (1977): 162. Only by making this mistake and using such a sample could the conclusion be drawn, as she does, that women's status is going up.

Portrait 1

MARY KOKO SOLOMON

Mary Koko Solomon was an energetic and forthright informant. She was in her late sixties in 1972, living in a small compound tucked away in the heart of Asere, with her brother, sister, nieces and nephews, and some other matrilateral relatives, mainly male. She was a good informant with an excellent memory and few inhibitions about her subjects. She talked straight to the point, while answering questions as fully as possible, illustrating when necessary by demonstration (making corn wine, for instance). She describes here perhaps the happiest marriage I encountered in any of the surveys. When I next saw her in 1978 she had had a paralytic stroke, was mainly incapacitated and very depressed. Her sister was caring for her with difficulty because of the terrible inflation in Ghana. I hope that others will find in this account of her life the vigorous and honest spirit which was hers. She was a delight to deal with, an enriching experience; the world is poorer for her passing.

Childhood (approximately 1906 to 1920)

My earliest memories have to do with the time I was with my parents, who provided everything I needed. My father had his own house at Ŋleʃi [James Town]; he was a carpenter and belonged to the family of Maŋtsɛ Kojo Ababio [a former head of that quarter of Accra], who presided at my outdooring. My mother lived with him there until he died when I was about eight years old, and then came back here to her own family house. My parents were very loving toward us and each other. They never quarreled with anyone. There were six of us and I was the eldest daughter.

I had a happy childhood. I used to play with a group of children and we would roam freely in the fields as far as the Kɔle Lagoon. At that time Accra was not as developed and there was a lot of open space and not as many people. James Town had some two-story houses, but Ussher Town had very few. There was no electricity or pipeborne water, and not even many streets. The houses were as close together as they are now; in fact, to make the street which you used to get here they had to tear down some houses. Many of the houses in Ussher Town are old; their design is the traditional one which we have used from time immemorial. Korle Bu Hospital had not been built yet, and the Post Office area was the eastern end of town. The area from Makola to Abose Okai was all open grass land. There were also some big trees which have now been cut down.

When we would play in these fields we would collect some wild plants called eŋmɛbii and pretend that they were plantain that we were selling in the market. We children liked holidays, especially Easter, Hɔmɔwɔ, and Christmas. We all received gifts then. We girls got brand new cloths and sometimes new jewelry to go with them. We dressed up very prettily and then we went out at Christmas and Easter to morning and evening church services. At Hɔmɔwɔ on the Thursday preceding Hɔmɔwɔ Saturday the villagers arrived in groups drumming and singing on the north side of town, where they would be met by people from the town drumming and singing also. Then everyone followed the drums through the principal streets of the town and dropped out when they reached their homes. Hɔmɔwɔ Friday was a day for twins, who celebrated a yam festival. On that day too the people of Asere[1] went to Okaikoi dressed in red cloth. The women carried vegetables and the men guns when they again returned drumming and singing to Bukom [Square in Asere] and the men formed a circle and fired their guns. On Saturday kpekple [Hɔmɔwɔ food] was prepared. On Sunday we visited friends and made up quarrels. I was particularly favored as a child at this time because my mother was the first of her mother's children to bring forth and I was the eldest daughter. My [maternal] aunts showered gifts on me.

Our mother was very careful concerning us. At the least sign of illness she would send that child to the hospital. I remember one day we went to

---

[1]Each quarter has its own rural villages under the jurisdiction of the Maŋtsɛ and its own Hɔmɔwɔ celebration.

the beach. We had a race on the way and I stumbled and fell. I was in the hospital for three days. I used to suffer from severe asthma, but my [maternal] grandmother cured it by buying medicines at the market. She ground them on a stone, mixed them with water, and I drank it. I was never taken to an herbalist. When the influenza came [1918] it frightened me; people who got it never survived more than a week and many people from this quarter died.

As children we were taught not to fight and to be humble and content with what our parents provided for us. We were told not to look for trouble. If we were rude we were beaten. It was our mother who usually disciplined us if we misbehaved since we were most often with her. I helped her; since I was the first born much of the work fell on me. She twice had twins so I always had to go out with her carrying a baby. I did not have much time for playing and no one ever thought of sending me to school, although in my time there were girls who went to school; they always wore cloth. I wanted to go to school but my mother needed me to help with the housework. I am glad that girls now go so they can stick up for their rights. My mother would send me to the market. I would go along with my girlfriends in the neighborhood. I had a few friends but the best ones were my sisters. I did not favor any one of my sisters over another, but treated them all equally.

Puberty and early years of marriage (circa 1920 to 1935)

When I had my first menstrual period I was frightened and told my mother. She did not tell me what caused it, but rather showed me how to keep myself clean under the circumstances by bathing three times or more in a day and washing and changing the pads.[2] It would be better if mothers told their daughters about it before it happened. After it my mother warned me not to run around with boys, but I did not ask her why. I only found out later after I had married and conceived.

The man whom I married first asked my parents for my hand. My parents consented and my father called me and told me about it. He was an apprentice carpenter to my father and about twenty years older than I was. He was from Nlefi. My parents wished me to marry the man. In obedience to them I agreed with reluctance, but as time went on we grew to love each other. He performed a full six-cloth customary marriage rite for me. Before I married I was ignorant of sex. That man gave me my first experience. To be frank, I struggled with him because I was scared of him when I saw him as a man.

It was three years before I first conceived. That did not worry me but my husband was upset and took me to a white doctor. We were then living in Liberia. Over there I was a foreigner and so, no matter what, I liked

---

[2]Usually rags or red cloth intended for the purpose.

Ghana better than Liberia. That very year I began medical treatment I got pregnant. I brought forth my first-born there.

While were were in Liberia I was smoking fish for sale and also frying and selling doughnuts. The doughnuts did well but the Liberians are not as used to eating fish as we are. I was trading with some Fantis from Ghana who were there also. After Liberia my husband's company transferred him back to Accra for four years and then to Victoria in Cameroon. It was a "dry" place as there was no work there that I could do. I gave birth to a child there too. Even though I was away from my mother, she had taught me much about childbirth to make it easier to give birth in a distant land. I had an elderly Fanti woman midwife who delivered the child and took care of it for the first week, giving it baths and so on. My husband was also very helpful; he would go for water and sweep the rooms and the compound before going to work every day for the first week after my delivery. After that week I did everything. We spent about five or six years in Victoria. When we were abroad my husband and I lived together, but when we would come back to Accra I would go back and live with my mother in her family house, and he would go back to his paternal family house.

Marriage (circa 1925 to 1952)

My husband was stout and black in complexion. We had a quiet and enjoyable marriage until his death. The marriage was, in fact, a family one. He was the son of my father's sister. We were of the same stock and therefore had a very cordial relationship. This kind of marriage strengthens the family circle and my father wanted it that way. It also keeps the property within the family. But family marriage [ʃia gbla] is not as common now as previously because some girls refuse to enter such a marriage.

Because at first I was unwilling to marry the [man who became the] father of my children, he made every effort not to give me cause to complain to my family. He lived peacefully with me. Sometimes my mother talked with me inside the house about marriage with no one else present. She shared her experiences with me and told me to be humble, obedient, and respectful toward my husband. I followed her advice. She never talked to me about my husband or asked me questions about him. My husband and I got along well. We never discussed matters having to do with his or my income and work. Once a husband gets to know about the finances of his wife the man begins to be tight with money. He will not be willing to take some of the financial responsibilities he previously was shouldering. Therefore, a safe practice is to keep the man in the dark. However, when I needed the help of a literate person I always asked him and he helped willingly.

My husband gave me monthly housekeeping money of £6 or 8 when the children started coming. Also, if I wanted a new cloth or something, and asked him, he would give me what he could. That was all right because he was also caring for his aged mother. I generally tried not to ask him for money to help my family. I only did it when someone was in dire need of help.

After our travels when we came back to Accra my husband took another wife. It did not worry me; I became friends with her and we visited each other at home.[3] Usually it is not good for a man to take another wife because the rivals quarrel all the time. But we did not; we even gave each other advice. I would not say that she helped me in my household tasks, however; we did not live together. As an only wife I gained respect, and also as a senior wife. She had three children with my husband, while I had six.

About twenty years ago my husband died. His death brought me greater grief even than those of my father and mother, because with it also came misery and poverty.

Childrearing (circa 1928-1972)

Before I had children I put no value on them. But after the second child I began to yearn that God would give me more children. When I was in Accra my mother helped me with my newborns. Among the Ga a mother should help until, say, the third child comes. She should train the new mother in childcare before letting her do it on her own. I myself raised my children as my mother raised me, which is the way things should be done.

My husband and I had six children altogether, but three died fairly young. He outdoored all of the children except the one who died too young.[4] He took more of the financial responsibility for bringing up the children than I did. As a result of this and because we were very cooperative we did not have many difficulties in rearing them. When a child did something wrong he liked to use persuasion to get the error corrected, but I used the cane a great deal. He did not like my caning the children. When I went out I would leave the children with any of my [biological or classificatory] sisters who happened to be home. But I did not like going out too much. Much of the time my sisters and I stayed home chatting and amusing ourselves. My husband and I had two girls and four boys. I gave the girls practical training in the vocations I followed. So even though they went to school they know how to prepare kenkey and corn wine.

All of my children finished Standard 7 [Middle Form 4] in school. Their father paid most of their school expenses, but he occasionally asked me to assist. I had a lot of worries with the children. They did not care about being punctual in going to classes. Sometimes I had to chase them with a cane to get them to go. It was not that they did not want to go to school; but rather that they were playing and did not have any awareness of time or its value. They did not mind being late for classes. This attitude is

---

[3]At their respective family houses.

[4]Under a week old.

probably common to children of all lands, including your country. Sometimes it amused me when the children would come home and imitate their
teachers. When a child was unwilling to continue with school we used persuasion and got him back to being interested in classes.

If I were advising a young mother regarding the upbringing of her children I would tell her to be patient with them since they learn gradually. She
should dress them neatly all the time. She should teach them to respect her
and to abide by her views. Because my children all do this I love them all
equally.

After their father died there was no one to help me with the children
any more and I had to work harder to make ends meet. At that time three
of the children were still young, while the older ones already had children of
their own. Sometimes the older girls assisted me with money for the younger
ones.

In the olden days people used to have larger families. It was fashionable
to have ten children. Today with the fourth child couples begin to think of
limiting the family. Sometimes parents have more children than they can
care for properly. Some women have children with men who run away. But
also there are women with responsible husbands who are prepared to have as
many children as they can. Our generation did not see the need to control
or limit birth. Your generation feels that it is good. With my background I
cannot judge the issue.

Work (circa 1918 to 1972)

I started work when I was about twelve years old helping my mother by
smoking fish, making kenkey, and taking our products to the villages to
sell.[5] We would go to places like Mangoase and Koforidua. At first, before I
started having children, we would go on foot, say to Nsawam, stay the day
and return the next day after having sold the fish. Sometimes we went twice
a week. I gave all of the profits to my mother since she clothed and fed me.
When I started I was only carrying maybe fifty fish on my head, but eventually I worked up to 300. After a while we started going by train, sometimes
even as far as Kumasi. When in the villages I stayed with other Gas I found
there and gave them some fish for their trouble.

I continued with the fish trade after I started having children. When
someone wanted to buy on a wholesale basis I did it that way, but usually I
sold the fish singly or in small batches. I used to make twelve shillings profit
on a batch of a hundred fish. I usually traveled once a week, sometimes
staying away for two days, sometimes a week. Once when I was gone for a
week some fish I had here got rotten. It had rained and there were worms in
it. The health inspector had me fined five shillings for the offense.

---

[5]Detailed descriptions of how to smoke fish and make kenkey and corn wine are included in Chapter IV.

Smoking the fish sometimes took three days, sometimes less. Occasionally I smoked a thousand fish at a time. My mother and I had three fish smoking pits which we used. I bought the fish at the seashore or the market from anyone who would give me a good price. We bargained over the price. Sometimes I paid cash for it and sometimes I used credit. As time went on the price of fish went up because nets got more expensive. I find it difficult to estimate my profits because it all went for necessities. Sometimes I would stop with the fish and make kenkey, which I sold at Bukom. To make kenkey you had to grind the corn by hand. I would start at the grinding stone at about five A.M. and finish by about eight A.M. It was tedious and fatiguing. Now the introduction of corn mills has made our work a little less tiring.

After the kenkey and fishsmoking I started making corn wine [ŋmɛdaa]. My mother-in-law taught me how to do it, and I still do it exactly the same way. I helped her for some time before starting on my own. It became profitable so I never wanted to switch to anything else. People usually order it from me in batches; once a whole batch was spoiled because the mill had had coconut in it previously; the corn got oily and useless. I like doing it because I am getting older and it is not too strenuous. I can rest between times. Also, one can prepare meals while the wine is cooking in order to have food ready for the children when they come home from school. I care for myself and my nieces and nephews with the proceeds from it.

My husband gave me capital to start with several times. It was, of course, a loan which I repaid later. If I were giving advice to young women starting out in trade now I would tell them not to waste the capital, concentrate on their work, and keep track of their profit position at all times. You have to watch the market constantly since it fluctuates all the time. We are all at its mercy. My own profits went up and down. Actually, I never considered my income in terms of profit. The work was to supplement what my husband provided.

Now I try to produce the same amount of corn wine all of the time, but it is getting difficult. There are shortages. Sugar formerly sold at one shilling a packet, now if you can find it at all you are lucky, and then it sells at three shillings [30 pesewas]. The cost of production of corn wine has risen considerably because of the rising prices of the raw materials. Perhaps it is the increase in the population which has driven prices up. In any case, the profit margin is much reduced after you deduct your costs. As a consequence I have cut down on the amount I spend for daily necessities.

Work is important for a woman. Do not women need to eat, keep their bodies neat and clean, and dress up on occasion? If a woman does not work, how would she have the means of procuring all of her necessities? As for me, my work gives me exercise. If I go for a week without preparing some wine I feel weak for lack of exercise. But sometimes the great heat from the fire bothers me and I go to the doctor. My daughter gives me medicine for it, and I also take anti-malaria drugs. But basically I attribute my longevity to the Lord. I owe it all to God.

IV

DECLINE IN THE TERMS OF TRADE:

A HISTORY OF FOUR TRADES

Trading as an occupation of West African women has a long, varied, and important history, most of which has yet to be written. A segment of this history as it pertains to Ga women is presented here, along with wider considerations about women in the Ghana labor force. The basis and great strength of this trade has been the maximal use of its chief resource, female labor organized in networks. This chapter will examine changes in the conditions and organization of trade in order to discern the implications for women's class position.

A Brief Historie of the Guinea Trade, 1600-1980

Ga (and some other coastal) women have been trading as far back as can be determined. Trade in such commodities as slaves, gold, and ivory was mainly conducted by men, but the trade in small luxury items was probably conducted by the women from the beginning of contact with Europeans, and the trade in fish and vegetables always was.[1] De Marees described in 1600 some of the commodities traded by the coastal women as "Linnen Cloth, Knives, ground Corals, beads, Looking-glasses, Pinnes, Arme Rings, and Fish . . . oranges, lemons, bannanas, backovens [?], potatoes, indianias [?], millia, mais, rice, manigette [cardamom], hens, egges, bread, and such like necessaries. . . ." He said that they were

> very nimble about their businesse, and so earnest therein, that they goe at least five or six miles every day to the places where they have to doe, and are laden like asses: for at their backes they carrie their children, and on their heads they have a heavy burthen of fruit, or millia, and so goe laden to the market, and there she buyeth fish to carrie home with her, so that oftentimes they come as heavily laden from the market as they went thith-

---

[1]D. McCall, "The Koforidua Market," in *Markets in Africa*, ed. P. Bohannan and G. Dalton (Evanston: Northwestern University Press, 1962), p. 697; F. A. Sai, "The Market Woman in the Economy of Ghana," Master's thesis Cornell University (1971), p. 7.

er . . . those women goe seven or eight together, and as they passe along
the way they are verie merrie and pleasant, for commonly they sing and
make a noise.[2]

They were obviously serious professional traders even at that time.[3]

Much later, in the mid-nineteenth century, there are further descriptions
of the commodities traded by the women and their devotion to trading.
Bridge in 1845 noted that the African wives of some of the merchants were
"sometimes left for months in sole charge" of businesses in their husbands'
absence.[4] These would probably have been profitable import/export
businesses. More typical were the Accra traders described by Cruickshank in
1853. "The whole population are traders to a certain extent. It is the
delight of the African women to sit in the market-places under the trees,
exposing their wares for sale, or to hawk them through the streets from door
to door, and from village to village."[5] In 1856 Daniell listed the commodities
traded by these women as plantain, bananas, peppers, limes, oranges,
groundnuts, local soap, pineapple, flax, tobacco, okra, cassava, kenkey and
other corn foods, soursops, berries, shallots, palm oil, shea butter, kola nuts,
dried and fresh fish, smoked deer and goat meat, beads, earthenware, guns,
copper basins, and local and imported cloth.[6] This list resembles commodities sold by the women more recently, although one should add more
varieties of vegetables, such as lettuce, cauliflower, carrots, tomatoes, and
avocados, and more imported goods, such as margarine, toys, toilet paper,
pots and pans, in fact, almost anything ever available in Ghana. While it is
still true that the majority of Ga women deal in foodstuffs of some sort, as
Henty noted in 1874,[7] imported goods probably accounted for an increasing
share of their business until recently.

How important market trading was and is as a profession for Ga women
is indicated by the census. In 1911, when the first attempt to record
women's occupations was made, 75% of the 4,000 women in Accra District
whose occupations were recorded were traders. In 1921 in the Accra Municipal area the corresponding figure was 65%, in 1931 for the Eastern Province,
59%, in 1948 for Accra only, 88%, and in 1960 for Ussher Town only, 78%.

---

[2]P. de Marees, "A description and Historicall Declaration of the Golden Kingdome of
Guinea . . .," in *Hakluytus Posthumus or Purchas His Pilgrimes*, trans. G. A. Dantisc, ed. S.
Purchas (1600; reprint ed., New York: AMS Press, Inc., 1965), VI: 286-87.

[3]R. Simms and E. Dumor, in "Women in the Urban Economy of Ghana: Associational
Activity and the Enclave Economy," *African Urban Notes* II, no. 3 (1976-77): 47, were incorrect in attributing the establishment of market trade on the Gold Coast to colonialism, a
mistake that largely invalidated their argument proving the parasitism of traders.

[4]H. Bridge, *Journal of an African Cruiser* (1845; reprint ed., London: Dawsons of Pall
Mall, 1968), p. 142.

[5]B. Cruickshank, *Eighteen Years on the Gold coast of Africa* (1853; reprint ed., New
York: Barnes and Noble, Inc., 1966), II: 280-81.

[6]W. F. Daniell, "On the Ethnography of Akkrah and Adampé, Gold Coast, West Africa," *Journal of the Ethnological Society of London* IV (1856): 29.

[7]G. A. Henty, in *Pageant of Ghana*, ed. F. Wolfson (London: Oxford University Press,
1958), p. 164.

Also in 1960, 73.2% of all Ga women in Accra were sales workers. In 1970, 79% of the employed women in Ussher Town were traders (including food processors).[8] It is safe to assume that approximately 70 to 75% of Accra Ga women were traders in the twentieth century.[9] Even those not listed in the censuses as traders had probably traded at some time in their lives. Whether or not this many women will continue to be traders is problematical. The proportion may go down, given the general direction of change in female labor force participation. Here again one encounters the paradoxical nature of women's position in Ghana.

Theoretically, Ghanaian women are in a relatively good position compared to many western and Islamic women regarding rights to work outside the home, own and convey property, and generally act independently of male permission. At independence all forms of legal discrimination against women were abolished, and subsequently liberal maternity benefits were enacted for wage workers.[10] Nevertheless, two factors have combined to create a great deal of sex segregation in Ghanaian employment with women clustered in low-paying jobs. One is educational disadvantage, and the other is discrimination in the labor market combined with inadequate child care facilities for working mothers. Discrimination in the labor market involves not only refusing to hire women, but also paying women less for the same work. Thus, women farm workers in Brong-Ahafo are not only paid half the daily wage of men, but also do not get the same fringe benefits of free meals, lodging, clothing, and medical care.[11] In 1967, 9.9% of all Ghanaians receiving wages or salaries were women, but they received only 8.2% of those wages or salaries. This trend was reflected even more strongly in the predominantly urban government administrative work force, which was 94.8% male in 1970.[12] Likewise, an overwhelming proportion of the work force in large-scale industrial enterprises is male--in 1970 it was over 95%. Those women who were employed were usually in low wage positions. In some cases the liberal provisions for maternity leave, combined with a higher female absenteeism rate caused by difficulties in obtaining child care, discouraged the

---

[8] *Gold Coast/Ghana Censuses*, 1911-70.

[9] The 1921 figure is probably too low since the census distinguished between makers and sellers of food, a distinction which is usually not valid. The 1931 figure is lower because it included a number of women who were farmers in the surrounding area.

[10] E. M. Ankrah, "Women's Liberation: Has the African Woman Settled for Tokens?" *New Blackfriars* LIV, no. 637 (June 1973): 207; M. Greenstreet, "Various Salient Features Concerning the Employment of Women Working in Ghana," background paper for Ghana National Council on Women and Development Seminar on Women and Development, Accra (July 1978), pp. 2-3.

[11] K. Andah, "Ghanaian Women in Agriculture," paper presented at Ghana National Council on Women and Development Seminar (Sept. 1978), pp. 22-23. They also had less access to bank credit and fewer basic farming tools. M. Nantogmah, a Ghana National Council on Women and Development representative, managed to remedy a similar situation near Tamale (personal communication, June 1979).

[12] M. Greenstreet, "Employment of Women in Ghana," *International Labour Review* CIII, no. 2 (Feb. 1971): 124; Greenstreet, "Various Salient Features," pp. 8-10.

employment of women.[13] To sum up the position, the proportion of men in industrial production, and clerical, professional, technical, administrative, and managerial occupations was more than double that of women in both 1960 and 1970.[14]

In Ghana, as elsewhere, the impact of government economic policies favoring large-scale, capital-intensive development has been negative for women. It can be argued, in fact, that these policies disadvantaged almost everyone, given the present parlous state of the economy. But the women (and children) have suffered more because they are more vulnerable. Their reaction to the decreasing per capita real income of the 1960s was to increase their labor force participation. Thus, female employment grew at a rate of 4.3% a year (versus 1% for males) in the 1960s. Older women, in particular, increased their activities.[15] In 1970 female labor force participation was 64% (of those aged 15 and above) as compared to 57% in 1960.[16] For men the figures were 89% in 1960 and 83% in 1970.[17] Women's employment was concentrated in the services and commerce due to the women's structural disadvantages.

Ussher Town was no exception in reflecting the general trends. According to the censuses, in 1901 19% of the men in Accra (which was then Central Accra only) were farmers, but in 1960 only 1% of the Ussher Town men were farmers and in 1970, 1.5% (the diminishing amount of farmland near Accra contributed to this difference also.) At the same time the number of male clerical and administrative workers went from under 7% in 1901 to about 15% in Ussher Town in 1960, and 19% in 1970 (this figure would have been higher without the male exodus to the suburbs).[18] Most men now have jobs which are in Accra, and many more people are employed in the complex of services and secondary industries in Accra. Meanwhile, in 1960 only 3% of the adult female inhabitants of Ussher Town were administrative, profes-

---

[13]E. Date-Bah, "Ghanaian Women in Factory Employment: A Case Study," International Educational Materials Exchange Paper No. 4137 (1976), pp. 2, 5.

[14]W. F. Steel and C. Campbell, "The Impact of Industrialization Policies on Women's Employment in Ghana," paper presented at African Studies Association Conference, Baltimore (Nov. 1978), pp. 6, 12.

[15]Ghana has a high labor force participation rate for persons over 65. In 1960 it was 42.6% for women and 71.3% for men compared to the respective rates of 10.1% and 29.7% for the U.S. S. K. Gaisie, "Population Growth and Its Components," in *Population Growth and Socioeconomic Change in West Africa*, ed. J. C. Caldwell (New York: Columbia University Press, 1975), p. 359.

[16]The urban and rural rates were almost identical. One should be wary of the census figures, however, since the job category of "housewife" usually claims more women than it should because it operates as a status symbol.

[17]Much of the preceding paragraph is based on information from W. F. Steel and C. Campbell, "Women's Employment and Development: A Conceptual Framework Applied to Ghana," paper (April 1979), pp. 23-25.

[18]*Ghana/Gold Coast Censuses*, 1901, 1960, 1970. The figures exclude male sales workers, who are often clerical; when included the figure is 33% for 1970.

sional, or clerical workers, none were farmers, and 88% were traders.[19] In 1970 the figures were respectively: 6%, .5%, and 79%.[20] More women were becoming domestic workers. This was reflected in the contrast in the occupations of women in the 1971-72 and 1978 Ussher Town samples. Among the 59 women 50 and over in 1971-72, 10% had ever been seamstresses, only 5% farmers, 3.3% unskilled laborers, and 1.6% each a domestic worker and spirit medium. All of these women were traders, along with the other 78.4% who had never done anything else. In 1978 5% of the 101 women 39 to 50 were seamstresses, none were farmers or unskilled laborers, 9% were domestics, 2% each spirit mediums and housewives, and 1% an actress. Approximately 5% had never traded, but 20% were not trading in 1978. This situation was unheard of in 1971-72, when even the oldest women were trading unless physical disability prohibited it. Since the alternative work to trading done by the women in 1978 did not require formal education, this change is more symptomatic of the decline in trading opportunities than the impact of education. This decline must be examined.

Changes in the organization of trade in various commodities are most strongly affected by the amount of processing a particular commodity must undergo before being sold. The amount of processing performed by a trader is associated with her function in trade; wholesale fish traders often perform no processing, while fish retailers often smoke the fish. In the fishsmoking and prepared foods industries this processing is essential; it is carried out within the compounds and relies on the compound organization for its successful pursuit. In contrast, the trade in imported goods usually requires no processing, whether canned meat or cloth is concerned. In the latter case, removing production from the compound has enabled women to concentrate on developing more sophisticated marketing techniques and to organize their businesses more tightly, without the compulsory levy exacted by the participation of large numbers of relatives. A shift from one trade to another may have definite implications for the economic independence of women, then; these implications will be examined here.

Another change in the organization of trade has been mainly at the compound level. Differential educational opportunities for men and women have meant a progressive separation of men and women into different spheres of activity. This process has helped to destroy cooperation between the sexes in economic endeavors and changed the division of labor. Ga women in Central Accra still operate largely within the context of the neighborhood, while the men are more likely to be socialized at their jobs in government or business offices, and therefore have a wider frame of reference. The results of these processes can be seen in changes in the organization of the fish, produce, prepared foods, and imported goods trades. These changes have interacted with social changes on a large scale to produce a new reality for Ga women.

---

[19]M. Kilson, "Variations in Ga Culture in Central Accra, *Ghana Journal of Sociology* III, no. 1 (Feb. 1967): 54.

[20]*Ghana Census*, 1970, Special Report A, Table 17.

The Fish Trade

Until the 1920s the trade in fish and produce in the Accra area were two facets of the same process. This trade was the most important component of the small market trade around Accra, and Ga women played the largest part in it. As far back as the fifteenth century, women were trading fish in the Accra area, as well as millet and salt.[21] In 1600 de Marees described the coastal women taking fish to the markets and bringing back vegetables.

> [The fish] which their husbands have gotten in the sea, whereof the women
> buy much, and carrie them to other towns within the land to get some
> profit by them, so that the fish which is taken in the sea is carried at least
> an hundred or two hundred miles up into the land, for a great present,
> although many times it stinkes like carrion, and hath a thousand maggots
> creeping in it.[22]

Lagoon fishing as an occupation for Ga men was probably an early development; deep-sea fishing was only introduced in the second half of the eighteenth century by Fanti. The fish trade obviously predates the latter development.[23] In 1817 Bowdich saw dried (smoked?) fish from the coast in the Kumasi market, and in 1847 Duncan described a popular fish called "pogie" at Accra, which was dried and sent to the interior, "even to Ashantee."[24] This trade is still one of the most important ones for Central Accra women. It developed from a small-scale circular process into a large-scale industry, where mechanization materially affected its organization. For analytical purposes the fish and produce trade will first be discussed together because of their unity, and then separated to consider the changes within the independent produce trade.

Understanding the fish trade is essential to grasping the economic position of Ga women in Central Accra. It had central importance for four samples in 1971-72 and 1978, as indicated in Table IV-1. Fishselling was the most important trade when combined with produce selling. It is worthwhile

[21]P. Ozanne, "Notes on the Later Prehistory of Accra," *Journal of the Historical Society of Nigeria* III (1964): 19-20, 23.

[22]De Marees, "Description," VI: 286-87.

[23]F. E. K. Amoah, "Accra: A Study of the Development of a West African City," Master's thesis Institute of African Studies, University of Ghana (1964), p. 11, n. 6; G. A. M. Azu, "The Impact of the Modern Fishing Industry on the Ga Traditional Fishing Industry," Master's thesis Institute of African Studies, University of Ghana (1966), p. 2; C. C. Reindorf, *The History of Gold Coast and Asante* (ca. 1890; reprint ed., Accra: Ghana Universities Press, 1966), p. 261; R. M. Lawson and E. Kwei, *African Entrepreneurship and Economic Growth, A Case Study of the Fishing Industry of Ghana* (Accra: Ghana Universities Press, 1974), p. 51. M. Johnson, "Census, Map and Guesstimates: the Past Population of the Accra Region," in *African Historical Demography* (Edinburgh: Centre of African Studies, 1977), p. 274.

[24]T. E. Bowdich, *Mission from Cape Coast Castle to Ashantee* (London: Griffith and Farron, 1873), p. 275; J. Duncan, *Travels in Western Africa in 1845 and 1846* (London: Richard Bentley, 1847), I: 88. This is probably what is now called *okpoku* in Ga, which can be false albacore, little tunny, or frigate mackerel, according to F. R. Irvine, *Fishes and Fisheries of the Gold Coast* (London: Crown Agents, 1947).

Table IV-1. Commodities Sold by Ga Women in Ussher Town.

Percent of Women	Commodities:					Sewing
	Fish	Grains, Fruits and Vegetables (Produce)	Imported Goods	Prepared Foods	Other	
1971-72 as main trade[a]	31.9	8.3	34.7	30.5	5.5	4.2[b]
1971-72 ever having sold commodity[a]	63.8	33.3	66.6	63.8	33.3	9.7
1971-72 having sold commodity as most recent trade[c]	26	12.1	37	31.6	2.8	3.2
1978 selling commodity at present in Salaga Market[d]	30	55	12.5	10	22.5	0
1978 selling commodity at present, women aged 30-50[e]	32.6	14	12.8	47.7	3.5	5.8

[a]No. = 72

[b]Answers do not add up to 100% because they were multiple. Most women traded different things at different times, and sometimes simultaneously.

[c]No. = 223. Some were selling the commodity at time of interviewing, and some had retired and named the last commodity they had sold.

[d]No. = 40 Salaga Market stallholders.

[e]No. = 86. Fifteen were not trading or sewing, and thus not included to make the sample more comparable to the others where all were trading or had traded.

noting, however, the approximate equivalence of numbers of women ever involved in the fish, imported goods, and prepared foods trades. This is an indicator of the tendency of women to diversify their options by both trading in many things simultaneously and/or changing commodities with changes in supply/demand conditions.

The fish trade can be subdivided into different categories, some of which coincide with periods of time. First there was the long-distance trade, walking to the local markets around Accra or farther away, which was then replaced (by the late 1920s) by the lorry or train trade to markets in the interior. All along there was a purely local trade in fish, wholesale and retail. In the 1950s and 60s the fishing industry was mechanized, which changed the structure of fish marketing, making it necessary for some women to travel to Tema to obtain fish. Of the fishsellers in the small 1971-72 sample, 57% had ever been in the long distance trade, 38% in the local trade, and 5% in the Tema trade.

Another classification one must make is the type of fish women traded, that is, what sort of processing the fish were subjected to before being sold. The main types are fresh, smoked, salted, and fried fish. In the 1971-72 sample 72% of the fishsellers sold smoked fish, 37% fresh fish, 7% salted, and 7% fried fish. It is not surprising that most of the women sold smoked fish since they were the chief item in the long-distance trade, the category showing the highest participation. The sellers of fresh fish mostly participated in the local trade, sometimes wholesaling them to the fishsmokers.

Until Tema Harbor opened in 1962, the main source of fish for the Central Accra area was Accra itself and Faana fishing villages just to the west of Accra. Figure IV-1 shows their location in the context of the markets and trade routes followed by these traders in the early twentieth century. Before World War II even people from east of Accra would travel to Faana to get fish to sell.[25] However, in the 1920s Tema began gaining in importance, which was magnified by the construction and subsequent opening of the Tema deep water port. It has now become the chief supply source for fish in the area.

Despite the shift in locale for the supply sources, fishselling has remained very important for women in Central Accra. This importance persisted in the face of governmental opposition. Until World War II the British colonial government mainly ignored the fishing industry,[26] except when sanitary or aesthetic considerations surfaced. Periodic efforts to remove the fishsmoking industry from Central Accra mostly failed. Before large numbers of metal barrels became available, women used swish smoking ovens, which were round and covered with thatch or zinc roofs. Some can still be seen in villages. The sanitary inspectors in Accra used to go on oven-destroying forays before World War I to enforce the government's edict that all fishsmoking should be removed to Tsokor, a nearby village. This caused a furor, and was never effectively enforced.[27] The government also wished to remove the fishermen to the outskirts of Accra, but their resistance was often the main obstacle to slum clearance in Central Accra.[28] In spite of these efforts, fishsmoking is still carried out in Central Accra, and fishermen can still be seen on Tuesdays mending their nets on the streets.[29] However, changing conditions are making this sight more rare.

Until the development of rail and road transportation as far as Kumasi in the 1920s, the long-distance fish trade was mostly conducted by women

---

[25]SNA 11/1089, "Coroner's inquest into death of one Karley-Bi by drowning," Dec. 20, 1924.

[26]Lawson and Kwei, *African Entrepreneurship*, p. 52.

[27]SNA 11/78, Petition from sixty Ga women to the Secretary for Native Affairs, Feb. 27, 1909; SNA 11/1209, letter Acting District Commissioner, Accra, to Secretary for Native Affairs, Dec. 8, 1920.

[28]Amoah, "Accra," p. 159; E. A. Boateng, "The Growth and Functions of Accra," *Bulletin of the Ghana Geographical Association* IV, no. 2 (1959): 9.

[29]The prohibition imposed by Ga religion on fishing or fishselling in Accra on Tuesdays is still observed. It is said that on that day the sea god bathes his children and must not be disturbed. Azu, "Impact," p. 63.

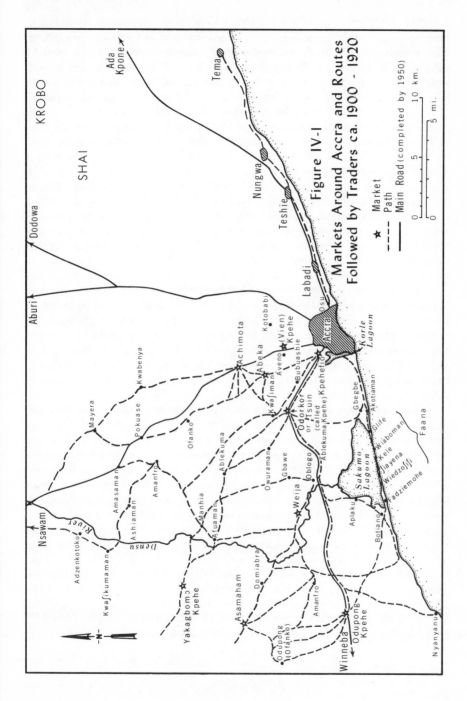

Figure IV-I
Markets Around Accra and Routes
Followed by Traders ca. 1900 - 1920

carrying headloads. Of necessity, this was a small-scale trade involving as many fish as could be carried by an individual and her relatives (or slaves, on occasion). I had no direct evidence of women having hired laborers to carry fish for them, but it may have happened. A headload of fish usually weighed about 60 pounds and contained 200 to 1000 fish, which the women sold in small quantities, two or three at a time. If someone wished to buy all of them, so much the better, but that was an unusual occurrence.

The long-distance trade involved relatively short relays; the farthest point one woman carried it was usually to Dodowa, Koforidua, or Kibi, some 60 miles from Accra. The upcountry buyers occasionally resmoked the fish to avoid the condition described by de Marees, and relayed them onwards. A typical trip might have taken a week and entailed visiting Adeiso, Nsawam, Pakro, Pokuase, and Koforidua until all the fish were sold. Others took three day trips twice a week. At the inland markets the women bought vegetables and fruit which they brought back to Accra for use or for sale. Sometimes it was necessary to change the currency they brought for the local one. In one case a woman had to get corals (perhaps beads) in order to trade at one place.

These women can be considered the professional long-distance traders; those who went only to the local periodic markets around Accra were not so profit-oriented. The local market traders were doing their daily shopping, in essence. They took along enough fish to pay for the vegetables they would need that week. Rather than traveling from market to market, they went to one market and came back on the same day, or even in one morning. Presumably they had little trouble in selling the relatively small quantities of fish they took with them.

The main items in the long-distance fish trade were and are smoked and salted fish. The time-consuming and tedious business of smoking fish is most easily accomplished with the help of the others living in a compound. It involves getting up at two or three in the morning, when the fish is brought by the fishermen, and smoking it until twelve noon. Women often have two to six fishsmoking barrels which they operate simultaneously. The main expense is for firewood, since the fire has to be kept going constantly. A women places the fish between layers of dampened sticks on a rack in the upper part of the barrel, while the fire is fed from below through an opening cut in the side of the barrel. The sticks are supposed to keep the fish from breaking. The oven is covered with a metal sheet. Usually fairly small fish, from three to nine inches long, are smoked in this manner. If they are smoked for a long time--three days or more--they will last for months. Otherwise, they must either be sold or resmoked within ten to eleven days.[30] For local use, short-term smoking is usually preferred to preserve taste.[31] Some women can smoke 5,000 fish in a day working them in relays in several

---

[30]N. Quinn, "Do Mfantse fishsellers estimate probabilities in their heads?" *American Ethnologist* V, no. 2 (1978): 212.

[31]U.N. Food and Agricultural Organization, "Market Women in West Africa," report (1977), p. 8.

barrels.

The fish which are salted are usually large, horse mackerel or shark being preferred. They are cut up in chunks four or five inches long and soaked in brine for two or three days. Then they are dried in the sun for several days. This method may preserve them for up to two years.[32] They are called *loosala*, or "stinkfish," and are very popular in the Northern Region.[33] Obviously, in both smoking and salting fish time is of the essence. In a tropical climate fish spoils rapidly. When women receive a load of fish they usually drop everything and smoke them immediately, with oven capacity and firewood supplies putting effective limits to the number they can handle at once. If they get impatient and do not do it thoroughly, they will lose the results of their effort. Therefore, great emphasis is placed on knowing how to do it properly. The residential system facilitates a novice gaining this knowledge by placing at her disposal the pooled experience of her female relatives.

Most often fishsmoking is a communal enterprise involving all of the women in a compound. Indeed, the space occupied by the fishsmoking paraphernalia makes it difficult for anyone living there to do anything else. Recently, because of the diminishing space available in Central Accra, some women have moved their fishsmoking enterprises to the suburbs or a village, usually Tsokor. Sometimes women have switched to another occupation when additions to a compound used up the area formerly devoted to fishsmoking.

Before the development of Tema and the shift of fishing away from Accra it was also common for relatives to help women obtain supplies. One author in 1947 described the division of labor whereby men fished and gave their wives the fish to sell as a "necessary consequence of their condition."[34] However, most women were pragmatic: they bought where a supply was available, as shown in Table IV-2. Over a fourth of the women used both kinship or marriage links and other persons as a supply source for their fish. The number of women who depended solely on relatives or husbands for their supply diminished in the younger age groups. One reason for this change is specialization. For instance, one woman in her fifties used to get the fish from her father, who then died and left the canoe and nets to his sons. They bought a new net with a finer mesh for catching small fish which are usually fried. She still prefers to sell large fish which she smokes. So, now she buys from other people most of the time except at Hɔmɔwɔ, when her brothers catch large ones. Another reason is the diminishing number of fishermen in Accra and the increasing importance of Tema as a supply center.

The women who bought fish from their husbands or relatives often operated on a commission basis. A woman might have agreed with her

---

[32]Lawson and Kwei, *African Entrepreneurship*, p. 75.

[33]Azu, "Impact," p. 52.

[34]A. P. Brown, "The Fishing Industry of the Labadi District," in *Fishes and Fisheries of the Gold Coast*, ed. F. R. Irvine (London: Crown Agents, 1947), p. 43.

Table IV-2. Sources of Fish Purchased by Women Traders.

Age Group	Source:			Total Number of Women
	Husbands	Relatives/ Others	Both	
90s & 80s	3	4	1	8
70s	3	1	3	7
60s	1	5	1	7
50s	1	5	2	8
40s	0	2	2	4
Total	8	17	9	34
Percent	23.5	50.0	26.5	100.0

husband that he would pay her a commission of one or two shillings on every pound's worth of fish she sold. The haggling came over how much the fish was worth. They struck a bargain and then the fisherman sent the fish to her house. She also might have taken a large basin to the harbor and fetched it herself. The commission was like a reduction in price, that is, if a man sold to a woman other than his wife he would charge her one or two shillings more per pound sterling worth of fish. With relatives or husbands the arrangement was invariably on a credit basis, and accounts were tallied up every Tuesday or so. If a woman made a profit over the agreed value of the fish, she might have kept it or given it to her husband. Usually she kept it.[35] If she was selling for her father she probably would have given him the profits because of his seniority within her family. Because of this sort of arrangement fishermen valued a shrewd trader as a wife, since she might have brought them more profit. Conversely, the women valued a husband who was a diligent fisherman, although they also bought from others if necessary.

A good fisherman was more likely to be able to purchase a canoe or a net. The use of the most common, or *ali* type, net was introduced in about 1870 by a Fanti fisherman.[36] The canoe and net owners got larger shares of the catch than the others, since their capital investment was larger. The number of shares varied; if it was ten the net owner might have taken four, the canoe owner two, and an owner one, the fishermen splitting three. The fishermen numbered four to twelve or so, depending on the size of the canoe. Thus, in that situation a person who owned both the canoe and the net got 8/11 of the catch. It was definitely an advantage, then, for a fishseller to be married to a canoe or net owner. Another advantage of dealing with

---

[35]Brown, "Fishing Industry," p. 43, and Azu, "Impact," p. 45, made the common mistake of assuming that all profits were handed to the husbands.

[36]Lawson and Kwei, *African Entrepreneurship*, pp. 51, 60. The head fisherman of Accra comes from this Fanti Cherekwanda family and has a stool and elders. He is called the *Woleiatsε* and is elected for life.

husbands or relatives was the extension of credit. If a woman took a loss they were more tolerant than others in delaying collection of the debt, in principle.

The women who bought from other people had several alternatives. They could go to the shore where the fish came in and buy directly from the fishermen. More commonly they bought from the fishermen's wives or sisters there. They could have gone to the market and bought fresh or smoked fish from the women there. It was more difficult to get credit in those transactions and sometimes cash was used.

A third method was to have a sort of partnership with some of the itinerant fishermen who came to Accra annually during the herring season (June-September). These were usually Fanti, but occasionally Ewe or Kru. Itinerant fishing seems to have been going on since the Fanti introduced deep sea fishing in Accra until recently. In 1896 the Ga fishermen in Accra formed a union to defend their rights to the waters around Accra, and again in 1916 they tried to get rid of them, all to no avail.[37] In 1953 Lawson estimated that about 100 boats of itinerant fishermen came to Accra. Some fishsellers in Accra evidently traveled to the Cape Coast area and gave monetary inducements to the canoe owners to come to Accra for the season.[38] The particular arrangement the women had with them varied. With some it was similar to that with relatives or husbands; the women lodged the men in their houses and got a commission plus their profits on the men's catch.[39] Others simply came, rented rooms from the women, and sold their fish to their hostess as they would to anybody else. With mechanization of the industry, however, migration has become less important since fishermen can more easily return long distances to their home villages. If a woman recruited fishermen she would have had the advantage of choosing those who caught the sort of fish she wanted. Because of the various types of nets there was considerable specialization in size and types of fish caught by different fishermen. The fishermen were sometimes called by the name of the net which they used. For instance, a man who used a *pɔli* net for catching small herring was called a *pɔliwole*.

Specialization is also evident in the organization of fishselling. Sometimes everyone in the compound, or even a lineage, had a role to play. The kind of specialization that evolved can be shown in one family, where the men had all been fishermen as far back as could be remembered. My informant, Naa Kɔdei, said that on both her mother's and father's sides the men fished and the women sold fish.

Naa Kɔdei was a soft-spoken, attractive woman in her fifties in 1972. As a young girl she sold fish for her mother, who smoked it and also prepared *tatale* (a sort of pancake) for sale. Her mother stayed home and watched

---

[37]SNA 11/810; SNA 11/602, letter from Asafoatsɛ C. B. Nettey to Secretary for Native Affairs, Oct. 5, 1916.

[38]R. M. Lawson (née Jackson), "The Economics of the Gold Coast Fishing Industry," Masters thesis, University of Birmingham (1953), p. 62.

[39]Azu, "Impact," p. 45.

the younger children while Kɔdei and her sisters walked to the villages or the market to sell fish. She then married a fisherman and smoked and sold his fish for him, as well as those that her father brought to her mother. When her brothers inherited the canoe from her father she continued to sell fish for them. Her daughter now is selling fish for Kɔdei's brothers, and her son is also giving Kɔdei fish to sell.

Naa Kɔdei sold fish mostly in Accra, but some family organizations covered the long-distance trade. On occasion one still finds all of the residents of a compound in Central Accra employed in the fishing industry, but that is getting rare with the decrease in gender linkages in production.

The local trade in fish mostly consists of fresh or fried fish, and some smoked fish. People used to buy the fish at the shore in Accra, for the most part, and sell them at Salaga Market. In 1971-72 people were more likely to buy frozen fish at Tema or at Salaga Market and sell at Makola No. 1. The local trade had the only women who could really be considered wholesalers: the women at the shore who sold the catch as it came in to other women; the passbook holders at Tema, who often resold as soon as they bought the fish; and some women who went early in the morning to Makola No. 1 to sell either fresh or smoked fish to others who resold in small quantities. Some of the oldest women used to sell wholesale from their houses also. The women who achieved preferred status with the State Fisheries Corporation or a private company like Mankoadze Fisheries have achieved a disproportionate influence over the trade, a phenomenon directly linked to the development of the mechanized fishing industry in Ghana.

The first fishing trawler in Ghana arrived in 1946.[40] In the 1950s and 60s the industry expanded, becoming important in the Accra area after the opening of Tema Harbor. The first effect was to make large supplies of fish available at lower prices to the wholesale fishsellers. Second, because of the larger amount of capital and the new skills involved, mechanized fishing severely damaged the local canoe fishing industry around Accra. The introduction of outboard motors for canoes helped the situation somewhat. Nevertheless, in spite of government loans which helped many fishermen to buy outboards, some could not afford the capital investment or higher maintenance costs. Those without outboards were severely impaired in terms of the number of fish they could catch. By 1966 about half of the 10,000 canoes in operation had outboard motors, and by 1974 only one-seventh were without one. While this enabled the canoe fishermen to triple their landings of fish in the ten years from 1962 to 1972, it is not clear that it improved their profit situation.[41] Why? Mainly for reasons associated with the distribution system.[42]

---

[40]Lawson and Kwei, *African Entrepreneurship*, p. 57.

[41]"The Economics of the Operation of Outboard Motors," report in University of Ghana Institute for Statistical, Social, and Economic Research archives (1977), pp. 11-12, 30; R. M. Lawson, "The Growth of the Fishing Industry in Ghana," *Economic Bulletin of Ghana* XI, no. 3 (1967): 9.

[42]Lawson, "Growth," p. 9, has also suggested that higher profits were inhibited by making up larger crews to share the earnings.

The introduction of trawling and outboard motors greatly increased the supply of fish; by the mid-1960s approximately one-fourth of the marine fish available in Ghana came from the State Corporation alone, less than a fourth was imported, and the rest were caught predominantly by canoes with outboards.[43] However, the perpetual indebtedness of the fishermen to the fishsellers became worse because more capital was required for operation of an outboard; fish prices fell with larger supplies; and the fishselling oligopoly became concentrated in fewer hands. This situation acted also to the detriment of the majority of the fishsellers, who became more dependent on the oligopolists. The old oligopoly took on new permutations, with side effects that largely removed wholesaling from Ga hands. The Abraham Commission Report in 1965 described the corrupt practices of SFC managers and officials at Tema, who sold large quantities of fish to a few preferred customers offering bribes.[44]

When the SFC got out of retailing fish itself in 1968 they went to a credit system where a ₵1,000 deposit was required for opening a wholesale account. Usually only the wives or close relatives of influential men could afford it.[45] Political influence became a factor in determining access to fish. This brought in some women who had previously never sold fish, but then saw the opportunities for profit in taking advantage of their connections.[46] The general change in fish wholesaling, then, has been from the fish being handled by a number of small-scale experienced wholesalers in the Accra area up until about the mid- or late 1950s, to a concentration of supply in the hands of a few by the 1970s, where experience in fishselling counted less. Meanwhile, the locale of this trade changed from the large markets to the frozen storage sites. Frozen storage facilities made fishsmoking less necessary and made a large pool of female helpers redundant for fish wholesalers. Processing fish, which is an aspect of production, became less important.

The specialization of functions in fishselling has become more pronounced over time. This is partly due to developments in the long-distance trade to which we must return now. Such specialization expedites the handling of the larger quantities of fish which can be shipped by motorized transport, as opposed to head porterage. It also absorbs surplus labor, and reflects the increased amount of time and effort Ga women put into marketing rather than production. Around 1900, when people were still walking to the villages to sell fish, there were two basic functions; buying and preparing smoked or salted fish, and selling it. The older women did the former and the younger unmarried or early married ones the latter, since they were stronger, and had fewer children to care for.

---

[43]Lawson, "Growth," pp. 4, 21; "Economics of the Operation of Outboard Motors" (1977), p. 2.

[44]*Report of the Commission of Enquiry into Trade Malpractices in Ghana* (Accra: State Publishing Corporation, 1965), pp. 35-36.

[45]Lawson and Kwei, *African Entrepreneurship*, pp. 239-40.

[46]Sai, "Women Traders," p. 8; Ghana National Council on Women and Development paper for Seminar on Women and Development, Accra (July 1978).

In the 1950s and 1960s it was more likely that one woman bought it, another bought it from her and prepared it, a third bought it from her and sent it upcountry via train or lorry, and a fourth sold it retail. A common fifth in the chain might have been a woman who bought from the fourth who sold it "wholesale." It may even have passed through the hands of six or seven traders before it came to the consumer.[47] Some of the links in this chain were often related, such as the fishsmokers and the recipients of lorry consignments. The most common combinations were mother-daughter or sisters. In the latter category were classificatory sisters, usually mother's sister's daughter to the dispatcher. Sometimes the women assumed fictive kinship ties of sisters, since the trust between partners should be like that between sisters.

The actual workings of these partnerships did indeed require a great deal of trust. Therefore, people usually preferred to deal with their relatives, since they were more amenable to social sanctions if they defaulted. Many women had only one partner, but some had several. The case of Lamle shows how the system worked.

> Lamle has been trading fish all of her life; she started when she was a girl walking to the villages to sell fish and bringing back vegetables. This was at the time of World War I. When she was about 30 she started on her own in the early 1930s. She had four partners to whom she sent fish, one each in Koforidua, Asamankese, Nsawam, and Akotiaman. Two were cousins and two friends. She sent them loads of 600 to 1,000 pieces of big fish via lorry. Her children, sisters, and her sister's children helped her prepare the fish for shipment. The fish were put in baskets in the lorry with a piece of cloth attached to the top containing stones and palm kernels, which indicated the purchase price of the fish plus her expenses in smoking them. The partner in Nsawam would recognize whose fish it was by the sort of cloth used, and pay the lorry driver the freight. Several days later, after selling the fish, she would send via the lorry driver the cost price of the fish to Lamle, plus more stones and palm kernels telling how much profit she had made. The partner kept the profits until Hɔmɔwɔ, when she and the other partners would come to Accra, and they would split them equally. Some of her partners sent her vegetables for her own use. These she also "dashed" to her helpers in Accra. She went on in this manner for some time, but eventually three of her partners died, and she got sick, so she quit. By 1972 Lamle was in the local trade only, smoking fish with her daughters, who sold them wholesale at Makola No. 1 early in the morning. Lamle was in her late sixties in 1972.

This history is typical in many respects. Some women whose partners wholesaled the fish were able to get their money back the same day. Some women trading at that time went by lorry or train inland and sold the fish themselves. They seem to have been the exceptions, though. This was the system used from about the 1920s to the 1960s.

Recently the situation has changed again, although some women still follow the older way. With the introduction of refrigeration facilities in the

---

[47]Lawson, "Growth," p. 16.

1960s, the seasonality of the fish supply was reduced. Wealthier women could leave a supply in cold storage at Tema until the market looked good, and then sell it. Cold storage facilities also became available inland; by 1966 Kumasi, Ho, Swedru, Tamale, and Koforidua had them.[48] This obviated the need for smoking the fish sent to partners upcountry. Some fish is now smoked by Fanti after being frozen in Kumasi.[49] Although the largest coastal fishsmoking industry in Ghana is still in the Accra area,[50] this industry was getting less important in the 1970s. The scarcity of spare parts for machines, however, may reverse this trend in the 1980s. Meanwhile, more Ga women are becoming involved in the local fish trade. In the 1971-72 small sample only 25% of the fishsellers in their sixties and over were in the local trade, as opposed to 65% of those in their fifties and forties. The Ga monopoly on the long-distance fish trade has been effectively broken.[51]

Before going into the produce trade, some mention of profits must be made. In the fish trade, as in others, women are leery of talking about their profits to each other or to outsiders. The imposition of an income tax on market traders in 1960 only reinforced this tendency. Some rough estimates can be made, however. Profit margins tended to be lower in wholesale trade, ranging between 15 and 25%, but turnover was much higher. These were the women who occasionally were able to branch out into controlling the supply of fish as well. Some purchased canoes and/or nets and hired crews to work them, thus assuring themselves of a steady supply of fish on profitable terms. Some women, by lending fishermen money at usurious rates of interest during the lean season, were able to mortgage their catch ahead of time and get it for a cheaper price than would ordinarily have been possible. In my sample two fishsellers were able to do this, and some other women in other occupations also became involved in moneylending (one fishseller who lent her husband money to buy a canoe and a net ended up divorcing him because he sold them without paying her back!).

Because of inflation in the price of imported goods, the cost of equipment like nets and outboard motors has gone up--not to mention the cost of fishing trawlers, which is beyond most people's purses. Even the cost of locally produced equipment went up more than the cost of living. Between 1890 and 1953 the cost of a canoe, the most expensive local item, went up by over 700%, compared to a rise in the cost of living of approximately 260%.[52] Such a phenomenon helped to further the dependency of fishermen

[48]Lawson, "Growth," p. 10.

[49]Lawson and Kwei, *African Entrepreneurship*, p. 152.

[50]A 1969-70 survey showed that 54% of the fish smoked on the coast in Ghana were done in the Accra-Tema area. G. Campbell-Platt, "The Development of Appropriate Food Technologies in Ghana: An Overview," Ghana National Council on Women and Development paper for Seminar on Women and Development, Accra (Sept. 1978), p. 11.

[51]Lawson and Kwei, *African Entrepreneurship*, pp. 151-52, noted this decline and stated that Fanti had assumed dominance over buying and smoking Tema Cold Store fish.

[52]Lawson, "Economics," p. 30; SCT 17/4/13, p. 54. In 1890 a canoe cost £5.10, in 1953 £30 to £50 plus £15 for transportation to the coast. See Table II-1 for the cost of living approximation.

or fishsellers on moneylenders and increase the price of fish, but there is no indication that it has affected profit margins.

Retail traders had profit margins ranging between 30 and 60% but a lower turnover. On occasion, if a woman was particularly clever or fortunate, she might have gotten a much higher profit. At the time of the long-distance foot trade this was likely to happen if a woman went to a less frequented place. One woman claimed to have made 2,000% profit on fish sold at a place not on her usual route. In the markets in Accra the profit margins are fairly standard, since there are agreements between traders on minimum prices, and considerable social pressure is exerted among traders to conform.[53] It was a woman's capital or credit which determined her turnover, and her number of dependents and carefulness in keeping track of her profits which helped determine her profits. The latter factors are very difficult to ascertain, even for some of the women themselves. There is no reason to believe, however, that most of the women are or were wealthy. In 1971-72 many of them seemed rather to have made enough for their needs and a few luxuries like new clothes. By Ghanaian standards they were probably comfortable at times and hard up at others, as is common in a seasonal trade. In 1977-78, however, times were unquestionably hard and supplies difficult to get and sell for small traders.[54]

The fishsellers are, nonetheless, generally better off than many fishermen, it seems. Even on motorized canoes, a 1977 report showed that crew members were earning well below the government minimum wage, and nonmotorized canoe crew members earned very little indeed.[55] No wonder, then, that Lawson and Kwei condemned the "traders' stranglehold on marketing" and recommended efforts to break the wholesalers' oligopoly. They noted, however, that the small fishsellers mostly remained poor and suffered from the same oligopoly.[56]

Produce

As in the fish trade, the long-distance foot trade in produce died out with the increase in motorized transport in the early 1920s. In the small 1971-72 sample, none of the women in their forties or fifties had ever

---

[53]Lawson, "Economics," p. 113.

[54]Possibly a gradual inflation in the numbers of fishsellers may have affected this. Lawson and Kwei, *African Entrepreneurship*, pp. 136, 150, noted that between 1952 and 1960 the ratio of fishsellers to fishermen went from 1:2 to 1:1, which they attributed partly to the increasing supply of fish. Population growth and lack of alternative employment opportunities for women may also have affected these numbers.

[55]"Economics of the Operation of Outboard Motors" (1977), pp. 11-12. The amounts were: ¢54 a month government minimum wage, ¢13.45 a month for motorized crew members, and ¢3.92 a month for nonmotorized crew members.

[56]Lawson and Kwei, *African Entrepreneurship*, pp. 83, 133. "It was the wholesalers and inland traders who reaped the benefits from increases in demand [in the 1950s], and not the fishermen or the fish 'wives', who remained poor."

participated in the foot trade in either trade. Most of the women who walked to the villages did so in the first two decades of the twentieth century. Some characteristics of the foot trade carried over into the lorry trade. In the 1920s and 1930s some women had their partners send them vegetables for their own use. This seems to have stopped by 1940, however.

Before the development of motorized long-distance transportation, the produce trade was quite similar to the fish trade in that people's participation in it depended largely upon their proximity to the source of supply. Many of the women in the long-distance trade did it while living in a rural area, where obtaining supplies was easy. Women traded vegetables like women traded fish, because they were performing an essential function in a largely familial production process. A few who lived in Accra were partners of people living in a rural area. At the beginning of the twentieth century, the Ga in Accra were more rurally oriented; many had close relatives in rural areas. The women who traded vegetables and fruit were often doing it for relatives or spouses who had farms. In the 1971-72 small sample, 37% of the women who traded in vegetables or fruit got their supplies from relatives or husbands. Most of these were in their sixties or older, however.

The arrangement for selling produce for a relative or spouse was similar to that in fishselling, except that no commission was given. The father or husband gave the vegetables to the wife or daughter, who sold them at the closest market in Accra, giving the profits to the men. It was, therefore, a less profitable occupation for the women than most others. The women also helped with the farming. Unlike in Accra, in the villages the women usually lived with their husbands. This coresidence of spouses sometimes was associated with the husbands' exercising greater financial control over the wives. Therefore, living in Accra appealed to some women as an escape from moral and financial supervision by their spouses.

The newer style of long-distance vegetable trade was less intimately tied to the family structure. Many women went themselves to the villages from Accra and bought vegetables or fruits.

> Akwele was in the produce trade from the 1920s to the 1950s. She used to go by lorry to villages near Accra twice a week and buy from six to twenty baskets of each sort of vegetable per trip. This included okra, tomatoes, garden egg (a small variety of eggplant), red peppers, and onions. She had to pay the lorry driver for each basket transported to Accra, where she sold them wholesale or retail.

Another woman did the same but bought corn, bananas, oranges, and palmnuts instead.[57] Another method used was a partnership system almost exactly like that for fish, except the direction of exporting the goods was reversed. A woman might have had a sister or daughter who went to live in Nsawam and started buying vegetables in the market there. She sent them

---

[57]Sai, in "Women Traders," p. 13, described the procedure as follows: they "started at dawn, travelled for two to five hours by mammy trucks or trotro to a rural market, bought the foodstuffs and returned by late evening. On the average they travelled sixty miles. . . ." On longer trips (4-6 days), they slept on the truck.

to Accra for her sister or mother to sell, and they made a reckoning once a year to divide the profits. One woman had six partners who were not relatives bringing things to her in the market at Accra to sell. In fact, the former arrangement, where women went themselves to buy vegetables, has now become more like the partnership system. Women now send their daughters to buy the vegetables. Sai commented that all of the Makola No. 1 produce traders in her survey who had been in trade longer than 10 years used to go themselves to the rural areas to buy produce, but in 1971 their daughters went for them. However, this may simply be specialization in tasks by age group, as Hill noted.[58]

The produce trade has become less linked to family structure than the fish trade, mainly because increasing urbanization has given Ga women in Accra fewer kinship links in the countryside, and there is no need to process the vegetables. Because of growth of Accra, the sources of food supplies are farther away. Whereas in 1961 Poleman described Asesewa, a town 60 miles north of Accra, as the heart of the maize-growing district, now much of the corn comes from the Northern Region, Brong-Ahafo, and northern Asante.[59] Even in 1961, 30% of the tonnage of the four main staples (maize, yam, rice, cassava) came from over 100 miles away.[60] Therefore, Ga people usually have no family connections with the source of supply.[61] This did not prevent them, however, from occasionally dealing in large quantities. Polly Hill described a Ga woman plantain seller in 1966, who sold several truckloads a day and had customers at Makola No. 1, Osu, Kaneshie, Labadi, Mamprobi, Adabraka, and Salaga Markets. She had been in business for twenty years, employed ten carriers, supplied credit to her customers (to be repaid within the week), and kept her accounts in her head. She was one of the largest wholesalers in Accra.[62]

More typical of Central Accra are the long-distance traders discovered in 1978. Since the interviewing conditions in 1971-72 and 1978 mostly eliminated the possibility of talking directly with those engaged in the long-distance trade, we gleaned indirect information about them from the 202 women interviewed in the 1978 house-to-house surveys. This gave an impression of the nature and incidence of more recent long-distance trading

---

[58]Sai, "Market Women," p. 54; P. Hill, in "Notes on the Organization of Food Wholesaling in South-Eastern Ghana B: Long Distance Trade in Plantains," paper (March 1966), p. 14, noted that collecting-wholesaling was essentially a young women's business.

[59]T. T. Poleman, "The Food Economies of the Urban Middle Africa: The Case of Ghana," *Stanford University Food Research Institute Studies* II, no. 2 (May 1961): 162. I am using corn here to mean maize, which is the general Ghanaian and American usage. G. Benneh, "Agricultural Land Use and Population in the Closed Forest Region of Ghana," in *Symposium on Population and Socio-Economic Development in Ghana*, ed. N. O. Addo et al., Ghana Population Studies No. 2 (1968), p. 71.

[60]Poleman, "Food," p. 169.

[61]Benneh, in "Agricultural Land," pp. 63, 75, noted that in the 1950s there was a 50% hike in the number of roadside villages within 50 miles of Accra supplying it with produce. However, he also showed that the area had a comparatively low density of available agricultural population (under 25 per square mile).

[62]Hill, "Notes," p. 22.

to compare with the more historical accounts from the 1971-72 survey. Fifteen percent of the compounds had one or more long-distance traders living in them. Thirty-two long-distance traders were mentioned in all, 78% of whom dealt in staples like cassava and corn and 56% in fresh vegetables and fruit. Only 12% dealt in fish, showing its declining importance in long-distance trade. Six percent dealt in imported goods and 3% (one woman each) in pottery and firewood. Most (79%) of the women went at least once a week to places within sixty miles of Accra in the Eastern Region, while 27% visited places in Ashanti Region. Only 16% went further than that, so perhaps "long-distance" is a misnomer in many cases. However, in the 1971-72 sample Kumasi was the most distant entrepôt visited, so the younger traders may have been forced to go farther afield.

In any case, these long-distance traders were not numerous. A guesstimate would put the number of economically active traders in an average Central Accra compound at at least three. If out of 202 compounds only 32 women were in the long-distance trade, then at most only 5% of the traders in the area were involved in it in 1978. Far more women are in the purely local trade. They bought the produce (corn, in particular) in Accra at the train station or at Makola No. 2, and sold it in smaller quantities. Some persons with larger capital than most produce traders have at their disposal have branched out into controlling the supply by starting farms on land they purchased inland. One 80-year old Central Accra man bought some land in Akwapim as a young man (using earnings from clerical work) and established some of his relatives on it growing vegetables. In 1972 he sold them to women who hired a lorry to bring them to Accra, and got part of their profits. However, control of the source of supply of the most profitable line in Accra, corn, has passed out of Ga hands. The wholesale yam trade, which is also quite profitable, has always been controlled by Akan women because they control the sources of supply; not one Ga woman in any of the surveys sold it.

For a few women, however, the growth of Accra provided new avenues for wholesaling produce, especially during and after World War II. The demand for services and supplies in Accra increased greatly during World War II because of the military presence. One woman in the 1971-72 sample took advantage of this by supplying pineapples to the Quartermaster's Division on a contract basis. In one week she would buy £60 worth of pineapples in Akwapim and send them down to Accra. Other women evidently also supplied other types of fruit, each specializing in one type. This sort of arrangement was also common with government offices in Accra. Some buyers supplied corn directly to large numbers of kenkey makers in Accra.[63] These women obviously had the largest turnover and probably made the most profits of any in the produce trace. Next largest in scale were the businesses of women operating concessions outside large stores in Accra and at other popular locations. They often specialized in European-type

[63]V. Nyanteng and G. J. van Apeldoorn, "The Farmer and the Marketing of Foodstuffs," University of Ghana, ISSER Technical Publication No. 19 (1971), p. 42.

vegetables, which restaurants and embassies purchased in large quantities. The proprietors of these concessions usually did not live in Central Accra but had houses elsewhere, an informal survey revealed. However, all of these women were dwarfed in numerical importance by the typical vegetable seller, who bought a small stock of tomatoes, onions, and peppers at Kantomanto Market daily or weekly, and then sold them on the street or outside the market, hoping to get rid of her whole stock that day. Their attractive trays of colorful vegetables were ubiquitous in Accra.

To sum up, the fish and produce trades underwent analogous changes in the twentieth century. In both women now rely less on relatives as a source of supply. Both were changed considerably, especially in terms of the bulk involved, by the advent of motorized transport. In both a system of partnership developed which successfully utilized new forms of transportation for the greater profit of the participants. There were some differences, however. While fishsmoking required the cooperation of all of the inhabitants of a compound on occasion, the produce trade was easily conducted by women with help from their daughters or nieces only. Produce never needed intensive processing in the compound, but fish did until frozen storage facilities made it possible for some large fish traders to dispense with the help of the compound organization. So, removal of production from the compound was in effect here. However, the most important difference between the changes in the two trades derived from the nature of the supply sources. In the fish trade, access to a supply of fish became a matter of political preference, which was possible because mechanized fishing has concentrated the largest supply of fish in a few hands. Cold storage facilities succeeded in cutting out the Ga middlewomen to some extent by making supplies of fresh fish directly available to inland traders. In the produce trade the control of supplies of some commodities ceased being a Ga prerogative altogether. Corn, which used to come from around Accra, now comes in larger quantities from elsewhere. Accra needs much more than the countryside immediately surrounding it can supply, especially since more land is built on and people go to Accra to work. Thus, for different reasons, the trend in both trades has been toward higher participation of the women in the local rather than long-distance trade, with an accompanying shift of emphasis to marketing, rather than production efforts.

In terms of profits, the change in both trades was from small-scale to large-scale ventures for some women with the advent of common motorized transport in the 1920s. However, the shift in the 1960s to higher participation in the local trade brought correspondingly less profits. Only a few women possessing some sort of monopolistic advantage still deal in large quantities. These women have become the objects of resentment on the part of farmers, who feel that they take unfair advantage of such factors as transport scarcity in buying the crops.[64] Whatever the vicissitudes of oligo-

---

[64]Nyanteng and van Apeldoorn, "Farmer," p. 48; J. North et al., *Women in National Development in Ghana*, USAID Women in Development Office study (April 1975), p. 43.

poly,[65] they have also affected the small retail traders in both fish and produce detrimentally, as their dependence on marketing rather than production becomes stronger.

Cloth, Beads, and Other Imported Goods

In the imported goods trade production has been completely removed from the compound. The process of imported goods replacing some locally produced goods started prior to the twentieth century. Many of the local products were sold at the same time, but then gradually phased out as imported goods gained in status. Ocloo claims that it was not until the 1930s that many imported goods became common, and the 1940s that they drove out local products.[66] Seers and Ross concurred with a note on the great increase between 1938 and 1950 in the import of "luxuries" and "semi-luxuries," especially foodstuffs.[67] The documentation is not vast, but it is available for some goods, and shows that the process was going on before the twentieth century. For instance, in the sixteenth century people in Accra were still making bark cloth,[68] but they later quit doing it. Metal pots largely replaced local pottery, although the latter is still used for grinding pepper and on certain ceremonial occasions. People in and around Accra used to raise pigs, but barrels of imported pickled pigs' feet replaced the homegrown variety for some uses.[69]

Until the early twentieth century local cosmetic preparations and soap were dominant, but now people in Accra mostly use imported cosmetics and soap. Ghana now has imported-type soap and cloth factories. The former are usually foreign-owned, however, so the effect is somewhat the same in that the profits are exported. Cloth is one field where import substitution has taken place in the 1960s, although cotton cloth is still imported. Aluminum pots are now manufactured in Ghana, but the aluminum is imported, despite Ghana's own bauxite reserves. Some imports produced local industries either dependent on imports, or concurrent with them. For instance, tobacco is now grown and cured in Ghana, but it is also imported. Imported small beads are used as a source for glass to make certain types of domestic beads. The history of imports in Ghana, then, has not always been one of

---

[65]One study has suggested that the farmers in the Kumasi area, at least, were receiving 55 to 60% of the consumer price for yams, while the traders got 15% (the other 30% went for transport and handling). FAO report, "Market Women," p. 14.

[66]E. Ocloo, "The Ghanaian Market Woman," paper presented at 14th World Conference of Society for International Development, Abidjan (Aug. 1974), pp. 1-3.

[67]D. Seers and C. R. Ross, *Report on Financial and Physical Problems of Development in the Gold Coast* (Accra: Office of the Government Statistician, 1952), p. 7.

[68]De Marees, "Description," p. 262.

[69]I. Wallerstein, in "The Three Stages of African Involvement in the World Economy," in *The Political Economy of Contemporary Africa*, ed. P. C. W. Gutkind and I. Wallerstein (Beverly Hills, Calif.: Sage Publications, 1976), p. 36, describes local products being driven out and local processing being forbidden by the colonialists.

substitution for local products, but the balance does seem to be on that side. "Foreign trade may actually destroy existing industries rather than create new ones."[70]

Thus, women increasingly concentrated more on marketing rather than production. While the marketing of imports has definitely created more jobs than it destroyed in terms of actual numbers (population increase alone took care of that), the development of a dependence in Ghana on goods manufactured elsewhere is not good, given the perpetual foreign exchange problems. Because most factories are elsewhere, Ghanaians do not get the benefits of jobs in the manufacturing process of imported goods that they use, or the profits from them to put into the economy. The industries that have been developed in Ghana are mostly secondary; the raw materials for them must be imported. Even some factories using local products, the tomato paste factory, for instance, have faltered because of lack of infrastructure and skills, and dependence on imported machine parts. Also, creating jobs in marketing rather than manufacturing has probably had a detrimental effect on certain groups in the population. It is interesting to speculate about the result if, for instance, the Europeans had not imported soap, which requires no imported raw materials to manufacture. The manufacture of local soap was a "cottage industry" carried on in the villages around Accra. The women made it by boiling the ashes of various substances such as plantain peel, cocoa leaf, or a tree called *onyaa tso* in Ga, and palm oil. It was called *ŋmɛsamla* or *Ga samla* ("palmnut soap" or "Ga soap"). If the village women now were supplying a large proportion of the soap used in Accra it might bring in considerable profits which would not be exported. They might themselves have established soap factories instead of leaving it to Procter and Gamble and Lever Brothers. As it was, at the time soap started being imported, local soap could not compete in quality and was gradually supplanted. Very few women were involved in the experimental intermediate-technology, small-scale soap factory set up in Kumasi for development purposes in 1973, although the technology was being transferred to a women's cooperative in Mali in 1979.[71]

What have been the changes, then, in a trade where local production was not involved, imported goods? Some of the changes resemble those in the fish trade, only they started earlier in the imported goods trade and have progressed farther. The big firms have opened branches even in small towns, thereby cutting out the middlewomen, the Ga women traders.[72] This process made women go into the local rather than long-distance trade. In the 1971-72 small survey more older than younger women were in the long-distance cloth and bead trade as their chief occupation. Forty-three percent of the 43 women involved in the cloth and bead trade were in the long-

[70]W. A. Lewis, *Anthropological Essays* (New York: Random House, 1970), p. 40.

[71]*Small Industry Development Network Newsletter*, No. 15 (June 1979), p. 7.

[72]This was noted also in the Ghana Ministry of Housing, *Accra Plan* (1958), p. 1, in a historical context. It claimed that the extension of colonial administration to the hinterland in the late nineteenth century broke the Ga monopoly on the trade in European goods.

distance trade and 57% in the local trade. In the 1978 sample of women 39 to 50 only 7% were in the cloth and bead trade of any sort. The cloth and bead trade is the best example because two-thirds of the 1971-72 imported goods traders were in it, and 56% of all the women ever involved in the imported goods trade. The single next most important trade was in provisions, which occupied only 13% of the imported goods traders as their chief trade; the rest were split evenly between aluminum pots, pigs' feet, and miscellany.

Cloth

In many ways the mechanics of the cloth trade resemble those of the fish trade, but there is one important difference. The amount of capital required to start in the cloth or other imported goods trade has always been higher than for other trades. In order to get the goods to sell it is necessary to establish a credit account with a large firm. Before World War I credit was given relatively freely by the big firms. This was the trust system, common in various parts of Africa, which relied on an educated relative or husband earning a salary vouching for the reliability of the customer. As the numbers of people wishing to peddle imported goods into the rural areas grew, the relationship was converted into cash. Customers starting in about the 1920s had to put down a cash deposit which opened a passbook account for them. They were allowed to take out up to 200% the value of the deposit in goods (this varied with different firms and the reliability of the customer), which they usually paid for in installments as they sold them. They got a commission on the goods of 1 to 5% plus any profits they made over that.[73] The record of a trader's transactions with the company were kept in a small passbook retained by the trader. By reviewing the passbooks every month or so when the customers came in for new goods the stores kept track of which lines were selling well, and used that information when deciding what to order from Europe. On closing an account a trader would receive the deposit back minus the value of any goods outstanding. In the "old days," the 1920s, people could open accounts with as little as £10. In 1952 £25 was required, whereas in 1978 at least £100 (¢200) was needed.[74]

Because of the need for a large sum of money at once, it was helpful to be subsidized by a wealthy husband or influential relatives. This occurred among 71% of the imported goods traders in the 1971-72 small sample. Before World War I a "gentleman," or literate person, had to vouch for a potential credit risk, often the trader's husband. Then there was the digging up of enough money to cover initial starting costs; artisans and clerks were more likely to have it or be able to get loans to obtain the necessary sum. Certain large Ga merchants were even more apt to be able to raise it. In

[73]*Report of the Commission of Enquiry into Trade Malpractices in Ghana* (1965), pp. 40-41.

[74]Lawson and Kwei, *African Entrepreneurship*, p. 139; Sai, "Women Traders," p. 15.

fact, what often happened was that a chief, or a merchant (sometimes the same person), would get passbooks for each of his wives, and set them up in small stores. The profits in this case would go to the husband. A consequence of this system was that the selling of imported goods came to be regarded as an aristocratic profession of sorts. One woman said,

A.   *When I was young I would have liked to do white man's work. I did not want to work with fish, corn, and so on, but I did not have enough money.*
Q.   Which type of white man's work?
A.   *Like the selling of cloth and handkerchiefs.*

This need for a large sum of money at once might have been instrumental in the formation of some voluntary associations. Those which operated on a revolving credit basis provided their members with just such a source of capital periodically. Another method of obtaining it was to form partnerships and pool resources.

As time passed there have been changes within the passbook system. There always was considerable flexibility in the amount of goods an individual trader was allowed to take out--if she had proved herself to be reliable she was given more. In the late 1950s, however, the big firms like U.A.C., U.T.C., and C.F.A.O. made lower ceilings on the amount over the security deposit which an individual could take out, usually a 50% maximum.[75] Also, whereas people used to be able to choose which goods they took out, the store managers subsequently began picking the goods for them. They often gave a customer some highly preferred goods on condition that she also take some slower moving, less desirable goods. The passbook holders are divided into categories, and those in the highest category usually got the "conditional" goods. These women often had no retail trade, but rather wholesaled the goods to other traders who retailed them.[76] The smaller traders then got left with the less desirable merchandise.

Such a system obviously lends itself to corruption. Men with powerful political connections or relatives in crucial positions within the firms have taken advantage of it to put their wives or female relatives into the highest categories. In some cases most of the goods supplied went to only a few women; everyone else had to buy from them.[77] With shortages endemic in Ghana, the women in these monopolistic positions can demand ceiling prices for their goods, causing great discontent.[78] Many imported goods are not

---

[75]Acquah, *Accra Survey* (London: University of London Free Press, 1958), p. 70. The initials here stand for: United Africa Company, Union Trading Company, and Compagnie Française de l'Afrique de l'Ouest.

[76]*Report of the Commission of Enquiry into Trade Malpractices in Ghana* (1965), pp. 42-43.

[77]*Report of the Commission of Enquiry into Trade Malpractices in Ghana* (1965), pp. 46-49.

[78]E. Dumor, in "Commodity Queens and the Distributive Trade in Ghana," paper presented at African Studies Association Conference, Baltimore (Nov. 1978), p. 5, reflects the resentment the traders aroused by classifying them as a parasitic enclave sector which exploits the local populace on behalf of foreign merchant capitalists. Seers and Ross, in *Report*, p. 15, commented, "Imported goods pass . . . through a shipping monopoly and an importing 'oligopoly' at one end, and at the other end, tens of thousands of traders doing inter-

covered by price controls, so these women can set the prices. If the price is controlled, as in the case of sardines, tomato paste, and evaporated milk, they can simply sell on the black market. Changes in supply conditions, then, have tightened credit terms and concentrated supplies in fewer hands. Both factors benefit the few big traders, and make it increasingly difficult for women with small resources to get started. Likewise, the police hassles over selling above control price which sometimes result in confiscation of a trader's whole stock, are devastating for small traders. A result--only 10% of the 1978 sample of 101 women aged 39 to 50 were selling imported goods, compared to the 42% of the 1971-72 small sample who had them as their main trade.

One reason the big companies instituted the passbook system was that they needed a relatively cheap method of distribution to the hinterland of the Gold Coast. The women fulfilled this need by carrying the cloth to villages inaccessible by road, and they also made cloth available at prices that buyers in the villages could afford by selling it on credit. Sometimes the terms were fairly easy; people could pay over a three month period. Most of the women who went to the villages appear to have been small-scale traders, who took only six or ten pieces with them (a "piece" of cloth is twelve yards). These traders would usually sell the cloth in half pieces or even less.

> Mother peddles cloth but I know she is not the fat rich market type. . . . In the villages you always have to settle for installments and money comes in in such miserable bits someone like Mother with four children just spends every penny of her profit as it comes. It is her favorite saying that she sells cloth for the fish-and-cassava women. There is always a threat of her eating into her capital.[79]

In general, the smaller the amount of cloth sold the higher the markup, and if it was bought on credit the price would be raised even further. In this way the women tried to compensate for a small turnover. Sometimes the larger traders would go upcountry also, but only to Nsawam or some other place with a market, where they would sell wholesale.

But more women were involved in the local wholesale cloth trade than the long-distance trade. The local wholesalers sold to village women who came in to buy and also hired other women to go to the villages for them. The best example of a large-scale wholesaler was Naa Klokai.

> The late Naa Klokai was a dignified woman in her seventies in 1972. She used to be a very active trader, but she had trouble with her legs and could not walk well enough to continue in 1972. In her heyday, from the late 1920s to the early 1950s, she had passbooks with C.F.A.O., U.A.C., and G. B. Ollivant. These she got by paying cash and using her jewelry as security. Her husband, a railroad manager, stood as guarantor for her, so she was allowed to take out more than the actual amount of her security. He

---

mittent business. This structure is the source of many of the country's problems, political and economic."

[79]A. A. Aidoo, *No Sweetness Here* (Garden City, New York: Doubleday and Co., 1971), p. 131.

also periodically checked her passbook to see that she was not being cheated.[80] Business was good in the 1920s. Many people came from the villages
and other market towns to buy from her at her stall in Makola No. 1. Her
turnover was between £600 and £1,000 a month at that point. She also
went to the villages herself to sell maybe once a month, taking a bale of
cloth (100 pieces) with her. These she sold both wholesale, usually at
Suhum, and retail. By the 1950s she no longer went herself to the villages,
but she had ten other women selling the cloth for her. They would take
out maybe £100 worth of cloth at a time and sell it at the market or in the
villages. They got the profits and she got the commission. At that time
her turnover was between £4,000 and £6,000 a month. In this way Naa
Klokai was able to pay for educating her five sons, even sending one to Britain. In 1978 she was the reigning head of an influential family with many
nephews working in high government or business positions. Her own
economic status, however, had fallen considerably with the cessation of her
trade. Part of her subsistence came from using or selling off cloth left over
from former years.

In the volume of her trade Naa Klokai was obviously not typical. She
was the most successful trader by far in any of the surveys. In her methods,
however, she was not out of the ordinary. Others did the same things only
on a smaller scale. More average was the type of small-scale trader who
worked for Naa Klokai. Of the 20 women whose turnover was given, 8 had
10 pieces or under a month, 4 had 11 to 25, 6 had 26 to 50, and only 2 had
over 50. These statistics, although based on only a few traders, are
confirmed by Addae's study of the cloth trade in 1954. She found that 80%
of the traders got less than £45 commission a year, and only three traders
made over £1,000 commission a year. Naa Klokai should be counted among
the latter. Those three traders at that time accounted for 14% of the total
allocation of textiles to passbook traders in Accra.[81]

In summary, then, the cloth trade was probably the most profitable
among the trades in imported goods. It was aptly described as "a market of
competitors full of semi-monopolistic tendencies."[82] The tendency toward
monopoly has become stronger in recent years. Conditions of supply have
changed to the detriment of small traders, as in the fish trade. There was
also a trend toward a higher concentration of traders in the local, rather
than long-distance trade, partly because the big firms opened branches in
towns upcountry. This has cut down the role of Ga women as middlewomen, which was so important in the 1920s, in particular. In any case,

---

[80]Some clerks of the big companies occasionally took advantage of the illiteracy of their
clientele by adding other items to their accounts, which they appropriated for themselves.
Report on the Commission of Enquiry into Trade Malpractices in Ghana (1965), p. 50.

[81]G. Addae, "The Retailing of Imported Textiles in the Accra Market," West African
Institute of Social and Economic Research Conference Proceedings (March 1954), pp. 55-56.

[82]Lawson, "Growth," p. 202; Sai, "Women Traders," p. 15; Lawson and Kwei, *African
Entrepreneurship*, p. 139; and Ocloo, "Ghanaian Market Woman," p. 2, all support this by
giving turnover figures or simply impressionistic assertions. Ocloo noted that it was mainly
wealthy textile traders who took over the shops vacated as a result of the Aliens' Compliance Order of 1969.

more women traded locally all along, probably because some were selling wholesale to women from the villages. In this manner the cloth trade differs from the fish trade with its development of partnership systems for the long-distance trade. The cloth trade also contrasted with the fish trade in requiring capital rather than labor for processing. With cloth women were therefore more likely to turn to their husbands and male relatives for help rather than to their female residential groups. Thus, participation in the upper levels of the cloth trade increasingly became the prerogative of those women with good connections in the upper levels of the male-dominated bureaucracy. Entrenchment of privilege was furthered because passbooks were often inherited, along with the good will of the trading firm. The conditions characteristic of the passbook trade also include trade in other imported goods. But it is possible for other changes to occur in supply conditions, as illustrated by the bead trade, with very different effects.

Beads

The number of people engaged in the bead trade has gone steadily down. While eight women aged in the seventies through nineties in the small 1971-72 sample sold beads as their chief commodity, none of the younger women did. The four women in their thirties through fifties who had participated in it did so only as girls when helping a relative. How did this trade die out?

The imported bead trade was built on an already existing local bead trade. Before the coming of the Europeans, people made beads from various stones. The most famous of these were the "aggrey" (*akori* or *kɔli* in Ga) beads, whose origins have been the subject of much debate among scholars[83] They were highly prized on the Gold Coast and already being traded in the sixteenth century when the first Portuguese traders arrived.[84] Another type of local bead, called *atsɛnte* in Ga, was of bauxite.[85] The Portuguese became the middlemen in the bead trade, as well as in the local cloth trade.[86] They and other Europeans started importing glass beads of various sorts. These can be divided into two categories, *millefiore* beads (large pottery beads pro-

---

[83]E. J. M. Van Landewijk, in "What was the Original Aggrey Bead?" *Ghana Journal of Sociology* VII, no. 1 (1971): 89, hypothesizes that they came from slag from abandoned iron workings.

[84]Van Landewijk, "What," p. 91. The Landers commented on "the famous Aggra bead [on sale at the Oyo-Ile market], which at Cape Coast Castle, Accra, and other places is sold for its weight in gold, and which has vainly been attempted to be imitated by the Italians and our own countrymen." R. and J. Lander, *Journal of an Expedition to Explore the Course and Termination of the Niger* (New York: J. and J. Harper, 1833), I: 170-71.

[85]These are still produced in small numbers upcountry.

[86]K. Y. Daaku, *Trade and Politics on the Gold Coast, 1600-1720* (Oxford: Clarendon Press, 1970), pp. 6-7.

duced at Murano in Italy), and small Bohemian glass beads.[87] The former, called *adiagba* in Ga, were polished and the edges were straightened and smoothed before they were strung and sold. This process was described by de Marees in 1600.

> They also use great store of Venice beads, of all kinds of colours, but they desire some colours more than others, which they breake in foure or five pieces, and then grind them upon a stone, as our children grind Cherrie stones; and then put them upon strings, made of Barke of trees, ten or twelve together, and therewith Traffique much: Those ground Corals they weare about their neckes, hands and feet. They also use round beads, and specially great round Counters, which they hang and plait among their haire, and let them hang over their eares.

These were one of the chief items of trade at that time.[88] The small beads helped to produce a new local bead ·industry in some villages. They were ground and the powder used for making a local variety of bead. The powder was put in layers of different colors in a mold, with pieces of stick stuck into each to make openings for stringing them. Then they were fired in a beehive-shaped kiln. These beads are usually opaque in color, in contrast to the clear glass of the imported small beads.

In the nineteenth century and perhaps before, the bead trade may have been the most important one pursued by women in Accra. In 1874 Henty remarked it as such, and described the women stringing beads on strips of palm leaf, and polishing them with sand and water.[89] Beadpolishing entailed the use of a large flat stone with water and sand to abrade them. Women rolled the strung beads back and forth on the stone to make them shiny. The processing made a basic difference in the organization of the bead trade. Whereas the cloth trade could easily be conducted by individuals (albeit on a small scale), the bead trade required the services of female relatives and/or others if a trader was to sell every day. Before World War II many women hired themselves out as beadpolishers, who were paid a standard rate per hundred beads. Occasionally beadpolishing was taught through a formal apprenticeship, the apprentice paying the teacher a fee.[90] Sometimes women used it as a means of picking up a little money on the side when their own trade was not flourishing, or even to get initial trading capital.

The example of Naa Dei is helpful to show organization and changes in the bead trade.

> Naa Dei was a formidable lady in her seventies in 1972 with a well-developed acquisitive instinct. She came from a prominent family in which her female relatives on her mother's side had been selling beads and cloth

---

[87]I am indebted to Professor A. Lamb, formerly of the Department of History, University of Ghana, and to Professor Jan Vansina of the University of Wisconsin for some of this information.

[88]De Marees, "Description," p. 282. An old Adangbe (Ga-related) song goes, "Kɔli is the greater, however plentifully *adiagba* is produced, kɔli is the child of another woman, kɔli is greater than all." Van Landewijk, "What," p. 90.

[89]G. A. Henty, *The March to Coomassie* (London: Tinsley Brothers, 1874), p. 285.

[90]*Ga Maŋtsɛ's Civil Court Record* (1922-24), pp. 185-86.

for at least three generations before her. As the oldest daughter in the family, and the only one not sent to school, she was groomed to follow in her mother's footsteps. She inherited her mother's wholesale business which centered in a shop near Makola No. 1. She and her mother sold only wholesale to traders who came from the villages to buy. Most of their business was done in imported beads rather than cloth. In the late 1920s, when business was very good, they employed four people steadily as bead polishers. In a good month they might have sold £2,000 worth of beads. In the late 1940s when she was trading on her own, she sold mostly small beads because the large ones were not available. The amount she sold was probably more, but the profit was less. In 1972 she was simply selling off her old stock, and claimed that the bead trade was ruined.

Naa Dei, like Naa Klokai in the cloth trade, is an example of a large bead trader with a well-articulated business. There were many more traders who sold only in small quantities, peddling beads in Accra or around to the villages. Those who dealt in locally produced beads usually got them from the main market in Koforidua, or from itinerant Kwahu or Hausa traders who hawked them around Accra. Those beads seem not to have been as popular, and were usually handled by small-scale retail traders, not wholesalers like Naa Dei.

The changes in the bead trade which made it moribund were mainly in supply and fashions. The supply of imported beads came from two areas in Europe which were adversely affected by World Wars I and II. As a result, the Bohemian beads stopped coming altogether during both wars, and the Italian beads during World War II. After World War II the Italians reduced their production and by 1967 had stopped it altogether.[91] These conditions had bad effects on the local suppliers. Unlike the cloth suppliers, which were mostly large firms, there appear to have been a number of small businesses who specialized in importing beads directly from Europe. The largest of these was a German firm called Jackel, whose proprietors were interned during World War II and later deported. There were also small firms run by Ga men, Amartey and Adjei being the most important. The only one of these businesses which still operated in 1972 was Sick-Hagemeyer, started by a Swiss in the 1920s; it imported small quantities of beads. The larger companies, like U.A.C., U.T.C., and C.F.A.O., drastically cut their importation of beads. Thus the *millefiore* beads, which were once the most popular type, are becoming rare. The small Bohemian beads were still available in 1972, but meanwhile styles changed in Ghana, especially in the urban areas, and beads are no longer an essential item of apparel for a well-dressed woman.[92]

On the streets in Central Accra in 1978 small girls wearing nothing but a string of waist beads were commonly found, but finding a woman wearing beads instead of gold or costume jewelry was another matter. Some elderly women still wear them, but they are not buying new ones. Some even wear

---

[91]*Annual Colonial Report* (1916), p. 17; *Ghana Trade Report*, 1967.

[92]The fashion for beads in the U.S. in the late 1960s caused a small renaissance in the bead trade, whereby some *adiagba* beads were imported from Africa under the mistaken impression that they were African in origin.

the full panoply: waist beads (small ones), ankle beads (large ones), and necklaces and bracelets. Women in their fifties and under have virtually stopped wearing beads. One reason for this trend is the wearing of European-style clothes. Somehow a heavy strand of beads looks out of place with a light cotton dress. The beadsellers have not adjusted their styles of stringing them to new fashions. Partly, it is simply a matter of taste--people prefer gold or costume jewelry. To wear beads is old-fashioned.

Because of this trend the large vocabulary which was once an essential part of the bead trade is falling into disuse and disappearing, along with the beads. Within the two large categories, *adiagba* (*millefiore*), and *manteŋlo* (small glass beads), there were many varieties named according to color, design, and/or function. For example, some were called *bihii ahɛrenii* (small beads for young boys), *anoma nomɛtɛtsrɛ* ("feather of a bird"), *ʃitɔ wui* ("pepper-seeds"), *nyaŋkunton* ("rainbow"), *koŋtomɛle* ("spinach stew"--green ones). Like the names given to cloth patterns, they were used as a marketing device.[93] I collected 45 of them from one woman, but different women knew different sets of names, depending on the kinds of beads they had sold.

In the sad state of the bead trade, then, we can see the baneful effects of both supply problems and unpopularity. After at least three and a half centuries of great prosperity, it is coming to a standstill. Since beads were the only imported good which created a considerable local manufacturing industry at the same time, this halt is probably not healthy for the local economy. Although the actual manufacturing of beads took place mostly in the villages in the twentieth century, beadpolishing was a common enough activity in Accra before World War II, and a fruitful source of beginning capital. Bead trading was one of the most profitable lines pursued by women, and those who knew it complained bitterly about its cessation. Nothing has developed with an analogous function to replace it. Since it was a trade in which both Ga men, as importers, and Ga women, as wholesalers, retailers, and processors were extensively involved, its ruin has been particularly grievous for them. A potential source of income for illiterate women has been removed, and one more compound industry has become defunct.

Kenkey and Other Prepared Foods

The trade in prepared foods used to be important for Ga women as a residual trade, but it is becoming a dominant one. While it accounted for only 30.5% of the chief occupations of the 1971-72 small sample, 63.8% of the women had participated in it at some time in their lives. In 1978 it was the most popular trade among the women aged 39 to 50. Why? It has low entry requirements in terms of capital and contacts, and it takes advantage of the cheap labor offered by the compound organization. Also, with the growth of Accra and a higher male-female ratio, the market for prepared

---

[93]C. C. Robertson, "Economic Woman in Africa: Profit-Making Techniques of Accra Market Women," *Journal of Modern African Studies* XII, no. 4 (Dec. 1974): 660.

foods has grown. Many single male migrants to Accra find prepared foods convenient. Meanwhile, the increasing difficulties with other trades have helped to push women into the less profitable but always needed trade in prepared foods. If a woman went bankrupt in another trade then she usually turned to prepared foods.

Prepared food makers can be divided into six categories according to commodity. The most numerous one is the makers of kenkey, or k‡mi, the fermented corn dough staple of the Ga. It also comes in two variations called ab‡lo and banku. Together the makers of these staples accounted for 50% of the prepared food sellers in the small 1971-72 sample. Another group is the women who run chopbars, or small restaurants serving what we would call fast food. They usually sell various sorts of stew, with fufu (the Akan staple) or rice. In this category also are the women who sell rice and stew, cooked yam, and fried fish without offering any seating amenities. Fried fish are usually sold as an accompaniment with stew or kenkey, either by their preparers or else by a woman who has bought them from the preparer. They are therefore being considered here rather than under the fish trade. A third category includes the makers of porridge, who usually sell on the street. The fourth is the sellers of fried foods such as plantain, doughnuts, and various sorts of pancakes. The bakers and sellers of baked foods are in the fifth group, and the sellers of cornwine, called ŋmɛdaa, in the sixth. Kenkey is the most important product and the focus of this section.

The process of making kenkey is still very similar to de Marees' description of 1600, except that millet used to be the main ingredient rather than maize.

> Overnight they steepe the Millia with a little Mais in faire water, and in the morning after they have washt, and made themselves readie, they take the Millia and lay it upon a stone, as Painters doe when they grind their colours, then they take another stone about a foot long, and with their hands grind the Millia as small as they can, till in a manner it be dough, and then it sheweth like baked Buckway Cakes, they temper their dough with fresh water and Salt, and then make Rowles thereof as bigge as two fists, and that they lay upon the warm harth, whereon it baketh a little, and this is the bread which they use. . . .[94]

Actually he abbreviated a little. It might be as well to go over it again in its modern form.

First the maize is bought and soaked overnight in water. Then it is ground, today usually by gasoline-powered mills owned and operated by men.[95] The change from handgrinding took place between the World Wars. The 1911 and 1921 censuses listed "corn grinders" as a category under

---

[94]De Marees, "Description," p. 272.

[95]A check on three cornmills operating in Ussher Town in 1978 revealed that two were owned by Ewe men and one by a Ga man. All were operated by males only. K. Campbell-Platt, in "The Impact of Mechanization on the Employment of Women in Traditional Sectors," paper presented at Ghana National Council on Women and Development Seminar on Women and Development (Sept. 1975), p. 11, gave cornmills as an example where even intermediate technology is dominated by men in Ghana.

women's occupations. In each case they numbered more than double the number of kenkey makers listed.[96] They were paid for their services. One woman said that at first people refused to eat kenkey made from machine-ground corn. The advent of cornmills reduced both the amount of time required to make kenkey, and the control over the whole process by the female network. Nevertheless, the process is still tedious and involves much labor on the part of many people. After taking the corn to be ground very fine, it is combined with water and made into dough. This takes place on the second day. The dough is allowed to ferment a bit overnight, which gives kenkey its characteristically sour taste. On the third day some of the dough is partly cooked (this dough is called *afrata*) and added to the raw dough in about equal proportions. Then this mixture is made into balls, which are wrapped in corn husks and then steamed over large metal barrels. Because of the great heat of the fire, women often get up long before daybreak to start cooking kenkey. This part of the process is particularly time-consuming and usually everyone helps. After this the kenkey is sold, either the same or the next day. It will keep for several days.[97]

Making kenkey, like smoking fish, involves a lot of bulky equipment which generally occupies most of the courtyard of a compound. It is a three-day process which lends itself easily to mass production. There is no indication that producing it on a large scale has changed. De Marees commented in 1600 that people made enough for their households only, but then he went ahead to say that,

> others that have not the meanes to have such bread, they goe to Market to buy it, and call it Kangues, when the Fisher-men come out of the Sea with their fish, then the women carrie it to the Market, where everie one comes to buy that and flesh, fruite, and other things.[98]

This may, then, be the original "fast" food industry. Precisely because it takes a long time to make, it is far more efficient for a few people to make large batches to sell to most of the people.

Kenkey production provides employment for many women. To minimize the amount of work done by the people in one compound, specialization arose dividing different stages of the process among different workers. The increasing use of cornmills, of course, eliminated the corngrinding specialty, but some women sold ready-made corn dough, and others boiled corn, thus reducing the amount of labor one set of people had to do. This was not common, however. None of the kenkey makers in the 1971-72 small sample availed themselves of these opportunities to shorten their labor, and only one woman mentioned a relative as having done so. Again, this specialization might help to absorb some surplus labor.

---

[96] *Gold Coast Census* (1911), p. 65; (1921), p. 57.

[97] *Banku* takes less time to make than kenkey as it is cooked through only once, and does not have leaves on it. It also keeps longer. *Abɔlo* has some of the same characteristics.

[98] De Marees, "Description," p. 272. The form of the word kenkey used here shows its Portuguese origins. Recently the English "corn" and Ga word *kɔmi* have been assimilated so that kenkey is referred to in Ga as *kɔm*.

Most kenkey was peddled around the streets; some was sent to other neighborhoods for sale. Before World War I, when Accra was only what is now Central Accra, there was a smaller market for kenkey, probably mainly the fishermen, as described by de Marees. In the 1970s much of it was "exported" for sale to workers in other neighborhoods, such as the industrial area, or the area around the big stores downtown. Usually the young girls, the daughters or granddaughters, peddled it in these areas, while the older women stayed at home working on the next batch and watching the younger children.

Because of the amount of work involved it helps kenkey makers considerably to have many female relatives available to aid in the process, making female compounds a great convenience. If for some reason no help was available, a woman usually did something else. One might suppose that, as in the fish and vegetable trade, relatives would be important in obtaining a supply of corn. This was not true in the 1970s, although in the nineteenth century it might have been. In the 1971-72 small sample only two women were ever aided by relatives in getting their supplies, and in those cases it was indirectly only. They used to buy corn at villages where a close relative was well known, so they could get easier credit terms. They and a few other women traveled to villages near Accra and bought their own supplies of corn. Even before World War II, however, most women bought the corn in Accra. Women who made kenkey after World War II bought the corn in the market or at the railroad station. In the 1960s many women bought from northerners who came around in a truck delivering bags of corn. Some got it from government cooperatives. Invariably the women bought on credit and paid back later, making kenkey one of the easier trades to begin.

The women in the 1971-72 survey regarded the prepared food trade as a reserve to be drawn upon in hard times. For instance, many women made kenkey when fish were not available, and regarded fishselling as their main occupation. Thus a woman might have made one batch of kenkey a week but sold fish at the same time. Because one could stay in the house most of the time when young helpers were available for selling, the prepared food trade was a convenient one for mothers of young children. Also, if a woman went bankrupt in the cloth trade, for instance, she could use credit to start again selling kenkey. Because a woman had to see about feeding her children or grandchildren anyway, it was quite easy if she had adequate help to run a trade in prepared food alongside something else. Indeed, the women viewed being able to feed themselves and their dependents and operate a business simultaneously as one of the main benefits of the trade.[99] This, however, was a factor which made it very difficult to determine the women's

---

[99]The great advantage of being able to eat your own product is shown in several estimates of the nutritional status of market women. Sai, "Women Traders," p. 17, commented that most were overweight. M. Fuchs-Carsch, in North et al., *Women*, p. 38, cited a study by Davey in 1961-62, showing that wage earners, self-employed men, petty traders, and self-employed women had the best nutritional status, farmers of both sexes, the worst. However, nutritional status is often measured solely by weight. Conceivably, on a diet primarily of a starchy staple one could be overweight and still undernourished.

profits, both for them and for us. Some women regarded the prepared food trade more as a convenience than a livelihood. The replies of this woman were typical.

Q. Do other people who sell kenkey make more profits than you do?

A. *I think they do.*

Q. Why do you think so?

A. *I'm not serious with it. I simply give it away to the household. All the children here belong to others and I have to feed them.*

Most of the women said that they gave food to other children and their relatives' children. Some even gave that as a reason for not knowing their exact profit position. In this trade, then, the compulsory levy exacted by the participation of relatives could sometimes be deadly for the business. However, most women accepted this as a fact of life and anticipated it.

Adding to the difficulties in estimating profits were supply and demand factors in the prepared food trade. On the one hand the cost of ingredients such as corn, tomatoes, and cassava, varied seasonally, and with the bargaining capabilities of the purchaser. On the other, the use of ingredients changed from day to day and week to week--a woman might have made a lot of *fufu* one day for her chopbar and not sold it all, so she cut down on the amount the next day. Therefore, the quantity of ingredients bought varied--a woman might have purchased four bags of corn for making kenkey in one week, and two the next. Even if one knew how many bags of corn she bought a week all of the time, the bags were not always standardized in size. Corn could be transferred into four different-sized bags on its way from the Northern Region to Accra.[100] For these reasons, as well as the reluctance of many women to even talk about profit margins, I will not even attempt a guess here. From other indications, however, the prepared food sellers were the poorest class of traders. They certainly were when judged by amount of capital invested.[101] For instance, one would expect that a kenkey maker, if she did well, might branch out into owning a cornmill so she would not have to pay to get the corn ground. One woman in her fifties said that she wanted to buy one for her son to operate, but had never been in a position to do so. Another woman accepted a cornmill as collateral on a loan she made to her husband, and seized it for debt when he defaulted, but she was not a kenkey maker.[102] No one had actually bought one. Considering that the cost of a grain mill in 1978 was ¢2,600 (or approximately $2,000

[100] J. van Apeldoorn, ISSER, personal communication, 1972.

[101] The low capital investment in prepared foods is fairly well substantiated by: Sai, "Women Traders," p. 10; N. Sudarkasa, *Where Women Work: A Study of Yoruba Women in the Marketplace and in the Home,* University of Michigan Museum of Anthropology Anthropological Papers No. 53 (Ann Arbor: University of Michigan Press, 1973), p. 85; K. Church, "A Study of Socio-Economic Status and Child Care Arrangements of Women in Madina," paper presented at Ghana National Council on Women and Development Seminar on Women and Development, Accra (Sept. 1978), p. 4.

[102] SCT 2/6/16, *High Court Judgment Book,* pp. 441-42 (case May 26, 1933).

at official rates of exchange), this is not surprising.[103]

There are, however, some factors influencing profits in the prepared foods trade that need discussion. The price of kenkey in Accra has always been a political football of sorts. Actually, it is not so much the price as it is the size of the balls that is important. Usually when corn is expensive the women make the kenkey balls smaller, rather than raising the price. The effect is the same, of course. This practice has helped to minimize the price rise for kenkey over time. Around 1900 a small one could be had for 1/2d.; at the beginning of 1979 it cost 12d. (15 pesewas). Because kenkey is such a vital food in Accra, complaints are long and loud if the balls get smaller or the price goes up.[104] Various governments have tried to remedy it perforce. For instance, in 1922 the Ga Maŋtsɛ had the gong-gong beaten around Accra warning the kenkey sellers to increase the size of the balls. The Asere and Sempe *maŋtsɛmei* then had a counter gong-gong beaten nullifying the first one.[105] It became an issue, in fact, in a political feud. In the next year complaints were rife because the cornsellers, who were told to move to Makola No. 1, refused to pay £1 for the stalls there, and were selling from their houses at high prices, driving the size of kenkey down. No one was informing on them for fear that they would quit selling corn altogether.[106]

Thus, while the cornsellers are in a fairly strong position, the kenkey sellers bear the brunt of public displeasure if the price goes up. There is considerable pressure for them to keep prices low, and occasional government interference in the form of price controls. It seems, then, that the price of kenkey does not rise as fast as that of other commodities if there is a shortage. And, there is no black market in kenkey in times of government control. This may be the reason why so many women complained about the lack of profits in kenkey. Inflation hit them worse than anyone else. In spite of price controls on corn, the black market flourishes.[107] But the kenkey makers now cannot double their prices; no one would buy. There are enough other prepared food substitutes, like rice and *gari* (a cassava product), so that they are caught in a bind. When the other substitutes did not exist they were in a stronger position, but people have developed a taste for staples not available previously in Accra.[108]

---

[103]Campbell-Platt, "Development," p. 21.

[104]See, for instance, *Accra Daily Graphic*, May 16, 1955, p. 3.

[105]SNA 11/1089, Interview of Gbese Maŋtsɛ with Secretary for Native Affairs, March 28, 1922.

[106]SNA 11/1089, Interview of *maŋtsɛmei* with Accra District Commissioner, March 9, 1923.

[107]For a discussion of the nature and effectiveness of Ghanaian government price controls in the 1960s and 1970s, see A. J. Killick, "Price Controls in Africa: The Ghanaian Experience," *Journal of Modern African Studies* II, no. 3 (Sept. 1973): 405-26. He concluded that the market women were too powerful for the government to enforce the price controls (p. 422).

[108]This development probably dates from the interwar years with the influx of migrants with diverse food habits into Accra.

Other Prepared Foods

These tastes are evident in the increasing diversity of food offered by women who run chopbars and sell rice and stew. Chopbars varied in size according to the labor and credit available to the proprietor. In larger establishments more varieties of food were offered. A typical selection was palmnut, groundnut (peanut) or light soup, with *fufu*,[109] kenkey, rice, or yam. The setting was usually the courtyard of a compound, which might have a sort of veranda to shelter patrons from the sun. One woman had sails rigged as a temporary shelter at the time her customers came, with benches for them to sit on. Often the customers brought their own utensils. Women usually provided only one meal a day in these establishments-- between about 11:00 a.m. and 1:00 p.m., or late in the afternoon. In one medium-sized establishment two young men and three young women were helping, in addition to the mother and daughter who ran it. Feeding these people took quite a chunk out of the profits. Even the women who ran the largest chopbars did not seem to be very well off. One woman said that her mother had done much better at it than she did. The mother catered extensively for clerks in government establishments,[110] sending her daughters there with the food, while at the same time she ran a prosperous chopbar in her home. Presumably, the market for such services should have grown, but among the 1971-72 sample there was no one who dealt on a large scale.

Selling rice and stew on a small scale was increasingly popular. Rice was particularly liked by the children, who got lunch money from their mothers when they went off to school, and patronized the women who sold rice and stew near the school. Cooked yam was peddled around the streets to people who were too busy to cook it themselves, or to men workers, who did not usually cook for themselves. Obviously, this sort of enterprise required less capital than running a chopbar, but it also brought in less profit. It also required less help, and usually only one or two women operated it.

Making and selling porridge was also most often a small-scale business operated by one person. Whereas women who ran chopbars could vary their menus and delete items which required expensive ingredients, porridge makers had the same dependence on corn as kenkey makers did. They had the corn ground, and then boiled it with water to make porridge. According to the texture, which varied from that of cream of wheat to that of oatmeal, it was called *koko*, *kpɔkpɔnsu*, or *akasa*. Again it was often children who bought ladlefuls of the porridge for their breakfasts, sometimes adding a purchase of sugar to put on it. These women usually sold outside their homes on the street in the morning. Their profits were quite small.

---

[109]*Fufu* is made out of pounded cassava, plantain, or yam, or any combination of the three. It has a viscous texture and is served in large globular portions.

[110]Contract arrangements for the selling of prepared foods may have a long history on the Gold Coast. Reindorf, in *History*, p. 149, mentions an incident at Keta in 1847, where as part of a conflict, "the mess-women in town were forbidden to cook for [the Danes at the fort]; however, they concealed food in their clothes" instead to relieve a siege.

The sellers of fried dough products provided desserts, in essence. These products took various forms, but all were made from roughly the same ingredients. Three kinds of doughnuts (*toogbee, akpiti,* and *kaklo*) were made from wheat flour, corn flour, or plantain. The first two contained sugar, while the last had red pepper in it. They were fried in palm or coconut oil. Pancakes (*tatale*) were also made from plantain. There were other, stranger forms, like *atsɔmo,* which are large slender rings of fried dough. Most of the doughnuts were peddled around Accra by young girls. Girls carrying screened wooden boxes on their heads filled with round fried objects were ubiquitous in Accra in 1971-72, but less common in 1978 due to the shortages of ingredients. A few women sold them from streetside tables or at tables in the market, but they were not common. The pancake makers were stationary, selling them fresh out of the pan at busy hours. They usually sold on the street, as did the women who made fried plantain.

All of these women, with the exception of the fried plantain sellers, had the same option as the chopbar owners did, of varying the ingredients if something got too costly. For instance, one woman switched from making *toogbee* to *akpiti,* because the former required wheat flour, which was scarce and too expensive. Like the chopbar owners, they bought their supplies on credit at the market, sometimes patronizing the same people regularly, sometimes different people. There was no indication that relatives played any part in providing supplies, although they did help with preparation. Most women operated on a small scale, but a few produced doughnuts in large quantities. If a woman had enough personnel to sell her products quickly it was possible. One woman interviewed in 1972 used the whole courtyard of a large compound for a *toogbee* business still extant in 1978. The space was occupied by trays and trays of raw balls of dough waiting to be put into a large vat of boiling oil. Her cousin's small daughter was helping her make them, and she and five or six other young girls were selling them. They were not paid for their services. Another woman's mother had supplied them to the pupils of the Accra Government School, so she had had a fairly large business.

Relatively little specialization has taken place in the fried foods industry; only one person ever encountered, a teenage hawker interviewed in 1978, purchased fried foods from someone else to sell. Their high perishability may have accounted for this to some extent. The baking industry, however, showed a higher degree of specialization. Whereas most women who made fried foods also sold them, most bakers did not. Baking with yeast is a skill which only became common in the twentieth century. The 1911 Census listed only 1.3% of the women in Accra as bakers, whereas in 1921 the corresponding figure was 7.9%.[111] Some Ga women were successful at baking because it was a scarce skill. They went with their husbands abroad and made a good living at it because the women in certain places in Nigeria, for

---

[111]*Gold Coast Censuses* (1911), p. 65; (1921), p. 57.

instance, did not know how to bake then.[112]

Bread is another European taste acquired by the Ga. Part of its appeal is that it keeps longer than kenkey. Like kenkey makers, most bakers only produced on a large scale with the help of numerous relatives and/or friends. One woman replied in this manner after we asked her why she did not bake, since her mother had; *Bread is not baked by only one person, and since I was alone I could not have done it.* She was not actually alone, but she was the only person who knew how to bake in a compound where everyone else made cornwine, so it was easier for her to switch than for them. In another compound a baking enterprise employed six adult women forming dough into rolls which were put into flat wooden boxes and then stacked, under the direction of its owner, who had six other women selling for her on a commission basis. Also, some women bought from her outright for resale later. Many women who had small provisions stores on the streets sold bread as one of their lines. Another common combination was selling bread and prepared tea on a small scale from one's home or at a stand in the street or market. In terms of methods and scale of production, then, bread must be classified with kenkey.

Baking is probably more profitable than selling kenkey, however. Bread, and more especially cakes, are still regarded as somewhat of a luxury and cost more than kenkey does relative to bulk, even considering the higher price of wheat flour as compared to corn. In 1971-72 people were starting to make a creditable corn bread, however, which was just as light as wheat bread, though a bit sweeter. The price of bread, like the price of kenkey, was fairly consistent. All over Accra one bought a certain size loaf at a certain price, and a certain size kenkey ball at a certain price. Such consistency cannot be coincidental, and no bargaining is allowed. There were probably price agreements, either explicit or implicit, among bakers and kenkey makers. One of the functions of the Accra Market Traders Association (now defunct) in 1958 was price-fixing for all commodities.[113] Competition was maintained, however, by varying the size of the kenkey or bread within narrow limits and its quality.

The last category of the prepared food trade requiring discussion is the making of cornwine. Ŋmɛdaa is a home brew used for special occasions by the Ga. It is particularly important for the outdooring of a baby, when it is used to anoint the baby's lips to signify that he or she will be brought up and live mainly on corn products.[114] It is only mildly fermented and not intoxicating.[115] Like kenkey making and baking, the production of ŋmɛdaa

---

[112]P. Kilby has done an interesting study of the large-scale producers in the Nigerian bread industry, *African Enterprise: The Nigerian Bread Industry*, Stanford University Hoover Institution Studies No. 8 (Stanford: Stanford University Press, 1965).

[113]Acquah, *Accra*, p. 86.

[114]Y. Manteko, *Out-dooring in Accra*, University of Ghana African Studies Institute Pamphlet Collection (1967), p. 11.

[115]The stronger local brew is called *akpɛtɛʃi*. Unlike in other parts of Africa, in Ghana it is not usually made by women, but rather by men using stills in the villages. Some women in Accra do sell it, however.

was usually pursued by a whole compound of women. Unlike the first two, however, it was not usually the sole profession followed by the women, since it often did not bring in that much profit. Following it was more a matter of honor and tradition. One woman explained that she did it because it was *adebonitsum⊃* in her family, "the work of the ancestors." Everyone back at least as far as her great-great-grandmother had done it. It does indeed seem to have had a long history, since de Marees reported people making "corn beer" in 1600, and Reindorf mentioned it by name ("*nmada*") as an indigenous drink of ancient origin, formerly made of millet.[116]

The process of making ηmεdaa takes less actual working time than making kenkey, although the elapsed time is similar. First the corn is soaked and then allowed to dry until it sprouts. Then it is coarsely ground, mixed with water, and strained. The first water is put on the fire, then a second water from the corn is added and it is boiled.[117] Sugar and salt are added to the mixture, some of the sugar having been browned first, which gives the cornwine its characteristic brown color. The whole is simmered for several hours. When it has cooled somewhat it is sold, usually in large kerosene tins. People made it to order for special occasions, so the profits varied. Most women made one or two batches a week according to demand. Making cornwine is not so time-consuming that many people are required, but it seemed to be a custom that everyone should participate. After the corn sprouted it only took a day to make it, or even a morning, and it was usually sold the same day. The customers came to pick it up or the maker delivered it. Thus often no one was needed to sell it either, although on occasion a hawker sold some of it iced in the market.

As in the other prepared food trades, supplies for making cornwine were purchased at the local market, and relatives did not seem to play any particular role in obtaining them at preferred rates. The cornwine makers were also subject to the tyranny of the cornsellers, but unlike the kenkey makers, they could raise the price more easily if necessary. Also, the price varied between different makers, probably because people were patronized mostly by friends and relatives. The industry was not really on a competitive basis but was more of a service performed by certain persons. People did not shop around for the cheapest cornwine, since a common attitude toward expenditure on ceremonies was that quibblers about price were cheapskates who lost face. All of these factors combined to make cornwine a steady but low income producer for its makers. Profits are generally higher, however, than for the fried food and porridge makers.

In summary, then, the trade in prepared foods contains wide variations. Of the six original categories, we find that in four (kenkey, chopbars, baking, and cornwine), the methods of production are and were largely communal. They would probably become unfeasible as occupations if the residential system changed drastically and women no longer had a large pool of female relatives to help them. The continuance of these trades in roughly the same

---

[116]De Marees, "Description," p. 274; Reindorf, *History*, p. 258.

[117]One variation is to strain it after having boiled it and let it sit for several hours.

form as they were at the time of the grandmothers of these women can partly be attributed to the degree of continuity in the residential system. The introduction of cornmills is virtually the only change which has taken place, and it has not had a large effect. People pay to have their corn ground now, but they used to pay corn grinders to do it anyway. The difference is that, whereas the money paid used to remain within the female nexus and was occasionally used as a source of capital for traders to start on their own, now it goes outside it to the men who own and operate the machines.

While I abandoned the attempt to judge actual profits in the prepared foods trade, it is still possible to make a rough estimate of relative profits. The bakers rank as a class at the top, with the kenkey makers and chopbar owners next and about equal. The cornwine sellers might be third. At the next level would come the rice and stew, and yam sellers, and the doughnut makers. The poorest group includes the pancake and porridge makers. This ranking is quite tentative, however; within each group there were variations according to the diligence of the individual, the location of her business, and the amount of credit she had available. Taken as a class together, the prepared foodsellers were the poorest of the three large groups under consideration here: fish and produce sellers, prepared food makers, and the sellers of imported goods. One of the most important reasons for this was the communal production system. While it reduced the work one person did, it also reduced her profits. It therefore was difficult to expand the business since money was not usually reinvested in it. In many of the prepared food businesses people started off big and gradually got smaller. A side effect of this process was the failure to branch out into subsidiary industries, like owning a cornmill, which might reduce costs and increase profits. Another reason for not expanding was the attitude of many women. They were satisfied as long as they made enough food to feed their families and profits to pay off their creditors. The prepared food traders as a group were less profit-oriented in their attitudes than the other women. The contrast was most sharp when they were compared with the traders in imported goods.

Another contrast with trades previously considered here came in the trend regarding specialization. In contrast to the fish and produce trade, specialization became less common in the prepared foods trades, if anything. The cornmills eliminated the corn grinders. In fact, one would expect specialization to be reduced if the residential system were changing and/or cooperation between women becoming less common. If people had fewer female relatives of all ages to call upon for various tasks they would have to do everything themselves. It is partly this situation which makes some forms of prepared foods appealing to women living with their husbands. If a woman had small children and lived with her husband (a likely combination), she wanted to earn some money but stay in the house and feed the children. Thus, making and selling porridge or fried plantain might have appealed to her. The 1971-72 data showed a slightly stronger tendency for younger women to do this, but was not sufficient to prove the hypothesis. A comparison of the occupations of the 1971-72 sample of 72 women, and those of the 101 Central Accra women aged 39 to 50 interviewed in 1978 is illuminating, however. The first sample was largely composed of women 50 or over (83%); in it 30.5% had prepared foods as their chief occupation. This compared to 42% of the 1978 sample pursuing it as their present occupation.

More significant, however, is the difference between the two samples in those engaged in selling prepared foods which were relatively easy to handle by an individual working alone or with minimal help from others (i.e., rice and stew, fried foods, porridge, and cornwine). Only 24% of the prepared food traders in the 1971-72 sample were in these categories compared to 49% of the 1978 sample. Given that the residential system seems fairly stable, these results suggest both that there is a higher likelihood that younger women will sell prepared foods, and that the cooperation of large numbers of women in an enterprise is becoming more rare. Also, kenkey making requires more capital than the small-scale endeavors pursued by individuals. Thus, while 54% of the 1971-72 small sample with prepared foods as a chief occupation sold kenkey or *banku*, only 38% of the 1978 sample did.

The other direction indicated by the results is the increasing popularity of selling prepared foods. The 1971-72 figure of 30.5% of the women selling prepared foods as their chief trade is a definite increase over the 20% of the 469 traders outside Salaga Market who were selling cooked foods and provisions, interviewed in a survey conducted by the Ministry of Housing in 1955.[118] In 1978 42% of the 101 women aged 39 to 50 interviewed were selling prepared foods. Steel, working with census data, found that between 1960 and 1970 local food preparation absorbed most of the increase in female small-scale employment. He attributed this phenomenon to the adverse impact of the government's favoring of capital-intensive production.[119] Under straitened circumstances when cooperation with relatives is becoming less common, it is easily understandable that women would opt for a trade with low entry requirements and a guaranteed market. Another predisposing factor is the more difficult conditions for small traders in the other trades described here, especially in recent years. The trend bodes ill for the future. Basically, more women are being forced into fewer, smaller scale, more local, and less lucrative occupations.[120] When this is combined with loss of control over supply sources and production, and lack of employment for middle school leavers or political power to change the situation, the signs become ominous.

*   *   *   *   *

In fact, the economic status of women traders has been going down. This was evident in the property ownership figures of women in the 1971-72

---

[118]*Accra Plan* (1958), p. 124. The breakdown into prepared foods only was not available. Sixty-nine percent were selling fresh foodstuffs of all kinds, and none cloth and textiles.

[119]W. F. Steel, "Female and Small-Scale Employment Under Modernization in Ghana," paper (Sept. 1979), pp. 14-15.

[120]Lawson and Kwei, in *African Entrepreneurship*, p. 140, observed, "Small-scale trade is a function of low levels of income."

small sample, presented in Table IV-3. Spending money on houses is probably the best indicator of prosperity among women traders. Real estate was
the most popular form of investment for these women; 75% of the women in
the 1971-72 small sample said that they would buy land and build a house if
they had the money to do it. Looking at house building or ownership
figures, this popularity endured throughout the twentieth century and even
rose a little. Between 1894 and 1899 in Accra, 15% of the building permits
issued for new houses went to women.[121] In 1905, 20% of the taxable houses
in Accra belonged to or were in charge of Ga women.[122] In 1953, 23% of the
9,000 houses in Accra surveyed by Acquah were owned by women (20% by
women only and 3% jointly with men).[123] In the 1971-72 large survey 52%
of the houses were built by men and 35.5% by women.[124] This increase in
the proportion of houses built by women was possibly one result of the prosperous 1950s, when more men were investing their money elsewhere than
Central Accra.

There are good reasons for investing in real estate rather than expanding one's business further. When a business gets bigger it cannot be run by
one person. People need other managers to work for them. Ghanaian
traders find it difficult to trust other people very far with their money.
Their trust is too often abused, both by relatives and nonrelatives. Real
estate, on the other hand, offers a high-yield investment which does not
require help from others in its management. In 1971 Garlick estimated that
it gave about a 10% annual return on the original investment, which was
second only to moneylending in profitability.[125]

Table IV-3.
Property Ownership by Women, 1971-72.[a]

Age Group	Percent of Women Owning:			
	House/[b] Room	Farm and/or Unimproved Land	Canoes and/or Nets	Jewelry
50s − 90s	27	47	5	54
30s − 40s	8	33	0	50

[a]Based on information from 71 women.

[b]Most of these were rooms, rather, and brought in minimal rent.

---

[121]SNA 11/1755.

[122]SCT 17/4/26, 102-10.

[123]Acquah, *Accra*, p. 48.

[124]The sex of the builder was unknown in the rest of the cases.

[125]P. C. Garlick, *African Traders and Economic Development in Ghana* (Oxford:
Clarendon Press, 1971), p. 56. With respect to men traders he noted that,

> The purpose of trading was not primarily to develop a business of size--though this might be
> possible--but to provide for immediate and future personal and family needs, particularly by
> means of the acquisition of real property. . . . A business was tied to the life of its creator;
> real property would endure with the family."

While real estate may be a popular form of investment, it is not attainable for everyone, as Table IV-3 shows. It might be argued that one of the reasons the younger women in 1971-72 owned less was the earlier stage of their careers. However, the women in their fifties were one of the more prosperous groups; they had mostly built their houses at least ten years before, when they were in their forties. Moreover, the women in their forties showed no signs of planning to build houses, such as half-built houses, and fewer of them owned land on which to build.[126] Buttressing Table IV-3 is the data concerning the nature of investments of the 71 women in the 1971-72 sample. When they had money saved, 82% invested in education (usually for sons), 70% lent money to relatives and 9% to friends, 36% bought land and only 26% built houses (some of these were never completed due to lack of funds, and some were additions only). Much of their savings, then, left the female networks to benefit male children and relatives, a theme which will be further developed in Chapter VI.

Further evidence of the poverty of most traders is available from other sources. It contradicts sharply the common stereotype of the wealthy trader put forth by the Ghanaian government-controlled media in the interests of blaming traders for the country's manifold economic ills. While it adds only a little to the chronology of their impoverishment, it does help to show us the position these Ga traders have within the distribution system, and also allows us to construct a rough hierarchy within which to place traders, who have all too often been carelessly lumped together into an undifferentiated mass.

It is quite clear that most traders' businesses are and were small-scale only. The Ministry of Housing survey covered 2,011 traders inside and outside Accra markets. It was conducted in 1955, at the peak of Ghana's prosperity, and found that the "great majority of traders have a small turnover and their profits may be as little as one or two shillings a day."[127] In 1960 Nypan claimed that half of the traders in her survey (dominated by the generally more prosperous traders in fixed locations) had a daily *turnover* of £2 or less.[128] Ewusi noted that in the subsequent period up to 1968 the relative distribution of income for self-employed persons in Ghana worsened so that the top 10% earned 43% of the sectorial income, and the bottom 10% only 1.8%.[129] Many traders would be in the bottom 10% and few in the top, along with successful businessmen and professionals. In 1967 an estimate put the number of wholesalers at no more than 2% of the traders,[130] while in

---

[126]Sai, in "Market Women," pp. 47, 104, noted that it was getting more difficult for Accra women traders to build houses. Many of these "houses" were only one or two rooms added on to a Central Accra building for the respondent to live in.

[127]*Accra Plan*, p. 61.

[128]A. Nypan, *Market Trade: A Sample Survey of Market Traders in Accra*, University of Ghana African Business Series No. 2 (1960), p. 40.

[129]K. Ewusi, *Economic Inequality in Ghana* (Accra: New Times Corporation, 1977), p. 73.

[130]R. M. Lawson, "The Distributive System in Ghana: A Review Article," *Journal of Development Studies* III, no. 2 (Jan. 1967): 202.

1971 Sai found that the profits of average traders were not substantial enough to raise their standard of living.[131] In 1977 Sethuraman found that about 45,000 traders in Accra were operating without any infrastructure, i.e., permanent fixtures of some sort, and concluded that a "substantial majority of informal trade activity uses very little capital, and is subject to severe infrastructural constraints. By implication, it follows that the earnings of participants in these activities are quite small."[132] With increasingly monopolistic conditions fostered by government policies and difficulties in accumulating capital, the number of prosperous traders now is indubitably even smaller. It may be a misnomer, then, to talk of "market traders," since most traders are not in the markets, and many even have very little trade indeed.

It is also clear from the foregoing discussion that there are very great differences between traders. Traders vary both in the commodities that they sell and in the functions they perform. We have seen here that there is a general correlation between the amount of profits and the commodity sold by traders, but women's profits are also associated with their functions in the distribution network. In order to classify women according to their profits, one must take into consideration at least three characteristics: commodity, function and location.[133] Of course, these are sometimes related; there is no need for the collector-wholesalers, or processors, of the produce trade in the cloth trade. The importance of function in trade undermines any strict association of one particular commodity area like imported goods with wealth. A hawker of imported matches is obviously going to be worse off than a wholesaler of locally-grown onions. The results of taking commodity, location, and function into account to construct a trading hierarchy based on wealth look something like Figure IV-2, where the size of the diagram represents roughly the numbers of Ga traders engaged at each level. The changes over the past thirty years are evident in the contrasting shapes of the diagrams. The minimum shown by all this is that all market women are not wealthy. Even to convey the impression of their universal wealth by devoting much space to considering the wealthy ones and none or little to the small ones is inadvisable, considering the increasingly violent persecution of traders in Ghana.[134] Most traders, even in the era of greatest prosperity,

---

[131]Sai, "Market Woman," p. 9.

[132]Sethuraman, "Employment," p. 23.

[133]L. Trager, in "Urban Market Women: Hoarders, Hagglers, Economic Heroines?" paper presented at African Studies Association Meeting, Los Angeles (Oct. 31-Nov. 3, 1979), p. 2, has suggested a more complicated classification including individual characteristics of traders.

[134]K. Little, *African Women in Towns* (Cambridge: Cambridge University Press, 1973), pp. 44-45; J. Gugler and W. G. Flanagan, *Urbanization and Social Change in West Africa* (Cambridge: Cambridge University Press, 1978), pp. 133-34.

Figure IV-2 The Ga Trading Hierarchy

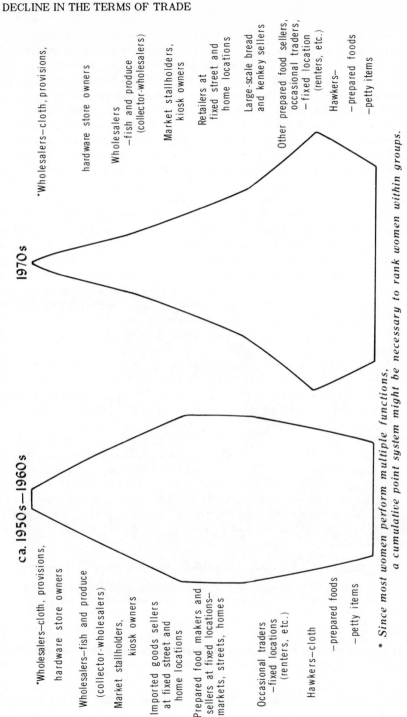

ca. 1950s–1960s

*Wholesalers–cloth, provisions, hardware store owners

Wholesalers–fish and produce (collector-wholesalers)

Market stallholders, kiosk owners

Imported goods sellers at fixed street and home locations

Prepared food makers and sellers at fixed locations– markets, streets, homes

Occasional traders –fixed locations (renters, etc.)

Hawkers–cloth

–prepared foods

–petty items

1970s

*Wholesalers–cloth, provisions, hardware store owners

Wholesalers –fish and produce (collector-wholesalers)

Market stallholders, kiosk owners

Retailers at fixed street and home locations

Large-scale bread and kenkey sellers

Other prepared food sellers, occasional traders, –fixed location (renters, etc.)

Hawkers–

–prepared foods

–petty items

* Since most women perform multiple functions, a cumulative point system might be necessary to rank women within groups.

were in the area from the middle of the scale downward.[135] Ga women traders were largely at the middle levels, due to their initial advantages in dominating trade in Accra, but now they are moving to the lower levels.

This evidence is strongly suggestive of relative poverty on the part of the younger women, then, and a progressive marginalization of the economic status of traders, a logical accompaniment to the decine in trade. Moreover, this decline has been shown not just to be temporary, attendant on the generally dismal state of the economy, but rather deeply rooted both in the expansion of international captalism, which removes production from marginalized countries, and in internal class formation. The latter manifested itself in the coopting of control over more lucrative trades by a male-dominated elite, whose women are more dependent on male-supplied capital than is the habit with most traders. Both of these processes mean a loss of economic autonomy at the macro-level for the people involved, and a consequent impoverishment of the victims, whether the whole state or its women are concerned. For the latter the decline in their trade is a dominant factor in placing them in an underclass.

A Porridge Seller

[135]K. Ewusi, "Women in Occupations in Ghana," paper presented at Ghana National Council on Women and Development Seminar on Women and Development, Accra (Sept. 1978), p. 7; D. D. Vellenga, "Non-formal Education of Ghanaian Women into Economic Roles," paper presented at African Studies Association Conference, Boston (Nov. 1976), p. 11; Simms and Dumor, "Women," p. 22; Sai, "Women Traders," p. 21; Seers and Ross, *Report*, pp. 13-14.

Portrait 2

NAA KOWA

A Woman and her Helper

The late Naa Kowa (she died in 1977 at the age of approximately 85) was an attractive, self-reliant woman with a good sense of humor, who looked much younger than her years. She was alert and intelligent but more reticent than some about certain details of her life. She was a respected member of a large and well-known family, and at various times served as foster mother to many children in it, supporting them to the point of paying for their education.

She lived in a spotless tiny whitewashed compound close to the large family house headed by her surviving full elder brother. They were very close and he was quite upset by her death, as was her daughter. When I returned to this area in 1978, her daughter (whom she disparages in this account as the "uneducated one") was still living in the compound, having inherited it, and could not speak of her mother's death nine months previously without crying. Naa Kowa did not reach her goal of living to be a hundred, but in the four score or so years that she did live those who knew her were privileged to partake of her wit and kindness.

Childhood (circa 1892-1906)

When I was about four a great tragedy happened which affected the rest of my life. My mother had a store which caught on fire, killing my mother's brother, my brother, and two other relations, and badly burning my mother. My mother's brother was a fair-skinned man whom she loved very much. One day he bought some barrels of wet gunpowder which he brought to my mother. They put it in the sun to dry. He decided to test it, took a small quantity and lit a match causing an explosion and fire which completely destroyed the store. After this my mother's face was scarred. She said she wanted to die and she had no money to care for us. She took my youngest sister with her and went away upcountry.

My mother first had three sons with my father, all of whom died. Then she bore my brothers, Ahima and Ahele, myself, and Lamle, my sister. When she left she sent me to her mother and gave my brother to our father. She vowed that she would never return to Accra because of the scarring and the sad memories. My father followed her trail to many villages but always missed her. She settled at several remote villages and married another man by whom she had two more children, Aba and Kwamla, who are both dead now. At a village called Atamlu my father's messengers finally caught up with her and managed to persuade her to return to Accra. But this was not until after I had had my second child.

After I was with my grandmother a short time, my father took me away from her and gave me to my half-sister, his daughter by another wife. I helped her with selling cosmetics, lavender, soap, and so on. But then she died giving birth to twins, so he gave me to my stepmother, his wife, who was a twin from Abola. When I was about ten I started helping my father with selling drinkables. We sold liquor, beer, and minerals [soft drinks] in large quantities to people from the villages, and they took them back home for sale. They brought rubber and parrots to my father, who purchased them for sale to the Europeans on the ships.

Since I did not have a mother I had to work as a child. I was always sad because I missed my mother. My father and stepmother treated me fairly well, though. She was much better than most stepmothers, considering that I was not really her daughter. They only beat me once, when I accidentally dropped the measure into one of the liquor barrels. I cried for such a long time as a result that I got sick, so they never beat me again.

I did not have much time for playing. If I was not selling I was making a farm at a place called Owula Kofi's valley, where we grew corn and groundnuts. But sometimes in the evening I had time to play games with the other children. We played *kwane-kwane*,[1] *adaawe*,[2] and *ampe*.[3] When we

---

[1] A form of hide-and-seek where two groups of children search for each other.

[2] A rhythm game involving clapping hands with your neighbor while standing in a circle and dancing in turns in the center.

[3] A rhythm and coordination game where a child jumps and claps in time with other children each in turn.

were returning from the fields sometimes we would play at marketing, using a kind of cactus called *aklati* which we cut into pieces and sold as meat. Broken pottery shards were our currency. We also enjoyed *olu* [skipping], and the boys played *otoosa*.[4]

As a child I was generally treated kindly. My stepmother loved me even more than her own children. The happiest times were at Hɔmɔwɔ and Christmas when we received gifts. My stepmother gave me all of my training. The first thing that she taught me was how to keep a house clean and tidy. I fetched the water, learned how to make the bed, and kept the things in the room tidy. At regular intervals I polished the floor. She taught me how to fold cloth. At one stage she taught me how to buy food at the market, and how to prepare food like *banku* and *dzidzi*,[5] and how to pound *fufu*. Another of my father's wives taught me how to make cake and pudding.

Because my stepmother was not my real mother I gave her the utmost respect. I was humble and she in turn affectionately corrected me whenever I went wrong. I stuck to her advice and seldom misbehaved. She taught me to use respectful language toward elderly people, not to pay them back in their own words. She taught me not to look a man directly in the eye when speaking to him. She said that you should always abuse a man who casually touches your body or holds your hand. The abuse will make him leave you alone. You should not go out at night. If you were not in bed by eight P.M. she shouted for you. And if you did not have a good excuse when you finally came back you would certainly be caned. She was so suspicious about men that she thought that if I attended Sunday school some man would seduce me. So I am an illiterate.

Puberty and marriage (circa 1907 to 1933)

At the time when I first menstruated I woke up in the morning and found that blood had soiled my bed. I was very frightened and started to cry. The girl with whom I shared my bed reported what had happened to my stepmother. I hid myself in a room and refused to eat. But then my father arrived and congratulated me on my coming of age. I was given pads to use for the blood. Mashed yam and eggs [*fotoli*] were prepared for me, a fowl was killed and we had a small party. I was given scented soap to use. Nothing specific was said about menstruation and its results, but after I started I noticed that people took care to give me more advice about not letting men hold my hand or seduce me in any way.

When a man started to be interested in me my parents would ask me whether I was interested in that man and wanted to marry him. On a number of occasions I gave no definite answer, but then I agreed to go to my first husband. He had talked to me when he came into the store to buy

---

[4]A team rhythm game.
[5]Made from cassava flour.

drinks and told me he liked me. So I told him I liked him and agreed to go to him. He is somewhat older than I am (he is still alive, though blind, and living at Amamomo). I was his first wife but he did not perform any customary rites for me. So I never stayed with him at his house.

I was somewhat apprehensive when I got married. I did not know what lay in the future. With us a bride who is going through the ceremony should break down in tears before the final handing over ceremony when her father's sister is bathing and dressing her. That was also the way I felt. But she usually becomes happy after she has settled down with the man and gotten to know him. The coming of the first child puts the seal on your happiness. Nevertheless, hard and trying times with misunderstandings and quarrels lie ahead. This may last as long as seven years and, if not handled wisely, break up the marriage.

In my case this is what ultimately happened. My husband was a very handsome man with big eyes. He was a goldsmith and fond of women. On the pretext of working on trinkets for the women he managed to seduce some of them and even had children with them. I did not pay attention to this even though the women sometimes got abusive toward me. I knew I was the senior wife and had enjoyed what there was to be enjoyed already. We loved each other very much, but sometimes he got very angry with me. Then he would become wild and uncontrollable. When we quarreled I would report it to my husband's father and mother. Usually no arbitration was called for and we patched it up ourselves. But finally some things happened which we could not patch up. He hurt me very much by what he did for his third wife. By that time we were five in number, which I did not mind as long as he fulfilled his financial obligations to me and the children. This he did by having his mother feed us. But he proceeded to have his marriage with that junior wife blessed by the church, ignoring me, the eldest wife. She was the daughter of a minister and he had gotten her pregnant. I took just offense and stopped being married to him.

Also, a very serious occurrence took place which developed into a [customary] court case. There was a courtship that resulted in marriage between my half-brother (my father's son) and a daughter of my husband's sister. This was against custom [incest taboos]. The woman died giving birth to the child, and my family was sued by my husband's family for damages. They claimed that my husband's niece had been killed by my half-brother. The result of all this, of course, was that I left him, taking the children with me.

The whole experience was so unpleasant that I did not want to repeat it. I was married for seven years and I stayed for another seven years without being married. I vowed never to marry again. I never expected that the man would act like that toward me. I became suspicious of men in general. The question uppermost in my mind was, what sort of trouble would another man bring with him? Ultimately I married again because the doctor told me that I had to if I wanted to stop having trouble with my menstrual periods. Every month I was getting sick.

My second marriage was a happier one for a while. The man performed a full customary marriage for me. He loved me. Any time I asked him for something he managed to buy it for me. He generally supported me and the children adequately. The monthly housekeeping money was thirty shillings. In addition the man bought all of the staples like oil, rice and onions. Each month he bought a full [100 pound] bag of rice. What I had to buy at the market was not expensive. Things like canned milk, corned beef and sardines were much cheaper then than they are today. The shilling had more value. If there was not enough money for food I would ask for more. If I did not get more I simply did not cook for him.

My second husband had been married twice before he married me, but by the time I was with him only one of his other wives was still married to him. He was a civil servant working at the secretariat. He was handsome, slim and wore his clothes well. He also liked flirting with women. In the end I also quarreled with him and the marriage broke up. Once when I went to spend the night with him he was there instead with my rival [co-wife] having intercourse. I had to return home. By then it was very late. As I was going along I was attacked and bitten by a monkey at the place where the Methodist Church is now. This was when my second daughter was small and still being carried on my back. The monkey wounded me badly, but my husband did not bother to visit me. After a week he sent word for me to come sleep with him, and I replied no, I would not stay married to him any longer. Thus ended my marriage with him, even though I was on good terms with his mother and sisters.

As a girl I knew that some day, as a woman, I would have to marry. That is nature. In my marriage I tried to follow the advice my father gave me. He told me to be humble and respect my husband. If I did not understand his viewpoint I was to approach him for an explanation. I was not to quarrel with him. If I were advising someone now I would tell them the same things, and also that meals should be prepared regularly once you have the money for it. A good husband should feed his wife and buy her cloth and other things for decoration. He should give her money at regular intervals. When she is ill he should take her to the hospital. He should support his children and see to it that they attend a good school. My first husband was good in that he made sure all of our four children attended school. One even went abroad. You see, if he is able to look after his children, it means he can care for his wives too.

In my experience many men do not do what they are supposed to. If a man acts as a brother you take him as such. But when he disappoints you once you will stop liking him. Men are great liars and frequently deceive people. Ga men are no different than other men that way. I did not trust either of my husbands at all. These days men are even worse than before. They lounge around and do not work; now the women support the men rather than vice versa. Things have changed greatly. At first a Ga had no right to marry a Fanti. But now if only you speak Ga and you want to marry me, I will agree if I love you. That is the only requirement. Then if the man is good to you and gives you all the things you want, it is all right.

Childrearing (circa 1912 to 1972)

I had six children but three died. I also had three miscarriages, the last one at Korle Bu Hospital. I would have liked to have had more children. Because many children die one needs to bring forth many children so that after death has taken its toll the parents will still be left with some children. But it is also bad to have more children than you can support. In such a situation the mother is put under unnecessary strain. My brother's daughter is a good example. She had seven children with a man who cannot support them. So the responsibility has fallen on my brother and the girl keeps on having children. However, there is no need to bemoan such a plight too much, since out of this batch of children will certainly come brilliant ones who might achieve fame. These will just have to help their less favored brothers and sisters.

My pregnancies were not easy. I always had strong pains in my head for at least three months. It was so bad that I had to go to bed. I lost my appetite. When I got big and my stomach protruded I also felt pain. In those days there were very few doctors and so expectant mothers were helped by experienced old women [midwives] at their homes. The final sign which showed me that the baby was ready to come was that I had to urinate frequently. I then left for the midwife's house. The first childbirth gives no pain at all, likewise the second. It is from the third on that delivery becomes painful. Once it was suspected that I would have twins. The baby came at 6 A.M. but the labor continued until evening when a large lump of undeveloped substance was removed.

Some men do not support their wives and children as they should. I see primarily two causes for this. First, rather than lack of love for the wife I would attribute it to lack of money. If a man has been lazy and not bothered to learn a trade he will not earn much. Second, some men are simply irresponsible. They use their income for things like drinking, dancing and women rather than on their children. This is a disgrace. My first husband was a responsible man this way. He has many children but every one went to school. The one working at Ghana Broadcasting attended Achimota [secondary] School for four years; one of the ones who died was very educated, and so is that one there. The only one who was not keen on schooling was this one who lives with me here. And that attitude has been passed on to her children. As a result of the type of training the parents gave the children they do not like school either. Also the child's intelligence is influenced by the sexual habits of the parents. Too much intercourse weakens the intelligence of the child. In fact, after the seventh month [of pregnancy], according to a published work, the parents should not have intercourse.

When my babies were young my relatives helped me to care for them. But as they got older the burden fell mainly on me and I paid for much of their schooling. One completed secondary school, two completed standard seven, and one did not even get to standard six. Usually they liked going to school, but sometimes I had to put my foot down and insist. I did not like to beat them, but rather used persuasion to get the children to behave. I praised them if they behaved well. If they played truant they had to go without their meal. I tried to be resolute and nip every bad habit in the bud. One has continually to set a good example for the child and remind it of what has to be done. You have to be vigilant all of the time. As the child comes of age the mother should begin with education in home management and married life. One should stress humility and submissiveness in both speech and action. A woman should not be extravagant but content to live within the means that her husband can afford. This education, of course, went to the girls. My boys were sent to their fathers when they were about three years old, as is our custom.

Among my children there is one whom I love best of all [the uneducated daughter]. She loves and respects me as her mother. I feel very sorry for her because she has not had a child yet. My prayer is that God should grant her a child but it has not been answered. As I sit by her I enjoy the company of my child. But she has none to share her company. To whom am I leaving her as I go to my grave? This makes me especially affectionate toward her.

Work

Since I am illiterate trading has been my work. I really regret that I have not had any formal education. I would have liked to read books and get knowledge from them. Now I can read just a little from the Ga Bible. Now that there is civilization there is a need for girls to receive education equal to that of boys so that they too can help.

My education in trading was mostly given by my stepmother. I not only helped my father with selling drinks but also traded in many commodities with her. We sold cloth, beads, [red] pepper and groundnuts, and smoked and salted fish. At certain seasons, especially Hɔmɔwɔ and Christmas, I sent wax prints to distant markets for sale. We often were given pieces of the wax prints that were left as presents to encourage us. She taught me also how to polish beads and smoke and salt fish. My brother and I kept a rum shop for my father at a place called "New Beedie." My wages for keeping the shop were five shillings. Some of the upcountry traders would buy as many as thirty caskfuls of rum at a time. We also had gin, schnapps, minerals and beer. Beer was one shilling a bottle. When I returned home from the shop I would polish beads, or smoke some fish if they were abundant.

When I was a bit older my father apprenticed me to a seamstress. There were a number of apprentices there. She gave us food and everything until we completed the course. When I had learned everything she could teach me, my father paid her £4 and that signified that I was then ready to sew on my own. This I did at the market in front of my brother's stall. I had completed the course and was following that trade as well as clothselling when I got married to my first husband. It was the profits from sewing that I used as capital to start trading on my own.

Actually, it was my mother's sister who taught me how to polish beads, and I traveled with her upcountry to sell them and the cloth. We would make several trips and then get tired and sell at home for four or six weeks. After a while I stopped selling cloth as it was unprofitable. Sometimes you got only a shilling profit per [twelve yard] piece. The children always wanted you to give them some. Beads seemed like a better commodity to sell as they were in fashion. The trades came in turns; one came and went, and then another. Also, there are good and bad times; when things change the only thing for you to do is change also.

I bought the beads from the shops in large boxes, then polished and strung them for sale. They sold best when strangers were in town, sometimes two or three hundred a day. People wore them at the waist and on the neck, knees and wrists for decoration. There were some reserved for special occasions which were very expensive. For instance, one set might cost £3, 4 or 5. We call those "proper beads." They are sometimes used when a chief is being installed. I have one set which cost £7 which is believed to protect you from lightning. Another type cost £6 for one bead.

It is difficult to say how much profit I got; it was important only to get enough to meet one's needs and to be able to buy more to sell. One can only know whether the business is showing a profit after a particular stock has been completedly sold out. If it has not, part of the capital and profit will be locked up in the stock on hand. It is also difficult to see the profit position because all along you use the profits for food, clothing and children's expenses. However, if you put aside some each week in the long run you will get a profit. This, even so, does not give a true picture of the situation. In the course of time I changed from imported goods to the sale of farm produce, but the profit situation showed little change. At Hɔmɔwɔ when I took stock of my position I had realized my capital all right but much of my expected profit had already gone in meals. On the whole, however, it was more profitable to deal in farm produce than in imported goods.

My stepmother taught me a lot about business strategy. I was trading at Koforidua, Kumasi, Mangoase, Dodowa, Aburi, and Akwapim Mampong. It was a lucrative business. I did not specialize in any one type of goods but tried out various commodities to see what sold best. You have to be constantly alert to seize opportunities and deal in as many goods as one possibly can. As a result one gets profits from many angles and will not feel worse off at any one time, especially in the case of farm produce which you can also use yourself. For example, once I was on my way to a women's church meeting when I happened upon an auction at the offices of the Accra Town Council. I bought £100 worth of goods there which I then resold immediately in a batch for £107. £7 was a nice profit then. Ah yes, I enjoyed my work sometimes, but if I had been rich I do not think that I would have worked. I did it to support myself and the children.

Some husbands object to wives working because they fear that through their work their wives might clandestinely take up with other men. For myself, my first husband did not object; he rather liked me to work since my earnings supplemented what he gave me. Also, I used to send his box of jewelry around for sale. My second husband once gave me capital for trading with the understanding that with it my monthly pocket allowance would stop. He wanted me to maintain myself with the profits. I made it plain to him that it would not work since I would have to eat into the capital. In the end I was proved right. The business did not last long.

Sometimes trading can lead to trouble. For instance, my mother was sent to court for profiteering once. And I myself with other market women took part in a demonstration against rising prices. This was when my late son was about seven years old. We marched to the castle at Osu to present our case. At the castle we were asked to wait to meet the governor. But before long the police waded in amongst us wielding truncheons and arresting many people. Some demonstrators were wounded and some pregnant women had miscarriages as a result. The arrested were put into custody that day, but released immediately because of an earthquake. For three weeks we made continuous pleas of not guilty; to avoid committing an offense we had not carried any weapons like cudgels or cutlasses. The chiefs together with lawyers, doctors, merchants and ministers of religion rose in support of the demonstrators. But no matter, I was fined £20. As a result of the shock I fell and hurt my leg, which is why I now walk with a cane. These demonstrations culminated in the attainment of self-government led by Kwame Nkrumah.

When I was trading in beads eventually I got into the pottery trade. This came about because some of my customers could not pay in cash but rather in kind; they were from the Weija area and were potters. So I took their pots and brought them to Accra for sale. When I got older and could not get around any more they started bringing them to Accra to my house. Clay pots still sell especially well around Hɔmɔwɔ, as the special food for it [kpɛkple] should be prepared in them. I still sell them from the house here, and beads also when I can, although now it is difficult to get them. Mainly I do not make a profit now.

*   *   *   *   *

If I had my life to live over again I would want most things to be the same. My character is good and I do not remember doing anything to offend anyone. I do not act foolishly or quarrel. I am very generous and have always been so. I have always been cheerful. I hate wickedness and do not remember fighting with anyone. The only person with whom I ever quarreled was my rival in marriage. There are some things I regret, however. The accident and the death of my mother affected me deeply. Also my [first] marriage did not turn out as successfully as I had wished. I had wanted a marriage where I shared the same roof with my husband and then served him. Once an unpleasant thing happened. A man, the Sanitary Inspector, entered my room when I was naked and I yelled at him and abused him for having done it. He sued me for damages in the Town Council Court but he lost the case.

In the end I attribute my long life to the good life I have led, a good and clean life. I always respected my elders and did what they wanted of me. I always watched my health and took castor oil as a purgative when needed. Occasionally I took Mist Alba, or boiled herbs for drinking. My father and [possibly step]mother both lived to be ninety-nine years old. I do not know if I shall reach a hundred. Finally I would say that I am looking to God.

A Men's Compound

V

CHANGES IN THE FEMALE HIERARCHY:

ACCESS TO CAPITAL AND

THE IMPACT OF FORMAL EDUCATION

Two contrasting themes have dominated so far in this twentieth century socioeconomic history of Ga women, an increase in economic independence from men expressed in the residential system, but a decrease in the autonomy of their trades which has caused them to become less profitable. Chronologically, until after the 1950s the gains of the traders made up for their losses. That is, the substantial profits to be made in trading, especially for the medium- to large-scale traders, both facilitated economic independence from men, and encouraged concentration on distribution rather than manufacturing. A number of Ga traders did well out of the cocoa boom and the tremendous increase in size of Accra, capitalizing on already established trade networks. However, their geographical advantage and consequent middlewomen functions inevitably disappeared with better transportation, technology, communications, and the advent of branch stores.

When hard times came beginning in the 1960s, the weakness of many traders' positions became evident. Their increased separation from the male-dominated upper class appeared as a disadvantage when they saw elite women assuming control (or being delegated authority) over some of the more lucrative trades. It is therefore a logical aspiration for young women to want to emulate elite women and obtain access to resources through men.

A third facet of the women's situation involves the implications of these changes for the strength of the female networks on which survival has so far depended. In this chapter these implications will be considered with particular concentration on women's access to capital and the impact and interrelationships of formal and informal education for women. Access to education and capital are two important determinants of class position. This discussion will center on changes in the women's apprenticeship system, which is responsible for perpetuating the strength of the women's trading networks.

The Apprenticeship System

Apprenticeship can take many forms. We interviewed apprentices who were trading in Salaga Market, doing paid and unpaid housework in Kaneshie, and doing sewing for their seamstress mistresses' businesses. Apprenticeship was the chief means for training girls, either inside or outside the family, before formal education began affecting them in large numbers. A girl usually started work by helping her mother. If the mother was dead or absent, she would have helped a grandmother, a stepmother, a more distant relative, or might even have been given to a nonrelative as a pawn in payment for debt.[1] If a mother wanted her daughter to learn a particular trade which the mother did not follow herself, she might have given her to a friend to bring up. Or, she might have felt that a friend or relative would be a better teacher. Thus, a successful trader would have been more likely to have had many young girls in her household, not only because she needed more help, but also because more people wanted her to bring up their daughters. These would most often have been granddaughters or small cousins, but nonrelatives were found on occasion. In the 1978 survey of 40 Salaga Market women, women claimed to have had helpers in 53% of their enterprises (38 out of 72).[2] In 45% of the enterprises the helpers were daughters; in 16% siblings' children; in 10.5% paid employees; in 8% sons, in 5.3% sisters; and in 16% other relatives. Conversely, the women themselves were usually taught to trade by a mother's side relative. Eighty-two percent of the women in the small 1971-72 survey were taught by their mothers, and many of the rest by a mother's side relative. Only 10% had ever been taught a trade by a nonrelative. In 1978 among the 40 Salaga traders 62.5% were taught by their mothers, fewer than in the 1971-72 sample, but more (30%) were taught by a mother's side relative. None had been taught by a nonrelative.

Most apprenticeships were informal between relatives. When the women in the 1971-72 small sample were asked to give a reason for the separation of sexes in the Ga residential system, more than half stated that the practice was for the purpose of training children in occupations proper to their sex. They were fully cognizant of the advantages of the residential system in allowing trades to be passed from generation to generation. Fifty-four percent of the women in the 1971-72 large sample had the same chief

---

[1]Girls were more likely to be given as pawns than boys, since if a girl's master seduced her, which often happened, the waiving of bridewealth was a convenient method for her lineage to rid itself of the debt. *Ga Maŋtsɛ's Civil Court Record* (1922-24), p. 114 (case 1922); M. J. Field, in *The Social Organisation of the Ga People* (London: Crown Agents, 1940), pp. 24-25, noted that in the 1930s pawning was common. I. Acquah, *Accra Survey* (London: University of London Press, 1958), p. 75, said that pawning still existed for girls in Central Accra.

[2]E. Schildkrout, in "Age and Gender in Hausa Society: Socio-Economic Roles of Children in Urban Kano," in *Sex and Age as Principles of Social Differentiation*, ed. J. S. LaFontaine (N.Y.: Academic Press, 1978), p. 118, found that women's occupational changes correlated with change in the age, gender, and number of children available to help them.

occupation as that of a daughter or mother, the majority being concentrated in the fish, produce and prepared food trades (71%). In most of the 119 cases (57%), a two generation correlation was involved, but 26% had three generations and 15% four generations. In two cases only were there five generations, but there might have been more, since some women simply did not know the occupations of their great-grandmothers. Probably because of the increased tendency among the middle age groups (fifties and sixties) to trade in imported goods, there was a noticeable diminution of women sharing occupations with their mothers or daughters as they got younger: 58% of the women in their seventies through nineties had at least a two generation correlation, compared to 46% of the women in their thirties through sixties. Also, many older women never thought of questioning the practice of mother-daughter succession in trade, like this one:

Q. Would you have liked to do any other work besides sewing and selling cloth?

A. *That was the work I did. I did not want to do anything else. That was what my mother was doing so that was what I did.*

Some apprenticeships, however, were formal, involving fees and nonrelatives. This was particularly true of sewing, probably because of the equipment involved. Such apprentices had to conform to the rules governing Ga apprenticeship: the apprentice could not make a profit but must give her earnings to her mistress; she must not squander her mistress' money, or work with anyone's tools besides the mistress'.[3] These rules typified the exploitative authority vested in the elders in the corporate kin mode of production. Although the rules dated from 1913, they were still applied by women in 1978. Most seamstresses had several machines and apprentices ranging in number from two to ten. The fees were low, and paid on a monthly basis by a relative of the apprentice. Breadbaking was taught by this arrangement also.

But the boundaries between formal and informal apprenticeship were vague in many cases. In this grey area fell the helpers of suburban women like the ones in Kaneshie. In theory, the arrangement by which elite women obtain domestic helpers is supposed to benefit the helpers because they are taught European-style housekeeping and sent to school in exchange for their help. The usual means of recruitment of helpers should be through relatives, and they are supposed to be treated as foster children. In practice, the system in 1978 was more like apprenticeship between nonrelatives. Among the sample of 230 helpers in Kaneshie in 1978, 80.5% of whom were female, we found that 62.4% were not related to their employers, and many were even from a different ethnic group.[4] Furthermore, only 33.6% of the female helpers were in school compared to 58.1% of the male helpers. Thus, when some women in Central Accra said that their daughters were fostered out to

---

[3]SCT 2/6/4, *High Court Judgment Book, Part 3*, p. 698 (case June 23, 1913).

[4]These results contradict Oppong's statement that maids were usually young relatives provided by senior relatives. C. Oppong, *Marriage Among a Matrilineal Elite* (Cambridge: Cambridge University Press, 1974), p 102.

suburban relatives and going to school, I was sometimes skeptical. Most of these servants were of school age. Also, it was questionable that they were learning skills which would help them to secure better employment. Routine housework and childcare were their usual duties. Dzidzienyo, in her study of Accra housemaids, found that most were female, had started working before age ten, and were not in school. Their pay went directly to their parents, who had arranged for their employment.[5] Girls were probably better off at home in an apprenticeship situation.

One of the changes in apprenticeship has been, of course, adding the most formal type, that is, vocational/commercial school. In this realm ideas of women's proper roles have constricted the opportunities available for women in Ghana. Table V-1 shows the sex ratios in 1976-77 for different types of courses at Accra Polytechnic and Accra Technical Training Center, the two largest institutions for post-middle school students. In business and catering, where the largest numbers of women were enrolled, the respective numbers of women were 680 and 804, smaller than the numbers of men in any of the other categories.[6]

Table V-1.
Sex Ratios in Accra Technical/Commercial Schools, 1976-77.

Course type:	Ratio of: Males to Females		
Pre-technical/technical (engineering, construction, etc.)	100	:	.3
Craft (electrician, welding, carpentry, mechanics, masonry, etc.)	100	:	.3
Business (accountancy, marketing, secretarial, etc.)	100	:	33.0
Catering (cookery, management, etc.)	100	:	40.0

[5]Dzidzienyo noted the implications for class formation of using such child labor.

> Housemaids are vital, they keep, especially the trained and educated women, free to use her talents and training. However, this is at the expense of and severely restricting the life chances of a whole segment of the children of the poor. . . . If we keep children in school and restrict child employment we raise the cost of household help to the point where it is prohibitive and drives many women out of work. If we do not, we guarantee illiteracy and underdevelopment for another segment of our Ghanaian womanhood.

S. Dzidzienyo, "Housemaids: A Case Study of Domestic Helpers in Ghanaian Homes," paper for Ghana National Council on Women and Development Seminar on Women and Development, Accra (Sept. 1978), pp. 4-6, 8, 13. D. F. Bryceson and M. Mbilinyi noted the same problem in Tanzania, "The Changing Role of Tanzanian Women in Production: From Peasants to Proletarians," paper (1978), p. 34.

[6]Ghana, Ministry of Education, Ghana Education Service, *Digest of Education Statistics 1976-77* (Accra: Government Printer, 1978), pp. 94-95. These covered all types of students (full- or part-time, day or evening, all levels).

North remarked with respect to girls' vocational training in Ghana, that
concentrating on domestic skills, as is done in the Women's Training Insti-
tutes and even in the new public vocational education program, not only
furthers the stereotype of women, but concentrates too much on the same
skills and creates unemployment.[7]

Thus we find the Social Welfare Department describing the Girls' Vocational
Training Centres, as "educational institutions which provide various trade
training courses in home science" for middle school leavers, school dropouts,
illiterates above school age, housewives who want home science training, gra-
duates, and those "expected to be self-supporting or better housewives." The
stated goal was to eliminate prostitution.[8] The S.W.D. Home Science Extension service offered courses in the early 1970s to perhaps 10 to 15% of rural
women in childcare, budgeting, housewifery, community health, nutrition,
family planning, basic agriculture, marketing and accounting.[9] Rural women
were better off than urban women in terms of vocational education, then.
Urban women like the Ga may be disadvantaged in some ways because they
have more access than their rural peers to a type of formal education that is
dysfunctional for them. Indeed, it is questionable if formal education,
whether vocational or academic, has benefited women on the whole. The
remainder of this chapter deals with this argument in the context of the
nature and development of formal education for women and its impact on
the apprenticeship system.

Access to Formal Education

Major changes in the apprenticeship system have been caused by the
impact of formal education on girls. Women must trade because of their
lack of other opportunities, not only due to the state of the economy but
also to their lack of access to formal education of the same type as men can
obtain. Both formal and informal education are critical in determining
women's fate and their class position. Formal education has been touted as
the panacea for all ills, a social investment which will bring infinite rewards
and better the status of women everywhere.[10] Men who have concerned
themselves with women and development issues have been most receptive to
the provision of at least a modicum of formal education for women, often

---

[7]J. North et al., *Women in National Development in Ghana*, U.S. Agency for International Development Women in Development Office report (April 1975), p. 119.

[8]Ghana, Department of Social Welfare and Community Development, Welfare Manual
No. 3, *Groupwork* (1973), p. 38.

[9]North et al., *Women*, pp. 109, 112.

[10]K. Ewusi, "The Size of the Labour Force and the Structure of Employment in Ghana," paper for University of Ghana Institute for Statistical, Social and Economic Research
(ISSER) (1975), p. 80; I. F. Rousseau, "African Women: Identity Crisis? Some Observations
on Education and the Changing Role of Women in Sierra Leone and Zaïre," in *Women
Cross-Culturally*, ed. R. Rohrlich-Leavitt (Paris: Mouton, 1975), p. 41.

because that education is seen as an indirect investment in the quality of children of both sexes. Even prior to colonialism, formal education of a European type facilitated entrance to the upper class on the Gold Coast because of the social and economic advantages it provided in the mercantile world. Educational level is now an essential part of a person's socioeconomic status. "Education is not only . . . a source of knowledge, but also the principal system of allocating status and chances in life."[11] Those without any formal education have their inferiority impressed upon them constantly, and sometimes even believe in it themselves. *I am only an illiterate so I cannot answer that*, was a common enough reply to various questions. Even those who seek important chiefships should be well educated, a university degree being preferable.[12]

Formal education in this context not only determines class membership, i.e., access to the capitalist means of production, but also exaggerates the differences between female networks and elite networks that are sexually integrated but dominated by men. Education serves as a "legitimation for inequalities of power" and "helps to socialize people into the different work habits, patterns of discipline and social demands of different positions in the production process."[13] It is no wonder, then, that improving the status of women has been unquestioningly associated with improving their access to higher levels of formal education. The questions here are, how successfully has the Ghana government accomplished its aim of providing universal education, and if successful, has that education substantially improved women's class position?

Compared to many colonies, the Gold Coast was well provided with educational facilities by the British; early on (relatively speaking) female education was a concern. Because of its status as an early coastal town and center of trade, Accra also was an early focus of European missionary efforts, including education. The first school founded by Europeans near Accra was at the Danish fort in Osu in 1722. Although it postdated the Dutch school established at Elmina in 1644, it survived as the oldest European-type school in West Africa.[14] The first effort to establish public education in the Gold Coast was the Education Ordinance of 1852, which said that females should be included. Its financing, however, was tied to collecting a poll tax, which

---

[11]P. Marris and A. Somerset, *The African Entrepreneur* (New York: Africana Publishing Corporation, 1972), p. 208; I. Schuster, in *New Women of Lusaka* (Palo Alto, California: Mayfield Publishing Co., 1979), p. 21, stated, "Occupation and income, which depend on amount and timing of education, are the chief factors that differentiate classes in modern Zambian life."

[12]In one case a youngish man with only a middle school education, who had become the "paramount" chief of a people, had much trouble in asserting authority over an older and better educated (secondary school) subchief, who had been one of his teachers. The status-role conflicts were insuperable.

[13]E. O. Wright and L. Perrone, "Marxist Class Categories and Income Inequality," *American Sociological Review* XLII (1977): 51.

[14]H. Meredith, *An Account of the Gold Coast of Africa* (1812; reprint ed., London: Frank Cass and Co. Ltd., 1967), p. 199; C. G. Wise, *A History of Education in British West Africa* (N.Y.: Longmans, Green and Co., 1956), pp. 1-2.

failed dismally.[15] In 1882 the first Education Ordinance to be carried out was passed, but public schools were not established on a large scale.[16] Basically education was left to the missionaries to develop. In Central Accra from 1874 on the Wesleyans opened schools with the aid of government subsidies. By 1900 the Wesleyans had 55 schools in the Gold Coast, mostly concentrated in and around Accra.[17] More boys than girls were sent to school, and more school places were available to boys. The missionaries had all of the European biases about the proper place of women. Even in the Basel Mission schools, where the sex ratio was more equal than in others and there was more concentration on vocational/technical education, the boys were instructed in "handwork" and the girls in sewing. Middle schools were available for boys only, from which they had "no difficulty in obtaining an apprenticeship in a mercantile business or . . . Government Office," according to Reindorf around 1890.[18]

Moreover, parents were not anxious to make their daughters, who had functional economic value, into luxury goods. The girls were needed at home for domestic duties and trading, and the new education did not fit them for better jobs, nor were better jobs available to them. In 1894 the headmistress of the Basel Mission Girls' School in Osu remarked, when complaining of truancy, that "the people persist in sending their children continually to the bush for provisions or to Accra shopping."[19] Reindorf noted that it was particularly difficult to persuade parents to send girls to school.[20] The single most important reason for not being sent to school or having to drop out (cited by 36% of the women in the 1971-72 small survey) was helping their mothers or other relatives. People developed different reasons for not sending them after some girls were sent to school. Sometimes the teachers were harsh and the lessons difficult so the children did not want to start or continue, as with 16% of the 1971-72 small survey. To prepare for their new roles as white collar workers, boys were encouraged to persevere but girls were allowed to quit, especially if money was a problem. One of these reasons applied to 43% of the women in the 1971-72 small survey.

In 1928 Collett, a Catholic missionary, summed up the situation for girls, having already criticized the quality of the education the boys were getting as too rote and time-wasting.

The education of girls is, as yet, far behind that of boys, since most of the

---

[15]H. O. McWilliam, *The Development of Education in Ghana* (London: Longmans, Green and Co., Ltd., 1969), pp. 26-28.

[16]G. E. Hurd, "Education," in *A Study of Contemporary Ghana*, ed. W. Birmingham et al. (London: George Allen & Unwin, Ltd., 1967), II: 218.

[17]*Annual Colonial Report*, 1900; North et al., *Women*, p. 101, cites Brokensha that there were 83 Wesleyan schools by 1880 with a total enrollment of over 3,000.

[18]North et al., *Women*, p. 101; C. C. Reindorf, *The History of Gold Coast and Asante* (ca. 1890; reprint ed., Accra: Ghana Universities Press, 1966), p. 222.

[19]Ghana National Archives, Basel Mission Papers, EC 7/18, *Logbook of Girls' School, Christiansborg, 1812-1901*, p. 98.

[20]Reindorf, *History*, p. 222.

parents seem to think it quite superfluous, if not harmful. This prejudice
has, perhaps, been increased, if not created, by the visible results of the European education which has been given to some of their girls, who have returned to their homes with a decided disinclination to take their share in
the household duties and with expensive tastes. . . . But, training which
will help the African girls to improve upon the domestic arts of their mothers, and which will, at the same time, train their minds so as to make them
suitable companions for their educated husbands, is very much to be
desired.[21]

The former part of his complaint we find echoed again and again among
Ghanaian women, in particular. "Mansa was a good girl. Not like one of
these *yetse-yetse* things who think putting a toe in a classroom turns them
into goddesses.[22] *There is one girl in that house over there, if she speaks
English you will have to bow to her*, a woman remarked acerbically. The
obvious answer to the latter part of his complaint is that teaching
European-style home economics and rudimentary letters with the aim of producing "cultured" wives was irrelevant to the needs of the local population
at that time.

There was a gradual rise in available school places before World War I,
although much local pressure was exerted to achieve more. However, it was
only in the interwar years that the educational take-off started. In 1920
Governor Guggisberg enunciated his 15 principles of education, which
included an increase in the number of places for girls. The culmination of
his policies was the opening of Achimota College in 1925. In actuality, nothing much was done about educating girls, although the government had radically increased its role in providing education.[23] Collett's post-Guggisberg
comment reflects this, and also the fact that very little thought, if any, was
given by the government to the appropriateness of formal education to local
needs. Instead, an attempt was made to import European culture (along
with language), lock, stock, and barrel. The needs of local women were certainly not considered, although such early political organizations as the
Aborigines' Rights Protection Society did pay attention to education for
boys to see that it measured up to European standards.

In fact, the early education of Ga women came more often at Sunday
School than daily school. In the 1971-72 small sample, while 74% of the
women had not been to any regular school, 70% had attended Sunday school
at some time. In 1891 there were already about 800 pupils of all ages in the
Accra Wesleyan Sunday Schools, and the *Gold Coast Chronicle* reported that
it was common to see groups of women in Salaga Market with alphabet

---

[21]Dom M. Collett, *Accra* (London: Society for the Propagation of the Gospel in
Foreign Parts, 1928), pp. 29-30.

[22]A. A. Aidoo, *No Sweetness Here* (Garden City, N.Y.: Doubleday and Co., 1971), p.
141.

[23]F. Agbodeka, *Ghana in the Twentieth Century* (Accra: Ghana Universities Press,
1972), pp. 101-03.

cards.[24] People were taught how to read Ga in order to read the Bible, translated into Ga in 1865 by the Basel missionary Zimmerman.[25] The appeal of Sunday school was great for girls, in particular. Mothers who did not feel they could spare their daughters to go to regular school were quite willing to send them to Sunday school, and besides, it was free. Some of the women were attracted by what they felt was the miracle of learning to read. Several were quite proud of being literate in Ga, and often could be found reading the Bible. Sunday school offered the first legitimate opportunities to socialize with boys. Not a few women met their future husbands there. For all these reasons, then, girls went to Sunday school long before it became popular to send them to regular primary school.[26]

Until after World War II it was not common to send girls to school. This is reflected in the different proportions of women who attended school in the 1971-72 large survey by age cohort. Among the women in their eighties and nineties, only 5% attended primary school, as opposed to 47% of those in their forties and thirties. No one went to secondary school, and only three or four women appeared to be functionally literate. The more general situation is indicated in Table V-2. The gradual change in sex ratios was succeeded by rapid change after World War II, which ultimately resulted in girls going to primary school at the same ratio as they are in the population.[27] This change was reflected in the educational level of children of the women in the 1971-72 small survey. Eighteen percent of the sons of women in their nineties and eighties had had no formal education, compared to 7% of those of women in their thirties and forties. However, for the daughters the proportion with no education went from 65% to 19%, a drastic difference. While a majority of the women 39 to 50 in the 1978 survey had had no education (70%), only 15.6% of their children of both sexes had had none, and these included preschoolers.

What caused this drastic change? After World War II people's attitudes about education for girls underwent a strong change, and the number of school places available to them increased. The women in the 1971-72 small survey reflected these changes, with very few differences according to age

---

[24]*Accra Gold Coast Chronicle*, Oct. 4, 1891, p. 2.

[25]Reindorf, *History*, p. 224.

[26]During most of the twentieth century the Gold Coast education system followed the British pattern of infant primary (classes 1-3), junior primary (Standards I-III), senior primary (Standards IV-VII), and Secondary (Forms I-VI). Children start school at age six. Later, in the 1960s, Standards VI to Form II became middle school, and primary school became six grades. G. B. Kay, *The Political Economy of Colonialism in Ghana* (Cambridge: Cambridge University Press, 1972), p. 299. Another change supposed to take effect in 1980 was that most children would finish school at age 14, after Junior Secondary, while the favored few would be sent on to Senior Secondary (then perhaps university), or vocational/technical schools for three years. Under the middle school system the normal age at leaving school is 15 or 16, so this is basically proposing to shorten the length of required education. Ghana, Ministry of Education, "The New Structure and Content of Education for Ghana" (Accra: Government Printer, 1974), pp. 1-4.

[27]J. C. Bryson, "Women and Economic Development in Cameroon," USAID report (Jan. 1979), pp. 69-70, noted that the change began at the same time in Cameroon.

**Table V-2. Ratio of Boys to Girls in Primary Schools in Accra[+]
and the Eastern Province,[*] 1890-1977.**

Year	Ratio of Boys to Girls		
	Boys	to	Girls
1890[*]	100	:	11
1919[*]	100	:	14
1930[*]	100	:	27
1938[*]	100	:	33
1955[+]	100	:	60
1960[+]	100	:	78
1965[+]	100	:	83
1970[+]	100	:	101
1976-77[+]	100	:	102

Sources: *Annual Colonial Reports*, 1890-1938, *Government Education Statistics*, 1965; *Ghana Census*, 1960, 1970; Ghana Education Service, *Digest of Education Statistics*, 1976-77. The Ussher Town ratio for 1960 was 100:96 for primary and 100:71 for middle school.

group. Eighty-eight percent of the women felt that girls should receive as much education as boys do, mainly for economic reasons. They felt girls should get good jobs in order to support their parents better, or to be able to keep accounts if they were market women, or to achieve higher status.[28] The next most frequent reason cited was to achieve equality of the sexes. Several women said proudly, *girls are equal to boys now*. Lastly, gaining knowledge was considered to be important, *because . . . it gives one self-respect, and prepares one for life.* Even among the negative answers women usually stated that girls need some education, especially if a mother had daughters only and wanted to be supported in her old age.[29] The change in women's attitudes can be attributed to a desire to widen their options for employment, but also to an awareness of the weakness of relying solely on female networks; they were covering their bets.

This change in attitude on the part of the women, combined with the expansion of schooling associated with Nkrumah's making primary and middle school education compulsory in 1961, drastically improved female school attendance. The women's changed attitudes were probably more important, however. It might be suggested that the change was due to men's attitudes rather than women's, since the men were supposed to pay the school fees. In

[28]Kirk (Fitzgerald) commented that education was more often seen as economically rewarding in Central Accra than the Ga villages, and that the regularity of school attendance there was intermediate between that of children in the villages and the suburbs. L. K. Fitzgerald, "Cognitive Development Among Ga children: Environmental Correlates of Cognitive Growth Rate Within the Ga Tribe," Ph.D. diss. University of California-Berkeley (1970), p. 20.

[29]In her 1969 survey of 57 market traders, Sai found that 61% felt that even middle school education was necessary for girls. F. A. Sai, "The Market Woman in the Economy of Ghana," Master's thesis Cornell University (1971), p. 64.

a few cases men refused to pay for the girls but not the boys. But in reality women played a dominant role in financing their children's education. They paid the school expenses for a majority of their children of both sexes (see Chapter VI), so their attitudes made the significant difference.

However, it does not do to derive too roseate a picture from simply looking at primary school statistics. For, stereotyped notions concerning women's roles and the progressive limitation of school places for girls at the upper levels still disadvantage girls. More girls than boys may start school, but fewer finish. If the 1976-77 ratio of boys to girls in Accra primary school was 100:102, the ratio in the last two years of primary school was 100:99, in middle school, 100:93, in secondary school, *100:51*, and in post-secondary teacher training, 100:37.[30] The higher the level the fewer the women; in 1970 at the University of Ghana 15% of the students were women, in 1976 at the University of Science and Technology at Kumasi, only 7.3%.[31]

A strong contributor to this pattern is the comparatively few places for girls at the upper educational levels. In the European tradition the system is highly selective; in 1969-70 only about 5% of the potential candidates for secondary school places succeeded in finding one, causing Gaisie and David to say, "in the light of present economic conditions a large proportion of children in the 13 to 19 age group will undoubtedly have to miss secondary education."[32] Asiedu-Akrofi and Atakpa have documented the change in allocation of school places to boys and girls in Ghana from 1968 to 1976. In middle schools the percentage of students enrolled who were girls went from 37 to 41%, in secondary schools from 26 to 30%, in commercial or business schools from 30 to 34%, in post-primary teacher training from 30 to 40%, and in universities from 11 to 13%. Between 1968 and 1976 there was no change in the percentage of students who were girls enrolled in: sixth form (16%), post-secondary teacher training (28%), or technical schools (14%). Because of the increases in overall numbers there was an increase in the *numbers* of girls enrolled in every sector, but the proportions did not change significantly. They noted that there were 28 boys' versus 17 girls' boarding secondary schools, that fewer girls' than boys' schools had sixth forms, and that in post-secondary or technical schools girls tended to do sex-stereotyped subjects, such as home sciences or secretarial training.[33] Given that there was a fourfold increase in the numbers of spaces for boys during that period,

[30]*Digest of Education Statistics 1976-77*, pp. 5, 12, 13, 76.

[31]M. Greenstreet, "Social Change and Ghanaian Women," *Canadian Journal of African Studies* VI, no. 2 (1972): 352; B. D. Houghton, "Women in Education in Ghana," background paper for Ghana National Council on Women and Development Seminar on Women and Development (Sept. 1978), p. 8.

[32]S. K. Gaisie and A. S. David, *Planned Fertility Reduction in Ghana: Structural Inter-Relationships, Potential Socio-Economic Impact and the Magnitude of the Needed Programmes*, University of Ghana Population Dynamics Program, Ghana Population Series No. 6 (1974), pp. 76, 79.

[33]K. Asiedu-Akrofi and S. K. Atakpa, "Practices Regarding Allocation of Places to Women in Schools and Colleges," research report for USAID/Ghana National Council on Women and Development (May 1978).

Houghton has appropriately questioned why more money was not spent on adding facilities for girls.[34] The answers lie in attitudinal factors.

Generally people do not regard provision of upper level education for girls as important. Some of the reasons for this are self-fulfilling prophecies, in that they help to create the very situation causing the parents' complaints. The labor value of girls is the prime suspect here. A girl's academic performance may suffer because of her domestic or trading activities, but no allowances are made to reduce those duties. The feeling is that girls can always trade in a pinch, and so schooling is less important for them, which in turn, of course, makes it more likely that they are trained to do nothing except trade. Thus, Houghton found in a survey of 62 sub-elite women in various occupations around the country that most, given limited resources, would educate sons over daughters, since girls can support themselves without schooling.[35] Likewise, as we shall see, husbands may skimp on chop money because they know that their wives will feed the children through their trading activities. In both cases, trading operates as an excuse to underprivilege women because no steps are taken to facilitate or improve the women's trading activities.

A second common attitude concerns the ideology of male support, expressed in this woman's statement. *A daughter will marry and be cared for, at least in part by her husband, whereas a son will have to take care of a wife, and will have more responsibility.* In Houghton's sample of female urban wage workers, even though most were self-supporting, they still felt girls' education to be less important.[36] When asked about the return rate on education by sex, the Central Accra women aged 39 to 50 were more dubious about the value for girls than for boys. Specifically, 8% felt that the girls' education expenses would not be repaid, compared to 2% for the boys'. Twenty-three percent were uncertain for girls, versus 16% for boys. They were less likely, however, than Houghton's sample of sub-elites to refer to the husband supporting the wife.

A frequent reason mentioned for not urging girls to go far with their schooling was that *a girl will just get pregnant and waste the value of her education.* Nonetheless, this persuasion did not engender giving daughters the sex education which would prevent pregnancy. Several women shrugged and said that this eventuality did not matter anyway, because then their sons-in-law might help them in their old age instead of their daughters. This situation is a forceful reminder of the Kenyan one described by Nelson, who attributed it to the women's incomplete consciousness of the social, economic, and political factors feeding into their low socioeconomic status.

---

[34]Houghton, "Women," p. 4. L. Weis, in "Women and Education in Ghana: Some Problems of Assessing Change," *International Journal of Women's Studies* III, no. 5 (Sept./Oct. 1980): 432, found that women's access to education was narrowing from 1961 to 1974 and that girls were disproportionately slotted to low status institutions.

[35]Houghton, "Women," pp. 10-11.

[36]B. C. Houghton, "Urban Wage Workers: Coping," profiles paper prepared for Ghana National Council on Women and Development (March 1980), p. 10.

The very women who have become pregnant out of wedlock because they had no access to methods of birth control deny birth control to their daughters, who in turn become pregnant before they finish their education. Women who are unable to find jobs because they have no education some-times educate their sons in preference to their daughters because they con-tinue to think of their sons as their future security.[37]

A lot of grumbling is heard about schoolgirls getting pregnant, and the scarce documentation supports the connection between girls' dropping out and their pregnancy. At two girls' middle schools in Central Accra with a combined enrollment of approximately 300 pupils, only one Form 4 girl was reported to have dropped out because of pregnancy in 1977-78. However, the teachers said that often pregnant girls simply stopped coming to school on their own without waiting to be told not to return, so they probably did not know about some pregnancies. The teachers also thought that the girls should be given sex education in the schools from Form 2 on, and be taught how to use contraceptives. Campbell-Platt, in a 1978 study of Accra school dropout rates, found that the female rate was higher than that for boys at every level, but especially for middle and secondary schools, where it was double that for boys. Twenty percent of the female dropouts were pregnant, lending some justification to the grumbling. Some of the secondary students got abortions.[38] In some cases male teachers or students were partially responsible for schoolgirl pregnancies, but no sanctions were imposed on them because of it.

The pessimistic view of the return rate on education, which might encourage parents not to send children to school, is supported by the ongo-ing job crunch for literates in Accra. Even back in the nineteenth century we saw there was beginning to be an oversupply of the clerically trained.[39] Guggisberg in his 1925 Annual Address commented on it.[40] A number of observers have noted the educational inflation in Ghana which has entailed a requirement of more and more education to get even lower level jobs.[41] The unemployment rate in Accra has tended to be higher for school leavers than for others. A 1967 study of middle school leavers found that eighteen months after finishing Form 4, 46.3% of the boys and 44.4% of the girls

[37]N. Nelson, "'Women must help each other': the operation of personal networks among Buzaa beer brewers in Mathare Valley, Kenya," in *Women United, Women Divided*, ed. P. Caplan and J. Bujra (Bloomington: Indiana University Press, 1979), p. 94.

[38]K. Campbell-Platt, "Drop Out Rates Among Girls and Boys at the Primary, Middle and Secondary Levels of Education in Selected Schools in Accra," research paper for Ghana National Council on Women and Development (1978), pp. 2, 18, 27.

[39]North et al., *Women*, p. 115, said that as early as 1850 there was an oversupply of literates to fill available jobs on the Gold Coast.

[40]G. Schneider et al., "The Volta Region and Accra: Urbanisation, Migration, and Em-ployment in Ghana," International Labor Office Urbanisation and Employment Programme Working Paper (Geneva: 1978), p. 12.

[41]G. E. Hurd and T. J. Johnson, "Education and Social Mobility in Ghana," *Sociology of Education* XL, no. 1 (Winter 1967): 58; J. C. Caldwell, "Introduction," in *Population Growth and Socioeconomic Change in West Africa*, ed. J. C. Caldwell (New York: Columbia University Press, 1975), p. 23.

were unemployed.[42] In 1970 in the Greater Accra Region the highest rate of unemployment was among those aged 15 to 19: 33.5%.[43] One might posit, then, that parents would be discouraged by this into channeling children either to vocational school or apprenticeships. In Ashaiman (near Tema) Peil found in 1968 and 1970 that parents were beginning to doubt the value of education.[44] Doubts appeared in 1978 in some answers to the question, "Does education help boys/girls to get better jobs?" One woman answered, *In principle, yes, but you need to pay bribes to get your son a job now. Because it's difficult to get work it might be better for a girl to marry. Many girls go far with school now but end up trading anyway.* This answer was not typical, however.

Echoing the majority of women in 1971-72 who felt that both sexes should get educated, 81% of the women aged 39 to 50 in 1978 were convinced that education would help their children of both sexes to get better jobs. Only 3% felt that this was not true for boys, and 5% for girls. The rest were uncertain. This percentage was even higher than the 70% of the urban older people interviewed by Caldwell in 1964 who felt that investment in children's education had brought a greater return than expenditure.[45] The convictions expressed by this woman were absolute, and mirrored in the replies of many others. *It's important for everyone to go to school so they know left from right. Schoolgoers get better jobs than non-schoolgoers.* This was not mere assent for the sake of agreeableness to a pesky question from an impertinent inquirer, but a true reflection of a belief held by many. This is why most girls in Accra now at least start school. This situation may be a reflection of the worsening economy in that everyone is looking for a way out of his or her troubles. For illiterates the financial rewards of literacy are the will o' the wisp to chase; for poorly paid literates trading may seem more appealing. In 1978 Houghton's poorly paid female urban wage workers saw trading as a more desirable occupation, but beginning capital was lacking.[46] In this way the present is vilified but hope is maintained. For the relatively few highly educated women, education usually brings a substantial return, thus creating a situation where women with the least and most education

[42]ISSER, *Survey of Middle Schools,* 1967 (Legon: 1968), p. 29. They found an overall unemployment rate of 53% for those who had passed the school leaving examination, and 72% for those who had failed (p. 52).

[43]K. Ewusi, "The Implications of Regional Seasonal Variations in Unemployment in Ghana," *Ghana Social Science Journal* IV, no. 2 (Nov. 1977): 110. Many statistics concerning unemployment are too low because they count only literates, that is, the unemployed registered with employment agencies. See W. F. Steel and C. Campbell, "Women's Employment and Development: A Conceptual Framework Applied to Ghana," paper (April 1979), p. 19; Gaisie, "Population Growth," pp. 358-59; R. Szereszewski, "Regional Aspects of the Structure of the Economy," in *A Study of Contemporary Ghana,* ed. W. Birmingham et al. (London: George Allen and Unwin, Ltd., 1967), I: 99.

[44]M. Peil, "Demographic Change in a Ghanaian Suburb," *Ghana Social Science Journal* III, no. 1 (1976): 72.

[45]J. C. Caldwell, "The Erosion of the Family: A Study of the Fate of the Family in Ghana," *Population Studies* XX, no. 1 (July 1966): 19.

[46]Houghton, "Women," p. 35.

show the highest labor force participation rates.[47] Meanwhile, people seem preoccupied with putting women among the minimally educated where their labor force participation rate will be the lowest, in yet another Ghanaian irony.[48] The assumption that access to formal education is crucial for women is logical, then, but the mechanisms for incorporating women equally into education and well paid jobs are lacking. Government rhetoric has been mistaken for reality. The answer to our first question is that universal education has not been achieved. The second question concerning the function of education for improving women's class position still remains.

The Impact of Formal Education on Marketing Knowledge

Because elementary education is becoming common for girls in Accra, it is important to discern its impact on informal education, the apprenticeship system, and their trading activities. The usual observation made concerning entrepreneurs in developing countries is that there is an inverse correlation between success in business and the level of formal education attained by an entrepreneur. Experience in business, rather than formal education, is the chief cause of the entrepreneurs' success.[49] There is further evidence that sending potential entrepreneurs to vocational schools is not as effective in developing that potential as had been visualized by those enamored of western models of development. In Western Nigeria Mabawonku found that it was more expensive and less effective to send young men to vocational schools to develop entrepreneurial skills than to train them through the indigenous apprenticeship system.[50] In 1977 in Ghana, Sethuraman found that most self-employed male entrepreneurs trained solely by apprenticeship. Those who went to technical training schools usually found wage employment.[51] Although the results below support the high value of experience in

---

[47]E. Date-Bah, "Ghanaian Women and Cooperatives," paper presented at Ghana National Council on Women and Development Seminar on Women and Development (Sept. 1978), p. 5.

[48]B. C. Lewis, "Economic Activity and Marriage among Ivoirian Urban Women," in *Sexual Stratification*, ed. A. Schlegel (N.Y.: Columbia University Press, 1977), p. 165, noted the same phenomenon in Abidjan.

[49]C Liedholm and E. Chuta, "The Economics of Rural and Urban Small-Scale Industries in Sierra Leone," Michigan State University Dept. of Agricultural Economics, African Rural Economy Paper No. 14 (1976), p. 103, have an interesting Sierra Leonean example of this phenomenon. Their sample included both men and women. Marris and Somerset, *African Entrepreneur*, p. 221, also noted the overweening importance of practical experience for Kenyan male entrepreneurs.

[50]A. F. Mabawonku, "An Economic Evaluation of Apprenticeship Training in Western Nigeria's Small-Scale Industries," Michigan State University Dept. of Agricultural Economics, African Rural Economy Paper No. 17 (1979), pp. 40-49. The return for apprenticeship training was almost twice that for trade school training.

[51]S. V. Sethuraman, "Employment Promotion in the Informal Sector in Ghana," International Labor Office World Employment Research Working Paper (Geneva: 1977), p. 11.

developing knowledge about marketing, they do not show a negative impact by formal academic education (no one had gone to vocational school). Rather, they suggest a more complex relationship, partly because the subjects are women and girls.

Much of the research to date has assumed that men have the most potential as entrepreneurs, and has therefore dealt exclusively with the making of male entrepreneurs. Researchers who have found a negative relationship between formal education level and male entrepreneurial skills often have a sample population whose literacy level is high compared with that of most women.[52] In Ghana Hakam found that even male apprentices usually had a middle school education in 1978.[53] In the case of women it is necessary to consider rather the impact of elementary schooling and literacy on their acquisition of market knowledge and skills. Marris and Somerset defined several stages at which lack of formal education became a handicap to Kenyan businessmen. Their first "threshold" was elementary literacy, i.e., reading, writing, and most important, arithmetic for keeping accounts.[54] It is this threshold which is of concern here.

To test the impact of formal education on marketing knowledge we compared two groups of girls in Central Accra, the Form I students, and the Salaga Market girls. The average age of both groups was 13, which made them old enough to have served most of their apprenticeship of whatever sort. The third sample of Salaga Market women was given a modified form of the questionnaire. All three samples were randomly chosen, but the Salaga Market women were drawn mainly from among stallholders, since we wanted well-established and presumably knowledgeable traders for purposes of comparison. The results modified considerably some preconceived notions about the market and schoolgirls.

Two striking characteristics came to light immediately in the background of the market and schoolgirls, and illustrated the intimate relations between the categories. First, 37 of the 41 market girls had been to school at some time; twenty of these were still attending school at the time of the interview. This was hardly, then, a group untouched by formal education; it became necessary in the results to differentiate according to the educational level of the market girls. Second, only one schoolgirl had never traded, and most (37 out of 42) were engaged in trading at the time they were interviewed. Rather than finding a segregation of the two activities of school attendance and trading, then, the two were overwhelmingly mixed. This aspect raised questions about finding significant differences in trading knowledge between the groups.

---

[52]Mabawonku's study should be faulted for omitting from his sample, with no explanation, the sole vocational school for women. His male samples were mostly literate. Mabawonku, "Economic Evaluation," p. 28.

[53]A. Hakam "Technology Diffusion from the Formal to the Informal Sector: The Case of the Auto-Repair Industry in Ghana," International Labor Organisation Working Paper (Geneva: 1978), p. 26.

[54]Marris and Somerset, African Entrepreneur, p. 216.

However, the background of the two samples showed that there were meaningful, not just geographical, differences between them, and also why the girls were employed in one activity or the other. The market girls were more likely to: have poorer less-educated parents, be in a fostering situation, live with their mothers only, have divorced parents, and have more siblings. They obviously had more pressure on them to help financially, reinforced by the higher likelihood of their being eldest daughters. There were also significant differences in exposure to trading.

Perhaps the most important impact of formal education on trading is that it has reduced the schoolgirls' exposure to trade. This was evident in the great differences in number of hours spent trading by the two groups; the market girls averaged 40.2 hours weekly in the market, the school-going market girls 26.2, and the schoolgirls who were trading, 15.4 (the Salaga Market women, 57.2). The age of beginning trade also differed; the market girls started at the average age of 9.3 years, compared to 10.7 for the schoolgirls, and had participated in 2.1 different businesses, compared to 1.6 for the schoolgirls. The market girls more often had sole responsibility for their trade. While 7.1% of the schoolgirls who were trading claimed to be doing it on their own, 23.8% of the market girls fell into this category.

Most schoolgirls who traded were helping their mothers (62.2%), while only half of the market girls did, a factor of their higher incidence of fostering. They were more likely than the schoolgirls to be helping a matrilateral relative (29.3%). More market girls sold fish, and more schoolgirls sold cloth and provisions, which reflected the commodities that their mothers or matrilateral relatives were selling. The market girls were far more likely to be hawking (83.3%) than the schoolgirls (33.3%). The schoolgirls were most likely to be selling at a stationary location (58.3%), while the market girls were less likely to help with that function (40.5%). The market girls were more likely to help with setting up and cleaning up, carrying the goods, and buying, and the schoolgirls with accounting and sewing. The market girls generally performed more functions than the schoolgirls, which may have been a factor of the increased amount of time they spent in the market. The schoolgirls often sold only on Saturdays or for a few hours after school each day. The different nature of the two groups' trading activities, then, showed the higher level of prosperity of the schoolgirls' families. The schoolgirls' trading activities were more likely to be higher up the trading hierarchy--at fixed locations and in imported goods.

Did reduced exposure to trading also mean that the schoolgirls brought in less profit? Probably. More market than schoolgirls had a turnover of ¢11 to ¢50 per day, and more school than market girls earned less than that. There were more school than market girls earning more than that, but the schoolgirls overestimated their profits by assuming that they always put in a full day of trading, as on a Saturday. The market girls were far more likely to be earning steadily.

What happened to their profits? Whether they were school or market girls, the vast majority, 97.5%, turned most or all of the money over to their mistresses. In 1958 Acquah reported that 98% of the working schoolgirls in

Accra turned over their earnings to a supervisor (compared to 87.5% of the working schoolboys).[55] This practice did not change much in twenty years, then. Twenty-two percent of both the school and market girls were allowed to keep some of the profits, while half of the market girls and 61% of the schoolgirls had an unspecified share of the profits returned to them as pocket money. Thirty percent of the market girls and 19% of the schoolgirls were given help or gifts in kind as a return--cloth, savings, etc. The fact that their mistresses kept control over the profits in most cases caused a majority of the school and market girls to wish to trade independently when they got older, so they could keep their own profits.[56] This suggests that many of the girls felt exploited by the system. It was a definite weakness that women did not generally use the share system to create incentives to raise turnover and profits. Also, some girls felt cheated by their mistresses. Both of these aspects made girls view the business as not their responsibility but rather a burden, and probably increased the likelihood of them cheating their mistresses. The disincentive to trade involved in this system operated equally for school and market girls.

Trading Knowledge

The questionnaire devised to test trading knowledge included objective questions about supply sources, cost and selling prices, passbooks, markets, market days and conditions, and turnover.[57] A more subjective open-ended section included queries about methods for making and improving profits and problems encountered while trading. It was felt advisable, in view of the sometimes hectic interviewing conditions in the market, to keep it fairly short and simple, but with enough scope that a highly motivated, intelligent trader could include in her answers as much as she wanted. The results were tabulated in several ways, first by question, and then each individual was given a box score based on her whole performance, similar to a grade on an examination.[58] Here the topical responses will be gone over first to show relative areas of strength and weakness in the groups' knowledge, and then

---

[55]Acquah, *Accra*, pp. 76-77, gives the only other data pertaining to this topic that I could find. She found that 30% of the schoolchildren of both sexes in Central Accra were working, most of them between the ages of 6 and 11. Sixty-four percent of the girls were hawkers compared to 42% of the boys. Thirty-six percent of the girls were stationary sellers, compared to 45% of the boys. Only .1% of the girls were carriers, compared to 7% of the boys. Another 7% of the boys were news vendors, an occupation reserved exclusively for boys.

[56]Those girls who were trading on their own were asked about when they formerly helped someone.

[57]I am much indebted to Victor Nyanteng of ISSER, University of Ghana, for helping with its creation. Because of excessive length, an appendix including copies of all questionnaires used was deleted from this monograph.

[58]It was not feasible to make qualitative numerical weights for the answers, which reinforced the necessity to do some topical qualitative analysis.

to analyze the differences according to educational level using box scores.

The most concise way of presenting some results is in tabular form, beginning with responses to the questions concerning supply sources and wholesale cost prices. Twenty-four point four percent of the market girls versus 7.5% of the schoolgirls claimed that there were no alternative supply sources for their commodity. Many of those market girls were selling fish. Even some of the market women concurred in this opinion, but upon further thought said that one could purchase fresh (or frozen) fish either at Tema or at the seashore, and get smoked fish at Makola. The latter explanation did not occur to the market girls. It was their answers in this category which accounted for most of their relative weakness compared to the schoolgirls, and weakness in this category, of course, carried over into the next one of the relative cost from different sources. In the other categories the market girls did a bit better than the schoolgirls, probably because they were more likely than the schoolgirls either to be helping their mistresses with buying, or buying for their own business.

In the next category, figuring out the sale price for their commodity, it was necessary to rate the answers on the basis of complete and correct, partial, or incorrect answers, the last including those who claimed ignorance. The market girls did better on correct answers (29.3% versus 19%), but of those who gave partial answers, almost half simply stated that their mistresses had told them a rote method for figuring it out (only a ninth of the schoolgirls did this). This method was what I came to call the "one fish" rule, commonly stated by the market women as, *if I buy four fish for ₵2.50 then I must sell three fish for ₵2.50, thus I get one fish profit.* Many of the market girls did not give it in its full form, but rather in the truncated one of, *if you buy at ₵1.50, then you sell at ₵1.60,* or even, *my mistress tells me,*

**Table V-3. Questions 1-5. Supply Sources and
Wholesale Cost Prices by Percent of Girls Answering Correctly.**[a]

Percent of Girls Naming	Schoolgirls (No. =40)	Market girls (No. =41)
1. Main supply source for commodity[b]	97.5	100.0
2. Alternate supply source for same	80.0	65.8
3. Relative cost from sources	75.0	56.1
4. Cost price of commodity 1978 per usual selling unit[c]	72.5	75.6
5. Cost price of commodity 1977 per usual selling unit[d]	47.5	58.5

[a]An answer of "no" or "I don't know" was judged incorrect.

[b]Any commodity the girl had ever sold.

[c]My thanks to Phyllis Nyanteng for helping in checking these prices.

[d]Specific prices were requested, not just general impressions. A few girls did not answer this because of fear of government agents uncovering price control violations.

and so got only partial credit. The other correct method, of course, was to add up all the costs, of materials, production, transport, etc., and put on an adequate profit margin, then figuring the unit price by dividing that total by the number of units for sale. When the market women answered this question they had a much higher complete rate (75%), of course, and were almost equally divided between these two correct answers, while a few opted for what might be called the catch-as-catch-can method of selling at one price one day, *and if the money doesn't reach, you raise the price the next day*. Because fish now often comes frozen in large blocks which cannot be sold in one day, it is impossible to count the units, so that this method is becoming increasingly popular. Also, under conditions of severe inflation such as Ghana has been experiencing recently, this last method might be more adaptable. In any case, only one of the girls considered this to be the best way.

The answers to the next question concerning how to obtain a passbook reflect the relative familiarity of the two groups of girls with trade in imported goods. Far more school than market girls gave a correct answer (33.3% versus 9.8%), although more market than schoolgirls gave a partial answer (39% versus 7.1%). More than half of both said they did not know, so the differences were not as great as they seemed. One schoolgirl commented, *You go to the store and pay money to the manager, have sex with him, and he will give* [the passbook] *to you*. Answers were judged correct even without the frills describing the corruption.

A correct answer to the question of whether high or low turnover is preferable, could consist either of "high," or a description of how profit and turnover are dependent on market conditions, an answer much more commonly given by market women than either group of girls. The differences in the answers were not significant; a few more school than market girls opted for a high turnover, but about two-fifths of both chose a low turnover. The market girls were more likely to say that it depended on the market for the item. The relatively high number of low turnover answers had to do both with economic conditions, which made people wary of buying large amounts lest they be stuck with it (and produce spoils), and the usual small scale of the girls' enterprises. Also, this question contained an implied hypothetical query, i.e., if you had a high turnover would you make more profits? Many respondents found it difficult to visualize such a situation and considered high turnover to be out of the realm of possibility. Even 20% of the market women opted for a low turnover as best.

On the questions about markets the results again were quite similar. The mean average number of markets named by schoolgirls was 6.5, by market girls, 6.9. The mean average number of market days named correctly was 2.8 for the schoolgirls and 2.5 for the market girls. Only on the question concerning prices on market days was there a significant difference; 92.9% of the schoolgirls as compared to 70.7% of the market girls claimed that things were cheaper on market days, with most giving valid reasons for this answer.[59] In this area it was interesting to note that 85% of the market women agreed with that, one of the few times the market women scored cumulatively below either set of girls.

The answers to the subjective questions were rated differently, every valid factor listed by an informant simply being added up cumulatively to devise the box scores. The results were surprising, since I had expected that degree of articulateness would materially affect them. It seemed logical that increased years of schooling would make the schoolgirls more articulate and less intimidated by what Harkness and Super called "the status differential between the adult and the child subject," which "interferes with free responses through the norms of obedience and respect."[60] The answers of the market girls forced the conclusion that this was not a serious impediment. The mean average number of answers given to the three subjective questions was 4.7 for the market girls and 4.1 for the schoolgirls. Kirk has suggested that the norms of "modesty, silence, obedience and respect for elders" among Central Accra children have broken down, which may be relevant here.[61] We experienced about an equal degree of reticence with the two groups, which was not very great. However, the relatively few answers of the market girls to the question about how to improve profits, as well as their higher acceptance of authority on the selling price question, were indicative of an unquestioning acceptance of authority not equally exhibited by the schoolgirls. Apprenticeship, then, may foster the older norms by reinforcing the ideas of respect for older relatives, while formal schooling has the opposite effect.

In making the quantitative ratings on the subjective questions, I did not impose judgments on how efficacious a suggested solution to the question was, but rather listed all relevant suggestions as having equal value. However, for purposes of discussion it is worthwhile to analyze the answers qualitatively. The answers to the first subjective question are given in Table V-4, with those from the market women for comparison.

The market girls were generally closer than the schoolgirls to the market women in their responses. In nine out of these eleven most frequently mentioned methods this is the case, and particularly in the first two instances, where the methods named are *not* the most efficacious. The only market woman who mentioned increasing prices as a method qualified it by saying, when the market conditions can bear it. Many of the schoolgirls seemed to believe that one could simply arbitrarily increase prices and still

---

[59]The usual reason things are cheaper then, of course, is that many sellers come from the villages and wish to get rid of their stocks quickly in order to return.

[60]S. Harkness and C. M. Super, "Why African Children Are So Hard to Test," in *Issues in Cross-Cultural Research, Annals of the New York Academy of Sciences,* ed. L. L. Adler, 285 (1977): 330.

[61]L. Kirk, "Maternal and Subcultural Correlates of Cognitive Growth Rate: The Ga Pattern," in *Piagetian Psychology, Cross Cultural Contributions,* ed. P. R. Dasen (New York: Gardner Press, Inc., 1977), p. 263. "Old-town children are rather unrestrained and raucous . . .", she says. At one point it was necessary to break up a fight among schoolgirls in order to continue interviewing.

Table V-4. Question A. How to Make a Profit, Percent of Answers Given by Schoolgirls, Market Girls, and Market Women.

Answer	Schoolgirls (No. = 73)	Market girls (No. = 94)	Market women (No. = 78)
1. Increase price/profit margin	28.8	6.4	2.6
2. Figure out profit margin	16.4	2.1	–
3. Be prompt/polite/patient/ nice with customers	9.6	11.7	23.1
4. Reduce prices to increase turnover	4.1	10.6	7.7
5. Dash[a] customers	–	9.6	9.0
6. Attract customers verbally	1.4	19.1	19.2
7. Hawk in order to sell/sell where many customers	6.8	12.7	1.3
8. Sell good quality merchandise	–	5.3	2.6
9. Attract regular customers	1.4	3.2	9.0
10. Attractive display/neatness/ cleanliness	1.4	6.4	7.7
11. God will help/pray	–	–	6.4
12. Other (none exceeding 4%)	30.1	12.9	11.4
Total	100.0	100.0	100.0

[a]Give them something extra.

sell well. Likewise, they attached great importance to figuring out the profit margin, which suggested a kind of mystical confidence that if you keep counting your money it might grow. Neither the market girls nor the women were as enamored with this fallacy. Rather, they opted for less formal and more effective means of increasing profit, like reducing prices to increase turnover, and paying more attention to pleasing and attracting customers.

In the answers to question C about traders' problems one can get a clear view of the contrasting viewpoints of hawkers and stationary sellers with their capital invested in a business,[62] as well as a comparison of level of trading knowledge. As one might expect, while the market women were more concerned with profits, costs, and scarcities, that is, the supply and viability aspects of trade, the girls were most concerned with the selling end of trade: infringement of police and sanitary regulations, which are mainly enforced against hawkers, and customer complaints over prices. In this case the market girls and the schoolgirls were about equidistant from the market women with no particular association between any two groups.

---

[62]The answers to question B are omitted, since they were quite similar to those for question A, the main difference being that the schoolgirls were more willing to make suggestions which would entail their mistresses in some way changing their actions.

Table V-5. Question C. Traders' Problems: Percent of Answers Given by Schoolgirls, Market Girls, and Market Women.

Answer	Schoolgirls (No. = 62)	Market girls (No. = 77)	Market women (No. = 61)
1. Police hassles (over control prices, licenses, street-selling regulations)	43.5	36.4	11.5
2. Taxes/rent	3.2	7.8	13.1
3. Unprofitable generally	3.2	1.3	11.5
4. Cost prices too high/low profit margin	1.6	1.3	11.5
5. Scarcities of goods to sell	1.6	—	9.8
6. Customer complaints (over prices, quality)	9.7	19.5	8.2
7. Few customers	1.6	5.2	13.1
8. Spoilage of merchandise	3.2	2.6	4.9
9. Sanitary regulations	9.7	13.0	—
10. Other (none exceeding 3.5%)	22.7	13.0	16.4
Total	100.0	100.1	100.0

Having considered topical performance by the groups on the questionnaire, it is then helpful to regroup the respondents according to educational level to derive their performance on the questionnaire as a whole. The box scores compiled for each individual are helpful for this purpose, although they take no account of the qualitative differences mentioned above.

The results are suggestive, although certainly not definitive statistically, the confidence levels being too low and the samples too small in some cases. The primary school attenders among the market girls and women did better on the subjective questions, while the middle school attenders did better on the objective questions. Among both market girls and women, those having schooling did better than those without to a marked degree. However, both market girls and women did better cumulatively than the schoolgirls, the market women at a 99% confidence level and almost 3 points higher. The main conclusion to be drawn from this is that experience plus schooling is the preferred combination. One cannot posit an inverse relationship between level of formal education and marketing knowledge, then, but rather a more complex interaction of the two, with mutual positive ramifications.

Table V-6. Trading Knowledge Box Scores - Schoolgirls, Market Girls, and Market Women by Educational Level.

Mean Average Score for:	Schoolgirls (No. = 42) Type of question			Market girls (No. = 42[a]) Type of question			Market women (No. = 40[b]) Type of question		
	Objective	Subjective	Total	Objective	Subjective	Total	Objective	Subjective	Total
Non-school attenders	-	-	-	7.1	2.8	9.9	10.7	3.5	14.2
Primary school attenders	-	-	-	8.6	4.3	12.9	10.5	5.5	16.0
Middle school attenders	8.6	3.0	11.6	9.1	4.1	13.2	12.1	3.3	15.4
Whole group	8.6	3.0	11.6	8.6	4.1	12.7	10.9	3.6	14.5

[a]Twenty seven market girls attended or were attending primary school, 10, middle school.

[b]Two market women attended primary school, 4, middle school.

The Interaction of Formal and Informal Education

We have seen that formal and informal education are not by any means mutually exclusive, but rather interactive in various ways. Not only do most schoolgirls trade and most market girls go to school, but many of the girls habitually play truant to trade.[63] Sixty-one percent of the school-going market girls claimed to have done so, as compared to 31% of the schoolgirls. Nevertheless, their commitment to schooling seemed strong, 93% of the schoolgirls claiming to prefer school to trading, as compared to 65% of the market girls, an unsurprising disparity. All of the schoolgirls and 86% of the schoolgoing market girls claimed to like school. With one exception, all of the market girls who wanted to be in school were. Furthermore, two-thirds of the schoolgirls and 62% of the school-going market girls felt that schooling helped to teach market skills, most of them citing mathematics as the most useful tool taught. Fifty-six point four percent of the market women concurred in this view.[64] These results look encouraging for the future of female literacy in Ghana, and might give the impression that things are only going to improve. This conclusion would be premature for a number of reasons, however.

---

[63]Campbell-Platt, "Drop Out Rates," p. 17, noted that even at the Achimota primary and secondary schools, and the Accra private secondary schools, which cater mostly to elites, girls sometimes went truant to trade.

[64]Over a third refused to state an opinion one way or the other on this question, claiming that their own lack of schooling disqualified them from answering.

One cannot assume that completion of middle school will create functional literacy, or even that literate skills will be applied to trading. Only one of the six market traders who had had some schooling kept written accounts. While on paper the curriculum looked adequate, in fact, inordinate amounts of time were spent on physical education and useless activities, to the detriment of instruction in the listed topics such as math, English, science, etc.[65] "Needlework" did not involve the use of sewing machines, and could more profitably be replaced by accounting. Truancy laws are not enforced.[66] It was not surprising, then, that 41% of the 32 schoolgirls who filled out forms were functionally illiterate (they could not write a coherent phrase in English). The blame for some of the manifold ills besetting the school system can be assigned to economic conditions. The intentions were good when compulsory free middle school education was introduced in 1961, but the system could not accommodate the subsequent quantum leap in the number of elementary students without a drop in quality. Teachers were promoted automatically and the shift system of attendance was adopted to meet the crunch. Osei attributed to the rapid expansion "a considerable fall in educational standards and mass unemployment as most school leavers were not trained to suit any employments."[67]

In times of exorbitant inflation, teaching is becoming an undesirable, underpaid occupation with a high turnover. None of the teachers at the two Central Accra middle schools in 1977-78 had been there the previous year. Often alternative efforts, including trading, occupied much of the teachers' time. Higher supervision was almost nil. Unfortunately, the attempt to raise the quality of teachers by requiring that they have secondary school (previously only middle school was required), has driven their quality down instead, because teaching attracts mostly the dregs who cannot get into a university or other post-secondary training. Also, it has made it far more difficult for women to become teachers due to the paucity of female secondary school openings.[68] Poor quality teachers tend to emphasize rote memory functions rather than creative thinking.[69] Likewise, "free"

---

[65]The prescribed curriculum in 1978 included the following, with their respective weekly hours of exposure: math--2 hours; English--3 hours; Ghanaian languages--3 hours; civics--1 hour; P.E.--1 hour; history--1 1/2 hours; needlework--3 hours; geography--1 hour; art--1 hour; music--1 hour; religious instruction--1 1/2 hours; science--1 hour. The new curriculum places more emphasis on practical skills such as agriculture, crafts, and vocations, but still differentiates between the sexes. Ghana, Ministry of Education, "The New Structure and Content of Education in Ghana," (Accra: Government Printer, 1974), pp. 4-5. Weis, "Women," p. 446, has stated that the girls' curriculum aims at "removing women from economic life and resocializing them for consumptive domesticity."

[66]Ewusi, "Size," p. 108.

[67]E. Osei, "Change in Education Composition of the Ghanaian Population from 1960-1970," Research Seminar paper presented at the U.S. Regional Institute for Population Studies, Legon (Sept. 1974), pp. 8, 12. Weis, "Women," p. 445, noted that as the number of girls in school increases so does their unemployment.

[68]North et al., *Women*, p. 114.

[69]Kirk, "Maternal and Subcultural Correlates," p. 259, noted this as a characteristic of schoolteachers in rural areas.

education was too expensive for the government and soon abandoned. Some
people cannot afford the fees, especially for the upper levels. It is not clear
how reforms can be accomplished in the face of so many obstacles, but more
must be done to help girls trade than simply adding accounting to an
already overburdened and underutilized curriculum.

It is clear, however, that acquiring basic literacy and (written)
mathematical skills would be a relevant advantage for traders, to protect
themselves against being cheated in business transactions or
exploited/maligned by politicians, and to facilitate the expansion of their
businesses.[70] School can also improve problem-solving capabilities, a definite
advantage. In a study comparing the cognitive results of formal and informal education, Scribner and Cole found that differences in the social organization of learning affect cognitive skills, most noticeably in the fact that
schools teach children to learn by classifying problems.[71] This was evident
among some of the more intelligent schoolgirls (who were often, but not
always, some of the best students). They had a far more innovative
approach to seeking solutions to the problems posed by trading, and obviously viewed the problems as being analogous to any other set of problems,
with solutions which could be sought logically. Only one market girl, who
was seeking a middle school place at the time, took this approach. Formal
education could be an advantage, then, for the many female school leavers
who, whatever their ambitions, will become traders given present conditions.
There is simply not sufficient alternative employment for them. It therefore
becomes particularly important that formal education fill the needs of
traders, as well as provide alternative skills for girls to widen their employment prospects.

However, formal education affects not only academic knowledge, but
also values. In this case it fostered lack of interest in trading as a career;
69% of the schoolgirls were not interested in it, as compared to 33.3% of the
market girls. Full-time trading is associated with illiteracy and low
socioeconomic status in the girls' minds, as in the adults'. This association is
important in damaging the economic possibilities of trading. Trading is not
seen as a vehicle fostering upward social mobility for the bright and ambi-
tious. If the bright girls go into other activities, then the creative possibilities in trade will not be realized to the detriment of the economy.

Formal education in Ghana promotes the notion of female dependency
on males, even though reality may be quite different.[72] Far more market

---

[70]K. Hart, in "Small-Scale Entrepreneurs in Ghana and Development Planning," *Journal of Development Studies* VI, no. 4 (July 1970): 115, commented, "Much of the characteristic dysfunctional behaviour of Ghana's entrepreneurs in the conduct of their businesses is ex-
plicable by reference to widespread illiteracy."

[71]S. Scribner and M. Cole, "Cognitive Consequences of Formal and Informal Education," *Science* 182 (Nov. 1973): 553, 557.

[72]In an interesting (though contradictory) study of Adabraka the Sanjeks found that
56% of the upper middle class women (by their definition) were housewives, versus 9% of
the others. Yet without questioning the type of education provided, they said that education would lead to *more* economic independence for women in Ghana. R. Sanjek and L. M.

than schoolgirls expected their work to provide the main source of support for themselves and their children (81% versus 50%). Forty-eight percent of the schoolgirls expected their husbands to provide most or all of that support, compared to 19% of the market girls. Encouraging the dependence of wives on husbands in this situation breeds undesirable results in every way. It is unrealistic; these girls will most likely have to bear the main responsibility for feeding their families. It also undervalues formal education for girls, and reduces the emphasis on improving and expanding it, and on girls' continuing in school. Related to this difference in expectations of support was probably the market girls' desire to have fewer children (4.2) than the schoolgirls (5.5). The market girls, in fact, had a stronger grip on economic reality, and, given the low quality of the schoolgirls' education, were being better prepared for their probable future than the schoolgirls. In addition, fostering unrealistic expectations is not conducive to anyone's happiness or well-being.

Access to Capital

There are also indications that formal education was affecting women's access to capital in harming the apprenticeship system. Most women got capital from several sources at different times. The sources of capital for women in the small 1971-72 survey and the Salaga Market survey of 1978 are described in Table V-7. In 1971-72 the usual source was a mother's sister or uterine sibling. In supplying capital as well as in apprenticeship, matrilateral female relatives played the most important role. Also, when a person started with her own savings, these often came indirectly from her mother. In two 1971-72 cases women admitted having withheld profits from their mothers to get capital to start themselves. The nonrelatives were mostly

Table V-7. Sources of Trading Capital, 1971-72 and 1977-78.[a]

Years	Percent[b] of Women Receiving Capital from:					
	Husband	Mother	Father	Other Relative	Nonrelative	Savings
1971-72[c]	31	32	10	18	19	21
1977-78[d]	42	37	12	15	40	37

[a]These results are quite similar to those of Nypan's survey in 1960. A. Nypan, *Market Trade: A Sample Survey of Market Traders in Accra*, African Business Series No. 2 (University College of Ghana, 1960), p. 31.

[b]These are percentages of answers, which were often multiple.

[c]No. = 72.

[d]No. = 40.

Sanjek, "Notes on Women and Work in Adabraka," *African Urban Notes* II, no. 2 (Spring 1976): 8-10.

persons who extended credit to beginning traders. Only one person patronized a moneylender. In 1977-78, the sample was noticeably younger, and also tended more strongly to get capital from husbands, nonrelatives, and savings, indicating a shift away from dependence on their mothers.

Younger women also tended to start with less capital, as a comparison of age cohorts in the 1971-72 sample shows in Table V-8. Because of inflation the minimum amount went up a bit over the twentieth century, but not nearly as much as the value of money went down, even considering the fact that the youngest women in the group were given the capital they spoke of in the 1940s and early 1950s.[73] Whereas the most common amount of capital which used to be given was £10 or under, after World War II it went up to between £10 and £50. At the same time the maximum amount went down, which may reflect the residential segregation of the wealthier women moving out. The mean average amount of capital given was £26.10 for women 50 and over, and £17.15 for women in their thirties and forties. It now takes more capital to get started, and the indications are that most women are not getting it.[74] This diminution also indicates a weakening of the reciprocal obligations between mother and daughter, possibly caused by a younger marriage age of the daughters, as well as formal education.

Capital is normally given to a girl when she starts trading on her own and no longer has to turn over her profits to her supervisor. For 63% of the women in the 1971-72 small sample this came when they married or bore

Table V-8. Amount and Range of Starting Capital by Age Group.

Age Group[a]	Percent of Women in Age Group with:				Range of Amount[b,c]
	Up to £10	£10.1 to £50	£50.1 to £100	Over £100	
90s & 80s	85	7.5	0	7.5	£1 - £140
70s	60	30	10	0	£1 - £100
60s	58	33	9	0	£2 - £100
50s	50	40	0	10	£1 - £300
40s & 30s	25	63	12	0	£4 - £52
Total %	59	31	6	4	100

[a]No. = 72.

[b]These amounts include the value of capital equipment provided.

[c]F. A. Sai, "Women Traders," background paper for Ghana National Council on Women and Development Seminar on Women and Development (July 1978), 10-11, noted that almost half of her 1969 sample of 57 Makola stallholders started with less than £5, or ₵10, capital.

[73]See Appendix A.

[74]R. Simms and E. Dumor, "Women in the Urban Economy of Ghana: Associational Activity and the Enclave Economy," *African Urban Notes* II, no. 3 (1976-77): 51.

their first child. The society considers them to be adults at that point. Thirty percent of the women, however, only became independent with the death of their mothers. In an extreme case in 1978, a 75-year-old fishseller said that she only had traded independently for the last six years since her mother died. Nonetheless, independence usually came when the woman was in her twenties, although there were a few who were orphaned before they married. Because the women's age at marriage was going down, the women became independent traders at a younger age, with detrimental results for the amount of capital they received. If one combines the age cohorts from the 1971-72 small survey and the 1978 Salaga Market women's survey (compensating for the chronological differences) for a sample number of 104, one finds that the 61 women aged 50 and over in 1971-72 started trading independently at an average age of 25.1, compared to 21.6 for the 43 women in their thirties and forties.[75]

Giving starting capital is viewed as a reward for past services to some extent. If a woman married at age 16 or 18 she stopped being of great service to her mother just at the time she was becoming most valuable, thereby depriving her mother of 5 or 6 years of help.[76] She might have kept on helping her mother unless she went elsewhere with her husband, which sometimes happened, but her small children impaired her effectiveness. Her productivity and profits went down.[77] Thus her mother received fewer profits from her and had less capital with which to reward her.

An adjustment which the women were making to this situation was to expect less capital from their mothers and more from their husbands. In the 1971-72 small sample 49% of the oldest age group (eighties and nineties) said they had expected to get capital from their mothers, compared to only 13.6% of the youngest one (thirties and forties), with diminishing numbers in between. Meanwhile, only 9% of the oldest women expected capital from their husbands, compared to 27.1% of the youngest cohort, with steadily increasing proportions in the intermediate age groups. These expectations mainly conformed to reality, but others did not. In all age groups people expected more help from their other relatives than they actually received, with the discrepancy growing larger as the groups got younger. Also, almost twice as many women thought help should have come from their fathers as actually received any. In fact, women who started in business during or after World War II got less help from their relatives with starting capital

---

[75]The correlation coefficient for this result is .18.

[76]See Chapter VI for an analysis of change in age at marriage.

[77]A U.N. Food and Agriculture Organization (FAO) report, "Market Women in West Africa" (Rome: 1977), p. 11, noted, "Young women rarely exceed small localized trading operations, often of intermittent character, on account of their dominant child raising commitments; while the large-scale long-distance traders usually are grandmothers at the age of 45 or above." N. Sudarkasa, in *Where Women Work: A Study of Yoruba Women in the Marketplace and in the Home*, University of Michigan Museum of Anthropology, Anthropological Paper No. 53 (Ann Arbor: University of Michigan Press, 1973), pp. 147, 156-57, also noted a strikingly similar relationship of trading activities to the life cycle.

than those who started earlier, as Nypan's findings support.[78] The abandon-
ment of reciprocal obligations in giving capital, then, is probably harming
not only extended family relationships, but also mother-daughter ones. Formal education, because it facilitated marriage at a younger age, as well as
diminished the trading input of young women, negatively affected the giving
of starting capital.

The reduction in mother-daughter cooperation is also reflected in the
attitudes of the established traders, as well as those of their daughters, where
again the impact of formal education was evident. In the 1971-72 small survey 57% of the traders wanted their daughters to take over after them,
while 46% reported that the daughters had. In 1978, 44% of the Salaga
traders wanted their daughters to trade. This desire did not necessarily
correlate with the amount of capital invested.[79] The women in 1971-72 who
did not want their daughters to continue with their business, some 20%,
often cited unprofitability as a reason. Others said that *an educated girl like
her should not do petty trading like I did.* Of the 44% of the Salaga traders
in 1978 who did not want their daughters to trade, most (65%) cited this
reason, followed distantly (18%) by profitability concerns. Education might
not only remove the desire on the part of the daughter to trade, but also the
pressure from the mother for her to do so.

*   *   *   *   *

Since formal education in its current form was neither significantly helping the schoolgirls' trading experience or knowledge, nor providing skills
likely to land them a job, it was of questionable use. Formal education has
taken away the benefits of full-time apprenticeship without substituting
those of a full-time job for a group which must be self-supporting. Weis
stated, "the very expansion of educational opportunities for females [in
Ghana] may, paradoxically, mean circumscribed options in the economy."[80]
It was, rather, helping to dissolve the cement which held together the chief
survival mechanism for women, the cooperation of mothers and daughters in
production and marketing. In terms of our original definition of labor control as a source of wealth and power, women were losing the capability of
recruiting labor. Two logical consequences ensued from this; both were
means of deriving financial help from men, especially elite men. First, there
was an increase in prostitution (without pimps) and informal liaisons with
wealthy men. Such practices have become acceptable, desirable means of
supporting oneself and educating one's children, while not-so-wealthy men

---

[78]A. Nypan, *Market Trade: A Sample Survey of Market Traders in Accra*, University of
Ghana African Business Series No. 2 (1960), p. 35.

[79]Sai, in "Market Woman," p. 63, found that just under half of the traders she interviewed in Makola No. 1 wanted one of their apprentices to take over after them, usually
their daughters. It was the more prosperous traders who desired it because of the capital involved.

[80]Weis, "Women," p. 446.

can at least supply subsistence needs.[81] Second, economic independence will
be sacrificed by those who can achieve it to the perceived higher status and
greater security of coresidence in a suburb with a white collar employee as
husband. Both strategies increased women's dependence on men, but the
first appeared more desirable because women retained more autonomy and
the security of the life in the suburbs was questionable. Therefore, formal
education, which might reduce inequality, was not doing so for these women.
Instead, it was reinforcing their subordinate position.

> We are dealing in books.
> The European
> Has brought stories.
> We are dealing in books.
> The European
> Has brought stories.
> We went, we did not understand;
> We came, we did not understand.
> Ga *kple* song[82]

A Women's Compound

[81]Both Bujra and Obbo have noted in East Africa the benefit of economic independence
that accrues to urban women with prostitution. J. M. Bujra, "Women 'Entrepreneurs' of
Early Nairobi," *Canadian Journal of African Studies* IX, no. 2 (1975): 215; C. Obbo, *African
Women, Their Struggle for Economic Independence* (London: Zed Press, 1980), pp. 105-06.

[82]M. Kilson, *Kpele Lala* (Cambridge: Harvard University Press, 1971), p. 269.

Portrait 3

NAA AFUWA

A Market Pharmacopoeia

Naa Afuwa is a medium-sized woman with a force of personality which makes her seem larger than she actually is. Her appearance is quite striking, in particular because she has a number of scars on her face. Her dynamism comes out in her busy life spent trading in fish, acting as a spirit medium,[1] and generally performing an important role in the community. There is no doubt that she is one of those unusual women who has achieved a level of importance in lineage affairs equal to that of a prominent man. Through her various activities she has become fairly well off, though it seems not to have changed her life style at all. She was the most prosperous woman in 1971-72 among the small sample.

She lives in a dark room belonging to the god off of a small courtyard in a rather anomalous compound inhabited by Ga and non-Ga tenants as well as some of her relatives. A constant stream of visitors waits to see her, and the interviews were always being interrupted by them. She was, however, very willing to keep talking and did not allow herself to be sidetracked. She talked to the point always, and did not ramble. Her comments were always intelligent; interviewing her was one of the more interesting experiences of my stay in Ghana. At our request she gave us some of the details of cases which had been brought to her recently. This account is based on eight interviews done in 1972, when she was in her late fifties.

---

[1]For a full description of the functions of Ga spirit mediums see M. Kilson, "Ritual Portrait of a Ga Medium," in *The New Religions of Africa*, ed. B. Jules-Rosette (Norwood, N.J.: Ablex, 1979), pp. 67-79, and M. J. Field, *Religion and Medicine of the Ga People* (Accra: Presbyterian Book Depot, 1937).

Childhood (circa 1914 to 1928)

The household in which I grew up was composed of my mother and father and my sisters and brothers. We all lived at Faana fishing villages west of Accra. My mother's mother also played an important role in the household. My mother was living with her at Kele when she married my father and moved to Fadziemohe, another of the villages. When I was somewhat grown I was sent to stay with her at Kele. She was always ready to give me advice and correct my manners. Later when she moved to Accra I came with her. My mother was quiet and soft-spoken. She was very hardworking and always busy with fishsmoking at one stage or another. She shared the same house with my father at Fadziemohe. Whenever any of the children got into trouble she would always, no matter who was the cause of it, try to make a peaceful settlement. My father, on the other hand, was a strict disciplinarian, especially with me since I was more than a son to him. He was more lenient with the boys, who were all younger than we girls. I was the third-born child of my mother, but the first one to survive infancy. The first two, a boy and a girl, died as babies. Because of this I was given these scars to make me ugly so the god would not take me too. A spirit medium performed the ceremony. That god had to be pacified when I became a spirit medium for this god.

As a small child I was like any other child, playing, eating, and whiling away the time doing what I pleased. When I had passed the toddler stage I became more active. I remember when our fathers used to go fishing; at their return we would go to the beach taking along small baskets and beg as many fish as we could. These we took home and gave to our mothers who would sell them for us. We also played games. The most common one was mock trading; we pretended that the beach sand was maize and the pebbles or pieces of paper were money. When I was about six the influenza came. My mother told me that I was the only one in the house who did not get it.

As I grew older I became tough; I was a tomboy. Many girls my age were frightened of me because I was very good at fighting (and still am). You see, my mother took a long time to conceive again after having me so my father said that I would take the place of the boy who had died. He therefore introduced me to the fishing business and taught me swimming, paddling, and how to mend nets. When the Sakumɔ Lagoon was calm he would take me out and teach me to paddle a canoe. Then we would have the swimming lesson. First he would get in the water and give me a demonstration, then he got back in the canoe and I would go in while he watched me to be sure I did not drown. Eventually I learned not only women's type of swimming, where one uses chiefly the legs, but also men's swimming using the arms. He even taught me how to rescue a drowning person, that one should always go behind them in the water to avoid being seized in panic so that you both drown. For all of these activities I wore pants instead of cloth.

But I also did women's chores as a child. My mother taught me to perform simple household tasks. I used to go with people from our village,

Fadziemohe, to Botianɔ to grind corn. We had no mills then. Fadziemohe is one of the group of villages we call Faana which is west of Tsokor. Going west from Tsokor you have the Faana villages in this order: Gbegbe, Akoteman, Glife, Wiaman, Kele, Mpemihuasem, ʃiayena, Wiɛdzoʃiʃi, Fadziemohe, then you cross the river [Densu] and get to Botianɔ, Oshiyie, and lastly, Kokrobite. In the olden days Faana was the main fishing center for Accra people. Tema is only important now because of the new harbor and the cold storage facilities.

Several bad things happened to me in my childhood, but by my intelligence and action I made them not as bad as they might have been. Once I was out with three other girls paddling on the lagoon when the canoe capsized. I righted the canoe while the others were struggling in the water and one of the girls, Obiɔkɔ, who was also a swimmer, climbed back into it while I rescued another of them. By the time I went to rescue the last girl she was wild with panic. I went under her in the water intending to lift her up above it but she clutched at my neck and shoved me deeper in the water. I let us go down further so that I managed, with some difficulty, to release her hold and surface, but I had to leave her. We paddled back to the village to report what had happened. A search party was sent out and they recovered her body, which was sent to Accra.

I was also witness to another drowning incident. Two boys and myself went to Aplaku, a nearby village, for water from the Humɔ. The water there is good for drinking. We used to gather it in canoes in the following manner. You took a good one without leaks and capsized it, then righted it almost filled with water. Then you paddled it downstream to Kele, pulled ashore and people collected the water. That day when I went with the two boys we each of us had a canoe. When we had filled the canoes and righted them we noticed that one boy was missing. We raised the alarm and people came running to the river bank. A message was sent and a search party quickly formed and went into the water. They searched for over an hour before they found his body caught in a thicket of water weeds near Kele.

The worst thing that happened, though, had to do with a younger sister who was about two years old. She suffered from asthma. One morning about sunup when my mother was away and my father had gone fishing I was alone looking after her. At that time I was about thirteen or so. She had an attack of convulsions. I rushed her to an herbalist in our village, who treated her. I returned home with her; she appeared to be asleep. I put her in bed and went to prepare *akasa* [corn porridge] for her. When next I went into my father's room to feed her she was dead. To die at Fadziemohe was forbidden. If a sick person is failing fast then he or she is rushed out of Fadziemohe to Kele or Botianɔ. In those days dead persons were buried heavily wrapped in cloth and tied up in a mat. Her dying like that was a tragic situation that had to be remedied. So I pretended that she was alive but sinking rapidly. I put her on my back and quickly crossed to the northern bank. When I got to Botianɔ I started screaming that my sister was dead. All of this happened within the space of about two hours. When my father returned he praised me for my courage. After her funeral I was cleansed by a rite involving slaughtering two chickens.

But there were happy times too. I particularly liked Christmastime as a child because we stayed at home at Faana. Hɔmɔwɔ was not as much fun because we had to go to Accra where we children were scattered among our families in different parts of town. But I got more presents at Hɔmɔwɔ. We would go to Accra for about two months before going back to Faana.

Puberty (circa 1928)

Another time I remember with pleasure was my coming-of-age celebration. My head was shaved clean and I was dressed richly to go about town visiting relatives and thanking acquaintances who had participated in the rites. Wherever I went people commented openly on my beautiful features. The ceremony and visiting were an advertisement to all that I had achieved marriageable age. I received many presents.

What went on before that was not so pleasant, however. When I found blood oozing from my private parts I was badly frightened. I showed my mother and she took me to the bathing room, got a pad for me, and showed me how to use it. She told me that it was called *yei anii* [literally, "women's thing"], and that it happened to every woman at a certain age. I had it for a week; when it stopped my mother boiled three eggs for me to eat. She invited me indoors and told me that a rite had to be performed for me, and that it was forbidden for a girl to conceive before its performance. She therefore warned me to keep away from sexual intercourse since I could conceive once I had had my first menstrual period.

Perhaps I should explain more about this rite. When a child falls ill frequently she is brought to the god here and given to it for protection--physical and spiritual. When she gets older--either before or after the menses--or even after her marriage occasionally, her head is shaved to show that she is being given a new personality free from the service of the god. The spirit medium in authority will charge £20 as an initial fee, to be paid by the parents of an unmarried girl or the husband of a bride. Every hair on her head is shaved off in the room where the god is; the hair is then tied up in white calico and placed under the stool of the god. The girl's body is smeared with white clay for good luck, and she is confined to the god's room for a full week. The only people permitted in during this time are the priestess and the bringer of food. After a week she is brought out into the courtyard and seated on a stool in the presence of her maternal and paternal relatives, friends and well-wishers, all gathered together for the ceremony. The candidate then dances three times and is subsequently adorned with many strings of beads which are tied to her wrists, elbows, knees, ankles, etc. She is bathed and from that time on pomade instead of white clay is applied to her body. She is dressed in rich *kente* cloth[2] and, shaded by a parasol,

---

[2]A beautiful heavy expensive handwoven cloth with geometric designs, which is Akan in origin.

goes forth to parade around the town expressing thanks to all well-wishers. It may take two or three days to complete this walk. At the end three sheep are brought, one for the confinement, one for the outdooring, and the third to be slaughtered for a feast. Fish is never to be eaten by the girl on that day. By the time the whole thing is over £40 or £50 will have been spent.

These customs are not obsolete. Just three days ago two girls and a boy were outdoored in this way. There is another custom called Otsentsi performed annually shortly after Hɔmɔwɔ for the god Dzafro-Otu. In it initiates are sent to the beach and pelted with balls of white sand. They go on a circuitous route to the beach past the entries to the groves and sanctuaries of a number of gods. From the beach they go to confinement for a week. People of all ages can have the rite done. When they are outdoored they also are dressed in *kente* but females wear a special headdress. They also parade thanking well-wishers. There is also another rite called Ayoobri.

All of these rites are Fanti in origin. My own ancestors who came down with the god were from Fantiland. It is difficult today to find a full-blooded Ga. The ancient people settled here and intermarried with other groups so that I would say that every Ga has either Fanti, Twi, Ewe or Ada blood. Intermarriage has gone on for so long that you cannot speak of a pure Ga today.

As a child, the adult I liked the most was my mother's sister. I imitated her as much as I could and she gave me much of my training. She would give me things like cloth when my mother was reluctant to do so. So when I became an adolescent I went with my aunt to help her. She was also in the fish trade, but she did not marry a fisherman. Rather she chose a health inspector who was transferred to Koforidua. She trained me in the chores of a clerk's household. When I finished the housework I was taught to go neatly dressed to the market. Before selling I changed into another cloth. She set me a good example, and I developed a disgust for unhealthy habits. It was there that I had my first menstrual period.[3]

Marriage (circa 1934 to 1972)

My father was very strict about my associating with men. He would beat me if he caught me plaiting my hair before I was betrothed. He also destroyed the hairdo roughly. Once I was impolite to a friend of his. We had gone to Nyenyenaa to inaugurate a drumming troupe; he was with some of his friends. A young man told him that he thought I was very beautiful and that he would like to marry me. The mention of the word "marry" led to my swearing at that man. My father became so incensed that he grabbed a length of rope right then and beat me so hard that he lacerated the skin.

Eventually, after many of my friends had already married, my father gave me to a fisherman to marry. My father came to Koforidua and asked

---

[3]When speaking of her "mother," while discussing her first menses, she was probably referring to her mother's sister.

me to return to Accra without explaining why. When I did he introduced the young man to me as a respectable and hardworking member of his fishing crew whom he would like me to marry. I refused. Because of my stay at Koforidua I wanted to marry a literate. But he beat me for refusing, so I changed my mind and resigned myself to his choice. The man married me in the full traditional way and also reimbursed my parents for the cost of the hair-shaving rite. After the ceremonies were over in Accra I was sent to my husband at Faana. We shared the same compound with his parents. In time I got pregnant. When my stomach was well developed I went to Accra to have a clinical examination. I was sent home as they said it was not time yet for me to deliver. That same day I gave birth to my first child at home. It had a rich growth of hair which delighted everyone.

Since my father had given me to the man I grew to love him. I was convinced that my father would not put me in a bad situation. As it turned out the man was nice to me and maintained me well. As man and wife there were naturally times when we quarreled but they were not serious. Our first quarrel was in connection with selling fish. Customarily if a fisherman offers his fish for sale at, say, 100 for five shillings, his wife would pay four shillings for it. But once when the fish were particularly large and fine my husband wanted more for them. We quarreled and he finally had to beat me. Beating your wife was accepted in that Faana community.

The second quarrel related to my being possessed by the god. He was not in favor of my becoming a priestess because he thought that I would be distracted from my duties as wife and mother. So he went with me to a village to perform a ceremony to save me from the god. I left him there, came back to Accra, and reported what had happened to my family. When my husband returned an argument developed over why I had left the village without telling him. Blows were exchanged over it. But eventually he resigned himself to it. He invoked the god which demanded a pacification fee from my husband for marrying one who is the wife of another person. This was two times 32 shillings, one sheep and drinks--the same as the adultery fine. He paid it before I was taken away to undergo training.

My first husband was dark-skinned like I am; we were about equal in height so that when we were out walking we looked like brother and sister. He was kind and generous to me and I was submissive to him. We understood each other. The happiest times were the outdoorings of our children. My husband was happy with my work. He acknowledged it as a joint venture in the interest of our marriage. There were even times when the fish were so numerous that he had to lend a helping hand with the fishsmoking. After all, it was the fish trade which supported all of us. His contribution to the household support was generally greater than mine, but when he was unable to work I provided meals from my own earnings. He therefore encouraged me to work so I would be better able to help. That was generally the way we lived at Faana since there was nothing like a monthly pay packet in the fishing community. He did not give me money, just fish.

We were not always at Faana, however. Sometimes we would stay in Accra--at Hɔmɔwɔ at our own family houses instead of together. I think I prefer it here. If you live together with your husband you feel ill at ease. When you go and see him occasionally it is better.

Nowadays things are different in marriage. We lived by our joint contributions and efforts, but women now want men to provide everything. Quarrels used to be settled by the families of the couple. Men were better about supporting their children. Now many men do not support their wives properly, and many women are unfaithful, even priestesses [spirit mediums]. They are greedy and want money. Now when the men fail to support their children, their wives go to the Social Welfare Department for redress instead of to the husband's family. But divorce cases still usually go to the Maŋtsɛ's courts. Sometimes I help settle disputes too.

I was married to my first husband for a long time. We had nine children. He took two more wives after I married him. But one day he saw me talking to another man and sent me away. That was the end of the marriage. After a while I married again, this time against the wishes of my family because the man did not do the marriage ceremony for me. My first husband paid money for the hair-shaving rite, plus £24, two bottles of schnapps and two dozen bottles of minerals; it was a six-cloth marriage.[4] He was from Gbese and about three years older than I was. He paid the money from his own earnings. He is dead now. But my second husband only did afayinodaa, the minimal door-knocking fee, which was £8 and drinks. He is a mason from Ŋleʃi and lives at Korle Gonno. He had three wives before I married him. But I have not slept with him for over a year now because he has not performed the pacification ceremony for marrying a priestess. A sickness attacked me, and a diviner told my mother's family that it was because my husband had not paid the adultery fine [to her god]. A message was sent to him telling him to pay it, but he asked for a month's grace before paying and never did it. My family has called on him many times to do it but with no success. I will not go to him unless he does it, or serious consequences might ensue.

The main reason I married was to have children. A woman must marry. Both of my husbands had girlfriends besides their wives. I did not like that because they gave money to them instead of to us [the wives]. A man should only have one wife and they should love each other. I trusted my first husband more than the second one because he took good care of me and the children. As a good husband should, he paid hospital and school fees, and for the funerals of the ones who died.

Childrearing (circa 1935 to 1972)

I was satisfied with the number of children I had, nine, but only four are alive now. My first husband was the father of them all. After a birth I would stay away from him for four months or so. I would usually nurse the child for maybe six months. Formerly it was popular to have big families.

---

[4]A full ceremonial Ga marriage (see below Chapter VI).

Today the cost of living alone should convince us that having big families is nothing but a bore. So, some of us use family planning, which is not new to our traditional medicine. If a couple approaches a priestess or herbalist with the request, there are herbs which can be given to stop procreation.

I not only took care of my nine children, but also of ten others belonging to my sister and brother. Two of my children died when they were infants, two as older children, and one as an adult. My husband and I took care of the children. Mostly I watched them, but occasionally he did. He provided most of the necessities for them. One son went to my husband's father who raised him and sent him to school. One daughter went to my younger sister at Hohoi and then moved around with her to Kumasi and Akyem Oda. I taught them proper behavior. When they misbehaved I beat them. But I did not do anything in particular if they were good. Sometimes when they ignored my advice it made me laugh, for by that they showed how inexperienced they were. I found it tiresome constantly saying "do this" or "do not do that." I remember being particularly angry with one of them once. I had asked my fourth son to go get some fish from his father to be used for the meal I was preparing. He refused to go because he said he was hungry. I grabbed him and beat him mercilessly. His skin was cut in a number of places. One eyelid was damaged. After the beating I put medicine on the wounds.

Only one of my children went to school, the sixth-born. The others all wanted to fish and so it was, even though I wanted them to go to school. The one who went to school started while he was staying with me, but then he went to stay with a female cousin of his father. One Christmas vacation he came to stay with us at Faana. He was in Standard 6 at that time. He went to the beach when they were dragging a fishing net ashore. His interest was attracted by a guitar fish [stingray?] in the net. Ignorant as he was, he went and grabbed hold of the fish which stung his hand. He started yelling and people rushed to see what was wrong. We did what we could for him for five days or so, and then sent him to Dr. Bannerman's clinic when we noticed that his face was turning blue. We came back from the clinic with him but by the following day he was dead. His father purchased the coffin and paid the funeral expenses. I was broken-hearted at his death, so much so that I almost went insane. For, my only child who was literate, whom I had hoped would educate me, was lost. His death and that of my mother are the worst things that have happened to me so far in my life.

Now I am taking care of some of my grandchildren who stay here with me. Their father is in town but he has proved himself to be irresponsible, so I am their sole guardian. I am strict with them; if they disobey they get the cane. The girls I invite indoors and tell them not to allow any man to lure them into mating. At night they have to stay in the house and go to bed early. I tell young mothers who come to me to do the same thing with their children. But above all I advise them to be patient and tolerant with the children, speak softly, and never molest them.

Work

I started work by helping my mother with the fish trade. She was selling my father's catch. This was when I was about eight or ten years old, before the Prince of Wales came [to Accra in 1925]. As I got older my mother gave me money to buy fish to smoke and sell. When there was a good catch she would give me maybe £10 to buy some. In this way I accumulated enough profits to start on my own when I got married, which is the usual custom. When I lived at Koforidua I sold jewelry for my aunt and also fish for my mother. When I started on my own I would buy maybe two to four thousand fish a day, early in the morning, and smoke them all day. The next day I would send them by lorry to my partners in Koforidua and Suhum. I also had a partner here. They were all Ga friends of mine. We would split the profits equally at Hɔmɔwɔ when we made our yearly accounting. What would happen is that throughout the year we kept track of the position by using corn kernels which were sent along with the baskets of fish to my partners to indicate its price. She would then add and subtract kernels to keep an account of her transactions with the fish, a separate account for each person with whom she dealt. My partner knew which fish to take from the lorry because I would tie a piece of cotton print to the baskets to identify them.

I sent the fish up every day in season, but only two times a week or so when the catches were small. I bought the fish at the shore at Faana. My father had a canoe and net and I got some from him at a reduced price, but I mainly bought from anyone who would sell cheaply. We did it as a credit arrangement, and every Tuesday we made accounts. I bought any kind of fish from different fishermen. The fishermen were named according to the kind of net they used, for example, *poliwole* for one who used a *poli* net, and so on through the other kinds of nets. I got the fish in large basins from the beach, smoked it, and hired porters to carry it to Accra for dispatch upcountry.

If a woman is lazy she cannot be a successful wife at Faana. My husband was pleased with my industry. I made a fair profit, but not as much as I get from being a priestess. Since fish decomposes easily and there is much competition in the market, I find that the best strategy is to minimize your per unit profit to outsell your competitors and achieve a fast turnover. That way in the end you get more customers and more profits. Now I have a canoe and a fishing crew who fish for me. Sometimes they return from the sea empty-handed. As an employer I must provide them with money to tide them and their families over. This is, of course, given against further catches. It is a worrisome responsibility sometimes. I also buy fish now in boxes and resell it to someone who lives here. I no longer send it upcountry. Now my daughter is carrying on with the fish trade.

As a fisherman's wife you cannot abandon the fish trade, but you can take on some other lines as well. For example, I also owned a small provisions shop and dealt in various goods such as *gari* [cassava flour], sardines, sugar, etc. Later I introduced beer, wine, and then *akpeteʃi* [locally distilled liquor]. No one had ever sold it before at Faana. It was illegal. We used to get it at Bajwiase and bury the drums in the ground to prevent detection. The policemen at that time [circa 1937-1942] who harassed the *akpeteʃi* sellers the most were Sergeants Tsutsubi and Kanjaga. At first it seemed as if they had a medicine which helped them to detect where the *akpeteʃi* was buried. We therefore got a counteracting medicine which confounded theirs. I was doing so well that I could easily pay the fine when I was caught. Once they confiscated forty tins of my *akpeteʃi* and fined me £60; I paid it on the spot. I even built a house with my profits. When *akpeteʃi* selling was legalized I bought a license for £5 and sold it from this house. But while possessed by the god it told me that it detested *akpeteʃi*, so I had to stop.

Another profitable endeavor also got me into trouble with the police. In the interwar years Accra was a port with many ships calling to discharge and load again. Then there came the torpedoing of the M. V. Sangara at Accra [May 10, 1940]. I was then a mother living at Faana and would come to Accra to get goods from the boat to sell. The Sangara had grounded and was half filled with water. At night fishermen would steal out to it. Taking along a hook and line, a diver would find his way into the hatch and hook a cargo which would be pulled up onto the deck by the rest of the gang. It would then be lowered down into a canoe and the crew paddled away and landed far from Accra to sell the goods and then returned. Many people were imprisoned for participating in this trade. I was caught and sent to court on two occasions for being in possession of smuggled goods from the Sangara, once it was wax prints. But like during the *akpeteʃi* days I was very well-to-do and could pay any fines outright to obtain my freedom. Some other people like myself got wealthy and a few put up buildings from the profits of this trade.

The main occupations I follow now are making *banku* and being a priestess. It is really the latter from which I get most of my income. I charge people four shillings if the god does not enter me and twelve shillings if it does. Many people come to me, usually one or two a day, and at Hɔmɔwɔ, two or three, since the evil spirits come out at that time. After I have cured someone they spread the word and that is how I get clients. Many people ask me to call their souls, cure a sick child or venereal disease, or promote fertility. Some illnesses are caused by witchcraft. The god tells me whether or not the witch has almost killed the person; if so, I do not even charge them the usual £10. Some women have *odeepnu* disease [a vaginal infection, perhaps venereal disease]; right now I am trying to cure a woman of it. I also diagnose and cure fever [usually malaria]. Spiritual church members often come here to find out what ails them. I help traders to make a profit again if they have been losing money. Sometimes when someone seems to be dying or has convulsions, I send the person to Korle Bu [Hospital] so that the doctor can sign [the death certificate] for him.

I know full well that at certain stages of some diseases patients should be referred to scientific medicine for treatment. Once I myself even rushed a baby with convulsions to the hospital. The mother had thought it was too late in the night to take her. By the following day at 5 A.M. the child was so much improved that she was discharged. The father of the baby gave me a guinea [£1.1] for that. Anyway, if the patient lives beyond the hospital visit then I will treat him with my medicines. Sometimes I do not need to make a divination for common ailments which I recognize immediately.

The god called me after I had borne my sixth child. I did not want to become a priestess but the god would not let me alone. You see, the three former incumbents of this priesthood were male and died young, so this time the god chose me, a female. It is a family god which comes from my paternal great-grandfather's side of the family. Only his descendant can be the resident of the god's house here. When I realized that I had to become a priestess I went for training to a "master" priestess. From her I gained much knowledge of herbal medicine, and over the years I have also added to it by my personal experience. During invocation the god prescribes the herbs for a particular ailment; that is the source of knowledge. I also learned how to deal with patients. In my state as a normal person I first talk sympathetically with the patient and affirm that with the god's blessing on the medicines the sickness will clear up in time. When I am possessed, of course, I am not conscious of what transpires around me. I do not know what the spirit says. It talks to those who wish to contact it. After the spirit has left me and I have regained consciousness I will divine what the spirit has said from the small pot which sits at the foot of the god, or the relatives [of the one whose spirit was called] may tell me. When I prescribe herbal remedies I use those I have gathered myself, which is part of our ritual, whatever the god has told me to get.

Women can become priestesses at any age if they are called. If a woman is still young enough to menstruate then she must go at that time to stay at her mother's house so as not to pollute the god and ruin the medicines. Afterwards she should kill a fowl to cleanse herself. The fowl's blood is mixed with sea water and an egg, which she uses to bathe herself. Then she can return to the shrine. Marriage with a priestess is also unique in some respects. The door-knocking fee is higher and then there is the pacification rite a husband must perform. It becomes very expensive.

I see you are interested in hearing about some of my cases. That may be the best way to understand what I do. Last week a pregnant woman who had been having pains came to me for help. I gave her a daily massage early each morning until she finally delivered safely at the hospital. When I help at a delivery I charge a guinea and a fowl for the blood which has soiled my hands. But since this woman delivered at hospital I only charged twelve shillings, a fowl, and a half bottle of drink. Also the young daughter of an Anglican priest was brought to me with convulsions early in the morning. I successfully treated her and by daybreak she was fully conscious again. I charge one goat, thirty-two shillings and one bottle of *akpeteʃi* for that, the usual convulsion-curing fee. But since goat is taboo for my god I substitute two big fowls. I did not do a divination in either case since I knew what to do from experience.

Yesterday two elderly women came to find out the cause of an illness which had attacked a relation. I divined and the soul of the invalid came to talk to the women. They should be back Tuesday with the things I prescribed for a rite to be performed to help the patient regain her appetite and eat again. We discovered that her soul was aggrieved because, although she had had ten children with her husband, he had refused to congratulate her by slaughtering a sheep as Ga custom requires. So she has stopped eating. The soul said that a sheep, fowls, four changes of cloth, and some money were required for a sacrifice.

Today some others came to invoke the spirit of a dead relative. The man had willed his house to some of his children leaving others no legacies, and they wanted to know why. His soul explained that the children of one of his three wives had ignored him while he was sick, while the others had cared for him. The third wife's children were the ones who came to me; they had been quarrelling with him which is why they had ignored him. When they clearly understood their father's point of view they wept a lot.

Another woman came to me to invoke the spirit of her brother. He was a mason who fell from a building at work and injured his arm badly. They treated him at Korle Bu but the arm withered. So he was pensioned off by his employers and used to pick up work at the beach helping the fishermen to drag in the nets with one arm. He was awarded compensation of £800 for his injury with which he intended to build a house to give him some income. He went with a friend to pick up the money and the friend cheated him by manipulating it so that he only got £200, taking the rest of it for himself. The mason's soul was so offended and aggrieved by the cheat that the mason died. At the invocation the soul identified the cheat, so the mason's family is going to try to retrieve the money from him.

A pregnant woman came, upset because the baby does not seem to be developing properly. I gave her a medicine for it. Sometimes a woman is not having her menses so she knows that she is pregnant but the stomach does not grow. In such a case the "old men" [the gods] will be consulted to reveal whether or not something has gone wrong. That is their mission.

Sometimes too a woman will have severe labor pains and the baby will not come. This is because she has been unfaithful to her husband and the baby is not his. If she confesses her adultery she will then deliver. In traditional treatment we insist on the confession, but medical science gives no value to that. All they care about is the fee. Today surgery is saving women from having to confess their infidelity. In a way, it is encouraging prostitution.

My status is almost like that of a *maŋtsɛ*. I have at this time been adjudicating a case where a mulatto woman borrowed £4 from a blind person. The blind man knew her. She refused to repay it and, to add insult to injury, abused him verbally. So the man brought the case to the god to achieve repayment. I sent word to the debtor to bring the money. She will also have to pay a pacification fine of thirty-two shillings, one fowl and a bottle of drink. If she does not she will be killed by the gods, and after her death her relatives will still have to pay the pacification fine, lest they be harmed also. But at that point it would cost them more: £14, one sheep, twelve yards each of calico, red cotton material, and wax print, twelve cloths used for menstrual pads, seven eggs, and two bottles of schnapps.

Last weekend was very busy. A man came to invoke his own soul. He had a disease which was not getting any better. He was shown a cleansing rite to be performed. I will do it tomorrow. A person came whose child was killed by a lorry. He wanted a rite to be performed to free the soul of the boy from the scene of the accident where he died. The rite requires one sheep, three times thirty-two shillings, one bottle each of schnapps and *akpeteʃi*, two fowls, two yards of white calico, palm fronds and raffia. All the things are tied up in the calico, then wrapped in the palm fronds. The bundle is taken to the place of the death and placed there, then dragged homeward three times. Then the sheep and fowls will be slaughtered and the blood sprinkled about the place; all of this frees the soul or spirit of the dead person so that it can then visit its former home. The meat of the sacrifices is all for me as the performer of the rite. The people will not expect to have any of the meat but you can give them some.

During Hɔmɔwɔ and Christmas people usually come to me so that I will invoke the spirits of the dead whose funeral rites or thanksgiving service days are drawing near. Another common request is the invocation of the souls of twins. Some people want their souls invoked because they have been losing money and want to know the cause; others feel bodily weak. Some want to know the cause of the death of a relative. Some pregnant women come because they have a light flow of blood monthly and want to know why. Yes, many people need my services.

I have become well-to-do through my various occupations. Of course, there was the occasional disaster, such as when I carelessly failed to put out the fire completely and it reignited feeding on the pile of fresh fuel nearby. All of the fuel burned along with a full drum of kenkey worth £8. But generally I did pretty well; soon after my marriage when I moved into my husband's house I was able to put up a four-roomed wooden structure. I was really making a lot then. There was a break when I went for priestess training for three years. Sixteen years ago I returned from that and in the subsequent four years I got rich. I was having at least four callers a day then. A decline followed, but starting two years ago the tide reversed itself again for the better. Now I even lend money occasionally to people, but I never borrow it. I charge 50% interest a month except for a relative or husband; then it is only 30%.

Through trade I became well off. As the eldest child I helped my juniors. I bought a canoe and gave it to my two brothers at Faana to manage. Of my two sisters I sent one to school but had to withdraw her because she was a dullard. I therefore set her up in business with capital; she has been dealing mostly in imported food items. Occasionally she gives me some of her profits, but I did not expect her to return the capital as such. She contributed to my fees for initiation into the priesthood, so to all intents and purposes she has more than refunded the capital. Thus we have fulfilled our mutual obligations. I am content.

VI

SOCIAL ASPECTS OF DEPRIVATION:

CHANGE IN MARRIAGE AND

DEPENDENCY PATTERNS, HELP FROM

DISPERSED FAMILY MEMBERS

The declining socioeconomic status of Central Accra Ga women is shown, not only in the conditions of their trading, but also in changes in their marital and dependency patterns. While marriage is becoming a less formal arrangement providing less security, the dependency burden on able-bodied women is growing heavier. In fact, change in marriage and dependency patterns, and relationships with residentially dispersed family members, are forcing women to bear a disproportionate share of the burden of family support, while education and the economic situation eliminate options other than trading. These factors are reinforcing the disadvantages of female autonomy and creating a dominantly female underclass.

The Fragility of Marriage

As in most societies, so in Central Accra marriage is not a choice but a social necessity. This has not changed. What has changed is the form that marriage takes. In Central Accra Ga society there have been large variations in forms of marriage for as long as can be determined. Differentiation according to social status in forms of marriage has probably been evident to some extent in Ga society as long as it has been socially and economically differentiated. The processes of residential segregation by social status and declining economic status accordingly were manifested in change in the forms of marriage used in Accra. Raymond Smith, in examining Guyanese village society, found that "common-law marriage becomes a symbol of class differentiation."[1] So it is in Central Accra. One judge, who refused to become embroiled in a long-winded court dispute of the kind which commonly arose when the validity of marriages was tested, stated in exasperation, "It is clear that by [Ga] custom there are wide variations in the way that marriage may be carried out, depending generally upon the

---

[1] R. T. Smith, *The Negro Family in British Guiana* (London: Routledge and Kegan Paul, Ltd., 1956), p. 181.

circumstances of the parties and their position in life, and that the requisites of a valid marriage are in fact extremely simple."[2] In the twentieth century socioeconomic differentiation has been expressed in a shift from elaborate to simple forms of marriage, which entail more economic independence for women.

In the late nineteenth and early twentieth century high status marriage in Ga society was mainly arranged for alliance purposes, to further the economic or political goals of the patrilineages. Such marriages involved elaborate negotiations, which commenced when the man sent a small sum of money and/or drink, called *weku daa*, "family drink," to the girl's parents; if they accepted it negotiations for the marriage were opened. The next step was (and is) called ʃibimɔ, which was composed of four or five different payments called *agboʃimɔ* ("door-knocking"), *kplemɔ* or *nkpɛle* ("consent"), *nyɛ ʃa moŋbo* and *tsɛ ʃa moŋbo* (giving the bride's parents cloth to replace those she dirtied as a baby), *hɛnɔbotoo* ("clothing the waist"), and *bladzo*, or *fotoli*, the fee for the girl's puberty rite.[3] These were separate payments made at different times, and parents could break off marriage negotiations by refusing to accept one of them. Next, *ga woo*, a further payment of money and drink, was sent. Lastly, *gblanii*, *sɛɛnii* or *yinii* ("marriage things"), was performed. It entailed by far the largest amount of money and drinks. Because one of the gifts involved was six cloths, a woman married by the full rite was often called *boi ekpaa yoo*, a "six-cloth woman." *Gblanii* was sometimes called *kpeemɔ* ("gathering") because it was ended by a ceremonial escorting of the bride by her female relatives to her husband's house. The culmination of the full marriage ceremony was the blessing by a priest of Ga religion and the *maŋtsɛ*. After this the richly dressed bride was carried around the town on the shoulders of her female relatives, or in a cart, and shown to the populace.[4]

A full marriage not only involved more ceremony, but also more obligations on the part of the two partners and their lineages, but especially for the women. The people arranging the marriage were very careful about the choice of a spouse. Thus a high status lineage would only accept a high status wealthy man who was willing to make their daughter his most favored wife by performing all of the customs for her. That usually meant she was his first wife. In return he expected her to be a virgin,[5] and sometimes proof of virginity was required. Cruickshank in 1853 said that the husband could

---

[2]SCT 2/6/18, pp. 177-81 (case May 8, 1934), decision written by Judge Deane.

[3]A. A. Amartey, personal communication, March 26, 1973; J. M. Bruce-Myers, "The Connubial Institutions of the Gas," *Journal of the African Society* XXX, no. 121 (Oct. 1931): 402; Alhaji Mohammed Makwei Laryea, personal communication, Feb. 18, 1978. Male puberty rites did not exist, and girls' puberty rites have become obsolete in Central Accra. They did not involve clitoridectomy.

[4]C. C. Reindorf, *The History of the Gold Coast and Asante* (ca. 1890; reprint ed., Accra: Ghana Universities Press, 1966), p. 45. Interview with the Ga Maŋtsɛ Nii Amugi II, June 25, 1972.

[5]J. M. Bruce-Myers, "The Origin of the Gas," *Journal of the African Society* XXVII, no. 105 (Oct. 1927): 73.

repudiate the wife and demand a refund of the marriage payment if the bride was not a virgin[6] Kwaku Niri described an incident in 1897 when a group of irate women came and flogged his daughter, probably because she was pregnant without any arrangement of marriage having taken place.[7] The husband of a "six-cloth woman" had absolute rights to any children born during the union and could demand a high fine for adultery with his wife.[8] This firm definition of rights was necessary in a vehicle which was often used by the wealthy and titled to cement alliances and consolidate property rights.[9]

In contrast to the multiplicity of formalities which attended a high status marriage, poor people and/or remarrying women (who had lower social status) used simpler and less expensive forms. Sometimes, instead of paying money, a man worked for his father-in-law as a marriage payment.[10] More commonly, a man sent drink to the parents of the girl, and paid for her puberty rites (which was part of ʃibimɔ above).[11] In 1926 the James Town maŋtsɛ declared that a woman was not legally married if her parents had not accepted something from the man, and that living together was not enough to create a legal marriage.[12] One woman who married her second husband in the early 1920s described the formalization of her liaison thusly,

Q. Did your second husband marry [in the sense of full marriage] you?

A. *No, we just stayed together. He came to "show his face" to my parents with an amount of £12, that meant that when my parents could not find me in the house, I was with him.*

Low status marriage also had fewer lineage and individual obligations attached to it. Daniell in 1856 made a distinction between concubinage, involving a small marriage payment, and marriage. The former, he said, was a common arrangement among poor people.

A wide separation . . . is to be made between this mutual compact and the ordinary nuptial rite, perhaps more clearly defined by the extent of control exercised by the husband. In the former, the woman is less amenable to the jurisdiction of her partner, less subject to restraint, and may at any moment leave him with her progeny, upon the infliction of any act of injus-

---

[6]B. Cruickshank, *Eighteen Years on the Gold Coast of Africa* (1853; reprint ed., New York: Barnes and Noble, 1966), I: 196.

[7]M. Kilson, ed., *Excerpts from the Diary of Kwaku Niri (alias J. Q. Hammond), 1884-1918* (Accra: University of Ghana Institute of African Studies, 1967), p. 32.

[8]D. G. Mills-Odoi, "The La Family and Social Change," Master's thesis University of Ghana Institute of African Studies (1967), p. 42; M. J. Field, *The Social Organisation of the Ga People* (London: Crown Agents, 1940), pp. 40-41; Cruickshank, *Eighteen Years*, I: 197.

[9]Bruce-Myers, "Origin," p. 399.

[10]Cruickshank, *Eighteen Years*, I: 197; Interview with Ussher Town Social Welfare Department (S.W.D.) social worker, August 14, 1972.

[11]Bruce-Myers, "Connubial Institutions," p. 402; *James Town Maŋtsɛ's Judgment Book*, p. 273 (case 1930); SCT 2/6/18, p. 178 (case May 8, 1934).

[12]*James Town Maŋtsɛ's Judgment Book*, p. 176 (case 1926).

tice or cruelty; in the latter case the reverse precisely applies.[13]

In the 1926 marriage case above the man whose "marriage" was declared invalid by the James Town *maŋtsɛ* could not collect an adultery fine.

While mutual consent was primarily a characteristic of low status marriage, as Daniell mentioned, arranged marriages for first unions were probably more common than otherwise in all classes. Bruce-Myers commented in 1927 that "a child should be given away only at the choice and instance of the male parent," without making the class distinctions he insisted on elsewhere.[14] There were reasons other than politics and economics that made even low status families desire arranged marriages: friendship pacts between the fathers, cross-cousin marriages, and certain ritual forms.[15]

Most of the drastic changes that have occurred in marital forms can be traced to the interwar years and show the declining power of the male elders of the lineages in controlling marriage, a logical companion to their reduced political power. If property ownership has become individualized, so has the arrangement of marriage. In the 1971-72 small survey there was a noticeable diminution in the number of arranged marriages as the women got younger. Sixty-five percent of the first marriages of the women in their sixties or over were arranged by their parents, as opposed to only 34% of the first marriages of those in their thirties through fifties. In the 1978 survey of women aged 39 to 50, only 29.5% of their first marriages were arranged. Mutual consent marriages, defined as unions in which the partners decided to marry independently of their parents/relatives, became the most common form in Ussher Town beginning in the 1940s.[16]

Linked to the increasing practice of mutual consent marriage in the years since World War II has been another change; the number of full marriages has diminished. While almost half of the women in the oldest 1971-72 age group (80s and 90s) had had full marriages, no one in the youngest cohort had had one, with the intermediate cohorts showing steadily decreasing proportions with one as the women got younger. In the 1978 sample only 3% of the women aged 39 to 50 had had one. At the same time, the proportion of women in 1971-72 who had had only minimum bridewealth or nothing done for them in their first marriages went from a third of the oldest group to half of the youngest. In 1978 they formed almost half of the sample (47%). However, full marriage now is not exactly equivalent to six-cloth marriage, in that mutual consent frequently has come to play an important role.

Full, or high status, marriage has evolved into an abridged form of the

---

[13]W. F. Daniell, "On the Ethnography of Akkrah and Adampé, Gold Coast West Africa," *Journal of the Ethnological Society of London* IV (1856): 13.

[14]Bruce-Myers, "Origin," p. 73.

[15]Mills-Odoi, "La Family," p. 44.

[16]However, some arranged marriages among older women, had an element of mutual consent. A woman manipulated her parents by getting pregnant and then sending her lover to her parents to arrange the marriage.

older Ga six-cloth marriage, with accoutrements added by Christianity.[17] Generally an initial drink is sent to the parents as part of ʃibimɔ, and the woman is "engaged" by a gift of jewelry and/or an engagement ring, a Bible and/or a hymn book, plus many bottles of spirits and "minerals" (soft drinks) and the sum of twelve guineas. This intermediate type of marriage, ʃibimɔ, was the most common form employed in the 1971-72 small sample (40.5% of all unions) but in 1978, with the generally younger and poorer sample, it had fallen to only 32% of the unions. The most common form of marriage after World War II was afayinodaa, "offering a drink," which went from 37.5% of the unions in the 1971-72 small sample to 59.7% in the 1978 sample. This is done usually after a woman has started cohabiting with her lover. In over two-thirds of the afayinodaa marriages in the small 1971-72 survey, the women were pregnant when the men sent a small sum of money and drink to their parents to indicate that they were assuming paternity for the children and were prepared to perform the rest of the customary rites at some indefinite future date.[18] More often than not, nothing more was done and the couple was considered to be married.

To what can we attribute this change in marriage forms? It is not only symptomatic of declining socioeconomic status, but also of a number of other processes. First, the increase in mutual consent marriages accompanied by the woman's pregnancy follows closely the increase in size and heterogeneity of the Accra population in the interwar years. This indicates a reduction in social control over the actions of girls which had formerly been imposed by physical supervision, for the most part. Further evidence can be found in a perceptible increase during the interwar years in overt Ga prostitution.[19] Second, the increase in education and diversification of opportunities for men gave them more economic independence from their male relatives in that they became wage earners. During the twentieth century bridewealth has always been monetized, giving wage earners a significant advantage in arranging their own marriages.[20] Third, formal education for women, whether Sunday or grammar school, has provided ways for girls to have contact with boys which did not exist before, while further reducing physical control. Some voluntary associations also provide coeducational social activities. A logical accompaniment, then, to the increase in mutual consent

---

[17]According to Kilson, Christianity played a large part in making the six-cloth marriage ceremony obsolete, as the Wesleyans disapproved of the essential part played in it by Ga religion. M. Kilson, "Urban Tribesmen: Social Continuity and Change Among the Ga in Accra, Ghana," Ph.D. diss. Harvard University (1966), p. 164. The British passed a marriage ordinance establishing a European type of marriage called Ordinance marriage, which is utilized by some elite Ghanaians. No one in either the 1971-72 or 1978 samples had had one, so this form is omitted here.

[18]Field stated that the custom of demanding proof of virginity at marriage was obsolete by 1940. Field, *Social Organisation*, p. 39.

[19]C. C. Robertson, "Social and Economic Change in Twentieth Century Accra: Ga Women," Ph.D diss. University of Wisconsin (1974), pp. 157-58.

[20]Field, in *Social Organisation*, p. 37, noted that the amount of choice a man had in picking his marriage partner was directly proportional to the share he was paying of the marriage payment.

unions, has been a fall in the age at first marriage: from 21.3 for the women fifty and over in the 1971-72 small sample, to 19.2 years for the women aged 39 to 50 in 1978.

It seems likely that the number of informal liaisons entered into by low status women primarily for economic benefits, without any formalization by marriage payment, will rise. They are one means by which a girl who has some education and finds market trading too unprofitable or low in status for her taste can support herself. Also, marriage in its current form, as we will see shortly, offers an insufficient amount of social and economic security to suit some women, which would only make informal liaisons more popular.

Conjugal Relations

In Central Accra, then, marriage is taking on many of the characteristics of extra-legal unions between higher-class men and lower-class women.[21] Conjugal relations are intimately entwined with economic reality, so that class formation has had a strong impact not only on the arrangement of marriage, but also its conduct. This is reinforced by the primarily economic functions and expectations of marriage in Ga society.

A woman's most important affective relationships are usually with her mother and her children; her siblings rank next in importance, her husband a poor third. In 1971-72 women in the small survey were asked what a good husband should do, what their own behavior should be, and whether or not their husbands had lived up to their expectations. An overwhelming 88% of the women used criteria based on the quality of economic support in judging the behavior of a husband. They expected their husbands to provide medical care, food and clothing for themselves and their children, and to pay for the education of the children. Twenty-three percent, who were mostly sixty or over, mentioned building a house for the wife and children as one of the obligations of a husband. Since this was a custom more honored in the breach than the observance, the younger women's expectations had adjusted to reality. Only 7% mentioned the provision of trading capital by the husband as an obligation, so it was not universally expected by any means. More women specifically mentioned support of the wives rather than the children as important, which was surprising, since other sources would indicate that husbands were supposed to provide food, an annual change of cloth only, and child support.[22] Women often mentioned providing *all* of the wife's needs as a desirable asset in a husband. Possibly this was not so much an expectation as an ideal for many women. The courts tended to enforce

---

[21]R. T. Smith has noted a parallel situation in Guyana in "The Matrifocal Family," in *The Character of Kinship*, ed. J. Goody (Cambridge: Cambridge University Press, 1973), p. 141.

[22]Field, *Social Organisation*, p. 55; Kilson, "Urban Tribesmen," p. 51; A. Nypan, *Market Trade: A Sample Survey of Market Traders in Accra*, University of Ghana African Business Series No. 2 (1960), p. 69. Probably this disparity is a factor of the differences between the women's and men's viewpoints.

less strenuous demands. For instance, in 1950 the High Court ordered a divorced man to pay his ex-wife £30 a year for her maintenance and that of their children, and to pay the school fees for their two youngest children.[23] There may be a general tendency for women to expect more from their husbands than the husbands feel obliged to give them, thus causing tension.

Just as the husband's obligations in marriage were viewed as primarily economic, so the women felt that the wife's value in exchange was also economic: the provision of services. This view coincided with that of Ghanaian society in general, which perpetuates strong sex-role distinctions concerning domestic chores. The menial labor of women is looked down upon as unfit for men. Women felt their primary obligations to be cooking, washing, watching the children, and being faithful to their husbands. Of these, the obligation to cook for the husband seemed most important; many women emphasized that the husband's meals should be ready on time. Some court cases arose out of the failure of wives to fulfill this obligation.[24] Refusal to cook for a man was a signal to quarrel, and perhaps separate, and cooking for another nonrelated man meant adultery. The men also placed great emphasis on cooking. One man was even willing to condone unfaithfulness on the part of his wife because she was a good cook.[25] Another man was willing to take back his wife, who had cohabited with and become pregnant by another man, but sued the man for "seduction and loss of services." He had had to hire another woman to do the housework and cooking since his wife was too pregnant when she returned to do it herself.[26]

Another obligation felt by the women was to trade and so earn money for household expenses. There were more older than younger women who felt this to be important, however. One woman expressed it this way,

> The woman should at times supplement the housekeeping money from her profits, besides buying her own requirements from them. In short, the ideal woman is not expected by Ga custom to depend wholly on her husband for everything. And naturally every man likes to marry an industrious woman because she is an asset and a prop to the man in hard times.[27]

As Koko Solomon said, Do not women eat, keep their bodies clean and neat, and dress up? If a woman does not work, how would she have the means to procure for herself all of her necessities?

In describing the proper behavior of women in marriage some of the women showed a contrast in their beliefs about how social, as opposed to economic, relations should be conducted. Some marital conflicts stemmed

---

[23]SCT 2/6/22, *High Court Judgment Book*, pp. 651-53 (case June 2, 1950).

[24]SCT 17/4/5, pp. 786-87 (case 1880); *Accra Daily Graphic*, March 12, 1960, p. 8; Dec. 19, 1960, p. 6.

[25]SCT 17/5/14, pp. 412-13 (case Jan. 16, 1895).

[26]SCT 17/4/16, p. 188 (case March 19, 1895).

[27]An even stronger statement along these lines was made by an Abidjan trader. "Even if women must suffer, they prefer to have their work . . . [Y]our work is your father, your mother and your husband; once you have work your life is secure. You must not count on a man!" C. Vidal, "Guerre des sexes à Abidjan. Masculin, Féminin, CFA," *Cahiers d'Etudes Africaines* 65, XVII, no. 1 (1977): 134 (my translation).

from this imbalance between submission on the one hand, and independence and occasionally even aggression, on the other. In her behavior and attitudes toward her husband a woman was supposed to be obedient, respectful, tolerant of his unfaithfulness, and sexually compliant. Many women emphasized that a wife should shut her eyes to a husband's unfaithfulness, and ignore troublemakers who came to report it to her. Not being extravagant was also considered a virtue in a wife. Respecting the husband's opinions and not quarrelling with him were thought to be very important. Some women emphasized that if one did quarrel with one's husband, one should not take the quarrel to one's relatives for settlement, but talk it out with the husband and submit to his judgment. The husband was seen as being dominant, and condescending toward the wife if he was a good husband. The wife was supposed to suppress unpleasantness and compromise more.

This submissive attitude toward husbands did not, however, extend to economic matters. The women were quite adamant about controlling the disposal of their own income, including that of the support money the husbands provided. What women did with support money was a sore point in some marriages. Some women felt that their husbands had rights to object to what they had done with it, but nevertheless did as they pleased. One woman confided, in the manner of one having conducted an illicit coup, that she had used some support money sent by her husband from abroad as capital to trade. A man in 1960 beat up his lover because she used the chop money he gave her to buy food for another man.[28] There is no community of property in marriage, and the women do their best to keep it that way. This position of asserting independence in economic decisions within marriage, while behaving submissively in other realms, is a difficult one to maintain. It has eroded among women who live neolocally with their husbands in the suburbs, where Oppong has shown that such independence is directly proportional to a woman's earning power relative to her husband's.[29]

Mutual respect, rather than romantic love in the western sense, was the highest form most women visualized the conjugal relationship could attain, and quite a few mentioned this as an important aspect of their successful marriages.[30] A woman who found happiness in her third marriage described the reasons for her satisfaction in the following manner.

We respected and understood each other. We even looked like brother and sister. He was nice to me and I was submissive toward him. He satisfied my wishes, was understanding, and generous, not only to me but also to my children by earlier husbands. He bought me clothes, footwear, etc., even before we had a child. The fathers of my children could have cared less about them and did not maintain them, but he shouldered the responsibility willingly.

Even respect was associated with the husband's behavior in fiscal matters, then.

---

[28]*Accra Daily Graphic*, Dec. 19, 1960, p. 6.

[29]C. Oppong, "Conjugal Power and Resources: An Urban African Example," *Journal of Marriage and the Family* XXXII, no. 4 (Nov. 1970): 676-80.

[30]Smith, "Matrifocal Family," p. 141, also noted this in Guyana.

A factor enforcing a wife's respectful attitude toward her husband was undoubtedly the Ga ethic governing proper behavior toward one's elders. Husbands are usually older than their wives, as was the case in 85.5% of the marriages in the 1971-72 small survey and 89.3% of those in the 1978 survey of women aged 39 to 50.[31] The sex and age differences both enjoin circumspect polite behavior upon the woman, and militate against a warm friendship. Another strong influence on conjugal relations was polygyny. From the women's point of view, polygyny and infidelity were mainly important for economic reasons, and they generally opposed both. Infidelity was opposed on the lesser grounds that *if he spends money on girlfriends he will not have enough for his wives.* Polygyny imposed the additional disability of competition for the children's inheritance, while not offering the cooperation available when coresidence with cowives is practiced. Older women, having had more experience with polygyny, tended to oppose it more: 58.2% of the 1971-72 sample opposed it, compared to 36.5% of the 1978 sample. The opposite was true for husbands' infidelity; while 24% of the 1971-72 sample approved of it as long as there was enough money to go around, only 8% of the 1978 sample approved. These attitudes were consistent with a slight drop in the incidence of polygyny; in the 1971-72 small sample 39% of 103 marriages were monogamous, as opposed to 42% of 197 marriages in the 1978 sample. Forty-one point six percent of the 101 women in 1978 were currently in polygynous unions.[32] Table VI-1 gives the distribution of husbands by the number of wives they had at the time they were married to the women in the samples.

Polygyny bred distrust in a marital relationship, even between monogamous spouses, because the husband could at will take another wife, thus worsening everyone's financial situation. A woman in 1978 said, *I don't trust my husband because any time he can take another wife.* Under such a threat women were hesitant to rely on their husbands' support or to have a close conjugal relationship. Sometimes the first wife resented the fact that she had helped her husband earn the money to get a new, younger and prettier, wife. A frequent result was that the marriage dissolved, through his

---

[31]These are percentages of husbands for whom information was given: 110 in the 1971-72 sample and 192 in the 1978 sample.

[32]Statistics on polygyny vary according to the viewpoint considered. Often men rather than women are asked about polygyny with the result that the incidence of polygyny is understated because it affects fewer men than women. S. K. Gaisie, "Population Growth and Its Components," in *Population Growth and Socioeconomic Change in West Africa*, ed. J. C. Caldwell (New York: Columbia University Press, 1975), p. 366, gives the proportion of polygynous marriages for Accra District in 1960 as 20%. J. C. Caldwell, *Population Growth and Family Change in Africa* (Canberra: Australian National University Press, 1968), p. 37, gives figures of 8% of the men versus 13% of the women involved in polygynous marriages for the Ghanaian urban elite. Kilson, in "Urban Tribesmen," p. 64, found that 13% of the men and 38% of the women in her Central Accra samples were in polygynous unions. D. I. Pool, "Conjugal Patterns in Ghana," *Canadian Review of Sociology and Anthropology* V, no. 4 (Nov. 1968): 247, found that the Ga had the highest rural polygyny rate for Ghana, and a relatively high urban one, being 85% of the rural women in polygynous unions, and 68% of the urban women.

**Table VI-1. Number of Wives per Husbands of Respondents,
1971-72[a], 1978.[b]**

| Years | Percent of Husbands, by Number of Wives | | | | Total |
Surveyed	1	2	3	4 or More	Percent
1971-72	12.1	39.8	29.6	18.5	100.0
1978	42.3	41.3	9.7	6.5	99.9

[a]No. = 108 husbands.

[b]No. = 196 husbands.

disinterest or her disillusionment.[33] To avoid this situation one female authority advised that a married woman should *keep some distance away from the husband to ensure a harmonious married life.*[34]

In general, if a man could fulfill his support obligations, the women did not object to polygyny. A common answer from those who approved of polygyny was, *It all depends on his financial ability.* One woman with halcyon views concerning a rich husband said,

> *If [a man] had three or four [wives] it would be good because the women would get clothing, money, and happiness with the man. . . . If you had, say, two girlfriends besides these, there is nothing wrong. But a woman should not have boyfriends because it is a sin. Your boyfriend cannot come to your aid when you are in need.*

She partook of the double standard of morality partly for practical reasons; a woman's lover could not be socially pressured to produce support, but her husband could!

Because of the economic importance of polygyny, we must consider further its incidence. Given the perilous state of the Ghanaian economy, it might be expected that the 1978 sample would show a drastic decline in polygyny because men could not afford to take more wives. Not so, as we have seen. The difference between the 1971-72 and 1978 sample was not large enough to be significant. Furthermore, the percentage of women never having had a polygynous union was similar for the two samples: 29% of the 1971-72 small sample versus 26.7% of the 1978 sample. This similarity, as well as that in the incidence of polygyny, indicate a relatively stable situation. Socioeconomic change has not brought about a decline in polygyny, contrary to the usual assumption.[35] If polygyny is stable or increasing in

---

[33]D. D. Vellenga, "Differentiation among women farmers in two rural areas in Ghana," *Labour and Society* II, no. 2 (April 1977): 204-05, found a similar situation among Ghanaian women cocoa farmers, whose husbands took younger wives and neglected the older ones.

[34]Interview with Naa Mannye, Jan. 19, 1972.

[35]It was impossible to figure out the intensity of polygyny for these samples, that is, the ratio of married women per 100 married men, because the marital histories were collected from women only. There was no way of determining how many of these women had the same husband. Even if the husbands' names had been collected, which they were not to

Ghana, then it is probably a symptom of the decreasing power of women.[36] Why? Goody has stated that "the reasons behind polygyny are sexual and reproductive rather than economic and productive."[37] This view, however, is male-centered. Polygyny serves reproductive functions more for the men than the women, since women in polygynous unions are usually less fertile than those in monogamous ones. In this situation the chief economic stress of child support falls on the women, so that the presumptive economic dysfunction of polygyny for men does not apply.[38] The younger women had often resigned themselves to its continuance. While only 6% of the older sample expressed resignation on the subject, 29% of the 1978 sample did, saying they left it up to the men to do what they wanted, the respondents' level of education making no significant difference in their replies. These answers may be linked to economic conditions and class formation, in that the younger women might have given up on ever achieving a high status/monogamous marriage, whereas more of the older women had had one. Several women in 1978 had been enticed into marrying a man on the false promise that he had no other wife, and got quite discouraged by it. Yet the women were usually, through moral and financial considerations (who would support a lover's child?), not willing to dispense with the double standard in their own sexual dealings. Ama Ata Aidoo expressed it aptly, in a dialogue between two sisters, one a proper married woman, the other a kept woman of several politicos. When the wife complains of her husband's infidelity, her sister replies,

Mercy: Men are like that.

Connie: They are selfish.

Mercy: No, it's just that women allow them to behave the way they do instead of seizing some freedom themselves.[39]

---

preserve confidentiality, so many Ga have similar or identical clan names that duplication would have been inevitable. Likewise, the incidence of polygyny, as measured by the number of polygynists per 100 married males, was not discernible. This is a disadvantage of working with single-sex samples. It is, however, permissible to present the women's point of view statistically, as long as readers exercise caution when making comparisons with statistics collected from the men's point of view.

    J. Goody, "Polygyny, Economy, and the Position of Women," paper presented at the University of Ghana African Studies Institute, Second Interdisciplinary Family Research Seminar (June 1972), p. 3.

    [36]Remi Clignet, in *Many Wives, Many Powers* (Evanston: Northwestern University Press, 1970), p. 17, noted that Ghana has one of the highest incidences of polygyny in Sub-Saharan Africa, and thought it was increasing. J. Van Baal, *Reciprocity and the Position of Women* (Amsterdam: Van Gorcum, 1975), p. 99, stated that polygyny is "clearly associated with male supremacy over women."

    [37]J. Goody, "Polygyny, Economy, and the Role of Women," in *The Character of Kinship*, ed. J. Goody (Cambridge: Cambridge University Press, 1973), pp. 181, 189. He also ignores the economic value of reproduction.

    [38]R. Clignet and J. Sween, "Social Change and Type of Marriage," *American Journal of Sociology* LXXV (1969): 124.

    [39]A. A. Aidoo, *No Sweetness Here* (New York: Doubleday and Co., 1971), pp. 184-85.

Marital relations, then, are directly rooted in economic reality. The fortunes of a marriage here have most to do with its finances. Nowhere is this more clearly shown than in divorce, when the expectations of the partners in a marriage have been betrayed by reality.

Divorce

Consistent with the change in marital forms, divorce has increasingly become a casually managed affair. This is related to the reduced interest of the lineages of the partners in maintaining a marriage which they did not arrange, and also to the reduction of patriarchal authority. The chief arbitrators in marital disputes were and are the immediate families of the partners and then the lineage elders. People consider it to be very important that efforts at reconciliation should be made before the marriage is dissolved. The courts have been known to dismiss petitions for divorce on the grounds that no such effort was ever made.[40] The party seeking a reconciliation is usually presumed to be in the right.[41] If a marriage partner is aggrieved he or she will probably first tell a sibling or a parent of the same sex about it. The confidante might then go to the other partner and discuss the grievances involved in order to seek some compromise arrangement. When marriages were important political instruments the grievances would probably have been taken quickly to the highest level, the *maŋtsɛ*'s court, or to the lineage or clan head. The more important the marriage, and the higher the status of the partners, the higher the level of the authority who tried to settle the quarrel. If a lineage still wields some influence the aggrieved party now might take the case to the eldest male member of the sub-lineage, or even to the lineage head. This person should then consult the elders in the other partner's family so that they will bring pressure to bear on the offending party.[42]

If arbitration fails and the marriage is dissolved by official means, the offending party is usually required to make some payment. The arbitrators determine who is more at fault and decide the amount of payment. If it is the husband he usually forfeits the bridewealth and is required to pay his wife *gbɛwoo*, or "send-off money." The customary amount was and is ₤25.[43] A full marriage must, in principle, be dissolved fully, with the participation of many more people than a marriage in which only *afayinodaa* was done. In Central Accra, with the number of full marriages dropping, we can expect that the number of formalized divorces will also be reduced. Unfortunately, due to imprecision in conducting the 1971-72 survey, the number of separations in which no formalities were taken was unclear. The 1978 sample

---

[40]SCT 2/6/16, *High Court Judgment Book*, pp. 153-56 (case Aug. 25, 1931).

[41]*James Town Maŋtsɛ's Judgment Book*, pp. 409-13 (case 1934).

[42]Mills-Odoi, "La family," p. 125; Field, *Social Organisation*, p. 28.

[43]Mills-Odoi, "La Family," p. 126; *James Town Maŋtsɛ's Judgment Book*, (case Aug. 16, 1921); ADM 37/4/11; Interview with Ga Maŋtsɛ Nii Amugi II, Dec. 16, 1971.

yielded information on 99 separations, 55.6% of which entailed no formalities, 42.4% arbitration by friends or relatives, and only 2% a court case.

In most cases the women left the men, that is, did not go to sleep with their husbands on request. For instance, among the cases in the 1978 sample where no formalities were performed, most (50.5%) were divorces in accordance with the unilateral decision by one partner. Of these (a total of 50 divorces), 72% were taken by women. This information is indubitably biased in that some women may not have wanted to admit to the humiliation of having had the husband tire of them. Nevertheless, in polygyny it is more likely for a woman to seek a divorce than a man.[44] She must do so in order to remarry, while he can simply take another wife and not bother to send for the old one. In the District and Maŋtsɛ's Court records there were 46 cases brought by women against their husbands and 35 by husbands against wives. One would expect the disparity to be greater, but the lineage structure and education made it more likely for men to use the court systems than women.[45] It is clear, then, that more women than men wanted out of marriages. Why?

In analyzing the causes of divorce an association must be made between claims by the women of nonsupport, desertion, difficulties caused by polygyny, and adultery. Altogether these accounted for 62% of the answers in 1971-72 and 68% in 1978. These factors are all interrelated in a complex manner, and which one a woman actually mentioned as a cause might have

---

[44]P. C. Lloyd, "Divorce Among the Yoruba," *American Anthropologist* LXX, no. 1 (Feb. 1968): p. 70; D. D. Vellenga, "Arenas of Judgment—An Analysis of Matrimonial Cases Brought Before Different Types of Courts in Akwapim and the Eastern Region in the 1930s and 1960s," paper presented at University of Ghana Institute of African Studies, Family Studies Seminar, Legon (Feb. 1971), p. 13; M. O. Saunders, "Women's Divorce Strategies in Mirria County, Niger Republic," paper presented at African Studies Association Meeting, Los Angeles (Oct. 31-Nov. 3, 1979), pp. 5-6. Lloyd, Vellenga and Saunders have all noted in other situations the higher incidence of women's instituting divorce cases. In Ibadan, Mary Bird found that out of 420 divorce cases in 1958, 419 were instituted by women. Mary Bird, "Social Change in Kinship and Marriage Among the Yoruba of Western Nigeria," Ph.D. diss. University of Edinburgh (1958), pp. 251-52.

[45]The vast majority of cases were between men. The paucity of divorce cases in the court records made it impossible to base any diachronic conclusions on them. I only examined cases between persons whose names were identifiably Ga, and did not consider those who were not from Central Accra, where possible. Because of time limitations and the huge bulk of material, I only considered one out of every five years from 1875 to 1960 in the District Court Records; the Maŋtsɛs' Records covered only from 1919 to 1937. The results were disappointing; the total number of cases involved was 17,279 (including 261 from the Maŋtsɛs' records), but only 81 dealt with marital disputes, 57 from the District Court and 24 from the Maŋtsɛs' records. The breakdown by type of divorce case was as follows, not distinguishing the source of the case. Cases brought by wives against husbands: maintenance, 11; suing for "send-off money," 17; breach of promise, 12; adultery, 2; miscellany, 4 (these do not include property cases). Cases brought by husbands against wives: return of bridewealth, 25; adultery, 10. In the District Court records such cases tended to be concentrated in a few years when, for various reasons, the local maŋtsɛ's court was not functioning. C. Bohmer, "Modernization, Divorce and the Status of Women in Bobodioulasso," *African Studies Review* XXIII, no. 2 (Sept. 1980): 84 ff., noted that informal methods of settling disputes were better for women in order to avoid the patriarchal authority expressed by and in the court.

been arbitrary. Women complained bitterly about husbands running around with other women, but they were more likely to use nonsupport than adultery as their "official" grounds for divorce. In fact, it was nonsupport that aggrieved them more than the infidelity. Everyone knows, of course, that a claim of nonsupport often means that the man is being consistently unfaithful.[46] Infidelity creates the possibility of polygyny. Polygyny, in turn, creates a competition between wives for the attention and support of the husband, in which the loser's children fail to be supported by the husband if his funds are limited. Desertion may be associated with him dropping the less favored wife. Or, a man may spend his money on other women without marrying them. One woman commented with disgust when asked if her husband had lovers, *No, he doesn't give money to women, so nobody loves him.* In any case, the wife may find it less humiliating to claim nonsupport as a grievance than loss of favor, even though people may surmise correctly that one arose from the other.[47]

Because of this common association, one informant claimed that many women were reluctant to report their husbands to the Social Welfare Department or to court for nonsupport.[48] Among my informants this tendency sometimes manifested itself in a claim that the husband was giving support when, in fact, he was not. This woman, who was unable to suppress her real feelings, showed this clearly.

Q. Does [your husband] help look after the children?
A. *Yes, in paying for school fees, buying books, etc., . . . but he does not do it. So why should I go there?*
Q. Were your husbands good men?
A. *No, they did not respect their wives. I do not have any quarrel with him [her second husband], but if I go there I might get pregnant and have another child, and he does not look after the children. So, he can stay there and I stay here.*
Q. Did your two husbands give you money when you lived with them?
A. *No, so I had to work and look after myself and my children. I have stopped living with husbands.*
Q. Did you want to marry when you were young?
A. *Yes, but I did not expect that this was what would come of it.*

Nonsupport caused many of the cases brought before the James Town Municipal Court in 1956-57.[49] Among the few divorce cases in the court records,

---

[46]Interview with Ga Maŋtsɛ Nii Amugi II, June 25, 1972.

[47]K. Church, "A Study of Socio-Economic Status and Child-Care Arrangements of Women in Madina," paper presented at Ghana National Council on Women and Development Seminar on Women and Development, Accra (Sept. 1978), p. 13, concurred with the comment, "'Chop money' is at the crux of financial arrangements in any Ghanaian marriage, and is a frequent source of strife." She went on to note that women did not want to admit that husbands were not providing all of it.

[48]Interview with S.W.D. worker, Ussher Town Branch, Aug, 14, 1972.

[49]Kilson, "Urban Tribesmen," p. 52.

nonsupport was given as a cause in *every* one where a woman instituted it.[50]

Has the worsening economic situation then raised the divorce rate because of increasing nonsupport? In the 1971-72 small sample, 70 women participated in 118 marriages. Of these marriages 44.9% ended in separation, 36.5% at the husband's death, and 18.6% were still continuing.[51] In the 1978 sample where 101 women aged 39 to 50 had entered into 198 unions, 52% ended in separation, 13.1% at the death of the husband, and 34.8% were still continuing. The differences in the proportion of marriages ended by death was due, of course, to the relative ages of the women in the surveys. Altogether we find that half of the marriages ended in separation. However, the intensity of divorce was rising for the younger women; exactly half of the older sample had ever experienced a divorce compared to 63.4% of the younger 1978 sample. Consequently, the women in the 1971-72 sample, despite their usually higher age, had had 1.7 husbands on the average, compared to 2 for the younger 1978 sample, a difference significant at the .5 level. Serial marriage for women was common, but is becoming more so.

Having answered the first part of our question positively, we then need to see if, in fact, there has been a lessening in husbands' support of their families. We get another affirmative answer. While younger women, the 1978 sample who were married after World War II, were getting more cash support, they got less in real terms. The 59 women aged 50 and over in the 1971-72 small survey averaged £4.15 a month in cash from their husbands, compared to the £16 averaged by the women aged 39 to 50 in the 1978 sample. However, these estimates tended to reflect good times; many (including half of the 1971-72 small sample) mentioned that on occasion no chop money was forthcoming, not just because of marital squabbles but also because the husband could not afford it. Also, they tended to estimate the situation at the beginning of the marriage, when it was likely to be the best. This factor, along with adjustments for inflation and a much higher incidence of help in kind among older women, made the benefits of the apparent rise in amount of money disappear. Women now receive proportionately less support than their predecessors did in terms of contributions to household expenses from

---

[50]SCT 2/6/18, pp. 553-57 (case Sept. 18, 1945); SCT 17/4/7 (case 1885); SCT 17/4/104, pp. 141-42 (case 1960); SCT 2/6/22, pp. 651-53 (case June 2, 1950); pp. 273-76 (case Aug. 27, 1948); *James Town Maŋtse's Judgment Book*, pp. 441-43, to give some examples. Saunders, "Women's Divorce," p. 7, also found nonsupport to be the primary cause for Hausa women in Niger seeking divorce, as did Obbo in Uganda. C. Obbo, *African Women, Their Struggle for Independence* (London: Zed Press, 1980), p. 39.

[51]If one compares this "divorce rate" with that of other cities in Africa in 1960, the Ga come in between Kampala with 32.5% and Kisangani with around 55%, according to P. Gutkind, "African Family Life," *Cahiers d'Etudes Africaines* III, no. 10 (1962): 192. These statistics indicate different phenomena, however. Gutkind was referring to the number of women in second or subsequent unions. One should be careful to define what one is calling the "divorce rate," so that it is comparable, as Barnes has noted. J. A. Barnes, "Measures of Divorce Frequency in Simple Societies," *Journal of the Royal Anthropological Institute of Great Britain* LXXIX, part I (1949): 37-62. Note the similarity when a comparable statistic is available for a sub-Saharan urbanized patrilineal society: 46% of Yoruba marriages ended in divorce, according to Lloyd, "Divorce," p. 78.

their husbands. In fact, since most of the women in the 1971-72 small sample were over fifty, and many were widows, they got more support from their children than their husbands. Fifty-seven percent received money from their daughters, 43% from their sons, and 64% provided most of their own support.

Other evidence for nonsupport comes from a consideration of the residential patterns of the children. Chop money may be a token amount (Aidoo called it a "nice joke"[52]), but husbands were supposed to support their sons, at least, by providing them with a place to live after the age of six or so. In practice things often did not work out this way. An examination of the residence of 240 sons of the women in the 1978 sample showed that 86% of those aged up to six years were with their mothers, 60% of those aged six to 12, 43% of those aged 12 to 18, and 26% of those over 18. Only in the oldest age group, when the sons could be expected to be largely self-supporting, was a sizeable proportion with their fathers, 26%, the same as the number with the mothers.

In cases of divorce or widowhood it was not common for many of the children to live with their fathers or fathers' relatives, which is obligatory, according to ideology. Field commented, "The children of divorce, if any, remain his." But she later stipulated that this was true *only if he had paid the full marriage fee*, which may be a clue to what is happening here.[53] Forty-four percent of the 500 surviving children of the women in the 1978 sample came from marriages which were no longer extant because of divorce or the death of the husband. Fifteen percent of these were with their fathers and another 8% with their fathers' relatives. Again, most of these children were male and over eighteen. The provision of residence (and presumably the majority of support) for male children was, then, another portion of ideology more honored in the breach than the observance by husbands.

So pervasive is the problem of nonsupport, in fact, that the Ghana government has tried to deal with it by ever more stringent laws making husbands or fathers accountable for their offspring.[54] To begin with, by a 1951 British law for the Gold Coast, only husbands in Ordinance (European-type) marriages were required to provide support, although customary law decreed it. In 1960 a section of the Criminal Code made it obligatory for all husbands. By the 1965 Maintenance of Children Act, fathers (whether married or not) were enjoined to supply at most ₡10 a month per child, and the Social Welfare Department was empowered to persuade them to comply. Lack of compliance could bring attachment of the husband's

---

[52]Aidoo, *No Sweetness*, p. 131.

[53]Field, *Social Organisation*, pp. 40-41.

[54]C. Oppong, "Parenthood in a Changing Context," paper presented at the Ninth Annual Conference of the Ghana Sociological Association, Kumasi (March 1975), pp. 7-9, cites the results of a large Accra survey showing that in half of the families of the 63% of the children with fathers present, these made no regular contribution toward their upkeep. At the same time over half of the 70 homeless children at the Osu children's home had employed fathers.

income. It was found impossible to enforce.[55] The 1977 Maintenance of Children Decree established family tribunals with jurisdiction to hear complaints regarding paternity, custody, and maintenance of children. According to their guidelines, the father of a child could be ordered to pay an allowance to the mother of the child during pregnancy and for nine months after the child's birth.[56] This last decree softened the sting of illegitimacy a bit, but still maintained the principle that even the fathers of illegitimate children were responsible for their upkeep to some extent. None of these measures has had a significant impact on men's actions concerning support.

Why did men often fail to support their children adequately? An underlying reason was probably the women's economic activity. The men knew that their children could look to their mothers for food if the chop money failed. Other causes lay in the husbands' stronger ties with their relatives by descent, as well as the superfluity of obligations incurred in polygyny. The economic situation and change in the nature of their occupations also affected their support capabilities. Even though more of the husbands of women in the 1978 sample were white collar workers (40.3% compared to 38% of those of the 1971-72 sample), and fewer were fishermen and artisans, they were more likely to be low-level white collar workers like petty clerks, and less likely to be small businessmen and cocoa farmers. The fact that more husbands of younger women lived farther away from their wives may also have accounted for some lack of support. Whereas 78.5% of the husbands of the 1971-72 sample were resident in Central Accra, only 44% of those of the younger 1978 sample were (34% of these husbands were living in intermediate areas like Osu and Adabraka and wealthier suburbs). Also, the higher likelihood of the younger women's husbands being non-Ga made them less amenable to pressure from the wife's family to fulfill their obligations.[57]

If marriage has become more fragile, then, it is largely because of a breakdown in the fulfillment of economic obligations by husbands. This is not only a logical accompaniment of the depression, but also a symptom of the shift away from conjugal economic cooperation because of the increasing differentiation of men's and women's jobs. When fishing and farming were the most important occupations followed by Central Accra Ga men, economic cooperation between spouses, or male and female relatives, was

---

[55]W. C. Ekow-Daniels, "Problems in the Law Relating to the Maintenance and Support of Wives and Children," University of Ghana Institute of African Studies, Legon Family Research Papers No. 1 (1974), pp. 286-89.

[56]*Ideal Woman* VII, no. 2 (Sept./Oct. 1977): 4. It is worthwhile noting that both by customary and written law, husbands are usually held responsible for maintaining their wives, so that my consideration of their support here is based on an already minimal view of their obligations. G. Woodman, "The Rights of Wives, Sons and Daughters in the Estates of Their Deceased Husbands and Fathers," paper presented at University of Ghana Institute of African Studies Family Seminar, Legon (Feb. 1971), p. 5. My informants were usually satisfied if the chop money was regular and an occasional gift or help in times of crisis, funerals, etc.) was forthcoming.

[57]In the 1971-72 small sample, 92% of the husbands were Ga, compared to 83% in the 1978 sample.

more the rule than the exception.[58] Even among the oldest group of women in the small 1971-72 survey more than half had cooperated with their husbands in some economic endeavor, usually fishselling or farming. Field remarked that a woman was supposed to trade her husband's agricultural surplus, and would help her husband with farming if they were on amicable terms.[59] Mills-Odoi and Azu, in their respective studies of the fishing communities in Labadi and Teshie, two Ga village-suburbs of Accra, noted the essential role of cooperation between spouses in carrying on the industry.[60] A symbiotic, conscientiously cooperative, relationship sometimes existed between husbands and wives for catching and marketing fish, aptly described by Naa Afuwa.

Q.   Who contributed most to the support of your children?

A.   *Both of us contributed, but he put in more since he was the man. As long as he could afford it he provided the money for meals. When he was unable to, then I bought the food with my own money. That was generally the life at Faana fishing villages because there was nothing like a monthly pay packet in the fishing community.*

Q.   Was your husband anxious at times because he thought that you were too preoccupied with curing the fish?

A.   *No, not at all. He acknowledged my work then as a joint venture in the interest of our marriage. There were times when he had to put in a helping hand, especially when the fish were plentiful.*

The possibilities for economic cooperation between spouses or male and female relatives have rapidly diminished because men are less often fishermen or farmers (from 25% of the husbands of the women 60 and over in 1971-72, to 16% of those of the women aged 39 to 50 in 1978), and because they are less likely to be self-employed. Forty eight percent of the husbands of the women 60 and over in 1971-72 were self-employed compared to 34% of those of the women aged 39 to 50 in 1978. Even in cases among the 1971-72 small sample of women where the possibilities existed for cooperating with their husbands or male relatives in economic endeavor, the women mostly did not do it. One reason for that was specialization; the men did not catch the type of fish the wives wanted. More important was that the relationship between fishsellers and fishermen had become more purely economic; in the past it was felt to be an obligation for a wife, daughter, or sister, to sell a man's produce, but not now. Thus, in the 1971-72 small survey only one-ninth of the women in the two youngest groups had ever cooperated with their husbands in some sort of work and fewer still with their male relatives. Logically enough, male capabilities of recruiting female labor dwindled along with their necessity for doing so. This reduction of

---

[58]Remnants of this situation still exist in fishing villages around Accra. G. Hagan, "Divorce, Polygyny and Family Welfare," *Ghana Journal of Sociology* X, no. 1 (1976): 67-84.

[59]Field, *Social Organisation*, pp. 62-63.

[60]Mills-Odoi, "La Family," p. 122; G. A. M. Azu, "The Impact of the Modern Fishing Industry on the Ga Traditional Fishing Industry," Master's thesis University of Ghana Institute of African Studies (1966), pp. 105-06.

cross-sexual linkages in production strengthened the dependence of women on female networks, increased the separation between the sexes, and made it less likely for a man to support his wife and children, especially in kind. If women asserted their independence in reducing their cooperation, they also felt the consequences in reduced support.

Given the primarily economic expectations of women in marriage, then primarily economic causes for divorce are not surprising. We tested other causes, such as the reduced interest of the lineages in marriage, but found that, for instance, more arranged marriages ended in divorce than mutual consent ones in the 1978 sample, and that arranged marriages in both samples were likely to be shorter.[61] Infertility was also not an important cause of divorce. Because it was usually blamed on women, a childless woman often felt herself lucky to have a husband and stayed with him. He could always take another wife. Reinforcing this view is the fact that in both the 1971-72 and 1978 samples women who had multiple marriages had more children in their first marriages than in second and subsequent ones.[62]

Another common explanation for marital instability relates to the economic independence of women. Economic independence is sometimes defined ambiguously as having something to do with the fact that women trade, Nadel's description of Nupe women inevitably being cited.[63] Not only divorce, but various evils, from uppity women to giving the men a feeling of "intense relative deprivation," have been ascribed to the trading activities of women.[64] Fortes expressed it this way, "Dare we draw the conclusion that too great a degree of social, economic, and legal freedom for women, too great equality with men, is detrimental to family life. . . ?" But this zero sum game (if you equalize the status of women, you detract from men's status) has gone too far. Women's trading does not necessarily create equality, in any case, nor did it have a positive relationship to divorce here.[65] Most of

---

[61]Probably because the husbands were older and the women widowed earlier than in mutual consent marriages. In the 1971-72 small sample mode of arrangement made virtually no difference to the fate of the marriage.

[62]In 1971-72 38 women with multiple marriages averaged 2.9 children in their first marriages, compared to 2.2 for subsequent ones. In 1978 the difference was not as great: 2.1 versus 2.0 for 65 women in multiple marriages.

[63]R. A. LeVine, "Sex Roles and Economic Change in Africa," *Ethnology* V, no. 2 (April 1966): 189-90, cites Nadel's pejorative description of Nupe traders' advantageous position with regard to their farmer husbands, where "sexual laxity" was associated with female traders (especially long-distance traders), and the wives often assumed "many of the financial responsibilities which should rightly belong to the men as father and family head. . . ." S. F. Nadel, "Witchcraft in Four African Societies: An Essay in Comparison," *American Anthropologist* LIV (1952): 21.

[64]J. C. Caldwell, "Population: General Characteristics," in *A Study of Contemporary Ghana*, ed. W. Birmingham et al. (London: George Allen and Unwin Ltd., 1967), II: 70; Daniel McCall, "Trade and the Role of Wife in a Modern West African Town," in *Social Change in Modern Africa*, ed. A. W. Southall (London: Oxford University Press/International African Institute, 1961), p. 298; Kilson, "Urban Tribesmen," p. 76; LeVine, "Sex Roles," pp. 192-93.

[65]M. Fortes, *The Family: Bane or Blessing?* (Accra: Ghana Universities Press, 1971), p. 9; Clignet, in *Many Wives*, p. 314, found the opposite, that labor force participation rates

the women traded whether they were married or not. Divorce gave them no particular economic advantage, rather the opposite, since they could expect less help from a divorced husband. Divorce usually happened when women were no longer receiving support from their husbands, in any case. Only one woman said that she had cut down her trading efforts because of her husband's support. The main impact of the women's trading activities on causes of divorce was to facilitate the husband's nonsupport of the children in a circular pattern, forcing the women to trade more.

Trading may offer some wives more avenues for infidelity, as in the stereotype of the immoral trader, but in this case husbands usually tolerated infidelity. A wife's skimping on her household duties because of trading, in combination with adultery, did cause divorce on occasion, and quarrels sometimes arose because of a husband's disapproval of trading. However, more husbands than not approved of trading. Also, because it was usually women who wanted divorces, their reasons were more important. For them, the decision whether or not to trade was moot and irrelevant to divorce, although the intensity of their trading activities could be affected by it.

In summarizing the developments in marriage and divorce in Central Accra it is tempting to opt for the set of characteristics so often described for the urban poor, and aptly condensed by Eames and Goode. They noted: (1) the development of consensual marriage with female-headed families, and illegitimate offspring; (2) reduction in the alliance and dowry aspects of marriage; and (3) instability of marriages, with a diminution in the role of father, while the mother's female kin often provide substitute childcare. While (1) has the fault that female-headed families already existed, there certainly has been an increase in consensual marriage and also a reduction in the alliance and bridewealth aspects of marriage among the Central Accra Ga population. Consistent with Engels' analysis, more people now are entering into unions involving less control by men over their offspring.[66] (3) is problematic as a change. Eames and Goode discuss it further. "Thus, from both the male and female point of view, marital instability can frequently be viewed as economically rational behavior when women have independent access to cash and males are in marginal positions."[67] Divorce was an economically rational decision for women who hoped to better their economic status by remarrying, but many of these men were not marginal; they were generally more educated and prosperous than their wives. This distortion of the situation from Eames and Goode's model has to do with the effect of polygyny on support, the differential access to formal education of men and women, and other appurtenances of male privilege, which have furthered the separation of the sexes in Ga society.

---

for single, divorced, and separated women in Douala and Yaoundé (Cameroon) were twice as high as for married women.

[66]See M. Barrett, *Women's Oppression Today, Problems in Marxist Feminist Analysis* (London: Verso, 1980), p. 46, for an analysis of Engels' thought regarding the relationship of property control to marriage.

[67]E. Eames and J. G. Goode, *Urban Poverty in a Cross-Cultural Context* (New York: The Free Press, 1973), pp. 173, 180-81.

The Growing Dependency Burden

> In the majority of cases your petitioners are without husbands or other
> male friends to support them in any the slightest degree whatever, and are
> compelled to maintain themselves and families by hard work which brings
> them weekly hardly enough to satisfy nature's wants; and even in cases
> where some of them have husbands, the cure has proved worse than the
> disease. . . .

This group of illiterate women in Central Accra who sent a petition to
the Secretary of State for the Colonies in 1896 was speaking for future generations when they portrayed their economic status in this manner.[68]
Although they were exaggerating their plight to obtain a reduction in taxes,
their complaint was the same as the most common one made in the 1970s by
women in Central Accra. They felt that they had been left bearing the
major part of the economic burden of raising a family, which was not fair.
The data concerning support for children and old people give substance to
their impression.

In Central Accra fewer able-bodied women are now having to support
more dependents, without question. The dependency age groups (aged up to
15 and 65 and over) have grown. Whereas in 1921 approximately 36% of
the Accra population fell in those ages, in 1970 46.5% did, with a steady
growth in the intervening years.[69] As mortality rates fell and life expectancy
increased, old people contributed more to this group. The dependency burden becomes clearer when the Ussher Town population is subdivided by age,
group and sex, as in Table VI-2.

The change in the sex composition of the population is particularly
noticeable. The 1970 results illustrate the effects of men moving out; the
proportion of men in the whole population fell by almost 4%. The biggest
changes were among those aged 15 to 54, where in 1960 men dominated in
every group. But in 1970, the only age group where men outnumbered
women was that of 25 to 34, probably due to a large number of single male
tenants. In 1960, 55.1% of the population aged 15 to 54 was male, in 1970
only 48.9%.[70] In the intervening years, of course, many suburbs grew where
not only the prosperous but also the poor could live. A consequence of this
development was that the whole population of Ussher Town may have

---

[68]Great Britain, Public Record Office, Secretary of State for the Colonies Papers,
96/298, petition Dec. 4, 1896.

[69]Among the total Ghana population, the dependency age groups went from 47.6% to
50.4% from 1960 to 1970. *Ghana Census*, 1970, II: xxxiii; K. D. Patterson, "Health in Urban Ghana: the Case of Accra 1900-1940," *Social Science and Medicine* 13B (1979): 259;
Ghana Census, Special Report A (1960), p. 3; Special Report A (1970), Table 7; I. Acquah,
Accra Survey (London: University of London Press, 1958), p. 38.

[70]The 1960 percentage of males 16 and over in the population was more typical of earlier years, when the respective proportions in the Accra African population were as follows:
1921--54.9%, 1931--55.5%, 1948--57.1%. Patterson, "Health," p. 259.

Table VI-2.
Sex and Age Structure of Ussher Town Population, 1960-70.

	Percent of Population in Age/Sex Group:							
	0-14	15-24	25-34	35-44	45-54	55-64	65+	Total
1960								
Female	20.9	9.6	6.8	4.9	3.0	1.9	2.2	49.3
Male	18.2	11.9	9.3	5.4	3.2	1.5	1.3	50.8
1970								
Female	22.9	10.4	6.9	5.0	3.4	2.0	2.5	53.0
Male	19.4	9.5	7.4	4.4	3.2	1.7	1.4	47.0

Sources: *Ghana Census* 1960, Special Report A, p. 3; 1970, Special Report A, Table 7.

decreased by 12.6% from 1960 to 1970, going from about 40,000 to 35,600.[71]
But the female population went down by only 5.8%, while the male population fell by 19.2%. The fact that a man was more likely to have his grown
sons with him contributed to this disparity. The net results of this trend for
the women in Central Accra are not good. While the population drop for
children up to age 14 was 5.6% from 1960 to 1970, and for old people 2.3%,
the number of women in the earning age groups of 15 to 64 fell by 7.5%, and
men by *26.7%*. In this section it will be shown that living nearby or
coresidence plays a crucial role in determining who bears the major share of
the dependency burden, meaning that women must do so.[72]

Dependency - The Young

The major part of the dependency burden is composed of young people
under fifteen. Ghana is part of the West African high fertility belt, and the
Ga are upholders of the rule. In 1960 Ghana's total fertility rate was 7.3 live
births per woman past childbearing age, the Ga urban rate was 5.7, and the
Ga rural one, 4.7, a contrast to the usual rule that urban rates are lower.[73]
In the 1971-72 small survey the 72 women in their thirties through nineties
had an average fertility rate of 6.3. In the 1978 survey of women aged 39 to

---

[71]However, the population decrease between the two censuses may have been due to
redrawing of the census district boundaries.

[72]This contrasts with Caldwell's supposition in 1967 that "the place of women, and
especially of children, in the home is improving, and children are absorbing more of the
family's money and attention." He was inordinately influenced by his studies of elite families. Caldwell, "Population," p. 161.

[73]This urban rate was above that for Accra as a whole (5.6), but below that for all
towns in Ghana (6.2). S. K. Gaisie, "Fertility Levels Among the Ghanaian Tribes," in *Population Growth and Economic Development in Ghana*, ed. S. H. Ominde and C. N. Ejiogu
(London: Heinemann, 1972), p. 87; Caldwell, *Population Growth*, p. 39; Caldwell, "Fertility
Attitudes in Three Economically Contrasting Rural Regions of Ghana," *Economic Development and Cultural Change* XV, no. 2, Part 1 (Jan. 1967): 231.

50 the average was six, not a significant difference and certainly not enough to indicate an overall drop in the birth rate.[74] There is even some evidence that the Accra birth rate may have risen over time, from an average of 30.2 births per 1,000 persons between 1913 and 1938, to 47.5 in 1967-68, yielding a population growth rate by natural increase of 2.8 to 3% per year. For urban areas in Ghana the population rose between 1931 and 1948 by 3.5% per year, and between 1948 and 1960 by 9.3%.[75]

This tremendous increase in population is disastrous, especially for the women. The population doubles or more in each generation (less than 25 years). The government is thus required to spend much money on providing urban amenities--housing, sewers, schooling, electricity, and water[76]--while individuals must use their capital for education and food, rather than both saving for development and investment. It would seem desirable, therefore, to achieve a decrease in population growth in Ghana and similar countries. Accordingly, family planning has been attempted by establishing clinics and distributing contraception devices, while ignoring the root causes of high fertility. It has therefore been a notable failure.

A more productive approach comes from considering demographic transition theory. Based on western historical models, it postulates that, as income increases, fertility will decline. Why? Because of rising expectations and investment in children, while children's mortality rates, labor and social security value decrease under urban conditions of more education, better health care and nutrition.[77] This theory has had widespread impact and sent scholars scurrying to prove that it applies in Third World countries. Unfortunately, the brunt of inquiry has been directed toward elite populations, operating on the assumption that they are only the first wave and everyone else's education and income will also rise to make fertility decline. Thus, when proof is discovered, as in Ghana, that elite populations have fewer children, the analysis of the problem often stops there.[78] It

---

[74]There were some differences in the 1971-72 small survey between age groups; the women in their eighties and nineties reported an average of 6.9 births compared to 5.8 for the women in their thirties through fifties.

[75]The 47.5 figure is for Ghana as a whole. Gaisie, "Population Growth," pp. 348, 340; Patterson, "Health," p. 260. Because of deficiencies in recording births the rate is probably underestimated. H. Page, "Fertility Levels—Patterns and Trends," in *Population Growth and Socioeconomic Change in West Africa*, ed. J. C. Caldwell (New York: Columbia University Press, 1975), p 52.

[76]Spengler has estimated that a 3% growth rate would absorb approximately 12% of the yearly national income in the provision of amenities. J. J. Spengler, "Population and Economic Growth," in *Population: The Vital Revolution*, ed. R. Freedman (Chicago: Aldine Publishing Co., 1964), p. 66. In 1975 approximately 20% of Ghana's total governmental expenditure went for education alone. UNESCO, *Statistical Yearbook 1976* (N.Y.: United Nations, 1976), p. 728.

[77]Caldwell, *Population Growth*, pp. 7-8; T. G. McGee, *The Urbanization Process in the Third World* (London: G. Bell and Sons, Ltd., 1971), p. 19. A pioneer article in this line was E. Sydenstricker and F. W. Notestein, "Differential Fertility According to Social Class," *Journal of American Statistical Association* XXV, no. 169 (1930): 9-32.

[78]Caldwell, *Population Growth*, pp. 38, 200-02; S. K. Gaisie, "Fertility Trends and Differentials" in *Population Growth and Socioeconomic Change in West Africa*, ed. J. C.

is not so simple. What happens when income distribution becomes *less* equitable and a majority of the people are getting poorer? In the current global perspective this kind of case is more typical and therefore warrants investigation. The most important question which needs answering concerns the impact of increased poverty on fertility patterns. Can one simply follow demographic transition theory to postulate that increased poverty drives fertility up and therefore increases the dependency burden? Little proof has been offered on this topic. The case of the Central Accra population therefore merits some attention.

The Central Accra samples offer the advantage of testing the impact on fertility both of overall declining economic status and of varying status according to particular periods. The results are inconclusive, as Table VI-3 shows. Much more reliable is the association of education level with fertility in the 1978 sample. Those with no education averaged 6.3 children, those with primary education, 6, and those with middle school education, 5, the combined average for the educated being 5.4. Fertility went down with higher levels of education, which supports demographic transition theory. But did it rise with lower economic status?

In fact, education level can be used as a proxy for income here, as elsewhere.[79] The women in the 1978 sample who had more education were also in more lucrative occupations, as Table VI-4 shows. We can expect, then, that poor, less-educated women will have more children. In this case, however, it is worth noting that higher income came mainly from trading activities in imported goods, not white collar jobs. However, the current situation in Ghana may possibly break the positive association of education level and

Table VI-3. Fertility Level
by Age Cohort and Economic Chronology, 1971-72, 1978.

Age of Women	Primary Childbearing Years	State of Economy	Fertility Level[a]
80+	1900s-1920s	Generally good	6.9
70-79	1920s-1930s	Generally bad	6
60-69	1930s-1940s	Moderately bad	6
50-59	1940s-1950s	Very good	5.7
40-49 (1971-72)	1950s-1960s	Fairly good[b]	6.1[c]
39-50 (1978)	1960s-1970s	Mostly bad	6[c]

[a]Mean average number of live births per woman.
[b]Bad from 1965 on.
[c]Fertility not completed in some cases.

Caldwell (New York: Columbia University Press, 1975), p. 343.

[79]D. W. Snyder, "Economic Determinants of Family Size in West Africa," *Demography* XI, no. 4 (Nov. 1974): 613.

**Table VI-4. Level of Education and Occupations
of 101 Ussher Town Women aged 39-50, 1978.**

Occupation[a] (by ascending economic status)	Percent of Women with level of education				
	None (No.=71)	Primary (No.=11)	Middle (No.=19)	All Educated (No.=30)	Total Percent (No.=101)
Unemployed	–	–	5.3[b]	3.3	1.0
Trade:[c]					
Prepared foods	31.0	9.0	15.8	13.3	25.7
Charcoal	1.4	–	–	–	1.0
Fish	38.0	9.0	–	3.3	27.7
Produce	11.3	18.0	5.3	10.0	10.9
Notions/sweets	7.0	–	15.8	10.0	7.9
Drinks/baked goods/provisions	2.8	45.5	15.8	26.7	9.9
Meat/eggs	–	–	5.3	3.3	1.0
Cloth/beads	5.6	–	10.5	6.7	5.9
Housewife	–	–	5.3	3.3	1.0
Domestic worker	5.6	18.0	15.8	16.7	8.9
Seamstress	4.2	–	10.5	6.7	4.9
Spirit medium	1.4	9.0	–	3.3	2.0
Actress	1.4	–	–	–	1.0

[a]Answers could be multiple.
[b]Outside the home, also counted under housewives.
[c]See Figure IV-2 for a ranking of traders.

income for women like these, because they are being hounded out of the imported goods trades, while employment in lower-level government jobs is quite scarce. If education level and income no longer are positively associated, the question will then become whether fertility levels will follow income or level of education. Because of the positive correlation between education level and use of contraception, unemployed middle school leavers form a poor group that would be more likely to use contraception. Therefore, while demographic transition theory seems to apply here, the factors of poverty and an education-associated increased use of contraception may eventually warp the situation so that decreasing income does not increase fertility, invalidating the theory.

At this point, however, Ga women have every incentive to *increase* their fertility, for reasons that need discussion. Because of patrilineal descent the factors of lineage prestige and perpetuation are not as important in promoting high fertility for women as they are for men. For women economic factors weigh more heavily, chiefly the labor and social security values of children, girls in particular. Girls (and boys to a lesser extent) contribute to the household economy by doing housework and trading. Historically boys contributed more when the male apprenticeship system was more important for Ga men. With the shift to formal education and literate jobs, however, boys' labor value decreased drastically while their maintenance costs went up. The labor of girls was and is used to help meet these costs, despite the fact that more girls are now sent to school. Girls who do not go to school put in long hours trading and doing housework, but schoolgirls also carry out considerable extracurricular duties. Therefore, the postulated impact of urbanization on fertility, that it will raise the costs and lower the labor value of children, does not operate to a large extent when women still carry out labor-intensive work like trading and/or home production.[80] Meanwhile, in a self-reinforcing process, the labor value of girls helps to alleviate the burden of caring for many small children and perpetuate high fertility. As in Nigeria and Cameroon (and unlike in western societies), there is a strong correlation between women working outside the home and high fertility.[81]

Other determinants of fertility are: age at marriage,[82] time spent in and out of marriage, monogamy versus polygyny, mode of arrangement of marriage, lactation practices, infant mortality, child support, and support in old age. Fertility would generally be increased by a younger age at marriage; the women in the 1971-72 small survey aged 50 and over averaged 21.3 years at marriage, compared to 19.2 for the 1978 women aged 39 to 50. Fertility would also be increased by a higher incidence of monogamous marriages; women in 1978 in monogamous marriages averaged 3.3 children, compared to 2.9 for women in polygynous marriages.[83] If there is a trend toward

---

[80] J. L. Simon, in *The Effects of Income on Fertility*, Carolina Population Center Monograph No. 19 (Chapel Hill: University of North Carolina Press, 1974), p. 116, noted that women's *wage* work outside the home usually does depress fertility, but cottage industry work does not. In a thorough review of the literature he found education the strongest variable in determining fertility.

[81] F. A. Ilori, "Urbanization and Fertility: A Case Study of Western Nigeria," paper presented at International Seminar on Integration of Theory and Policy in Population Studies, University of Ghana (1977), pp. 2, 9; V. DeLancey, "The Relationship Between Female Labor Force Participation and Fertility: Compatibility of Roles on a Cameroon Plantation," paper presented at African Studies Association Conference, Baltimore (Nov. 1978), p. 17. E. Schildkrout, "Age and Gender in Hausa Society: Socio-Economic Roles of Children in Urban Kano," in *Sex and Age as Principles of Social Differentiation*, ed. J. S. LaFontaine (N.Y.: Academic Press, 1978), p. 118, found that the labor of children appreciably raised Kano women's income, especially that of lower class women.

[82] I am omitting age at menarche here because there may be a relatively high incidence of premarital induced abortions. Age at menarche is reduced with better diet, and therefore is related to socioeconomic status. In the 1978 samples of 42 market and schoolgirls, the schoolgirls menstruated at age 14, on the average, compared to 14.5 for the market girls, a result compatible with their socioeconomic status differences.

W. Bleek, "Induced Abortion in a Ghanaian Family," *African Studies Review* XXI, no. 1 (April 1978): 113, found in a rural Akan family that the highest instance of induced abortion was among young unmarried girls.

[83] Usually more polygynous marriages are infertile. Here 17.7% of the 113 polygynous marriages were infertile compared to 9.6% of the monogamous ones. Also, more monogamous marriages were superfecund; 18% produced 7 or more children, compared to 12.4% of the polygynous marriages. R. R. Kuczynski, *Demographic Survey of the British Colonial*

monogamy, then it may help increase fertility. However, the increasing fragility of marriage meant that more younger women spent more time outside of marriage, which might cancel any fertility gains due to monogamy.

Mode of arrangement of marriage had a significant impact on fertility in both samples. In the 1971-72 sample, women in arranged marriages averaged 4.2 children compared to 3.3 for mutual consent marriages. In 1978, the women in arranged marriages averaged 3.9 children compared to 2.9 for mutual consent ones. Much of this difference is due to the fact that more mutual consent marriages were polygynous and infertile. The trend toward mutual consent marriage, then, should help depress fertility.

Lactation generally depresses fertility by inhibiting ovulation, while keeping the infant healthy. The women in the 1971-72 small survey reported an average lactation length per child of 17.6 months, compared to 14.1 months for the 1978 women.[84] However, any resultant effect of increasing fertility was negated by the negative correlation between lactation length and infant mortality in the 1978 sample; most babies who died were still being nursed. Lactation does not give immunity to malaria and many other endemic diseases, the most important killers of children. Also, the impact of shortened lactation length seems insignificant compared to the spectacular drop in infant mortality in Accra. From 1913 to 1960 the number of infant deaths per 1,000 live births in Accra went from 399.5 to 96, a 400% drop.[85] However, the impact of the economic downturn of the late 1960s and 1970s is not represented here. The infant mortality rate among the children of women aged 39 to 50 in 1978 was 71 per 1,000 live births, suggesting that the conditions of the late 1960s and 1970s had not affected it greatly.[86] Now the scarcity of medicines has long since reached crisis proportions, while nutrition has been rapidly deteriorating under the impact of inflation. Unfortunately, the gathering and publishing of statistics is also a casualty of the crisis, so that hard evidence may be a long while coming. The evidence available here shows no particular impact of decreased lactation length on fertility, but possibly a decrease in fertility due to decreased infant mortality.

The statistics concerning Ussher Town birth rates, then, indicate stability at a relatively high level. In contrast, the decrease in Accra infant mortality indicates a significant increase in the women's dependency burden.

Empire (London: Oxford University Press, 1948), I: 467, cites two reports written in 1850 and 1858 respectively by Lt-Gov. Bannerman (who was from Accra), and Dr. Clarke, the Colonial Surgeon, both of whom stated that polygyny reduced the number of births greatly.

[84]The U.N. Food and Agriculture Organization Report, "The economic value of breast-feeding" (Rome: 1979), p. 50, shows that in 1965-66 the average age at weaning of babies of educated Accra women was 10.2 months, of uneducated women—14.5 months.

[85]Patterson, "Health," p. 260; G. M. K. Kpedekpo, "Some Observations on Infant Mortality in the Urban Areas of Ghana," *Ghana Journal of Child Development* II, no. 2 (Dec. 1969): 16.

[86]This included infants dying at less than a year of age, to make it comparable to Patterson's Accra rate cited above. The statistic may have been lowered by the underreporting of infant deaths many researchers have noted, although we tried to be as thorough as possible. The 1971-72 data on infant mortality was not complete enough to be reliable.

Nonetheless, the support patterns give a clear indication of strong pressures toward continuing high fertility for these women. The social security function of children may even be most important in causing high fertility. In the absence of governmental social security, women look to their children and investments to provide support in sickness and old age. One childless woman said, *My houses are my children; they support me now that I am old.* But most women cannot afford investments and must rely on their children. The most frequent reason for having children cited by women in 1971-72 was to achieve economic security. In times of hardship it is even more crucial that they have children to help them. Thus, one might expect present economic conditions to reinforce an ethic which already promotes high fertility because of ideas of social status, maturity, and respectability. Infertility continues to be considered a tragedy.

A Comparison of Factors Promoting High Fertility

It has often been suggested that extended family links help to make high fertility feasible by spreading the burden of child support over a wide range of relatives.[87] The 1978 survey of women aged 39 to 50 yielded detailed information about the residence of 500 surviving children, and some about their support, while the 1971-72 small survey included more information about child support. All of this information led to the conclusion that high fertility was more a consequence of lack of child support by the children's fathers than of spreading the burden among relatives. The financial responsibility for the children a man propagates can easily be escaped by him, meaning that economic considerations will not usually affect his sexual activities. One woman commented, *Ghanaian men want many children, but they don't take care of them.* Meanwhile, the woman may leave the man because of lack of support, only to marry again in the hopes of finding someone who will help. She will then have more children who may end up not being supported either. Because of her concern about support in old age, she will still want many children. While there is an ethic which says that husbands should support their wives, it is almost never observed; a woman's grown children are her most important resort in time of crisis. In the face of this reality, the actions of relations in fostering children paled to insignificance as a cause of high fertility. Such actions, in any case, were not usually undertaken because the suppliers of foster children sought to relieve a heavy child support burden, but rather because their users sought help, or children to relieve sterility. We need to look, then, at some of the evidence supporting these assertions.

---

[87] J. C. Caldwell, *The Socio-Economic Explanation of High Fertility*, Changing African Family Project Series Monograph No. 1 (Canberra: Australian National University, 1976), p. 108; S. K. Gaisie, "Some aspects of fertility studies in Ghana," in *The Population of Tropical Africa*, ed. J. Caldwell and C. Okonjo (London: Longman's, Green and Co., Ltd., 1968), p. 245.

Paying school fees was the most important responsibility which the man was supposed to fulfill, and yet most women in 1971-72 reported that they had paid most of them themselves. Among the 42 Form 1 schoolgirls interviewed in 1978, the payment of school fees was mostly attributed to the fathers or a father's relative (57.1%), but a substantial number (40.5%) reported that their mother or a mother's relative paid them. More important, in 57.1% of the cases the mothers gave them pocket money, compared to 19% where the fathers did. The pocket money was cumulatively larger than the public school fees. Also, the relatives who helped (other than the parents) were all women.

Coresidence can be used as a fair proxy for financial help for and from children, depending on their age. Table VI-5 shows the residence of the children of the 101 women in the 1978 sample. Of the 130 children living with persons other than their parents, half were living with female, and 6% with male relatives, showing again the overwhelming preponderance of women in childcare. The remainder were elsewhere. By the time the women were in their forties, 7.4% of all the children were independent and elsewhere, not an overwhelming number available to help them finance the younger siblings. More help probably came from the 84.5% of the girls and 26.2% of the boys over 18 who were still living with their mothers. In that case they were more likely to be unmarried and sharing the family food. However, not a few of the women were grandmothers because their elder coresident daughters had children. They were supporting grandchildren as well as children, while their elder daughters' earnings were cut by the exigencies of childcare. The child-related dependency burden for women with children averaged three children per woman, omitting grown (over 18) and fostered children, and grandchildren. Two cases illustrate the situation.

**Table VI-5. Residence by Age and Sex of Child
and Relationship to Caretaker, 1978.[a]**

Children		Percentage of Children of Same Sex Living with					
Age	Sex	Mother only	Father only	Both parents	Matrilateral Relatives	Patrilateral Relatives	Other
0.1-6 years	female	84.4	6.2	3.1	6.2	–	–
	male	85.7	4.8	4.8	2.4	2.4	–
6.1-12 years	female	73.1	4.5	3.0	9.0	9.0	1.5
	male	59.6	17.5	8.8	8.8	5.3	–
12.1-18 years	female	61.6	2.7	1.4	19.2	9.6	5.5
	male	42.6	24.6	8.2	8.2	4.9	11.5
18.1 and over	female	54.5	9.0	2.3	6.8	3.4	23.9
	male	26.2	26.2	5.0	6.2	7.5	28.7

[a]No. = 500.

Akuɔkɔ was a 46-year-old fishseller bearing a particularly heavy dependency burden in 1978. She had had ten children by one husband, all of whom were surviving and eight of whom lived with her. The two oldest daughters, respectively 28 and 26, were living with her, plus five grandchildren belonging to her first-born daughter, a *banku* seller. The second daughter had managed to complete middle school and get a job as a printer. She was the only child in a position to contribute to the household. Akuɔkɔ got fish to sell from her husband, but no cash. On occasion she made loans to him, as well as to her eldest son, a fisherman. Although she did reasonably well as a fishseller, she had a very difficult time simply feeding her chief dependents, the five children thirteen and under and some of the grandchildren. She wished that her husband would help more, but realized that he could not afford it. She felt that there was no one to turn to for money in a crisis, and worried a lot.

Another type of situation was experienced by Obliɔkɔ, a woman with a light dependency burden relative to others in the sample.

Obliɔkɔ was also 46 years old and a fresh fishseller in 1978. She had had five children, four of whom aged seven and four were living with her (two sets of twins). Her 25-year-old eldest daughter lived elsewhere and was not contributing to the household. The father of the first set of twins, her third husband, refused to pay child support, but the father of the second set, a medical dispenser, was giving her ¢30 a month, even though they were separated. He had given her ¢100 a month before the separation, but they separated because he often got drunk and beat her. Her mother tried arbitration to save the marriage but died before accomplishing it. Obliɔkɔ felt that she was just getting by, with some help from her brothers. Even so, she had had to reduce the amount of food she bought and had had to stop buying cloth altogether.

Neither of these women was completely destitute by any means, but for both only the variable profits from fishselling stood between them and a serious catastrophe. The fact that they both had at least one child old enough to help financially did not get them very far, nor did the existence of husbands or ex-husbands.

Some women (35.6% of the 101 in the 1978 sample) were helped by relatives' taking their children, usually daughters, to serve as domestic helpers to wealthier female relatives in the suburbs.[88] The mothers who fostered out children had bigger families than those who did not, 6.2 compared to 4.7 children. However, because most women did not have children fostered out, fostering may not have made that much difference to fertility, or to the dependency burden; only 11.2% of the surviving children were being fostered. The maturing of the older children (33.6% of the children were over 18) was more important in alleviating the dependency burden, and might even have encouraged some women to have yet more children when they saw their burden lessening. Half of the women were under 45 and could probably have done so. It may be, then, that the bearing of children throughout the entire childbearing period actually encouraged high fertility by moving older

---

[88]The percentage of women in 1971-72 who had fostered out children was similar: 31%.

children out of the dependency range as younger ones were coming in. It was not unusual to find a twenty-year age gap between a woman's oldest and youngest children, and 14.8% of the surviving children of the women aged 39 to 50 were six and under. It seems unlikely, then, that the child-related dependency burden provided a motive for reducing fertility, but fostering was not necessarily an important contributor to increasing fertility.

The most important factor in promoting women's high fertility is clearly the social security function of children. As long as women remain in jobs where no pensions are provided and the labor value of children is still considerable, there is very little rational justification for limiting their fertility, in their view. Some men might see differently because of fixed salaries or pensions. Thus, in three cases in the 1978 sample of women aged 39 to 50, marriages had broken up or fights had arisen because a husband wanted a wife to get an abortion and she refused. However, polygyny gave husbands more children and young wives to support them, so their motivation for reducing fertility was also questionable. In fact, the data concerning support for the elderly show just how necessary children are.

Dependency - The Old

The dependency burden for old persons seems also increasingly to fall on the younger women. While Caldwell in 1966 indicated that sons were more likely than daughters to be helping both parents, the 1978 data taken from 101 old or retired people in Ussher Town showed daughters in this role.[89] Caring for the old and infirm is by far the lesser of the two major dependency burdens; attrition makes them less numerous than the young, and habit, as well as necessity, enjoins that they work as long as possible.[90] Nevertheless, they add to the burden borne by the working-age population, especially the women.

The 1978 survey of 101 elderly/retired persons in Ussher Town yielded specific information about their sources of support. Eighty-four women and 17 men were included with the respective mean average ages of 72.3 and 66.8 years. All were at least semi-retired needing some help. The results disproved the common assumption that urbanization necessarily reduces the social security value of children.[91]

---

[89] J. C. Caldwell, "The Erosion of the Family: A Study of the Fate of the Family in Ghana," *Population Studies* XX, no. 1 (July 1966): 19.

[90] K. Ewusi, "The Size of the Labour Force and the Structure of Employment in Ghana," paper for University of Ghana Institute of Statistical, Social and Economic Research (ISSER) (1975), pp. 31-32; "While government social legislation are [sic] forcing those over 55 years into early retirement, economic pressure during the decade [1960-70] has rather forced them to look for alternative means of income and thus they . . . remain in the labour force."

[91] Usually accompanied by the rising incomes assumption. Simon, *Effects*, p. 113; Caldwell, in "Population Prospects and Policy," in *Study*, ed. W. Birmingham et al., p. 160,

Women and men exhibited markedly different support patterns, although similarities outweighed differences in a few areas. Both relied primarily on their children for support, the majority of whom were helping in some manner (72.5% of the women's children and 51% of the men's).[92] Both sexes received help most often from their daughters, followed next by their sons. Seventy-five percent of the women's daughters were helping them and 59% of the men's. Of the sons 70% were helping the women and 44% the men. In the 1971-72 large sample support for women was also derived from a higher proportion of their offspring than for men. This can be attributed partly to the women usually keeping the children after divorce. As a result the children's contacts with their fathers were often limited.[93] Field stated in 1940 that women did not mind divorces as much as men did because they knew that the children would always help them anyway.[94] Caldwell in 1966 also found that, in a survey of 800 Ghanaians over 60, men got help from a smaller proportion of their children than women did, despite the fact that they had more children.[95] Another more simple explanation for this phenomenon comes out of that last clause. Since men do have far more children than women, even if a lower percentage of those children contribute to their fathers in old age, enough may be provided. Men in fact got help from *more* people on the average than women did (4.9 versus 4.4 persons), mainly because of their differential fertility.

Women received help from a far wider range of relatives than men did, among whom the female network is outstanding. Women of all ages were most concerned that they have *daughters* to look after and cook for them in their old age. Their sisters' children and grandchildren were even more likely to help them than their own grandchildren were. The reason for this lay primarily in the fact that childless women (17% of the elderly women had no surviving children) were most likely to have been helped by their sisters and their children. In two such cases, old feeble women just managed, one by sharing with a marginally employed sister (also childless), and the other by help from two unemployed sisters who were receiving support from their children. Of necessity, then, the women had to look to a wider range of relatives and nonrelatives for support than the men did; there were no

---

also unwarrantedly assumed that "in the long run the government will undoubtedly shoulder these social welfare burdens."

[92]The bias in this data, if any, would be toward overestimation of help, because some people found it humiliating to admit that their children were not fulfilling their support obligations.

[93]Robertson, "Social and Economic Change," p. 196n.

[94]Field, *Social Organisation*, pp. 25-26.

[95]Caldwell, "Erosion," p. 12. Unfortunately, Caldwell succumbed to the western male's "housewife" complex in providing an explanation for this data. He gave as the reason "the greater traditional acceptance of women not working in gainful employment [!], and hence needing support from relatives at every stage in their adult lives" (p. 14). He found that only 52.2% of the surviving children were helping 241 urban parents (p. 15). The contrast with my results hints that hard times have spread the dependency burden of old people further, although not necessarily increased the amount they get. However, there is perhaps a simpler explanation—the contrasting sex biases of the samples.

childless men. The men also had younger wives to care for them, while it was virtually unknown for an elderly woman to have an older or younger husband who helped.[96] It was more likely, although quite rare, that a well-off older woman would attract a younger husband by supporting him.

In fact, the reasons for high fertility for women come through clearly in the fertility statistics from the sample. Men had, on the average, 14.1 children from multiple marriages, of whom 7.5 were surviving in 1978 (men's children born outside of marriage were not recorded). Women, in contrast, bore an average of 6.8 children, of whom 3.6 survived in 1978, an uncanny resemblance to the 3.7 surviving children of 215 women in the 1971-72 large survey. Even a woman with surviving children was not always guaranteed an income. In one case a 76-year-old woman had three surviving daughters and one son, none of whom lived in Accra, and got no help from them. A brother had helped her, but his death three months prior to the survey left her dependent on tiny earnings from selling sponges and an occasional dash from a friend.

That more women than men helped these older people illustrates the skew of the dependency burden. The responses of both men and women were similar in this respect. Fifty-four point six percent of the supporters of the women were female compared to 60% of those of the men.[97] This was despite the fact that the female supporters were less educated and less likely to be employed in well-paid jobs than the males. Because more of the supporters were women, the women respondents were more likely to be living with their supporters than the men. Thirty-four percent of the supporters of the women lived in the same house with them, compared to 11% with the men. The supporters of both the men and the women were most likely to live in Central Accra (46%), and next likely to live in the far suburbs (32%), the rest being scattered equally about the near suburbs, Ga villages, and other locations in Ghana and abroad. Living nearby or coresidence were positively related to support, then.

There were also differences in the type and amount of help given by female and male supporters. Women could generally afford to give less money but gave more in kind--sharing food, for instance. Men gave more clothing, which might involve the outlay of a single large sum of money. Was this help adequate? The mean average amount of money received by women respondents per month from all sources was ₵46.32, for men, ₵53.09.[98] This seems reasonable (although certainly not luxurious), *provided that the respondent was supplementing his or her income from other sources.* In fact, some got income from part-time work or other sources, as indicated in Table VI-6. The rents received were often minimal, as for a room in a

---

[96]Caldwell, "Erosion," p. 11, noted that aged males often got their chief support from younger wives. J. North et al., *Women in National Development*, U.S. Department of State AID report (April 1975), p. 84, made a similar observation about Larteh, Ghana, and commented on the superior financial resources of men as compared to women.

[97]The number of supporters whose sex could be determined was 369 for the women and 85 for the men.

[98]For 79 women and 16 men (not available for others).

Table VI-6. Sources of Support by Sex in Percent of Respondents.[a]

Source:	Women (No.=84)	Men (No.=17)
Work	41.7	52.9
Pension	–	23.5
Rent	3.6	11.8
Friend	9.5	–
Savings	–	5.9

[a]Excluding help from relatives.

Central Accra compound. The men not only got more monetary help from relatives, but also had more sources of help external to the family: pensions, rents, savings. Almost two-thirds of the men had three or more types of income, while more than two-thirds of the women had only one or two. More men were still working, probably because of their younger average age and lack of childcare responsibilities for grandchildren. Approximately the same proportions of men and women reported getting help in kind, so the women had no advantage there.

Given these results, it is not surprising that when the respondents were asked whether or not the help they got was sufficient for their needs, two-thirds of the women replied in the negative compared to half of the men. These responses were undoubtedly linked to economic conditions; in the 1971-72 small sample, 83.3% replied affirmatively to this question. In 1978 those who replied negatively were then asked how much would be sufficient for them per month, yielding an average amount of ₵230 for the women and ₵330 for the men. Furthermore, more men than women reported that there were people who should be helping them and were not, which was partly due to the smaller proportion of their children giving help.[99] The women seem, then, to have made fewer demands than the men did, yet their needs were probably greater because of the lopsided dependency burden. In a few cases women only got regular donations to the household budget because they were caring for (grand)children belonging to the donors. The men were far more likely than the women to be spending their money mostly on themselves. Two examples will suffice, the first fairly desperate, the second a bit better, neither comfortable.

---

[99]A brief comparison of the characteristics of supporters versus nonsupporters (those named by the respondents as owing them support but not fulfilling the obligation) is instructive. Generally the nonsupporters were younger than the supporters by about five to eight years (43.9 versus 38.2 mean average age for the supporters versus nonsupporters of the women and 34.9 versus 26.5 for the men). More of the nonsupporters than supporters had a middle school education, were skilled laborers, students, or unemployed. More lived in a far suburb or abroad. Supporters more often had secondary education, were traders, fishermen, or white collar workers, and lived in the same house with the respondent. Above all, more nonsupporters mentioned by both sexes were male (58.7%), indicating that people felt that their sons had shirked their responsibilities more often than their daughters.

Naa Koshie was a 68-year-old breadseller in 1978. In spite of help from two children and three of her sister's children or grandchildren, she was having great difficulties with survival on a budget which had to feed not only herself, but also her elder sister with two of her daughters and their children, another sister's son, and a granddaughter. Her earnings and their contributions were simply not enough to feed them all adequately.

Tawia was simply trying to keep the household together and did not have the time to work outside it in 1978. Her former trade, selling fishing nets and thread, had become impossible because of shortages, and no capital was available to start a new one. At age 62 she was responsible for feeding herself, two grown children, her husband, and two grandchildren, on contributions from her husband and seven of their eight children. Inflation was making great inroads on the fixed contributions of the household members. She complained that the standard of their nutrition was declining, while buying cloth had become impossible.

At every age, then, women were bearing more of the dependency burden than men, with fewer resources to support it. Not only did they have fewer resources but they were also more likely to *perceive* themselves as resourceless; over a quarter of the women said they had nowhere to turn in a crisis, compared to only 5% of the men.[100] The Social Security Act of 1965, which made it compulsory for establishments employing five or more workers to pay social security to the government for their workers,[101] was irrelevant in this context; most women were self-employed.

Because the most common means of birth control used in Ghana, abortion, must be sought by women, it is the women's decisions which mainly determine fertility. In an attempt to shore up their vulnerable economic position these women often wanted to have as many children as possible. The saddest and poorest cases were women with no surviving children who begged their subsistence from reluctant relatives and acquaintances. One woman had alienated all of the other residents of a large compound in this way. They felt guilty and therefore resentful of her mere presence (she had only a marginal right to live there, in any case). She said, *I starve some.* Another one scraped by on an earned pittance and an occasional small donation from a friend. In contrast, the man who complained most loudly of poverty was getting a pension of ₵30 a month, as well as help from children. This was admittedly not much, but definitely more than many women were getting. Moreover, he had a guaranteed source of income, unlike their irregular donations which had a tendency to dry up in the economic drought. The residential system constantly presents such examples to the eyes of all women, reminding them to have children.

---

[100]The men, mostly fishermen and skilled artisans, were more familiar than the women with the outside world and alternative resources, probably because they were more educated than the women and participated in networks including white collar relatives.

[101]G. Aryee, "Small Scale Manufacturing Activities: A Study of the Interrelationship Between the Formal and the Informal Sectors in Kumasi, Ghana," International Labour Office World Employment Program Working Paper No. 23 (Geneva: 1977), p. 25.

Women often believed that having more children increased the probabilities of having one who would become rich and support them. Economic theory supports this conviction--or at least the probability that persons of high fertility will be better supported in old age--by saying that the same number of benefits accrue to individuals from having a large family of low quality children or a small family of high quality (better educated and employed) children.[102] The elderly women's experience compared to that of the men here also supports this belief. However, the women's feelings about bearing a disproportionate share of the consequent dependency burden were often ambivalent. A recent survey of literature written by African women found that one of the dominant themes was "men using women's sense of responsibility to enslave them."[103]

Sharing the Same Bowl? Help from Suburban Relatives

We need to explore further the nature of the help received from residentially dispersed family members to see whether or not the dependency burden is mitigated significantly by help from wealthier suburban relatives, which was suggested by the fostering results. Below the argument that ties between extended family members inhibit class formation by redistributing wealth is addressed.[104] The ties between residentially dispersed family members will be tested by exploring the connections between Ga families in Central Accra and in Kaneshie, a prosperous suburb originally settled by Ga. Kaneshie mainly grew up during and after World War II; from 1956, when it had a population of 8,800, it grew to be approximately 30,000 in 1970.[105] My choice of this area was determined by the number of people in Central Accra in 1971-72 who mentioned having relatives there. In fact, one area, the housing estate built to accommodate the 1939 earthquake victims, was largely populated by people from Asere. An elderly woman living in Old Kaneshie said, in reference to Asere, *We are one people; we eat from the same bowl.* The results did not bear out her contention.

Kaneshie is a bewildering complexity, a vast sprawl encompassing everything from a sports complex to the Ga Maŋtsɛ's palace, with secondary

---

[102]Snyder, "Economic Determinants," p. 618.

[103]B. Berrian, paper presented at National Women's Studies Association Conference (May 1980).

[104]Caldwell, *Population Growth*, p. 184; T. Kumekpor, "Marriage and the Family in a Changing Society: A Case Study of Attitudes of Students of the University of Ghana to Marriage," University of Ghana Institute of African Studies, Legon Family Research Papers No. 3 (1975), p. 74; R. Genoud, *Nationalism and Economic Development in Ghana* (New York: Frederick A. Praeger, 1969), p. 36; P. J. Foster, "Secondary Schooling and Social Mobility in a West African Nation," *Sociology of Education* XXXVII, no. 2 (1963): 150-71.

[105]Ghana, Ministry of Housing, *Accra Plan* (1958), p. 46, noted that Kaneshie could accommodate a population of approximately 28,000. *Ghana Census* (1970), Special Report A, Table 7; *Ghana Census* (1960), Special Report A, p. 3. It is not mentioned in the 1948 census.

schools, factories, and demure residences in between. It had, according to
the 1970 census, more white collar workers, skilled laborers, and homemakers
than Ussher Town, and fewer unemployed, fishermen, and traders. The sex
ratio for Ussher Town was 88 males for every 100 females, compared to
105:100 for Kaneshie. Many of the excess males in Kaneshie were in their
prime earning years, while the excess females in Ussher Town were more
often in the dependency age groups. The dependency ratio in Ussher Town
in 1970 was 128 persons 0 to 19 and 65 and over per 100 aged 20 to 64, compared to 121 for Kaneshie.[106]

We surveyed 280 houses in three areas in Kaneshie: Old Kaneshie, the
earthquake housing and lowest in socioeconomic status, Awudome Estates, a
middle class housing estate mostly built in the 1960s, and New Kaneshie, an
area of mixed estate and owner-built houses dating from the 1970s. Table
VI-7 sums up the socioeconomic characteristics of the three areas, which
were chosen to provide as much diversity as possible. Old Kaneshie was
ethnically Ga, and the only area having a predominance of one group. The
proportion of Ga houseowners went down as the socioeconomic status of the
area went up, from 94% Ga in Old Kaneshie to 26% in Awudome Estates
and only 16% in New Kaneshie.[107] This could be accounted for by the fact
that government estate houses predominated in the latter two areas; in areas
of exclusively owner-built houses more Ga were present because of their
advantage in access to land.[108]

There was quite an age range among the owners, but the average age
went down according to the newness of the areas. This age supports what I
found among the traders, who were most likely to have built or bought
houses in their forties or fifties. Also, because of inheritance patterns
(women were more likely to have inherited houses, men to have built or
bought one), the proportion of female houseowners went down with the newness of the areas. This also had to do with relative wealth, since women
traders were formerly more able to afford houses. In Old Kaneshie, women
were more likely to have bought a house themselves or inherited one from a
female relative; in Awudome and New Kaneshie they sometimes got them
from their husbands. One prosperous cloth trader in New Kaneshie was
engaged in an acrimonious court battle with her husband's relatives for possession of the house. Both she and her husband had contributed to building
the house, but he had died intestate a few months previously. She and their
children were in possession; the relatives were doing their best to evict them.
This sort of case arises frequently and provides yet another incentive for
women to keep their money separate from their husbands'. Reinforcing male

---

[106] *Ghana Census*, 1970, Special Report A, Table 7.

[107] The proportion of Ewe and Asante houseowners went up with increase in socioeconomic status, while Fanti were strongly represented in both Awudome Estates and
New Kaneshie.

[108] Such is the labyrinthine complexity of Kaneshie that I only discovered such an area
when I was almost finished with the interviewing, too late to include it in the survey. A
spot-check there revealed that in ten houses there were 7 Ga and 3 Ewe owners, with two
Fanti tenants and one Ewe tenant.

**Table VI-7. Kaneshie: Education and Occupation
of Houseowners in Three Areas, 1977-78.**[a]

	Percent of Houseowners in			
	Old Kaneshie	Awudome Estates	New Kaneshie	Total
Education	(No. = 63)	(No. = 135)	(No. = 51)	(No. = 249)
None	41.3	10.4	5.9	17.3
Primary	6.3	–	–	1.6
Middle	30.2	37.8	17.6	31.7
Post-middle/technical/ teacher's training/ nurse's training/ commercial	14.3	25.2	33.3	24.1
Secondary	7.9	15.6	17.6	14.1
University	–	11.1	25.5	11.2
Total	100.0	100.1	99.9	100.0
Occupation[b]	(No. = 65)	(No. = 149)	(No. = 59)	(No. = 273)
Unskilled laborer	1.5	–	–	0.4
Farmers	–	4.0	–	2.2
Homemakers	–	4.0	1.7	2.6
Traders/small business owners				
food/produce	33.8	7.4	5.1	13.2
imported-type goods	10.8	11.4	6.8	9.9
Skilled laborers	18.5	14.8	16.9	12.5
White Collar				
low-status[c]	32.3	51.0	52.5	49.1
high-status[d]	4.6	15.4	20.3	16.1
Maŋtsεs, elders, priestesses	4.6	0.7	1.7	1.8
Total	106.1	108.7	105.0	107.8

[a]Numbers indicate those where numbers were given. The sizes of samples were partly determined by the size of the neighborhood. All of Old Kaneshie and Awudome Estates were covered, plus part of Kaneshie Estates adjoining Awudome Estates. While the largest physical area was covered in New Kaneshie, it encompassed the fewest houses. There I worked until I reached the end of Kaneshie. Thirty-two point six percent of the owners were non-resident and 17.7% of the houses were occupied by tenants only.

[b]Answers could be mutliple.

[c]Clerks, draughtman, teachers, etc.

[d]Doctors, lawyers, professionals, managing directors, large entrepreneurs, etc.

authority was the higher incidence of conjugal households in all three areas than downtown. Thus, Kaneshie presented in microcosm the increase in economic dependency for women associated with elite status.

From among the 280 households surveyed we selected 67 Ga families to examine further concerning their help to relatives downtown. They comprised three-quarters of all Ga families in the sample, and all of the ones who had relatives in Central Accra. In the end, only 40 families completed the whole survey, including the household economy section which required keeping track of all expenditures (44 did everything except that section). Since the main goal here is to consider financial help going from Kaneshie downtown, rather than the differing nature of the three areas, I will henceforth mostly consider the sample in the aggregate. The sample is biased toward Old Kaneshie with 21 households; 15 households were in Awudome Estates, and only 4 in New Kaneshie. Its socioeconomic characteristics are given in Table VI-8. The respondents were either owners themselves or related to the owner; none were tenants. More respondents than owners were female because women were more likely to be in the house and have the time to reply. The household expenditure surveys were supplemented by

Table VI-8. Characteristics of Kaneshie Ga with Central Accra Relatives.[a]

	Respondent	Owner
Mean average age	52.4	58.5
Sex:		
Female	68.9%	45.5%
Male	31.1	55.5
Education		
None	31.1%	27.9%
Primary	6.7	4.7
Middle	33.3	34.9
Secondary	2.2	2.3
Post-middle technical/commercial	24.4	27.9
University	2.2	2.3
Total	99.9	100.0
Occupation[b]:		
Trader - prepared foods	25.9%	24.5%
- imported goods	20.4	10.2
Domestic	1.8	–
Housewife	5.5	2.0
Skilled labor	14.8	14.3
Low-status white collar	22.2	36.7
High-status white collar	7.4	10.2
Elder	1.8	2.0
Total	99.8	99.9

[a]No. = 67.

[b]Answers could be multiple.

information from other household members when necessary.

We calculated the amount of monetary help given to nonresident relatives in two ways--by percentage of income, and by percentage of estimated
annual expenditure derived from our household expenditure survey. At
2.2% of expenditure, the amount of help given to nonresident relatives was
not high, and ranked third lowest in importance, as can be seen in Table
VI-9. This proportion was directly related to income. Those who gave no
help (25% of the sample) had an average annual income of ₵3,200, those
whose help was up to 4% of expenditure averaged ₵8,300, and those with
5% or over averaged ₵16,600. In fact, it might be more accurate to double
the percentage spent. Because spouses kept their money separate in most
cases, the contributions listed usually came from only one of the major
household earners. Even doubled, however, the proportion amounted to only
approximately ₵30.50 a month per household going to nonresident relatives,
if one takes percentage of income, and ₵37.50 a month if one takes

Table VI-9.
Household Expenditure in 40 Kaneshie Households, 1978.[a]

Item	Percent of Expenditure	Item	Percent of Expenditure
Food and fuel (for cooking)	61.7	Clothing	2.9
Education fees and pocket money	6.3	Taxes	2.8
Transportation, including car mainte-nance	4.2	Housing, including maintenance, utili-ties, taxes	2.4
Charitable donations (church, voluntary associations, etc.)	4.0	Services, including servants' pay, medi-cal care, etc.	2.3
Savings	3.3	Financial help to non-resident relatives	2.2
Other	3.3	Consumer goods (ra-dio, T.V., etc.)	1.6
Entertainment, in-cluding tobacco, al-cohol	2.9	Organization dues	0.2
		Total[b]	100.1

[a]Based on one week's record kept in January or February, 1978, plus supplementary information about annual or other regular expenditures.

[b]As it turned out, 100.1% seemed incorrect, since on the average households reported
that expenditure exceeded income by about 33%. Even considering that people probably
underreported income, debt was indubitably a persistent problem for many.

percentage of estimated annual expenditure.

The respondents were also asked about other types of help they were giving to nonresident relatives. This yielded a broader picture of the outflow of help among 45 respondents, but still 27% said that they were not helping anyone financially, a higher percentage than those who omitted help to non-resident relatives from household expenditure. However, the request implied *regular* help, which might explain the difference. Eighty-six percent of the recipients were getting money or money and help in kind, the rest in kind only. Most got help with their subsistence needs, but 15% got help with education expenses. When amounts were cited (in 32 cases) the mean average sum given monthly was ¢15.96. Cumulatively, the most help went to persons younger than the respondents, especially grandchildren, siblings' children, or siblings. However, those older than the respondent also received a fair share, especially mothers and mothers' sisters (classificatory mothers).

Having derived an impression of the scope of help, we then sought information about types of help ever given. Asking about help with educational expenses netted the following results. Forty-two percent of the respondents claimed that they had never helped anyone except their own children with educational expenses. These were distributed fairly evenly throughout the three residential areas (as were those who had not helped others financially). Altogether, the 26 respondents who did help aided some 63 persons to get an education. Those helped were related to the helpers as follows: brother--11.1%; sister--9.5%; grandchild--27% (15.9% were daughter's daughters); sister's child or grandchild--22.2%; brother's child--9.5%; spouse's relative--9.5%; and other--4.8%. Siblings and their children received the most help here, even more than grandchildren. This may be because people did not always feel it necessary to mention helping grandchildren, that being taken for granted. Also, grandchildren were more likely to be coresident, and thus fall outside the scope of the question. When respondents were asked what type of education they had sponsored, 71.4% stated that they helped with primary school expenses, 42.9% with middle school, 14.3% with secondary school, 3.2% with post-middle school training, and 4.8% with apprenticeship fees. On the average help was given for 6.3 years, a respectable duration. No one expected to be directly repaid, reciprocity entailing a more involved exchange of later help.

People were also asked about help to nonresident relatives in the form of services. Here more information was gleaned than expected, although some was a bit vague. In 36 cases people said that they had helped an unspecified number of people, although in 44 specific individuals were mentioned. The type of services performed in the 80 cases were as follows: finding a job/school place--43.7%; cooking (especially for ceremonies)--32.5%; teaching skills (apprenticeship)--11.2%; doing paperwork--8.7%; obtaining goods/housing--3.7%, settling disputes--2.5%; other--1.2%. The help people gave to relatives was supplemented by that to friends, which 36.4% of 44 respondents said they had given in services, but none in the form of regular contributions. Six point eight percent of the sample had helped friends with education expenses.

While cumulatively, all of this help seems impressive, most of it did not go to persons in Central Accra. Why? Forty-three percent of the 40 respondents had no *living* immediate relatives in Central Accra. Nineteen percent had a mother, 2% a father, 26% a sister, 17% a brother, 7% a daughter, 5% a son, and 2% a grandparent, living in Central Accra in 1977-78. Those who had any living immediate relatives in Central Accra averaged 1.7 apiece, with a slightly higher average for Old Kaneshie. Only 23% of the sample had an elderly person, a parent or grandparent, living there whom they could help. This was because many of the respondents' parents were dead, a few lived in Kaneshie with them, and some lived elsewhere than Central Accra, often with a sibling or child in another suburb. The respondents' siblings who were living in Central Accra were often younger, although a few were retired or unemployed. Their children downtown had sometimes taken up on rights to live in a family house or gone to be with husbands. Most often, whole families (defined as any of the common residential groupings) had moved out, leaving no immediate relatives downtown, or new families had formed neolocally. This sample did not offer a tremendous number of natural opportunities, then, for help going to Central Accra. This was why we broadened our inquiry to deal with help to any nonresident relatives.

The general rule we found in examining support patterns among Central Accra old people, that support was most often associated with living nearby or coresidence, was upheld in these results. Six percent of the families were fostering a child of a relative, and 6% had a coresident elderly relative (senior to the owner) who had been invited to live with them in Kaneshie. In addition, 15% of the households were those amorphous conglomerations of matrilaterally or patrilaterally related persons usually containing elderly or young persons not necessarily closely related to the coresident able-bodied adults. Then there were the 16% of the conjugal or single-parent households which included either grandchildren or siblings (and maybe a few of their children) of a core parent. Altogether, in almost 40% of the Ga households help was being provided in the context of coresidence to relatives other than a couple/parent and children core, i.e., to members of an extended family.

While the nature of the dependency burden was somewhat different from in Central Accra, it was equally significant for these households. The mean average number of active earners in the households was 2.3, so that each person was supporting an average of 2.2 other coresident persons, a small improvement over Central Accra. Unlike in Central Accra, many households (60%) had no retired persons in them. If the dependency burden of old people was lighter, that of young people made up for it by being heavier, perhaps due to higher survival rates for children. The respondents had an average of 5.7 living children apiece, 56.6% of whom were coresident. Because of education expenses, the children were more costly to support than in Central Accra. Many families had at least one child at a secondary boarding school, which is quite expensive. In a case of scarce resources, education for the children would probably take priority over other obligations. In an extreme case, a woman trader in New Kaneshie whose husband had abandoned her, had four teenage sons and two daughters to support, as well as an elderly mother. Because she had sold everything she could, she presided over a house with one broken chair and a table for furniture. But her children were all in school, even though the two eldest sons were easily old enough to work.

Another reason for only small amounts of help being given in 1978 was, of course, the economic situation. When looked at historically, as in the results for help *ever* given anyone, the help seems substantial. But for 1978 alone, it is not impressive. In fact, the results dispute Engel's law, that expenditure on food is inversely related to rising income, a logical consequence of the runaway prices of foodstuffs in Ghana. Table VI-10 sites these results among those from other Ghanaian household expenditure surveys. The mean average number of persons composing a household was 7.4, and the mean average amount spent weekly (including the prorated items) was ₵213.04. Compared to other household expenditure surveys in Accra, the proportion spent on food was high for a sample with perhaps a quarter of the

Table VI-10.
Household Expenditure in Accra/Urban Ghana, 1953-1978.

Year	Location	Percent of Expenditure on	
		Food	Help to Non-resident Relatives
1953	Accra	64.1	n.a.[a]
1961	Accra	56.1	n.a.
1965-66	Ghana[b]	65.5	1.1
1965-66	Ghana[c]	57.0	n.a.
1970	Ghana[d]	21.0	7.3
1971	Legon[e]	21.1	n.a.
1978	Kaneshie[f]	67.1	2.2

[a]Not available.
[b]Average size household 4.5 persons.
[c]White collar workers.
[d]Upper and middle income Ghanaians.
[e]Senior staff households.
[f]Households covered in this survey.

Sources: R. Szereszewski, "Patterns of Consumption," in *A Study of Contemporary Ghana*, ed. W. Birmingham et al., I:111; Dutta-Roy and Mabey, *Household Budget* (1968), p. 42; K. Ewusi and S. J. Mabey, "Expenditure Patterns of Upper and Middle Income Groups in Ghana," University of Ghana, ISSER Technical Publication No. 26 (1972), p. 68; K. Ewusi, "Changing Patterns of Household Expenditure in Ghana," paper presented at Conference on Innovation in African Economic History, Legon (Dec. 1971), p. 9.

households earning over ₵10,000 a year.[109] Expenditure on food ranged from 23% to 89%, with only a tenth of the households below 40%, but almost half above 70%. Inflation is undoubtedly eroding even the position of highly paid salaried workers.

Another reason these Kaneshie households were not able to spare large amounts of cash was their own need for help. There was a large proportion of female-headed households in the sample (47.5%). When the respondents were divided by sex we found that women spent more on food, education, and charitable donations, while the men spent more on clothing, transport (because some owned cars), help to nonresidents, consumer goods, entertainment, savings, and taxes. In fact, the men's expenditures were generally indicative of their greater prosperity, which allowed them more excess to devote to nonessentials. We also asked about sources of household income, and found that 42% of the 19 households with female heads were getting help from outside, compared to 24% of the 21 male-headed ones. The average yearly income for female-headed households was approximately ₵7,300, compared to ₵8,500 for male-headed households.[110] These figures included income from all sources, which was derived as follows (mean averages): husband's earnings (of conjugal household), 32.1%; wife's earnings, 25.1%; earnings of a single head, 15.8%; children's earnings, 11.7%; outside help, 4%; rents, 11.3%; other, 0.4%. However, they omit many poorer households, where the nature of self-employment made income quite difficult to estimate. Given that 32.5% of the households were themselves in need of and receiving help from elsewhere, it is not surprising that little was given to nonresident relatives.

How did people feel about giving help to their relatives? Most (60%) expressed satisfaction with the amount of help they were giving to relatives; those who were not satisfied usually wanted to give more. Here the strong ethic about help to kin was evident. When asked if their relatives pressured them to help, 42% replied affirmatively, that pressure usually coming in the form of a visit from the needy person who begged for help. Ten percent claimed that the help given strained their resources, meaning that only about a seventh of those who were helping felt that they could ill afford it. Eighty-four percent said that they could afford to give less help in 1977-78 than they had previously, and many went on to complain about the condition of the economy. While it is impossible to measure the contrast in amount of help, certainly more of the help with educational expenses was given in the past than the present, partly as a factor of the age of the head of household. In some households older heads had already become, or were

---

[109]Three households in Awudome Estates and New Kaneshie could *not* be considered elite. They were headed respectively by a retired injectionist, a small trader, and a retired kenkey seller. On the opposite side, two households, one each in New Kaneshie and Awudome Estates, were very wealthy indeed.

[110]Compare these to the personal incomes for Ghana estimated by the U.N. report, "The economic value of breast-feeding," p. 50, in 1970. The average annual earnings for male wage workers were ₵1300, for self-employed men ₵1100, and for self-employed women ₵800.

in the process of becoming, pensioners of their children. However, the drastic slide in the economy would certainly pare help to nonresident relatives to
a minimum.

What conclusions can we draw from this data concerning Central Accra
and class formation? We need to look more closely at the data regarding
Central Accra before venturing any. Forty-seven point seven percent of the
sample were helping a relative in Central Accra. This meant that most people who were helping anyone numbered among them a relative in Central
Accra. The residents of Central Accra who were helped were related to the
helpers as follows: mothers--26.6%; mother's side relatives (usually mother's
sisters)--36.7%; sisters or their offspring--30%; fathers or father's side
relatives--3.3%; and brothers--3.3%. The total number of people helped was
30, or an average of .7 apiece for the sample. They thus formed only 43% of
all persons helped, probably because the main direction of help was to persons younger than the giver. Most (63.3%) of those helped in Central Accra
were older than the giver.

Was financial help accompanied by a warm personal relationship linking
together these people? After all, 28.3% of the immediate relatives (siblings,
children, parents or grandparents) of the initial 67 respondents had lived or
were living in Central Accra, and 80% of the respondents had once lived
there themselves. One might expect that Kaneshie Ga people would maintain a relationship with some of their family downtown, especially those they
were helping. However, this did not necessarily follow: 34% of the sample
helped financially and visited, 2.3% helped but did not visit, 18.2% did neither, and 45.5% visited but did not help. The highest proportion of those in
the last category lived in Old Kaneshie, where immediate relations were not
likely to live in Central Accra but they shared a common lifestyle and similar economic status. The visiting pattern, then, upholds Eames and Goode's
thesis that close ties are likely to be maintained between kin of the same
socioeconomic status, but the pattern of financial help contradicts it.[111] One
woman in Central Accra said about a man who had moved to the suburbs,
He's so rich he doesn't need to go to funerals any more, meaning that he no
longer had need of the reciprocal bonds established by funeral attendance
and giving.

Summing up this data, two facets are most striking. First, it is impressive that almost half of a sample composed mainly of comfortable to less well
off households (32.5% of whom were themselves being subsidized) were helping at least one relative in Central Accra in a time of great hardship. People
who had more usually gave more. In doing so, they were sometimes fulfilling
reciprocal obligations because those relatives had helped them to get educated. They were upholding the strong social obligation to help kin.[112]

[111]Eames and Goode, *Urban Poverty*, p. 194.

[112]A. C. Smock, "Ghana: From Autonomy to Subordination," in *Women Roles and
Status in Eight Countries*, ed. J. Z. Giele and A. C. Smock (New York: John Wiley and
Sons, 1977), p. 193, in a 1972 survey of 1,757 school children, found that at all levels they
expressed "overwhelming support" for the idea that it is wrong under any circumstances to
refuse assistance to a relative.

Furthermore, this help was not usually exacted through pressure, but freely and unresentfully given. This help was undoubtedly influenced by the fact that most people had lived in Central Accra themselves at one time, and so were not far removed from it. The wealthy and comfortable among the sample were mainly self-made "nouveau riche." There had not been enough time for increasing generations of education and affluence to cut most persons completely off from their background. They generally honored their family obligations.[113] However, the impressions derived from conversations with young people in Kaneshie are that they know and care little about Central Accra, so that this help may be severely truncated in the next generation.[114]

Second, if this honoring of extended kin obligations is the positive side of the coin, the actual amount of help provided is the negative side. People in Kaneshie may have been helping to the best of their abilities, but this did not result in a large amount of financial help going downtown. Commonly people would give an elderly relative a cedi or two on a visit, except for those who had parents there. Thirty percent of the recipients of help were parents, and no one was helping a child living in Central Accra with educational expenses. If one judges actual amounts of monetary help (and in half the cases the respondents were giving money only),[115] by their own account the average amount given monthly to a recipient in Central Accra was ¢10.70. Calculating it from percentage of expenditure, one comes up with a figure of only ¢.27 per individual per month,[116] with a grand total of about ¢4,100 annually going from Kaneshie downtown from all of these households.[117] Whichever estimate one accepts, the amount of help is certainly not enough to inhibit class formation by raising the standard of living of those downtown to an appreciable extent. More help, in fact, went to coresident relatives in Kaneshie, who at least got free room and board. Coresidence, then, plays a crucial role in help to relatives, not only in Central Accra, but also in Kaneshie. Given the probable truncation of contacts

---

[113]C. Oppong, in "A Note from Ghana on Chains of Change in Family Systems and Family Size," *Journal of Marriage and the Family* XXIX, no. 3 (Aug. 1977): 617, found that increasing generations of education were accompanied by a reduction in financial obligations to kin outside the conjugal family.

[114]R. Sanjek, in "Cognitive maps of the ethnic domain in urban Ghana: reflections on variability and change," *American Ethnologist* IV, no. 4 (Nov. 1977): 616, found that very few Ga residents of Adabraka, an older suburb where many Ga have grown up, could name the seven quarters of Central Accra.

[115]Thirty-six point seven percent of the recipients got both money and in kind contributions, 13.3% in kind only.

[116]To arrive at this amount I took .022 times the average annual expenditure and average annual income for all households, which I then averaged to get ¢227.80 annual expenditure on help to all relatives. Then, because the Accra recipients of help formed 43% of those helped, I took that percentage of the total to get ¢97.95, and divided that by 30 to get the annual amount given to them individually, or ¢3.26. When divided by 12 one arrives at the monthly amount of ¢.27 per individual.

[117]This is using the .044% figure to calculate the results, which one must do for the whole household. However, for the calculation above, the .022% figure was used because the information about help to relatives usually came from one respondent in the household only.

with increasing generations of residential separation, the narrowing access to higher education, and the worsening economic situation, I predict no reversal of this situation, but rather its reinforcement.[118]

* * * * *

Women must trade, then. Changes in the institution of marriage, which have made it more fragile and reduced conjugal economic cooperation, in the apportionment of the dependency burden, which have followed those in residential patterns to segregate the sexes both financially and geographically, and in education, which has segregated them socially and economically, have weakened the women's networks. If one looks at the situation in terms of monetary flows, one finds that money is steadily accumulating with the male-dominated elite and leaving female networks. A prime mechanism for removing capital from female networks is women's investment in their sons' education. Educated men have control over most land and other resources, along with the skill to manipulate them. They receive wages which they supplement with entrepreneurial activities, on occasion. This should contribute to capital formation in Ghana. But the Ghana government has persistently discouraged large indigenously owned businesses by threatening nationalization, while leaving multinational corporations alone. Thus foreign investment and real estate have been more appealing, a good explanation for the phenomenal expansion of luxury housing on the northern fringes of Accra in the midst of the worst economic situation Ghana has ever experienced.

Meanwhile, most women spend their money to feed and educate their families, providing their sons with the wherewithal to raise their social status. When their sons become absorbed in elite lifestyles the women look to their daughters for help. These children provide vital social security functions. Poorer people had more children and made less use of fertility reduction measures, thus supporting the obverse side of demographic transition theory.[119] The inverse relationship between income/level of education and level of fertility disputes the assumptions of such theorists as Caldwell, Goode, Beaver, and Morgan, expressed most aptly by Caldwell, "The rate of social change determines economic change and this in turn determines the

---

[118]B. Marshall, in *Bukom* (London: Longman's, 1979), presents a roseate picture of an early 1960s Ga family living near Bukom Square and helping each other, *except* for the member who chose to move out.

[119]More detailed results of the KAP (Knowledge, Attitudes and Practice concerning contraception) surveys will be published elsewhere. D. A. Ampofo, in "Abortion in Accra: the Social, Demographic and Medical Perspectives," in *Symposium on Implications of Population Trends for Policy Measures in West Africa*, ed. N. O. Addo et al., Ghana Population Studies No. 3 (1971), pp. 84, 87-88, found that Ussher Town and James Town had two of the highest abortion rates in Accra. Abortion users were most often better-off traders, stall-holders being disproportionately represented. He estimated that one out of every four or five pregnancies ended in abortion.

value of children and hence fertility change."[120] Economic change, in fact, and economic status, would seem to influence social change, and poverty plays a causal role in high fertility. The poverty of women, in particular, is of crucial importance when considering fertility.[121] In the absence of other resources, the dependence of women on their children is growing, a trend which may increase fertility. The posited "crumbling of the strength of the extended family," which was supposed to reduce fertility, may possibly have the opposite effect here, making it that much more important that women have children as buttresses against ill-fortune.[122] Raising their income rather than the availability of contraceptives, would probably be most successful in reducing their fertility.

Faced with heavy burdens and hard times, these women survive because of determination and their ability to manipulate scarce resources using cheap labor. Increasingly in Ghana it is only the disadvantaged who make full-time trading their occupation, although many of the advantaged use it to supplement their incomes. In the face of educational disqualification from many jobs, trading remains a live option but also bears the stigma of low social status. The paradox is that, while many women aspire to the male-dominated elite, most will remain in female networks where they are economically independent from men, and poor as a consequence. Westerners should not mistake such independence for privilege. That women have been able to survive so far has largely depended on the strength of those networks. However, socioeconomic forces are weakening that strength and making it logical for younger women to trade off economic independence for the anticipated greater security of dependence on a man. Unfortunately, neither the weakened female networks nor the marital situation offer most women the long-term security they are seeking for themselves and their children.

---

[120]Caldwell, *Socio-Economic Explanation*, pp. 77-79. W. J. Goode, in *World Revolution and Family Patterns* (New York: Free Press of Glencoe, 1963), p. 183, says, "As some approximation to a western conjugal family becomes widespread in Africa, one might expect some control of fertility." S. Beaver, in *Demographic Transition Theory Reinterpreted* (Lexington, Massachusetts: Lexington Books, 1975), p. 50, says, "Natality decline is facilitated to the degree that a pre-development culture is predisposed to modernizing influences and has the opportunity for contact with more developed societies.[!]" T. Morgan, in *Economic Development: Concept and Strategy* (New York: Harper and Row, 1975), p. 231, put forth the popular theory and advice that resources used to retard population growth will contribute more to increasing per capita income than those used to accelerate production.

[121]Simon, *Effects*, p. 172, is one of the few people concerned with such questions to take women into account as a separate factor, the habit of classifying women's socioeconomic status with that of their husbands being so ingrained.

[122]Caldwell, *Population Growth*, p. 601. K. D. Patterson, in "The Impact of Modern Medicine on Population Growth in Twentieth Century Ghana: A Tentative Assessment," in *African Historical Demography* (Edinburgh: Centre of African Studies, 1977), p. 439, stated that birthrates have changed very little in Ghana since 1945; if anything they rose slightly.

You eat you don't give me.
He said I should go chew stone.
Because he has money and I haven't any.

Has money come from stone? Or is it because of poverty?
This is the problem.

Hɔmɔwɔ song[123]

Outside Salaga Market

[123]M. E. Kropp-Dakubu, "Akaja: A Ga Song Type in Twi," University of Ghana Institute of African Studies *Research Review* VIII, no. 2 (Jan. 1972): 55.

Portrait 4

KATE MENSAH

In 1971-72 Kate Mensah was an old, feeble, rather portly woman living in an indifferently cleaned tiny room in a small compound shared with some of her grandchildren. Her only surviving daughter lived at Mamprobi, a suburb of Accra. There was a lot of friction between her and the other residents of the household, as shown in her account. She depended on the neighborhood children to run errands for her and they resented it. Her memory was somewhat impaired, which made her narrative confusing at times. The tapes and notes of the eight interviews in which she gave me this information had to be drastically reorganized and condensed to come up with the results here. There are probably more inaccuracies in it than in the other accounts, and there are fewer direct quotes. Kate Mensah had a certain dignity and a profound belief in Christianity. Often we would encounter her reading her Ga Bible, which seemed to provide her with solace for the many tragedies which scored her life. She died in 1976, to the sorrow of many who knew her, at the age of approximately eighty-five.

Childhood (circa 1891 to 1905)

I was born at Ŋleʃi. My mother had four children; I was the youngest. When I was about three or four the man then married to my mother decided that I was not his child and disowned me. My father did it because I did not resemble the other children. He cursed my mother, demanding that she tell the truth about my birth on pain of death. This he did secretly but someone saw him doing it and came to tell us. He then took the case to the Sempe Maŋtsɛ's court (that Sempe Maŋtsɛ has now been succeeded by four others). He broke the marriage with my mother and in addition asked for repayment of every expense he had incurred on my behalf. My mother's elder brother came to collect us and repaid the sum spent for my outdooring. My father was wrong, which was shown by the events which followed. That Sempe Maŋtsɛ died a week after pronouncing judgment in favor of my father, and so did several of his elders, as well as my father's mother. My mother then went to stay at her mother's family house taking all of us with her. We stayed there until my uncle built this house, then we came here. He was our guardian.

When I was a child I was very agile and liked to run and play. Often a group of us would go to the beach and swim in the sea. When we returned we were beaten by my uncles because the adults said that it was dangerous. In fact, it was. Once we were swept out by the waves and some men in a canoe came to save us. But one of us drowned. The body was taken to the hospital, which at that time was near where the stadium is now. A police officer interrogated us but found that we were too young to give any useful statements. We were just innocent children. So we were released and after that I never went to the beach again.

I usually played with a group of girls and the boys played with boys. I was brave and could fight anyone who challenged me. I did not look for fights, but if I was passing and noticed some kid picking on another one I would butt in and say that the bully had done something to me before for no reason. Then if the bully kept it up I would beat him or her up for revenge. I hated to see a weaker person being bullied. I even fought boys. My own older sister could not win a fight with me.

Most of my childhood was spent in Accra, but at one time we moved to Nsawam for a while. My uncle, the one who built this house, was working there. It was at the time of the outbreak of the Kaiser War [World War I] and the soldiers were dragging even old women out of their houses and molesting them. So we all went to Nsawam to take refuge. We had no land there; my uncle had simply gone there to stay with a relation. When that relation died we all came back to Accra.

I was born at the time that they were starting to build roads in Accra, when all of the houses were roofed with thatch. Cowries were the currency then. There was a market near the bank of Kɔle Lagoon and another at Mukpɔnɔ, which was attended by people from the villages. Makola Market was only built later. Near where it is now, on the present-day site of the power house, was a big pond. The place was [and is] called Kiŋbu [lit., "king's well"]. That provided the water supply during the dry season. There were also many deep wells where you had to use buckets to draw up the water. If you fell into one you died. When pipeborne water was put in the wells were filled in. Also, there were very few electric lightposts and those far apart, making it a very favorable situation for thieves.

At that time people dressed differently. If you saw old photographs you could see for yourself. Some women put beads in their hair, which was plaited. Young girls parted their hair and wore one cover cloth and a blouse. Until your menses you could not wear a headkerchief. You would not dare put on the cloth used by your mother. Grown women wore a top and a cover cloth, plus the "middle" cloth, and a headkerchief. Dresses were only for the educated. To make the woman's outfit you need eight yards of cloth--two for the cover blouse and three each for the middle and lower body coverings. Then women also wore earrings, ankle and waist beads, and a loin cloth. While in the house you did not wear any of the outside cloth. Very old women did not use a cover blouse at all. Powder was not in use, but women rubbed their shoulders with a kind of ground [green stone] stuff called *krobo* mixed with lavender.

Uneducated men wore a type of flowing loin cloth which left the sides of the hips and thighs bare. Over this he threw a cloth if he was going out. It took eight yards of material for the outside cloth. Educated men used belts and put on wrist watch drawers [?]. Then you could easily tell a man from a woman, but today it is easy to make a mistake. Also then we had facial marks [scars] which differentiated one group from another. Ewe marks were quite different from Hausa ones. These helped greatly with the identification of strangers.

I cannot recall any specific happy incident of my childhood. As a child you have to sweep the room and the compound, remove the dustbin and empty it, and fetch water. When you were big enough you washed the clothes. But when the chores were done you were free to go and play. As long as our mothers did not bother us we were happy with them and ourselves. We had age group companions with whom we played happily and went about. There might have been six children from one house, four from another, three from yet another and then six from our house. You kept to this group until you married. We would play *ampe* and other games. Sometimes we would go to market to buy or sell. We would play until it was time for bed, when everyone returned each to his or her own home. The boys went to their fathers and the girls to their mothers. The next morning it was more of the same.

I did not like being scolded and punished. I did what I was told to avoid it. I did not brag or look for trouble by joining in a bad kind of play. I did not loiter in the evenings. When it was time for bed I was always there. When an errand had to be run and someone else refused, I volunteered. I laid my mother's bed in the evening and washed her clothes, which my sisters and brothers did not do. My mother favored me as the youngest. She did not remarry, as she was afraid that to do so would make me die. Also, I was quite different from the other children and with us the child who

comes with tragedy receives special attention. For all of these reasons my
sisters and brothers developed a hatred for me.

Our mother disciplined us in the following manner. The first offence
merited a reprimand. After that you were scolded or beaten. This was supposed to change the child for the better. When you befriended a bad child
you were asked to end the friendship. Some young girls were morally weak
and some were disrespectful to older persons. If you still stayed friends with
them you were beaten. Before you went anywhere you had to ask permission, likewise if you took anything from the house. A child had no purse of
its own. You could only buy bread with money from your parents. We were
told not to visit in other children's homes because it was the stranger who
was accused if something was missing. We were taught to be submissive and
humble. When it was reported that you had been insolent to an older person or refused to run an errand you were given a good beating. You did not
dare then to look your mother in the face. It was an abomination. This was
the training our mothers gave us, and they had received the same training
from their mothers.

There were many bad diseases around when I was a child. There was
one disease like chicken pox. It went after the skin, stomach and brain causing madness. Many died from it; those who survived were left with spots all
over the body.[1] There was another disease caused by some bad type of air.
Externally it appeared to be like a boil. If you did not get a cure immediately the result was always fatal. So heavy was the death toll that at the
burial of the dead no rites were carried out at all.[2] Yes, many many diseases
broke out. Malaria was prevalent in my youth. There were herbalists with
potions which cured it quickly. As a child I often suffered from it and would
be ill for some time, too weak to do anything. Another one was guinea
worm, but I did not get it, I thank God. The only disease I keep having is
piles.

When I was a child I loved all of my relations. But I associated more
with those with whom I stayed on good terms and kept away from those
who quarreled with me. When my mother was away the older women of the
house, even though they were not Christian, knew God and did not allow
anyone to bother me.

Puberty and early married life (circa 1906 to 1918)

We were innocent children when our first menstrual periods came.
What would happen is that when you suddenly noticed the blood you
started crying and ran to your mother to say that you had urinated blood.
You would only be given in marriage when you had menstruated; it is a sign
that you have come of age. After menstruation we still played with boys but
never had intercourse with them. If anyone had been caught doing it the

---

[1]She is talking about smallpox.

[2]She is talking about the bubonic plague, probably the 1908 Accra epidemic.

punishment was severe. You could receive Christmas presents from them given without motives. Their friendship was enjoyed until one of the two of you got married; then you had to end it.

When I first married I was over twenty years old, fully grown. My husband did a full customary marriage ceremony for me; his parents paid £8 to my parents for me. He arranged it with my parents and I did not know him before we got married. He was a drunkard from Asere quarter. At that time it was not acceptable for people to marry non-Gas because there was no way to find out about the family background and character of a stranger. Why, he could have been the biggest thief in the world and you would not have known it! But today people marry non-Gas.

At that time also your family was more important in deciding your marriage. A man wishing to marry a girl would approach her mother. If the mother approved of him she arranged the marriage. The girl had no choice. She accepted her mother's choice believing that no mother would present a child with a bad thing. If a man was courting you personally, unlike in my situation, and your family disapproved, then you were told to end the friendship. But if they did not know anything about it and you got pregnant, then they had to accept the man. A responsible man who put a girl in the family way without the customary approaches would ultimately go forward and perform all of the rites.

In any case, I was not happy at getting married and wept because of it. We all did. I was completely ignorant of what marriage meant and felt shy. Having a husband is no small thing; I did not know what to do for him. Such feelings made me keep as far away as possible from the house where my husband-to-be lived until the day my hand was given to him formally, and besides, that was the proper way to behave. Before I married I was advised that in my marriage I should be obedient to the man, respect his wishes, and cook and serve him diligently. My grandmother [her mother's mother's sister] told me not to argue with the man or run to complain about him to my mother. She also said not to use the chop money on myself and not to run around with men. The man was advised that he was to be the breadwinner and clothe and feed his wife and children.

I was with my first husband for three or four years. He was a goldsmith and already had one wife. Your joy after marriage depends on how your husband treats you. You may not be happy. This man did not provide enough chop money. He was a drunkard and we had no children. For these reasons my parents said I should leave him. The marriage becomes fulfilled when a child arrives. Nothing surpasses the joy of a woman at having her own child. The man may leave you but you still have a child to console you. It is usual to have a marriage broken up if after two years or so there is no child. If the man leaves you then you find another man.

Marriage (circa 1918-1933)

My second husband was that Otublohum Maŋtsɛ whose corpse was stolen. We arranged it ourselves and started living together. We had two children. We used to go on cocoa buying trips together, since that was his job. I worked for him cleaning the money (coins) so it could be used. Sometimes the white men he worked for would give him money to give to me but he kept it for himself.

I shared my room in the village with an aunt of this Maŋtsɛ. She had joined me because she was quarreling with her sister. This woman had a son who said that he had put £5, or two months' wages, into a box for savings. He went to the box later and found only £2.10 there, and accused me of having taken the rest. But later on he realized that he had used £2.10 to repay a debt owed to the Maŋtsɛ for clothing. They apologized to me for the false accusation. It was strange, therefore, that still later when he divorced me this man claimed that he did it because I was a thief. At the time he had exonerated me! Anyway, a short time after this incident the marriage broke down. I had gone back to Accra because of the incident. The man did not bother to visit us or inquire after the children's welfare. Why, he would come to visit someone next door and not even stick his head in here! He also did not give me any allowance for the children. When a child fell ill I sent word to him, but he never cared. He had a "Mrs." [woman married in church] and two other wives to spend his money on. It was his irresponsible behavior that ended the marriage. I was with him for maybe five years.

It was after we were divorced that he became the Otublohum Maŋtsɛ. A long time later when his father died our grandchildren attended the funeral. I quarreled with one of the grandchildren subsequently and she told me that her grandfather had told her that I had stolen someone's money. That was when I found out that he had believed it. I did not, therefore, attend his funeral.

For three years after that divorce I was not with anyone. During that time I converted to Christianity. There was a time when I was always bemoaning my fate. But I have been happy ever since I came to know God. Because I have held to my God I am happy. God is wonderful; I have been cursed four times but I am alive. If you are truthful, not afraid of the devil, and innocent, God will Himself judge the devil. One should not fear the devil but some people do. It all depends on belief. What you believe in becomes a god. If you believe in it, then the effects follow. But if you have no belief in curses, they will have no power over you.

The first time I was cursed was the business when I was with the Maŋtsɛ and his aunt did it. I was shown to be innocent; not only did they apologize, but also not long after my departure for Accra the belongings of that woman were all stolen by thieves. Another incident had to do with a woman friend who lives in our house. Her sister had a sore and could not walk, so she sent her two small children to beg that I go buy her something to cook. When I returned, 2s./6d. worth of beads had been stolen. Another time six strings of beads were gone. She recovered and accused me of having

stolen £2.10 that she had put under her pillow. She did this because a
malam[3] told her that the thief was a person who usually came to her. She
accused me and started scolding me whenever we met. She would even follow me to my husband's house at night. She put a curse on me and stopped
her children from coming to see me. I was innocent; the curse rebounded
and killed her two children. My friend, her sister, believed the charge and
quit coming to see me. But then the woman accused my friend of having
killed her children with witchcraft. So my friend sought refuge in this house.
That woman later left for Nsawam to trade, and when she returned she was
insane and remained so until she died. Even her only surviving daughter is
mad and in the asylum.

The third time had to do with my father, which I already explained.
The fourth had to do with a Christian friend of mine. She had quarreled
with her family and moved here to share my room. She had a wardrobe
where she kept her money, for which she bought a lock from a Hausa man.
She took money to pay for the lock and then claimed that I took it, that no
one else could have had access to the drawer where it was. I denied having
done it. My own children even believed her and took me to task for it; her
children censured her, for in her time of need I had given her a refuge.
Thank God that He protected me through all these trials! Had I been evil I
would have been dead long ago.

My third husband was the best one. When he approached me about
marriage I told him that, according to the rules of the [Wesleyan] church, I
would be expelled if the marriage was not confirmed by customary rites and
blessed by the church. I showed him the responsible person in our family for
him to contact about the marriage. He accordingly did so and the marriage
was contracted and blessed. He gave my parents £6 and some drink to
confirm it. I only became pregnant after we were officially married. While
my first two husbands were quite a bit older than I was, this man was about
the same age. He was a Ga man and a clerk by profession. The marriage
was very happy; we got along quite well. He satisfied my wishes and was
understanding and generous. He even bought me clothes and footwear
before we had a child. In addition, he not only took care of his own children, but he also supported my children by the Maŋtsɛ, and my sister's children. All this he did willingly. Unlike the others he was honest with me and
always told me what he was going to do. Unfortunately, he died when our
son was in elementary school.

There are a few things in my life which I regret. One was having as a
child insulted people older than myself. But more important was having had
three husbands. When I was young I always said that I would marry only
one man. But that is the way it is sometimes; not all husbands are good
ones. Why, there is a girl who lives here who got pregnant by a man who
denied responsibility for the child. So the girl's parents did everything for
the baby, naming it, and so on. Her mother took her to Winneba to apprentice her to a bread baker, and this man came and said he wanted to marry

---

[3]Hausa Islamic teacher cum herbalist or diviner.

the girl. He did and the girl had another child with him. But that man did not look after his children properly, so the girl went to his family house to ask her husband for money. He refused and his mother beat her with her slippers. About two weeks ago they took the case to court. Ah, marriage can be a heavy thing!

Childrearing

I had three children of my own. They are all dead now except one. The middle one was the mother of that granddaughter who lives here and has mulatto children. This daughter was very tall and strong, much fairer in color than myself. She married without customary rites and had many children with the man. Twelve of her children are dead along with their mother. She had a son who worked at the court at Adjabeng. At one time he stayed with me alone in this house. He got sick and was admitted to Korle Bu [Hospital]. Before going to the hospital he had me hide £400 for him in his mattress in the presence of his mother [probably classificatory--his father's sister]. He also had some gold ornaments in his wardrobe. They discharged him from the hospital before he had recovered. I nursed him at home for a long time. His mother never came near him the whole time he was ill. Finally his body could no longer bear the illness and he died. When I went to the family to report the death his mother and her brother came and removed not only the money, but also all of my gold ornaments. After his burial I demanded their return without success. They took possession of everything that had belonged to the deceased, leaving nothing for his only surviving child, who was staying with me. I took care of him by the sweat of my brow as a tobacco seller. He grew up and I sent him to school. He finally got a job.

I also had a son by my third husband. I paid for educating him through Standard 7 since his father died while he was in elementary school. He worked hard. He was sent on transfer in his work a number of times. His absence made me cry a lot. There was no one to whom I could refer cases involving him. At long length I convinced him to come home and he got a job at Achimota. During World War II he was in the army in Burma. Later he was transferred to Tema as a pioneer worker but was sent back to Achimota subsequently because the person who had replaced him was inefficient. When he reported to Achimota for work that time and greeted the Osu man he was replacing, they shook hands. When he came home that day he started to bleed and that was the end. He died, leaving me not a single child. All my toil therefore went for nothing. Now I am left with only my oldest child alive. Were it not for her and her children I would have no one at all to go buy me something to eat.

Children can be ungrateful. Take that one sitting over there. She is my own grandchild. She only speaks to me to abuse me. But I took care of all of her children for her. Yet today she asked me not to send any of her children on an errand. Children of strangers run my errands for me. That

one lying down over there also has children but they are all with their
fathers. And so I am alone here in this house.

Once my daughter brought an Ewe girl to live here who had been put in
the family way by an expatriate. But my daughter later would have nothing
to do with the girl when she fell ill. My children demanded that I should
drive the girl out, but I refused because she was in a pitiful state. So I cared
for her until she gave birth, and even acted as her foster mother sending her
to the maternity ward at Korle Bu. After she came back she stayed on for
two weeks. At one point she got in a fight with someone at the water stand-
pipe and was taken to the police station. I went and put up bail for her.
She was cautioned and allowed to go with me. Another Ewe woman came to
fetch the girl away to her father. My children were all encouraging her to
leave. I went to the police station to get permission for her to leave and
they said it was all right and to send the baby with her. So we sent them off
with the baby on the back of the Ewe woman. But the nursing mother ran
away leaving the Ewe woman with the baby. She brought it back here; neither of us had breast milk to give the baby, so it died. The tragic incidents
in my life were many; if I tell you all of them I will end up screaming.

Work

Very early on I realized that my mother had a difficult time caring for
us, so I decided never to add to her worries. I hawked kenkey and *abɔlo* for
my mother. Sometimes she tried to dissuade me from going, but I was
determined because I knew what a help it was. Otherwise she would have
had to provide me with everything. In those days prices were very low so I
could provide for all of my necessities through trading.

Long ago trading was different than it is now. We walked as far away
as Nsawam with headloads of foodstuffs. Salaga was the old central market
place in Accra; London and Makola Markets were introduced by the Europeans. Later a building was put up at Salaga and the sellers began to pay
taxes. During the renovations Salaga people sold at Bukom Square. At one
point there was a tiny market at a place in Asere called ʃunɔ as a result of
the [1939] earthquake. It was patronized chiefly by older people who could
not walk all the way to Salaga or Makola.

I traded with my mother until I married. Then I started on my own
selling tobacco, cloth, and soap. But eventually I lost money on that, so I
switched to selling beads which turned out to be the most profitable commodity. Actually, before I started selling the beads I knew all about the trade
because I had polished them for other people. In fact, that was how I got
the capital to go into business for myself. I was paid according to the quantity polished. When I went into business myself I bought a polishing stone
which came from one of the pits around town. They cost from three to five
shillings each depending on the size. You used water and sand and rolled
the beads back and forth on the stone to polish them. Before that I was
working for someone else as a hired laborer.

Formerly the bead trade was much bigger than it is now. Supplies could be had from many importing firms: CFAO, Jackel, Sick [-Hagemeyer], and about four of them run by Ga men. They would import for the customer to order. We bought from them and then retailed the beads after polishing, stringing, and pricing them. But today bead importing has stopped; many of the firms have gone out of business. You cannot even find the polishing stones now and have to use discarded ones. So we are only selling off some of the old stock. The old times were better. Now I mostly earn money by making dusters from cloth scraps that people give me.

The main thing that I liked about the bead trade was that it was profitable. Profit is what every person in business looks for; as long as the profits keep coming you stick to the enterprise. To figure out your selling price you add together the cost price of each string of beads, the cost of the thread for stringing them, the labor cost, and a margin added on which is your profit. In fact, with all commodities that is how you get the selling price, that is, the cost of all elements which went into its production plus a margin which is the seller or producer's own pay. Anyone who ignores this will incur a loss in business. This I was taught by the people who hired me as a beadpolisher. Once you were initiated by the older sellers into the trade you kept to the advice given. And if you had problems as a newcomer you consulted with them.

I did a good business, unlike my sister, who spent a lot of time traveling on trading expeditions. But she always came back empty-handed. This provoked her to be jealous of me. Her grandchildren even argue with me constantly, and none of them contributed a cent toward my mother's funeral expenses.

Sometimes, of course, you could not avoid taking a loss and had to sell back stocks of beads to the stores. Such factors as not being able to string them in time to supply the demand might have led to such a situation. The best times for selling were Hɔmɔwɔ, Christmas, and after the cocoa harvest. You had to keep up with a high demand then. We gave the beads names to describe them, which helped people to ask for what they wanted. People liked wearing them for holidays. But now things have changed and the bead trade is spoiled. My plight is a hard one, but by the grace of God I know how to trade and that lightens my burden.

Reflections on the present

Civilization was not as widespread in the past as it is today. Today if someone offends you and you go about cursing them, you will be reported by your victim and dealt with severely. It was a very bad way of seeking redress for your wrongs since often it was third parties who first suffered from the curse. I cannot explain how, but cursing can lead to the death of both adults and children. Today, therefore, society demands that redress must be sought only in court.

Some things in our day were better than they are today, and some things today are better than they were in our day. Stealing was not as common before; if you were caught stealing then even your own relatives would beat you severely. A curfew kept people inside after eight P.M. Swindling was unknown. People did not carry tales about others. Children were not forward and disrespectful. When chided by an older person they did not answer back. The behavior of the present generation astonishes me. In our day an older person did not need to be a relative of the child to have the right to scold or punish him for bad behavior. His mother would side with you if you reported the behavior to her. But now children talk back to me for scolding them. This is very bad. Children who are working now do not even feel an obligation to maintain their parents.

Why, when I was young I stayed here and took care of my uncle until he died. To reward us he made a will leaving my mother this house; his younger sister resented that. I let her children live here and they quarrel with me. They do not pay their share of the taxes and they refuse to let their children run errands for me. They do not even speak to me. They are ungrateful. That one who lives there even has an Nkrumah estate house at Mamprobi which he rents out, while living here rent-free with all of his relatives.

However, now we have more amenities in Accra, like pipeborne water, electricity, more roads, and better transportation. More people are educated. Those not literate in English try to get literate in Ga. I learned it from a young man who had gone to Sunday School, where he had learned it. This is good.

But we are poor now. Ungrateful children spend their money on drink, not on you. Because they decide to enjoy their income alone they are compelled to pay for every necessity in life, even drinking water. Whereas if they gave their mothers an allowance the mother would willingly prepare them meals. This is a savings in kind and a blessing. But notwithstanding all you have done for them, they show you no gratitude.

And the prices!!! In our day hoarding of commodities was unknown. Now women are selling a packet of sugar for almost ten shillings, not because the supply is bad, but because they hoarded it. This is close to highway robbery! The traders forget the poor. Therefore, I think the good old days were better. Even to survive now is difficult. I surrender all my troubles to God for him to solve.

A Street Scene Near Bukom Square

VII

CONCLUSIONS

"The government can do anything except change a man to a woman."
An Nkrumah minister.

"My government is a victory for the common man."
Head of State Flight Lt. Rawlings, December, 1981.

Studying women has forced the rethinking of old categories, especially those concerning class formation. Barrett has commented that, "The oppression of women under capitalism is grounded in a set of relations between . . . the economic organization of households and its accompanying familial ideology, the division of labour and relations of production, the educational system and the operations of the state."[1] In this study I have dealt with all of these relations and attempted to explore their mutual ramifications. In doing so I have had to depart from common assumptions in several respects. First, exchange relations do characterize the household economy, which then allows the household to be disaggregated for purposes of analysis of socioeconomic status.[2] Second, it is not always the monogamous family that is basic to women's subordination;[3] polygyny may also reinforce that subordination, an area that needs more research. Third, residential units are not always coterminous with lineage groupings; rules of descent, inheritance, and residence interact in complex ways to determine the impact of greater penetration of capital on a society. Conversely, the greater penetration of capital may change these rules or determine which of a number of alternatives already present becomes most popular. As Bloch has said, "since . . .

---

[1]M. Barrett, *Women's Oppression Today. Problems in Marxist Feminist Analysis* (London: Verso, 1980), p. 40.

[2]Harris has a good discussion and critique of Sahlins' views that households are self-sufficient units. O. Harris, "Households as Natural Units," in *Of Marriage and the Market*, ed. K. Young et al.(London: CSE Press, 1981), p. 54.

[3]Leacock, in an uncharacteristic departure from cross-cultural perspectives, has associated monogamy with a class society, and therefore with women's subjugation. E. Leacock, *Myths of Male Dominance* (N.Y.: Monthly Review Press, 1981), p. 306.

kinship [under communal production] is itself part of the mode of production, it changes directly in reaction to changes in the mode of production."[4] The interaction of macro-economic change with micro-economic and social organization has been a prime focus of this work.

We began here with a suggested chronology for socioeconomic change involving three stages, an initial precolonial one of cooperation of male and female hierarchies in a corporate kin mode of production, an intermediate one of weakened male patrilineage authority[5] combined with an assertion of independence by the female hierarchy, and the present one of reassertion of male authority buttressed by a shift to a capitalist mode of production. This study has focused chiefly on the intermediate and present stages concerning women and class formation. The intermediate stage should be further divided into separate periods demarcated by the World Wars and characterized by different degrees of penetration of international capitalism. It is a period where the sexes were generally further segregated.

Prior to World War I Accra was a small town with a rurally oriented, largely homogeneous population, although class differentiation was already well begun. Ussher Town was inhabited by more economically heterogeneous people than at present, but was also more ethnically Ga, a tightly knit community sharing a common set of values. Women tended to follow the trades pursued by their mothers and were more likely to choose a spouse in accordance with their parents' wishes. Young men were already breaking away from the authority of the male elders by converting to wage jobs. The female hierarchy had begun a bid for independence from the male elders, encouraged by increased trading opportunities and British suppression of lineage political power and certain social institutions. Around 1889 Reindorf noted that among the British laws disliked most by Ga men, the first was "against the cruel treatment of wives [who] had now the option of leaving their husbands." The second was the 1874 law freeing the pawns and domestic slaves.[6] The latter were mostly women at that time, and the abolition of slavery had a significant impact in improving the status of lower class women, although ultimately it may have weakened the female hierarchy by reducing its power to recruit cheap labor.[7] In any case, during the pre-World War I period there are obvious cracks in the façade of lineage authority also evident in court cases and petitions cited here, as well as in some of the life histories of the women interviewed in 1971-72.

Between the wars the geographical expansion of Accra helped to express increasing class differentiation. Developments in transportation, in

---

[4]M. Bloch, *Marxist Analysis and Social Anthropology* (London: Malaby, 1975), p. 222.

[5]I have avoided the use of the term patriarchy because of definitional problems and its association with particular feminist theory which I do not feel applies in entirety in this case.

[6]C. C. Reindorf, *The History of Gold Coast and Asante* (1890; reprint ed., Accra: Ghana Universities Press, 1966), p. 323.

[7]C. C. Robertson, "Post-Proclamation Slavery in Accra: A Female Affair," in *Women and Slavery in Africa*, ed. C. C. Robertson and M. A. Klein (Madison: University of Wisconsin Press, 1983).

particular, revolutionized the methods of conducting trade employed by Ga women. Many changes began which accelerated later after World War II, such as the move to the suburbs, and the weakening of the effectiveness of social sanctions controlling the behavior of Ga women. Central Accra saw the influx of a heterogeneous population of workers and was becoming a less cohesive community than previously. After World War II the Central Accra Ga population was exclusively urban. The compound as a unit of production had often been supplanted by a more individualistic organization of trade for the women, while their middlewomen functions were being eliminated by branch stores. Their movement out of production became more pronounced as distributive activities occupied most of their time. A period of great prosperity for some and increasing access to education in the 1950s raised women's expectations.

The benefits of this intermediate stage, however, were not universally applicable to all women under colonialism. These Ga women were in an advantageous position to take up on increased opportunities for economic independence because of: the possibilities of the residential and trading systems, the separation of property in marriage, their rights to own and convey property, and their semi-autonomous precolonial female hierarchy, which provided them with leaders and a method of labor recruitment. Geiger (Rogers) has suggested that increasing the separation between the sexes was part of the "divide and conquer" strategy pursued by the colonialists.[8] But given colonialist lack of understanding of indigenous social structures, it was probably rather an unintended consequence of colonial rule. Other women not possessing the same combination of advantages as Ga women sometimes went straight from lineage to capitalist male dominance, such as the Baule and Lusaka women, and many Latin American women.[9] Nonetheless, in a quite different situation in rural Tanzania, Bryceson and Mbilinyi discerned a very similar periodization relating the socioeconomic status of women to that of men. Of the intermediate period they say, "the lineage relations of production, the basis of control over women in precapitalist social formations, was being destroyed by the process of capital penetration partly through the active agency of the colonial state."[10]

In the postindependence period, however, things changed again. The high hopes of the 1950s were frustrated in the 1960s as the value of cocoa fell. For Ga women, whose economic position had generally been improving

[8]S. G. Rogers, "Anti-Colonial Protest in Africa: A Female Strategy Reconsidered," *Heresies* III, no. 1 (1980): 24.

[9]Mona Etienne, "Women and Men, Cloth and Colonization: The Transformation of Production-Distribution Relations among the Baule (Ivory Coast)," in *Women and Colonization, Anthropological Perspectives*, ed. M. Etienne and E. Leacock (Brooklyn: J. F. Bergin, 1980), p. 232; K. T. Hansen, "When sex becomes a critical variable: married women and extra-domestic work in Lusaka, Zambia," paper presented at African Studies Association meeting, Los Angeles (Oct. 31-Nov. 3, 1979), p. 15; J. Nash and H. I. Safa, eds., *Sex and Class in Latin America* (New York: Praeger, 1976).

[10]D. F. Bryceson and M. Mbilinyi, "The Changing Role of Tanzanian Women in Production: From Peasants to Proletarians," paper (1978), p. 18.

during the century, the depression of the 1960s and the disaster of the 1970s emphasized the disadvantages of the two basic changes that had occurred. Economically they were more independent of spouses and relatives and had fewer persons with whom reciprocal obligations were honored. But they were becoming more dependent than previously on distributive rather than productive activities, where they had less control. The economic situation also exacerbated the tendency toward monopoly in the fish and cloth trades, which made the lot of the small trader more difficult. These factors then influenced more women to go into the less profitable small-scale local prepared foods trade.

After World War II, mutual consent, low-status marriage at a younger age became the most common form of marriage in Central Accra, a manifestation of the class differentiation taking wealthier people to the suburbs. In the postindependence stage women were seeking methods for extracting resources from elite men, who had superior access to the capitalist means of production. Informal liaisons, rather than marriage, became a common strategy for retaining autonomy but obtaining male-controlled resources. This trend also is becoming common in many parts of Africa, and has been noted among such diverse groups as Nairobi, Haya and Atu prostitutes, Abidjan, Beti, and Accra women of all classes, and others.[11] It therefore makes sense to analyze monetary flows in terms of female and male networks, just as Guyer speaks of a "women's economy."[12]

In the present stage women continue to look to their children for social security, while help from wealthier suburban relatives is negligible in ameliorating their situation. Elementary formal education, which women started getting in large numbers after World War II, reduced cooperation between mothers and daughters in business, but did not provide women with significantly better economic opportunities. The interactions between all of these simultaneous processes are difficult to grasp; only a few have been explored here. The most crucial questions raised concern the role of coresidence vis-à-vis economic dependency, the nature of monetary flows between men and women in the aggregate and within households, and the economic marginalization of women in class formation. In this case the three factors are inextricably linked as the coresidence of multiple generations of women becomes symptomatic of lower class status. Whereas in many societies female-headed households are a symptom of poverty because the male supporters are absent, in Ga society female-headed households seem to

[11]Bryceson and Mbilinyi, "Changing Role," pp. 19, 33; J. Bujra, "Women 'Entrepreneurs' of Early Nairobi," *Canadian Journal of African Studies* IX, no. 2 (1975): 213-34; and "Production, Property, Prostitution: 'Sexual Politics' in Atu," *Cahiers d'Etudes Africaines* 65, XVII, no. 1 (1977): 13-39; C. Vidal, "Guerre des sexes à Abidjan. Masculin, Féminin, CFA," *Cahiers d'Etudes Africaines* 65, XVII, no. 1 (1977): 144; J. I. Guyer, "Household Budgets and Women's Incomes," Boston University African Studies Center Working Paper No. 28 (1980); C. Dinan, "Pragmatists or Feminists? The Professional 'Single' Women of Accra, Ghana," *Cahiers d'Etudes Africaines* 65, XVII, no. 1 (1977): 168. Guyer (p. 17) noted that women explicitly search for reliable ways of gaining access to men's incomes and discuss the advantages and disadvantages of different strategies.

[12]Guyer, "Household Budgets," p. 11.

have always existed, but only recently have come to be associated with poverty because of the economic marginalization of women.

Sex segregation has become a characteristic of lower class affiliation, and such women's class position is not mediated by men to any significant degree. In contrast, elite and sub-elite women have become class fractions, whose status is more dependent on that of their husbands. Their relationship to the means of production is mediated by their husbands, from whom they receive sub-rewards.[13] Thus Ackah, Asiedu-Akrofi, and Atakpa, all members of the Ghanaian elite, implicitly or explicitly state that a woman's status in Ghana is dependent on her husband's achievement.[14] Elite women's loss of autonomy is replicated elsewhere, sometimes among poorer women when migration to cities and lack of employment opportunities deprive them of economic functions outside the home.[15]

New types of skilled labor requiring literacy are needed; the workers failing to obtain these jobs sometimes form a sort of bourgeois proletariat, that identifies with the elite but does not have access to the means of production. Towards the top of the new hierarchy the sexes are integrated into a competition for advantage, which the men usually win because they have greater access to resources such as education. The women's integration, in any case, is only marginal. A woman may, however, be able to buttress her elite position by using labor resources gained from female networks. A teacher who trades would be a good example. But most women remained within segregated female networks in the 1970s, while the corporate kin mode of production became subordinate to the capitalist mode.

---

[13]Bryceson and Mbilinyi, "Changing Role," p. 32, noted "Wives of men in government and parastatal posts, many who [sic] rose from the ranks of the peasantry have newfound class interests tied up with their marriages. Unlike [sic] women workers, divorce is undergone at very high costs; hence, their fear of losing their husbands."

[14]C. A. Ackah, "Social Stratification in Ghana," Ghana Journal of Sociology V, no. 2 (Oct. 1969): 4; K. Asiedu-Akrofi and S. K. Atakpa, "Practices Regarding Allocation of Places to Women in Schools and Colleges," research report for USAID/Ghana National Council on Women and Development (May 1978), p. 1.

[15]A. C. Smock, "Ghana: From Autonomy to Subordination," in Woman Roles and Status in Eight Countries, ed. J. Z. Giele and A. C. Smock (New York: John Wiley and Sons, 1977), p. 191; C. Oppong, Marriage Among a Matrilineal Elite (Cambridge: Cambridge University Press, 1974), p. 116. J. Bryson, "Women and Economic Development in Cameroon," USAID report (Jan. 10, 1979), p. 45; K. T. Hansen, "Married Women and Work: Explorations from an Urban Case Study," African Social Research, no. 20 (Dec. 1975), p. 786; J. O'Barr, ed., Third World Women: Factors in Their Changing Status, Duke University Center for International Studies Occasional Paper No. 2 (Durham, N.C., 1976), p. 27; D. Remy, "Underdevelopment and the Experience of Women: A Nigerian Case Study," in Toward an Anthropology of Women, ed. R. Reiter (N.Y.: Monthly Review Press, 1975), p. 371; A. Rubbo, "The Spread of Capitalism in Rural Colombia: Effects on Poor Women," in Toward an Anthropology, p. 357; R. Clignet, Many Wives, Many Powers (Evanston: Northwestern University Press, 1970), p. 284; C. Sutton, S. Makiesky, D. Dwyer, and L. Klein, "Women, Knowledge, and Power," in Women Cross-Culturally, ed. R. Rohrlich-Leavitt (Paris: Mouton, 1975), p. 588; R. A. LeVine, "Sex Roles and Economic Change in Africa," Ethnology V, no. 2 (April 1966): 186-87; I. Schuster, "Marginal Lives: Conflict and Contradiction in the Position of Female Traders in Lusaka, Zambia," paper presented at Women and Work in Africa Symposium, University of Illinois-Urbana (May 1979).

We now arrive at the problem of the relationship between the sex-segregated networks and the nominally integrated elite. Increasingly in Ghana educational inflation has made it so that formal education does not insure high class status, and economic conditions have damaged the financial situation of those on fixed salaries, with the result that recourse to female/male networks is necessary for many upper and lower level government employees, especially women. The interweaving of economic relationships between wage and self-employment has become even more complex, and requires a great deal of research. We do not know enough about any of its characteristics. The formal-informal labor market dichotomy used by economic analysts has obscured what really happens in terms of monetary flows between the two, while the use of the "traditional-modern" division has equally obfuscated social relations. Central Accra Ga women are still mostly in self-employment, but their connections with elite members--a few of their children and other relatives--have helped to make them aware of "how the other half lives," while not improving their economic status to any significant degree.

The present stage, then, can be seen as a logical outcome of the general post-independence reassertion of male power in every sphere. The assertion of female independence in the intermediate stage was analogous to the freeing of the slaves under colonialism. It was gradual and the results were unintended by the colonialists. Economic independence, nevertheless, did not provide equality because both slaves and women suffered similar socioeconomic disabilities, chiefly lesser access to the means of production. It was also only logical that once this assertion of female independence began, the female elders themselves would lose power as junior women used the same principles to declare their independence. Thus, the authority which used to come automatically with age has largely disappeared. Gender has supplanted age as the primary determinant of a person's access to resources.

The direction of socioeconomic change in twentieth century Accra, then, while initially benefiting Ga women, has by now become detrimental to them. The advantages embodied in their trading history and long-established residence have mostly evaporated with the help of repressive government policies. In fact, gender identity is increasingly being used by the governments of Ghana in an ideology which objectifies women traders into a class which can be blamed and persecuted for causing the enormous economic problems. In 1970 the Busia government expelled alien traders in one of the first major moves in a campaign to blame small local retailers for the defects of the international market.[16] Since this measure did not remedy the problems (and left the dominance of the multinationals even stronger, if anything), the Acheampong government imposed more stringent price controls (first begun by Nkrumah), which mainly applied to canned imported

---

[16]S. Katz, *Marxism, Africa and Social Class: A Critique of Relevant Theories*, Occasional Monograph Series No. 14 (Montreal: McGill University Centre for Developing Area Studies, 1980), p. 97, noted that the same phenomenon in Tanzania concerning Asian businessmen helps to obscure the fundamental problems of dependence in a neocolonial economy.

"essential" foods like sardines, tomato paste, and condensed milk. From the beginning to the end of the Acheampong government, its newspapers head-lined charges against petty traders of violating price controls and hoarding essential goods while people starved. A typical gesture was the Acheampong government decree of 1976 ordering the street sellers to buy kiosks from the government; only the larger traders could afford one at an annual rate of ₵10 to ₵150. Even some of them then went under(ground) when the government ordered all kiosks abolished in a move worthy of Catch-22.[17]

The persecution heightened during the first Rawlings government. In a symbolic act on August 18, 1979, soldiers bulldozed Makola No. 1 Market and reduced it to a pile of rubble. "That will teach Ghanaian women to stop being wicked," a soldier said. Makola No. 1, built in 1924, was the center of trade in Ghana, and the chief wholesale and retail market in Accra, having replaced Salaga Market in that function. In 1966 the 13 markets in Accra had a daily attendance of over 25,000 traders and 70% of the food for Accra households came from them.[18] In 1978 Makola was the chief among the 19 markets in the Accra area, with no indication that its importance had dwindled over time, despite many efforts by various independent govern-ments to remove control of the distributive system from the women traders.

Another aspect of Ghanaian government policy toward traders could be called malevolent neglect. This tradition was established in the latter years of colonial rule and furthered by independent governments. In the mid-1960s the Accra City Council largely ignored market supervision and spent less than one third of the revenue collected from the markets on maintaining or improving them.[19] These revenues could be substantial; in August 1976, ₵51,000 was collected from hawkers and vendors in fixed locations and ₵10,400 from "casual" traders by the Council, of which very little was put back into the markets.[20] Thus, a progressive decay in the physical accom-modations of the markets is very evident. In Salaga Market the fishsellers have been evicted from the sole building due to its poor condition; it now echoes emptily the play of a few children and youthful hawkers inside to escape the broiling sun. There are virtually no adequate restroom facilities and the aisles are littered with chunks of broken cement and even ordure, on occasion. The sole new construction, Kaneshie Market, was not completed at the time of the destruction of Makola, and since its opening has not really

---

[17]K. N. Afful and W. F. Steel, "Women in the Urban Economy of Ghana: Comment," paper (1978), p. 8; S. V. Sethuraman, "Employment Promotion in the Informal Sector in Ghana," International Labour Office World Employment Programme Research Working Pa-per (Geneva: April 1977), p. 31.

[18]R. M. Lawson, "Inflation in the Consumer Market in Ghana—Its Cause and Cure," *Economic Bulletin of Ghana* X, no. 1 (1966): 11; Lawson, "The Supply Response of Retail Trading Services to Urban Population Growth in Ghana," in *The Development of Indigenous Trade and Markets in West Africa*, ed. Claude Meillassoux (London: Oxford University Press/International African Institute, 1971), p. 381.

[19]J. E. M. Bartels, "Accra Market Surveys, Part I, Organization and Management," pa-per for Stanford Food Research Institute Economics and Marketing Section (Oct. 22, 1968), p. 16.

[20]Sethuraman, "Employment Promotion," p. 22.

replaced it.

The bulldozing of Makola, then, was actually only one of the later events in a long line of repressive measures aimed particularly at the traders in imported goods. Thus, the cloth market on the street next to Makola No. 1 mostly vanished even before Makola was bulldozed. Such measures (which at times included the summary execution of traders for price control violations), combined with an overvalued currency, have made the best places to buy Ghanaian-manufactured cloth the markets in neighboring countries at Abidjan and Lomé. By now even the produce markets have been severely damaged; under the second Rawlings government mobs attacked the main markets in Kumasi, Koforidua, and Sekondi. Government repression has mainly hurt the small traders, because they cannot afford to pay bribes, and the distribution system as a whole, to the further detriment of the economy. Most traders do not have sufficient capital to hoard goods, and must buy those covered by price controls at above the control price because of the long chain of distribution. Some corrupt government officials themselves have sold goods at the control price. The largest price hikes, in any case, have been in fresh produce, which is neither suitable for hoarding nor subject to price controls. Attempts to establish a competing government-run distribution system have mainly failed due to supply problems and corruption, as have supermarkets.

The results, then, of a weak attempt at socialism have been the further privileging of multinational corporations at the expense of indigenous businesses, the creation of a number of capital-absorbent parastatal corporations that extract profits for the benefit of the elite, and the giving of monopolistic advantages to certain male-subsidized privileged women, who are not usually traders by avocation. Their profits often feed directly back to the male elite. Nowhere more than in the attack on Makola--which was safe because the traders have become politically powerless--is the attempt of reconstituted male authority to reassert power over uppity low-status women more evident. The illusion of the power of market women collapsed in the Makola rubble, but the witch-hunt continued.[21]

Thus, the reversal of the trend toward improvement of the socioeconomic status of traders was not due solely to general economic deterioration, or increased penetration of capitalism, but also to their gender, which defined their relationship to the means of production. Ga women increasingly find themselves sharing the fate of female urban migrants in Ghana and elsewhere: truncation of links with residentially dispersed family members, less education than men, narrowing employment opportunities,

---

[21]Sexist rhetoric was evident in the campaign against Makola. The *Ghanaian Times* described the bulldozing as a "happy tragedy" producing "tears of joy" for the "worker, the common man" [who] "was helpless at the hands of the unfeeling Makola conspirators" (Aug. 20, 1979, pp. 1-2). Nii K. Bentsi-Enchill, "Losing Illusions at Makola Market," *West Africa* (Sept. 3, 1979), p. 1590. More thorough exploration of the issues involved is in my "The Death of Makola and Other Tragedies; Male Strategies Against a Female-Dominated Distributive System," paper presented at Canadian Association for African Studies meetings (May 12, 1982).

and lack of access to the products and profits of land.[22] Such trends entail an increased need for support from husbands, often unfulfilled. Rural women also suffer some of the same sex-imposed disabilities. In fact, if Third World peoples suffer the penalties of underdevelopment, their women also suffer those of so-called "development," the combination of indigenous and imposed sex-stereotyping which deprives them of socioeconomic viability. Although women's status has many culturally-bound permutations, it also has many common features.[23] This commonality more than justifies a thoughtful consideration of women as belonging to class fractions, whose access to the means of production is mediated by men, or to classes with distinct nonmediated access to the means of production.

The access to the means of production of the vast majority of the Central Accra women in this study was not mediated by men to any significant degree. Women in this situation, in contrast to those with mediated status, do not often develop class-consciousness, although they often possess solidarity and carry out group actions. These women marched, petitioned, and demonstrated on their own behalf at various times from about 1890 to 1980. However, the decline in power of women elders means that their solidarity will have to be recast in more democratic terms to survive. Solidarity is not the same as class consciousness; a female hierarchy may possess considerable female solidarity but its women probably will not have class consciousness because its upper levels have better access to the means of production than its lower ones. The fact that a female hierarchy still remained does not vitiate the usefulness of considering these women as a class; there are variations within any class. Because of the weakening of the basis for their economic autonomy we can expect the variations within the class to lessen, which may help the arousal of class consciousness. Their persecution by the government and the persistent lack of help from husbands would help in developing female class consciousness by maintaining their nonmediated status. But the decline in female solidarity may impede women's development of a sense of class consciousness which is linked to awareness of a particularly female plight. I expect that the more they move into the lower levels of the male-dominated sexually integrated hierarchy with the acquisition of minimal education, the more they will become class fractions with weak female solidarity. Dependence on pleasing males has a splintering effect among women which is not easy to overcome. One problem facing many societies where class consciousness has developed is that that consciousness

---

[22]In a survey of development-related literature Tadesse found overwhelming evidence that "in most cases women . . . are denied access to land, farm produce, farm inputs, credits, cooperative membership and other technological innovations [including formal education]." Z. Tadesse, "Women and Technology in Peripheral Countries: An Overview," in *Scientific-Technological Change and the Role of Women in Development*, ed. P. M. D'Onofrio-Flores and S. M. Pfafflin (Boulder: Westview Press, 1982), p. 85.

[23]M. K. Whyte, *The Status of Women in Preindustrial Societies* (Princeton: Princeton University Press, 1978), has an excellent critique of the generalized notion of "the status of women," and discussion of its various components and their interrelationship cross-culturally.

developed within a sexually integrated hierarchy and is therefore also male-dominated, thus accounting for the failure of many revolutionary programs to implement effective equal rights for women.

Lack of formal education for this developing underclass also makes class consciousness problematical in that it impedes knowledge of women else-where and also the self-confidence that reifies action. However, with increasing access to formal education, but blockage of better opportunities, class consciousness may be facilitated. This issue was not dealt with directly in my data collection, and remains open. Many of these women certainly perceived themselves as being different from, and lower in status than, educated people, in particular, but we did not attempt to obtain refinements on that perception. Thus, the definition of class used here was an objective rather than subjective one.

Another dimension of class that has often been included in definitions is the capability of a class to reproduce itself. This dimension has been used to eliminate the possibilities of women being a class, on occasion.[24] The use of this criterion should perhaps be discarded, because it implies status group endogamy and equality of men and women. It also implies equality within conjugal families. In this case, a woman's male children, depending on their access to education and jobs, might have moved into almost any level of the integrated hierarchy, or remained in the sexually segregated hierarchies. Social mobility was perhaps facilitated because of the bureaucratic nature of the upper class which made formal education of supreme importance.[25] There was, in fact, a lot of upward social mobility reflected in some of these family histories over the twentieth century. However, access to the upper levels of the elite is narrowing for children of *both* sexes of these progressively disadvantaged women, precisely because of the uneven dependency burden. These women are becoming an underclass, a perpetually overworked and underemployed labor reserve which is not needed in a stagnant economy, and their children have lessened access to resources as a result.

Gender, Change in the Mode of Production and the Sexual Division of Labor: a Model

Where do we stand, then, in finding answers to the difficult questions posed in Chapter I? We have already seen that as a descriptive model the above periodization of the changing relations of women to the means and

---

[24]H. I. Saffiotti, "Women, Mode of Production, and Social Formations," *Latin American Perspectives* IV, nos. 1-2 (Winter/Spring 1977): 28; J. Samoff, "Class, Class Conflict, and the State: Notes on the Political Economy of Africa," paper presented at African Studies Association/Latin American Studies Association meetings, Houston (Nov. 1977), p. 15.

[25]Magubane and others have called African elites an "administrative bourgeoisie" which Magubane says has "the apparatus of political power, but [is] without the economic foundations for true class rule." B. Magubane, "The Evolution of the Class Structure in Africa," in *The Political Economy of Contemporary Africa*, ed. P. C. W. Gutkind and I. Wallerstein (Beverly Hills: Sage Publications, 1976), pp. 186-87, 193.

mode of production has value and general relevance within African, and some other Third World countries. In fact, the description fits nicely into the emerging world pattern concerning female labor force participation, whereby under conditions of early industrialization, high female labor force participation is maintained. Then in an intermediate period local commerce and home production are undermined and damaged, rural-urban migration increases, and female labor force participation goes down. Under conditions of advanced industrialization, female labor force participation goes up again because the tertiary (service) sector has expanded, and some women of the bourgeoisie enter well-paid employment.[26] Third World countries, however, are not industrialized to a large extent and so have the disadvantages of both the intermediate and advanced stages; female labor force participation goes down. But if the model works as description, does it also work as analysis?

The first question posed was: What is the relationship of gender stratification, or the subordination of women (if present), to class formation? The answers are: (1) This varies according to the time, the culture and the classes concerned. (2) In this case gender stratification for poor women is becoming class formation by gender because of the systematic deprivation of women's access to resources, while bourgeois women are becoming class fractions in Poulantzas' sense, an embodiment of class contradictions. Acker has stated that, "sex divisions in the production system emerge as structural characteristics over time . . . and present individual women and men with different work realities. It is not just that women constitute a disadvantaged estate, but that the structure itself is constituted in terms of sex differentiation, and this has consequences for men, as well as for women."[27] The question then arises as to whether increased penetration of capital invariably leads to this conclusion. This in turn relates to the second question: Is there some point at which gender stratification becomes class formation along gender lines? The answer here is more complex.

Increased penetration of capital entails the creation of a proletariat, but the lower classes in Third World countries like Ghana do not generally earn wages. Rather they are mainly confined to the tertiary sector and are often self-employed. In fact, the tertiary sector is created out of an undifferentiated mass of manufacturing and service activities conducted by people like these women, whose activities have largely become tertiarized as they have moved out of manufacturing. Perhaps we need to change our definition of a proletariat to include those in the lower levels of the tertiary sector, who are being exploited as a reserve labor force and underpaid providers of necessary services to "productive" laborers. In fact, their labor creates surplus value because men can therefore devote more time to wage-

---

[26]P. M. D'Onofrio-Flores, "Technology, Development, and Division of Labour by Sex," in *Scientific-Technological Change*, ed. P. M. D'Onofrio-Flores and S. M. Pfafflin, p. 193. See also A. Oakley, *Woman's Work* (N.Y.: Vintage Books, 1974), Chs. 2 and 3.

[27]J. Acker, "Women and Stratification: A Review of Recent Literature," *Contemporary Sociology* IX (Jan. 1980): 30.

earning tasks. Women are exploited when they are forced into contributing the surplus value of their labor to others, whether they are selling prepared foods or performing domestic labor. Wage laborers in Africa are usually better off than the self-employed. In this sense, then, the worldwide tertiarization of women's work into low-paid jobs, which are either self-employed or wage labor, is a manifestation of the proletarianization of women. Since it has come about almost universally with the increased penetration of capital, there is definitely an association of the two.

But, the question may be raised, why women? This leads us to the third set of questions raised in the introduction: What is the relationship between the sexual division of labor and the mode of production? How has this changed over time? With the increased penetration of capital, the sexual division of labor is usually transmuted by the continuance of sexist ideology into a ghettoization of women into certain unskilled or semi-skilled jobs, as we see developing among women in wage jobs in Ghana.[28] As Tadesse stated, "[T]here is growing cross-cultural empirical evidence that indicates a sharp sexual division of labour attributing certain tasks and differential power to men and women. Penetration of capital invariably accentuates these patterns in the direction of enhancing male dominance and the subordination of women."[29] Ideology, which is rooted in both economics and magico-religious thought, and which plays a crucial role in withholding political power and technological knowledge from women, makes the transition from a cooperative sexual division of labor to a female work ghetto a logical one. The early sexual division of labor, often seen as blameless, efficient, and necessary in a kind of functionalist approach, frequently expresses in practice an ideology of male superiority, and is therefore easily transmuted into a "pink collar ghetto" for women. Barrett has stated, "Capitalism did not create domestic labour, or the 'feminine' areas of wage labour; but it did create a set of social relations in which pre-existing divisions were not only reproduced but solidified in different relations in the wage-labour system."[30]

Mode of production is intimately related to level of technology. Technological knowledge is mostly not transmitted to women because of a combination of indigenous and imposed sex-stereotyping. It is no accident, then, that women often remain in a labor-intensive mode of production while men assume control, or participate in, capital-intensive activities. Technology is the vital link between the sexual division of labor and the mode of production, while ideology controls the dissemination of technological knowledge.

We end with the attempt to relate all of these processes in answering the fourth question: How are changes in women's class position related to changes in the sexual division of labor, modes of production, and class

---

[28]Bryceson and Mbilinyi, "Changing Role," p. 27, noted rampant sexual discrimination in the wage labor market in Tanzania because (1) mechanical jobs were felt to be beyond women's capabilities; (2) employers felt that female labor productivity was lower than male, which was reinforced by the 1975 maternity leave act; (3) women lacked education. All of these factors are also present in Ghana.

[29]Tadesse, "Women and Technology," p. 80.

[30]Barrett, *Women's Oppression*, p. 182.

formation in general? What we come to, in effect, is a model which can best be described visually, as in Figure VII-1.

Not all economies pass through the slave mode of production phase, but many experience an intensified need for labor which then spurs mechanization. Early metropolitan capitalism generates increased penetration of capital, and arrives accompanied by ideology which limits the access of women to technological knowledge and other resources. Ideology filters perceptions at every level to determine sex role allocation. Colonial capitalism takes place after early metropolitan capitalism, of course. Peripheral economies like that of Ghana move from phase IIIb to IVb, from colonial to peripheral capitalism, and remain in IVb until or unless they become substantially industrialized. Because of the workings of international capitalism/ neocolonialism, many countries are likely to remain in phase IVb indefinitely.

The coexistence of two modes of production in phases IIIb and IVb should not be taken as yet another static two-tier economic model. The capitalist mode of production interacts with the corporate kin mode of production to such effect that it transforms and ultimately destroys it. The transformation in phase IVb entails tertiarization of many of the activities performed by corporate kin groups, so that for Ga women, as one case, it might now more appropriately be called a corporate kin mode of distribution.

This model mainly applies to capitalist countries and their colonies or ex-colonies, but the role of ideology and unequal dissemination of technological knowledge in transforming the more egalitarian early sexual division of labor into a pink collar ghetto has been similar in socialist/communist countries. Women workers in the USSR only technically "own" the means of production because they have no power or authority to control or manipulate them to achieve true equality. They are largely confined to low-status jobs, even though their labor participation is very high. Tadesse continues:

> [P]ositive changes in the status of women and thereby the transformation of a given country depend on the use of technology within a totally different socioeconomic framework . . . [H]istory has shown that no societal transformation is complete if it fails to focus on the special needs of women and redress the gap and the resultant inequality that is reproduced via the existing sexual division of labor.[31]

Although the official political ideology may say otherwise, and women in socialist countries may continue or move into agricultural and manufacturing activities, the sexual division of labor is still determined by sexist ideology, which assigns women to low-status positions. For most countries, then, the socioeconomic transformations required to achieve equality of the sexes are drastic, and certainly will not occur without both female action to promote them and a rearrangement of national and international priorities. Unfortunately, most policymakers have yet to be convinced that such equality would benefit the economy as a whole.

---

[31]Tadesse, "Women and Technology," pp. 105-06.

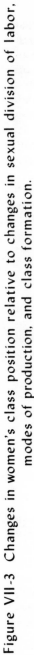

Figure VII-3 Changes in women's class position relative to changes in sexual division of labor, modes of production, and class formation.

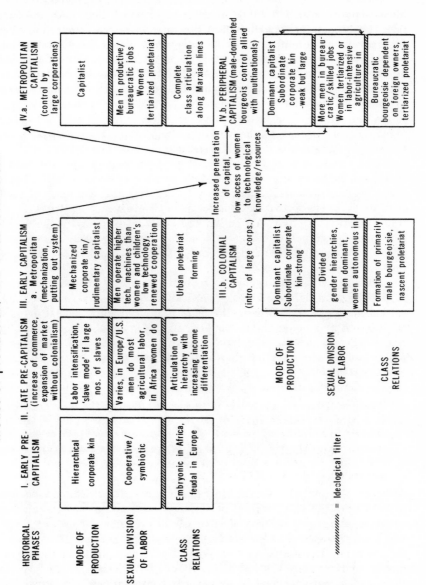

* * * * *

   Meanwhile, these Ga women continue their increasingly difficult survival efforts, largely forgotten in the overall world scheme of things. Although their solidarity is being undermined, it still stands as a powerful symbol of what can be accomplished by sharing the same bowl. If both sexes and all nations could do that the world would be a better place. But a glance at the world situation chillingly resurrects the fate reserved for those who are alone by choice or accident, by acting solely in their own self-interest, or because others have abandoned them.

   She told me that I might die. I retorted that, since all my relations were dead, I could care less if I died that very day.

A 90-year-old Woman

APPENDIX A

COST OF LIVING AND CURRENCY

Cost of Living

Column I of Table II-1 gives the retail price index for Accra for food only, which includes the prices of corn, plantain, fowls, oranges, flour and sugar, with the relative weights of 40, 24, 12, 12, 6, and 6, according to approximate proportions in the local diet. Until 1938 the price data were taken from the *Annual Colonial Reports* for the Gold Coast. Because of gaps in the Ghanaian data it was necessary to bridge the time between 1938 and 1948 by using British cost of living data taken from the *United Nations Statistical Yearbook for 1950*. Again, food only was used, but no breakdown by weights or commodities was available. The Ghanaian data picked up again in 1948, but this time they were derived from the *Ministry of Labour Report, 1953-54*, and the *Statistical Yearbooks of Ghana*, 1961, 1963, and 1965-66. In these sources weights and breakdown by commodities were given, and it was possible to differentiate food prices from others. The relative weights of 82 and 18 were given to local and imported foods, respectively, which were adopted here. The years 1970 to 1977 were extrapolated from Kodwo Ewusi's figures (see Chapter II, footnote *h* under Table II-1). The weights for the 1978 data, which I collected, had to be adjusted because it was impossible to get flour or sugar at most of the 20 markets surveyed in Accra. The 1978 figure, then, includes only local food products. For purposes of incidental information, the change in cost of living for all items is also given here, which includes services, clothing, fuel and light, household goods, etc., but only the food prices were used for computing the real wage index in Part III because it was a more consistent index.

Column III of the table gives the rise in wages using 1903 as base 100. The data until 1948 were taken from the *Annual Colonial Reports*, using wages paid to Public Works Department domestics, carpenters and masons, day laborers, and junior grade civil servants with the respective weights of 3, 8, 3, and 6 as being typical of the Ga male population. The *Report of the*

Gold Coast Ministry of Labour for 1953-54 was used to get wages for private sector day laborers and junior grade clerks, using 3 and 6 as their respective weights, combined with public sector carpenters with a weight of 8 from the *Annual Colonial Report* for 1952-53. The difference between public and private sector wages, whenever it was given, was not significant, so it seemed acceptable to use private sector data when those for the public sector were not available. Lastly, the *Republic of Ghana Labour Statistics* for 1964 and 1970 gave the wages for public sector daily and monthly rated workers, which were given the respective weights of 3 and 6. For 1970 only central government African workers were used because they are mostly in Accra. It was impossible to determine exactly which workers were subsumed under which category, but day laborers certainly came under the first, and junior grade civil servants under the second. 1974 was derived from the *Economic Survey of Ghana* and applies to workers in establishments with over 10 employees, so is not as reliable and gives an overly optimistic real wage index.

Column IV is the result of dividing the wage by the price index to get some idea of the relative position of salaried workers--realizing, of course, that a two year difference is ignored in most of these calculations. This qualification and the others given above about this data amply illustrate why it is so difficult to construct anything but the crudest of cost of living estimates for the Gold Coast/Ghana during the twentieth century. The data are inconsistent and, therefore, frustrating, to put it mildly. I found myself literally tearing my hair out at one point. It is comforting, however, that the results of both the wage and price indices came out to be as close as they are, which might indicate that the margin of error is smaller than one might think. Also, there was a rough correspondence with results obtained by others, and by using them as an independent check on my data I was able to spot some mistakes.[1]

Currency

Using the retail price index one can then approximate the changing value of currency in the Gold Coast/Ghana. Throughout this study, when the price of an item is given at the rates prevailing when it was quoted, it can then be factored by the difference in the price index to get the approximate value of the item in 1978 cedis, or 1964 pounds. The factors thus derived are in Table A-1.

---

[1]W. Birmingham, "An Index of Real Wages of the Unskilled Labourer in Accra, 1939-1959," *Economic Bulletin of Ghana* IV, no. 3 (March 1960): 3; N. A. Cox-George, *Studies in Finance and Development: The Gold Coast (Ghana) Experience 1914-1950* (London: Dennis Dobson, 1973), p. 145; N. K. Adyanthaya and J. T. Kodua, "New Series of Consumer Price Index Numbers for Ghana," *Economic Bulletin of Ghana* VIII, no. 2 (1964): 16; Ghana Central Bureau of Statistics, *Economic Survey, 1972-1974*, p. 14; *Accra Catholic Standard*, Jan. 1, 1978, p. 4.

Table A-1. Multiplier Factors for Determining 1964/1978 Prices.

Year:	1901	1911	1921	1931	1938	1948	1954
£	339	305	216	329	314	240	139
¢	10,063	9,066	6,410	9,770	9,318	7,137	4,142
Year	1960	1964	1970	1974	1977	1978	
£	122	100					
¢	3,633	2,968	1,717	1,153	223	100	

In the nineteenth century at Accra, as elsewhere along the West African coast, various sorts of currency were used. Gold dust was the prime medium of exchange during most of the nineteenth century, but by 1889 cowries had supplanted it.[2] In 1903 cowries were still in common use and people were unwilling to accept copper coins, even though cowries were getting scarce. Silver and gold coins were commonly accepted.[3] After World War I the British introduced paper currency, which was not popular because it mildewed. Women in the markets refused to accept it.[4] By this time, of course, the British pound sterling was the official currency. It remained the basis of the Ghanaian currency until 1965, when the cedi was instituted at the rate of ¢2.40 to £G1, or £1 British pounds, or $US2.80.[5] In 1967, the National Liberation Council established the new cedi at the rate of N¢1 to $US.98. In 1971-72 the new cedi was revalued twice more, once by the Busia government so that N¢1 equaled $US.48. When Busia was overthrown by the National Redemption Council, the cedi was readjusted to be worth $US.76, where it stood until Acheampong was overthrown by the Akuffo government, who devalued it to $US.36 in 1978. These changes in the currency reflected the drastically worsening economic situation in Ghana. An inevitable accompaniment to an overvalued currency in the 1970s was the development of a flourishing black market. In 1978 from January to April the unofficial exchange rate went from about 7 cedis per $US1.00 to 12 or 14. Even further deterioration was evident by early 1983, when $US1.00 was worth 60 to 70 cedis at black market rates. Under pressure from the International Monetary Fund the second Rawlings government devalued the cedi to be worth about 5 cents.[6]

---

[2]F. A. Sai, "The Market Woman in the Economy of Ghana," Master's thesis Cornell University (1971), p. 2.

[3]*Annual Colonial Report*, 1903, p. 13. SNA 11/1775, interview of Governor Nathan with Osu Maŋtsɛ Noye Ababio, Dec. 31, 1903.

[4]SNA 11/1088, welcoming speech of Ga Maŋtsɛ and maŋtsɛmei to Governor Guggisberg, Nov. 28, 1919.

[5]After 1965 the people in Accra still used the terms pound and shilling to refer to ¢2.00 and 10 pesewas respectively (100 pesewas = ¢1.00). Even threepence is used to refer to 2 1/2 pesewas, and sixpence for 5 pesewas.

[6]"End of a Dream: Ghana, Once Pride of Africa, Now is Nearing Collapse," *Wall Street Journal*, March 28, 1983, p. 1. *Africa News* XX, No. 22 (May 30, 1983): 6.

SELECTED BIBLIOGRAPHY*

Ghana

Ackah, C. A. "Social Stratification in Ghana." *Ghana Journal of Sociology* V, no. 2 (Oct. 1969): 1-7.

Acquah, Ione. *Accra Survey*. London: University of London Press, 1958.

Addae, Gloria. "The Retailing of Imported Textiles in the Accra Market." *Proceedings of the West African Institute of Social and Economic Research Conference*, March 1954. Ibadan: University Press, 1956.

Addo, N. O. "Household Patterns Among Urban and Rural Communities in South-Eastern Ghana." University of Ghana Institute of African Studies, Legon Family Research Papers No. 1, 1974.

_____. "Some Demographic Aspects of Urbanization in Ghana, 1931-1960." *Ghana Jour. of Social Science* I, no. 1 (1971): 50-82.

_____. "Urbanization, Population, and Employment in Ghana." In *Population Growth...*, pp. 243-51. Edited by S. H. Ominde and C. N. Ejiogu. 1972.

_____, Ampofo, D. A., Gaisie, S. K., Benneh, G., and Kpedekpo, G. M. K. *Symposium on Implications of Population Trends for Policy Measures in West Africa*. Ghana Population Studies No. 3, 1971.

_____, Gaisie, S. K., Benneh, G., and Kpedekpo, G. M. K. *Symposium on Population and Socioeconomic Development in Ghana*. Ghana Population Studies No. 2, 1968.

Adjetey, J. N. N. "Improving the Traditional Method of Smoking." Ghana Ministry of Agriculture *Fisheries Research Report* I, no. 1 (1962): 8-11.

Adyanthaya, N. K., and Kodua, J. T. "New Series of Consumer Price Index Numbers for Ghana." *Economic Bull. of Ghana* VIII, no. 2 (1964): 3-19.

Afful, K. N., and Steel, W. F. "Women in the Urban Economy of Ghana: Comment." Paper, 1978.

Agbodeka, Francis. *African Politics and British Policy on the Gold Coast 1868-1900*. London: Longman Group, Ltd., 1971.

_____. *Ghana in the Twentieth Century*. Accra: Ghana Universities Press, 1972.

---

*In this bibliography USAID stands for United States Agency for International Development, which is part of the State Department, NCWD stands for the Ghana National Council on Women and Development, and ISSER for the University of Ghana Institute for Statistical, Social, and Economic Research.

Ahmad, Naseem. *Deficit Financing, Inflation and Capital Formation: The Ghanaian Experience, 1960-1965.* Munich: Weltforum Verlag, 1970.

Aidoo, Ama Ata. *No Sweetness Here.* Garden City, N.Y.: Doubleday and Co., 1971.

Allott, A. N. "A Note on the Ga Law of Succession." *Bull. of the London School of Oriental and African Studies* XV, part 1 (1953): 164-69.

_____. "Marriage and International Conflict of Laws in Ghana." *Jour. of African Law* II, no. 3 (1958): 164-84.

_____. *Essays in African Law.* London: Butterworth and Co., Ltd., 1960.

Amarteifio, G. W., Butcher, D. A., and Whitham, David. *Tema Manhean, a Study of Resettlement.* Accra: Ghana Universities Press, 1966.

Amartey, A. A. *Omanye Aba.* Accra: Bureau of Ghana Languages, 1969.

Ammah, Charles. *Ga Hɔmɔwɔ.* Accra: Advance Publishing Co. Ltd., 1968.

Amoah, Frank E. K. "Accra: A Study of the Development of a West African City." Master's thesis, University of Ghana Institute of African Studies, 1964.

Ampofo, D. A. "Abortion in Accra: The Social, Demographic and Medical Perspectives." In *Symposium on Implications...*, pp. 79-105. Edited by N. O. Addo et al. 1971.

Appiah-Kubi, Kofi. "Monogamy: Is it Really So Christian?" *Africa Woman*, no. 5 (July/Aug. 1976), pp. 46-48.

Arhin, Kwame. "The Ashanti Rubber Trade with the Gold Coast in the Eighteen-Nineties." *Africa* XLII, no. 1 (1972): 32-43.

Armah, Ayi Kwei. *The Beautyful Ones Are Not Yet Born.* N.Y.: Collier Books, 1969.

Aryee, George. "Small Scale Manufacturing Activities: A Study of the Interrelationships Between the Formal and the Informal Sectors in Kumasi, Ghana." International Labour Office World Employment Program, Geneva. Working Paper No. 23. June 1977.

Asiedu-Akrofi, K., and Atakpa, S. K. "Practices Regarding Allocation of Places To Women in Schools and Colleges." Research Report for United States Agency for International Development (USAID)/Ghana National Council on Women and Development (NCWD) Research Project, May 1978.

Azu, G. A. M. "The Impact of The Modern Fishing Industry on the Ga Traditional Fishing Industry." Master's thesis, University of Ghana Institute of African Studies, 1966.

Azu, Gladys Diana (see also Mills-Odoi). "Women and Contraception." Paper presented at NCWD Seminar on Women and Development, Accra, July 1978.

Bartels, J. E. M. "Accra Markets Surveys, Part I, Organization and Management." Paper for Food Research Institute Economics and Marketing Section, Oct. 22, 1966.

Bartle, P. F. W. "Modernization and the Decline in Women's Status: An Example From a Matrilineal Akan Community." Paper presented at NCWD Seminar on Women and Development, Accra, Sept. 1978.

Beckman, Bjorn. "Ghana, 1951-78: the Agrarian Basis of the Post-Colonial State." In *Introduction to Rural Development in Tropical Africa*, pp. 143-67. Edited by J. Heyer, P. Roberts and G. Williams. N.Y.: St. Martin's Press, 1981.

Benneh, G. "Small-Scale Farming Systems in Ghana." *Africa* XLIII, no. 2 (April 1973): 134-46.

Bentsi-Enchill, Kwamena. "Abortion and the Law." Paper, ca. 1974.

_____. *Ghana Land Law*. London: Sweet and Maxwell, 1964.

Bentsi-Enchill, Nii K. "Losing Illusions at Makola Market." *West Africa* (Sept. 3, 1979), p. 1590.

Birmingham, Walter. "An Index of Real Wages of the Unskilled Labourer in Accra, 1939-1959." *Economic Bull. of Ghana* IV, no. 3 (March 1960): 2-6.

_____, Neustadt, I., and Omaboe, E. N., eds. *A Study of Contemporary Ghana*. 2 vols. London: George Allen and Unwin Ltd., 1967.

Blomquist, A. G. "Foreign Aid, Population Growth, and the Gains from Birth Control." *Jour. of Development Studies* VIII, no. 1 (Oct. 1971): 5-22.

Boateng, E. A. "The Growth and Functions of Accra." *Bull. of the Ghana Geographical Association* IV, no. 2 (1959): 4-15.

Bourret, F. M. *Ghana, the Road to Independence, 1919-1957*. London: Oxford University Press, 1960.

Bowdich, T. E. *Mission From Cape Coast Castle to Ashanti*. London: Griffith and Farran, 1873.

Bridge, Horatio. *Journal of an African Cruiser*. 1845. Reprint ed. London: Dawson's of Pall Mall, 1968.

Brokensha, David. *Social Change at Larteh, Ghana*. Oxford: Clarendon Press, 1966.

Brown, A. P. "The Fishing Industry of the Labadi District." In *Fishes and Fisheries of the Gold Coast*, pp. 23-44. Edited by F. R. Irvine. London: Crown Agents, 1947.

Bruce-Myers, J. M. "The Connubial Institutions of the Gas." *Jour. of the African Society* XXX, no. 121 (Oct. 1931): 399-409.

_____. "The Origin of the Gas." *Jour. of the African Society* XXVII, no. 105 (Oct. 1927): 69-76. No. 106 (Jan. 1928): 167-73.

SHARING THE SAME BOWL

Caldwell, John C. "The Demographic Implications of the Extension of Education in a Developing Country: Ghana." In *Symposium on Population...*, pp. 90-100. Edited by N. O. Addo et al. 1968.

_____. "The Erosion of the Family: A Study of the Fate of the Family in Ghana." *Population Studies* XX, no. 1 (July 1966): 5-26.

_____. "Extended Family Obligations and Education: A Study of An Aspect of Demographic Transition amongst Ghanaian University Students." *Population Studies* XIX, Part 2 (Nov. 1965): 183-99.

_____. "Fertility Control." In *Population Growth and Socioeconomic Change...*, pp. 58-97. Edited by J. C. Caldwell. 1975.

_____. "Fertility Differentials as Evidence of Incipient Fertility Decline in a Developing Country." *Population Studies* XXI (July 1967): 5-21.

_____. "Population Change." In *A Study of Contemporary Ghana* II: 78-110. Edited by W. Birmingham et al. 1967.

_____. "Population: General Characteristics." In *A Study of Contemporary Ghana* II: 17-77. Edited by W. Birmingham et al. 1967.

_____. *Population Growth and Family Change in Africa.* Canberra: Australian National University Press, 1968.

_____. *Population Growth and Socioeconomic Change in West Africa.* N.Y.: Columbia University Press, 1975.

_____. "The Socio-Economic Explanation of High Fertility." Australian National University Changing African Family Project Series, Monograph No. 1. Canberra, 1976.

Campbell-Platt, G. "The Development of Appropriate Food Technologies in Ghana: An Overview." Paper presented at NCWD Seminar on Women and Development, Accra, Sept. 1978.

Campbell-Platt, Kiran. "Dropout Rate Among Girls and Boys at the Primary, Middle, and Secondary Levels of Education in Selected Schools in Accra." NCWD Research Paper, Accra, 1978.

_____. "The Impact of Mechanization on the Employment of Women in Traditional Sectors." Paper for NCWD Seminar on Women and Development, Accra, Sept. 1978.

Cardinall, A. W. *The Gold Coast, 1931.* Accra: Government Printer, 1931.

Chi, I-Cheng, Ampofo, D. A., and Koetsawang, Suporn. "Incomplete Abortions in Accra and Bangkok University Hospitals, 1972-73." Paper presented at International Planned Parenthood Federation Africa Regional Conference on the Medical and Social Aspects of Abortion, Accra, Dec. 12-15, 1973.

Church, Katie. "A Study of Socio-Economic Status and Child-Care Arrangements of Women in Madina." Paper presented at NCWD Seminar on Women and Development, Accra, Sept. 1978.

Claridge, W. Walton. *A History of the Gold Coast and Ashanti.* 2 vols. 1915. Reprint ed. N.Y.: Barnes and Noble, 1964.

Collett, Dom Martin. *Accra.* London: Society for the Propagation of the Gospel in Foreign Parts, 1928.

Cox-George, N. A. *Studies in Finance and Development: The Gold Coast (Ghana) Experience 1914-1950.* London: Dennis Dobson, 1973.

Cruickshank, Brodie. *Eighteen Years on the Gold Coast of Africa.* 2 vols. 1853. Reprint ed. Barnes and Noble, 1966.

Daaku, Kwame Yeboa. *Trade and Politics on the Gold Coast, 1600-1720.* Oxford: Clarendon Press, 1970.

Daniell, W. F. "On the Ethnography of Akkrah and Adampé, Gold Coast, West Africa." *Jour. of the Ethnological Society of London* IV (1856): 1-32.

Date-Bah, E. "Ghanaian Women and Cooperatives." Paper presented at NCWD Seminar on Women and Development, Accra, Sept. 1978.

_____. "Ghanaian Women in Factory Employment: A Case Study." International Educational Materials Exchange paper No. 4137, 1976.

_____. "Some Features of Marriage Patterns Among the Members of One Elite Group in Ghana." University of Ghana Institute of African Studies, Legon Family Research Paper No. 3, 1975.

Debrunner, H. "The Church of Christ at Accra Before 1917." MS. in Basel Mission Papers. Ghana National Archives (EC 7/19). N.d.

de Marees, Pieter. "A Description and Historicall Declaration of the Golden Kingdome of Guinea...." In *Hakluytus Posthumus or Purchas His Pilgrimes* VI: 247-353. 1600. Translated by G. Artus Dantisc. Edited by Samuel Purchas. Reprint ed. N.Y.: AMS Press, Inc., 1965.

Dickson, K. B. *A Historical Geography of Ghana.* London: Cambridge University Press, 1969.

_____. "Evolution of Seaports in Ghana: 1800-1928." *Annals of the Association of American Geographers* LV, no. 1 (March 1965): 98-111.

Dinan, Carmel. "Pragmatists or Feminists? The Professional 'Single' Women of Accra, Ghana." *Cahiers d'Etudes Africaines* 65, XVII, no. 1 (1977): 155-76.

Dodds, Maggie, ed. *Ghana Talks.* Washington, D.C.: Three Continents Press, 1976.

Dua, H. S. "Report on Population and Earnings Survey of Faana Fishing Villages of Accra (Feb./March 1961)." *Fisheries Research Report* I, no. 2 (1962): 8-26.

Due, Jean M. "Development Without Growth--The Case of Ghana in the 1960s?" *Economic Bull. of Ghana* III (1973): 3-15.

Dumor, Ernest. "Commodity Queens and the Distributive Trade in Ghana." Paper presented at African Studies Association Conference, Baltimore, Nov. 1978.

Duncan, John. *Travels in Western Africa in 1845 and 1846*, Vol. I. London: Richard Bentley, 1847.

Dutta-Roy, D. K. *Eastern Region Household Budget Survey*. University of Ghana Institute of Statistical, Social, and Economic Research (ISSER), Technical Publications Series No. 6, 1969.

_____, and Mabey, S. J. *Household Budget Survey in Ghana*. ISSER Technical Publications Series No. 2, 1968.

Dzidzienyo, Stella. "Housemaids: A Case Study of Domestic Helpers in Ghanaian Homes." Paper presented at NCWD Seminar on Women and Development, Accra, Sept. 1978.

Ekow-Daniels, W. C. "Problems in the Law Relating to the Maintenance and Support of Wives and Children." University of Ghana Institute of African Studies, Legon Family Fresearch Papers No. 1, 1971.

Engberg, Lila. "Household Differentiation and Integration as Predictors of Child Welfare in a Ghanaian Community." *Jour. of Marriage and the Family* XXXVI, no. 2 (May 1974): 389-99.

Ewusi, Kodwo. "Changing Patterns of Household Expenditure in Ghana." Paper presented at the Conference on Innovation in African Economic History, University of Ghana, Legon, Dec. 14-20, 1971.

_____. "The Determinants of Price Fluctuation in Ghana." ISSER Discussion Paper No. 2, Dec. 1977.

_____. *Economic Inequality in Ghana*. Accra: New Times Corporation, 1977.

_____. "Expenditure Patterns of Upper and Middle Income Groups in Ghana." ISSER Technical Publications Series No. 26, 1972.

_____. "The Size of the Labour Force and the Structure of Employment in Ghana." ISSER paper, 1975.

_____. "Road Transport Facilities and Their Effects on Local Food Prices in the Sixties." *Economic Bull. of Ghana* I (1971): 24-32.

_____. "Women in Occupations in Ghana." Paper presented at NCWD Seminar on Women and Development, Accra, Sept. 1978.

Field, J. J. "The Asamanukpai of the Gold Coast." *Man* XXXIV, no. 211 (Dec. 1934), 186-89.

_____. "The Otutu and the Hionte of West Africa." *Man* XLIII, no. 18 (March/April 1943): 36-37.

_____. *Religion and Medicine of the Ga People*. Accra: Presbyterian Book Depot, 1937.

_____. *The Social Organisation of the Ga People*. London: Crown Agents, 1940.

Fitzgerald, Lorraine Kirk. "Cognitive Development Among Ga Children: Environmental Correlates of Cognitive Growth Rate Within the Ga Tribe." Ph.D. dissertation, University of California, 1970.

Fleischer, C., and Wilkie, M. B. "Specimens of Folk-lore of the Ga-people of the Gold Coast." *Africa* III (1930): 360-68.

Fortes, Meyer. *The Family: Bane or Blessing?* Accra: Ghana Universities Press, 1971.

Foster, Philip J. *Education and Social Change in Ghana*. Chicago: University of Chicago Press, 1968.

_____. "Ethnicity and the Schools in Ghana." *Comparative Education Review* VI, no. 2 (Oct. 1962): 127-35.

_____. "Secondary Schooling and Social Mobility in a West African Nation." *Sociology of Education* XXXVII, no. 2 (1963): 150-71.

_____. "Secondary School-Leavers in Ghana: Expectations and Reality." *Harvard Educational Review* XXXIV, no. 4 (1964): 537-58.

Fraker, Anne, and Harrell-Bond, Barbara. "Feminine Influence." *West Africa*, Nov. 26, 1979, pp. 2182-86.

Gaisie, S. K. *Estimating Ghanaian Fertility, Mortality, and Age Structure*. Ghana Population Studies No. 5, 1976.

_____. "Fertility Levels Among the Ghanaian Tribes." In *Population Growth and Economic Development*. Ed. Ominde and Ejiogu. 1972, pp. 84-92.

_____. "Population Growth and Its Components." In *Population Growth and Socioeconomic Change...*, pp. 346-66. Edited by J. C. Caldwell. 1975.

_____. "Some Aspects of Fertility Studies in Ghana." In *The Population of Tropical Africa*, pp. 238-46. Edited by J. C. Caldwell and C. Okonjo. 1968.

_____, and David, A. S. *Planned Fertility Reductions in Ghana: Structural Inter-Relationships, Potential Socio-Economic Impact, and the Magnitude of the Needed Programmes*. Ghana Population Studies No. 6, 1974.

Garlick, Peter C. *African Traders and Economic Development in Ghana*. Oxford: Clarendon Press, 1971.

Golding, P. T. F. "An Enquiry into Household Expenditure and Consumption and Sale of Household Produce in Ghana." *Economic Bull. of Ghana* VI, no. 4 (1962): 11-33.

Goody, Jack, ed. *Changing Social Structure in Ghana: Essays in the Comparative Sociology of a New State and an Old Tradition*. London: International African Institute, 1975.

Gould, Peter R. *The Development of the Transportation Pattern in Ghana.* Evanston: Northwestern University Press, 1960.

Graham, C. K. *The History of Education in Ghana.* London: Frank Cass & Co., 1971.

Greenstreet, Miranda. "Employment of Women in Ghana." *International Labour Review* CIII, no. 2 (Feb. 1971): 117-29.

_____. "Social Change and Ghanaian Women." *Canadian Jour. of African Studies* VI, no. 2 (1972): 351-55.

_____. "Various Salient Features Concerning the Employment of Women Workers in Ghana." Paper presented at NCWD Seminar on Women and Development, Accra, July 1978.

Grier, Beverly. "Underdevelopment, Modes of Production, and the State in Colonial Ghana." *African Studies Review* XXIV, no. 1 (March 1981): 21-47.

Grove, David, and Laszlo Huszar. *The Towns of Ghana.* Accra: Ghana Universities Press, 1964.

Hagan, G. "Divorce, Polygyny and Family Welfare." *Ghana Jour. of Sociology* X, no. 1 (1976): 67-84.

Hakam, A. N. "Impediments to the Growth of Indigenous Industrial Entrepreneurship in Ghana: 1946-1968." *Economic Bull. of Ghana* II (1972): 3-31.

_____. "Technology Diffusion from the Formal to the Informal Sector: The Case of the Auto-Repair Industry in Ghana." International Labour Office World Employment Programme, Working Paper, Geneva, July 1978.

Hart, Keith. "Informal Income Opportunities and Urban Employment in Ghana." *Jour. of African Studies* XI, no. 1 (1973): 61-89.

_____. "Small-Scale Entrepreneurs in Ghana and Development Planning." *Jour. of Development Studies* VI, no. 4 (July 1970): 104-20.

Henty, G. A. *The March to Coomassie.* London: Tinsley Brothers, 1874.

Hill, Polly. *The Migrant Cocoa-Farmers of Southern Ghana.* Cambridge: Cambridge University Press, 1963.

_____. "Notes on the Organization of Food Wholesaling in South-Eastern Ghana: Long Distance Trade in Plantains." Paper, March 1966.

_____. "Women Cocoa Farmers." *The Ghana Farmer* II, no. 2 (May 1958): 70-71, 76.

Hopkins, Anthony G. *An Economic History of West Africa.* N.Y.: Columbia University Press, 1973.

Horton, James Africanus. *West African Countries and People.* 1868. Reprint ed. Edinburgh: University Press, 1969.

Houghton, B. D. "Urban Wage Workers: Coping." NCWD paper, Accra, March 1980.

_____. "Women in Education in Ghana." Paper presented at NCWD Seminar on Women and Development, Accra, Sept. 1978.

Hurd, G. E. "Education." In *A Study of Contemporary Ghana* II: 55-79. Edited by W. Birmingham, et al. 1967.

_____, and Johnson, T. J. "Education and Social Mobility in Ghana." *Sociology of Education* XL, no. 1 (Winter 1967): 55-79.

Hutchinson, Thomas J. *Impressions of West Africa.* London: Longman, Brown, Green, Longmans, and Roberts, 1858.

Irvine, F. R., ed. *The Fishes and Fisheries of the Gold Coast.* London: Crown Agents, 1947.

Jackson, R. M. (see also Lawson). "The Economics of the Gold Coast Fishing Industry." Master's thesis, University of Birmingham, 1953.

Jahoda, Gustav. "Boys' Images of Marriage Partners and Girls' Self-Images in Ghana." *Sociologus* VIII, no. 2 (1958): 155-69.

_____. "Love, Marriage, and Social Change: Letters to the Advice Column of a West African Newspaper." *Africa* XXIX (1959): 177-90.

_____. "The Social Background of a West African Student Population." *British Jour. of Sociology* V, no. 4 (1954): 355-65. VI, no. 1 (1955): 71-79.

_____. "Urban Adolescents' Views on Social Changes in the Gold Coast." *West African Institute of Social and Economic Research Conference Proceedings No. 2.* Ibadan: University Press, March 1953.

Johnson, Marion. "Census, Map and Guesstimates: the Past Population of the Accra Region." In *African Historical Demography*, pp. 272-94. Edinburgh: Centre of African Studies, 1977.

Johnson T. J. "Protest: Tradition and Change, An Analysis of Southern Gold Coast Riots 1890-1920." *Economy and Society* I, no. 2 (May 1972): 164-93.

Kay, G. B., ed. *The Political Economy of Colonialism in Ghana.* Cambridge: Cambridge University Press, 1972.

Kaye, Barrington. *Bringing Up Children in Ghana.* London: George Allen and Unwin, 1962.

Killick, A. J. "Ghana's Balance of Payments Since 1950." In *Readings...*, pp. 107-27. Edited by E. H. Whetham and J. I. Currie, 1967.

_____. "Inflation and Growth." In *A Study of Contemporary Ghana*, I: 413-22. Edited by W. Birmingham et al. 1966.

_____. "The Economics of Cocoa." In *A Study of Contemporary Ghana*, I: 365-90. Edited by W. Birmingham et al. 1966.

_____. "The Monetary Effects of Recent Budgets in Ghana." In *Readings...*, pp. 94-106. Edited by E. H. Whetham and J. I. Currie, 1967.

_____. "Price Controls in Africa: The Ghanaian Experience." *Jour. of Modern African Studies* II, no. 3 (Sept. 1973): 405-26.

_____. "The State Promotion of Industry." *Ghana Social Science Jour.* III, no. 1 (1976): 18-34.

Kilson, Marion. *African Urban Kinsmen, The Ga of Central Accra.* N.Y.: St. Martin's Press, 1974.

_____. "Continuity and Change in the Ga Residential System." *Ghana Jour. of Sociology* III, no. 2 (1967): 81-97.

_____, ed. *Excerpts from the Diary of Kwaku Niri (Alias J. Q. Hammond), 1884-1918.* University of Ghana Institute of African Studies, 1967.

_____. "The Ga and Non-Ga Populations of Central Accra." *Ghana Jour. of Sociology* II, no. 2 (Oct. 1966): 23-28.

_____. "The Ga Naming Rite." *Anthropos*, 63/64 (1968/69): 904-20.

_____. *Kpele Lala.* Cambridge: Harvard University Press, 1971.

_____. "Ritual Portrait of a Ga Medium." In *The New Religions of Africa*, pp. 67-79. Edited by B. Jules-Rosette. Norwood, N.J.: Ablex, 1979.

_____. "Urban Tribesmen: Social Continuity and Change Among the Ga in Accra, Ghana." Ph.D. dissertation, Harvard University, 1966.

_____. "Variations in Ga Culture in Central Accra." *Ghana Jour. of Sociology* III, no. 1 (Feb. 1967): 33-54.

Kingsley, Mary H. *Travels in West Africa.* 1897. Reprint ed. N.Y.: Barnes and Noble, 1965.

Kirk, Lorraine. "Maternal and Subcultural Correlates of Cognitive Growth Rate: The Ga Pattern." In *Piagetian Psychology, Cross Cultural Contributions*, pp. 257-95. Edited by P. R. Dasen. N.Y.: Gardner Press, Inc., 1977.

Kpedekpo, G. M. K. "Some Observations on Infant Mortality in the Urban Areas of Ghana." *Ghana Jour. of Child Development* II, no. 2 (Dec. 1969): 5-20.

_____. "Tables of School Life for Ghana 1960." In *Population Growth...*, pp. 336-40. Edited by S. H. Ominde and C. N. Ejiogu. 1972.

Kropp-Dakubu, M. E. "Akaja: A Ga Song Type in Twi." University of Ghana Institute of African Studies *Research Review* VIII, no. 2 (Jan. 1972): 44-61.

_____, and Phyllis Riby-Williams. *Ga Adesai Komei, Stories in Ga.* University of Ghana Institute of African Studies, 1972.

Kumekpor, M. L. "Family Planning in Ghana." Paper presented at University of Ghana joint seminar, ISSER and the Dept. of Sociology, 1971-72.

_____. "Marriage and Divorce Under the Matrimonial Causes Act (1971)." ISSER paper, 1972.

Kumekpor, Tom K. "Marriage and the Family in a Changing Society: A Case Study of Attitudes of Students of the University of Ghana to Marriage." University of Ghana Institute of African Studies, Legon Family Research Papers No. 3, 1975.

Lawson, Rowena M. (see also Jackson). *The Changing Economy of the Lower Volta 1954-67.* N.Y.: Oxford University Press, 1972.

_____. "The Distributive System in Ghana: A Review Article." *Jour. of Development Studies* III, no. 2 (Jan. 1967): 195-205.

_____. "Engel's Law and Its Application to Ghana." *Economic Bull. of Ghana* VII (1963): 22-34.

_____. "The Growth of the Fishing Industry of Ghana." *Economic Bull. of Ghana* XI (1967): 3-24.

_____. "Inflation in the Consumer Market in Ghana--Its Cause and Cure." *Economic Bull. of Ghana* X, no. 1 (1966).

_____. "The Supply Response of Retail Services to Urban Population Growth in Ghana." In *The Development of Indigenous Trade and Markets in West Africa*, pp. 377-98. Edited by C. Meillassoux. London: Oxford University Press/International African Institute, 1971.

_____, and Kwei, Emmanuel. *African Entrepreneurship and Economic Growth, A Case Study of the Fishing Industry of Ghana.* Accra: Ghana Universities Press, 1974.

Leith, J. Clark. *Foreign Trade Regimes and Economic Development: Ghana.* N.Y.: National Bureau of Economic Research, 1974.

MacMillan, Allister. *The Red Book of West Africa.* 1920. Reprint ed. London: Frank Cass and Co., 1968.

Manoukian, Madeline. *Akan and Ga-Adangme Peoples: Ethnographic Survey of Africa.* West Africa, Part I. Edited by D. Forde. London: International African Institute, 1950.

Manteko, Yimma. *Out-dooring in Accra.* University of Ghana Institute of African Studies Pamphlet Collection, 1967.

Marshall, Bill. *Bukom.* London: Longman's, 1979.

McCall, Daniel F. "The Effect on Family Structure of Changing Economic Activities of Women in a Gold Coast Town." Ph.D. dissertation, Columbia University, 1956.

_____. "The Koforidua Market." In *Markets in Africa*, pp. 667-97. Edited by P. Bohannan and G. Dalton. Evanston: Northwestern University Press, 1962.

_____. "Trade and the Role of Wife in a Modern West African Town." In *Social Change in Modern Africa*, pp. 286-99. Edited by A. W. Southall. London: Oxford University Press/International African Institute, 1961.

McElrath, Dennis. "Societal Scale and Social Differentiation: Accra, Ghana." In *The New Urbanization*, pp. 33-52. Edited by S. Greer et al. N.Y.: St. Martin's Press, 1968.

McNulty, Michael L. "Urban Structure and Development: The Urban System of Ghana." *Jour. of Developing Areas* III (Jan. 1969): 159-75.

McWilliam, H. O. *The Development of Education in Ghana*. London: Longmans, Green and Co. Ltd., 1969.

Meredith, Henry. *An Account of the Gold Coast of Africa*. 1812. Reprint ed. London: Frank Cass and Co. Ltd., 1967.

Metcalfe, G. E. *Great Britain and Ghana: Documents of Ghana History, 1807-1957*. London: Thomas Nelson and Sons Ltd., 1964.

Mills-Odoi, D. G. (see also Azu). "The La Family and Social Change." Master's thesis, University of Ghana Institute of African Studies, 1967.

Munger, E. S. "Land Use in Accra." *Zaïre* VIII, Part 2 (1954): 911-19.

Nathan, Matthew. "The Gold Coast at the End of the Seventeenth Century Under the Danes and the Dutch." *Jour. of the African Society* IV, no. 13 (Oct. 1904): 1-32.

Nii-Aponsah, D. A. *The Gbese People in History*. Accra: 3ª Publications, 1972.

Nketia, J. H. "Historical Evidence in Ga Religious Music." In *The Historian in Tropical Africa*, pp. 265-83. Edited by J. Vansina. London: Oxford University Press/International African Institute, 1964.

_____. "Progress in Gold Coast Education." *Transactions of the Gold Coast and Togoland Historical Society* I, Part 3 (1953): 1-9.

Nkosi, Lewis. "Polygamy." *Africa Woman*, no. 7 (Nov./Dec. 1976), pp. 24-25.

North, Jeanne, Fuchs-Carsch, Marian, Bryson, Judy, and Blumenfeld, Sharna. *Women in National Development in Ghana*. USAID paper, April 1975.

Nukunya, Godwin Kwaku. "Women and Marriage." Paper for NCWD Seminar on Women and Development, Accra, July 1978.

Nyanteng, V. K. "The Storage of Foodstuffs in Ghana." ISSER Technical Publications Series No. 18, 1972.

_____, and G. J. Van Apeldoorn. "The Farmer and the Marketing of Foodstuffs." ISSER Technical Publications Series No. 19, 1971.

Nypan, Astrid. *Market Trade: A Sample Survey of Market Traders in Accra*. University of Ghana African Business Series No. 2, 1960.

_____. "Market Trade in Accra." *Economic Bull. of Ghana* IV, no. 3 (March 1960): 7-16.

Ocloo, Esther. "The Ghanaian Market Woman." Paper presented at the 14th World Conference of Society for International Development, Abidjan, Aug. 11-16, 1974.

Ofosu-Amaah, S. O. "The Menarche at Aburi Girls' School." *Ghana Jour. of Child Development* II, no. 2 (1969): 48-52.

Ollennu, N. A. *The Law of the Testate and Intestate Succession in Ghana.* London: Sweet and Maxwell, 1966.

Omari, T. P. *Marriage Guidance for Young Ghanaians.* London: Thomas Nelson and Sons. Ltd., 1962.

_____. "Role Expectations in the Courtship Situation in Ghana." *Social Forces* XLII, no. 2 (Dec. 1963): 147-56.

Oppong, Christine. "The Conjugal Family 'Open' or 'Closed': A Preliminary Analysis of Changes in the Prescribed Norms for Conjugal Relationships of a Sample of Ghanaian University Students." University of Ghana Institute of African Studies *Research Review* VIII, no. 2 (Jan. 1972): 18-28.

_____. "Conjugal Power and Resources: An Urban African Example." *Jour. of Marriage and the Family* XXXII, no. 4 (Nov. 1970): 676-80.

_____. "The Crumbling of High Fertility Supports: Data from a Study of Ghanaian School Teachers." In *The Persistence of High Fertility: Population Prospects in the Third World* II: 331-60. Edited by J. C. Caldwell. Canberra: Australian National University Press, 1977.

_____. "Education of Relatives' Children by Senior Civil Servants in Accra." *Ghana Jour. of Child Development* II, no. 2 (Dec. 1969): 43-47.

_____. "Ghanaian Women Teachers: Workers, Kin, Wives, and Mothers: A Study of Conjugal Family Solidarity--Norms, Reality and Stress." Paper presented at Conference on Women and Development, Wellesley, Mass. June 1976.

_____. "Joint-Conjugal Roles and Extended Families: A Preliminary Note on a Mode of Classifying Conjugal Family Relationships." *Jour. of Comparative Family Studies* II, no. 2 (Autumn 1971): 178-87.

_____. *Marriage Among a Matrilineal Elite.* Cambridge: Cambridge University Press, 1974.

_____, Okali, C. and Houghton, B. "Woman Power: Retrograde Steps in Ghana." *African Studies Review* XVIII, no. 3 (Dec. 1975): 71-84.

Orraca-Tetteh, R. "Effects of Rapid Population Growth in Ghana on Nutritional Needs." In *Symposium on Implications of Population...*, pp. 57-68. Edited by N. O. Addo et al., 1971.

Osei, E. "Changes in Education Composition of the Ghanaian Population from 1960-1970." Paper presented at U.N. Regional Institute for Population Studies, Legon, Sept. 20, 1974.

Ozanne, Paul. "Notes on the Early Historic Archaeology of Accra." *Transactions of the Historical Society of Ghana* VI (1962): 51-70.

_____. "Notes on the Later Prehistory of Accra." *Jour. of the Historical Society of Nigeria* III (1964): 3-23.

Pappoe, Matilda E. "Women and Abortion." Paper presented at NCWD Seminar on Women and Development, Accra, July 1978.

Patterson, K. David. "Health in Urban Ghana: The Case of Accra 1900-1940." *Social Science and Medicine* 13B (1979): 251-68.

_____. "The Impact of Modern Medicine on Population Growth in Twentieth Century Ghana: A Tentative Assessment." In *African Historical Demography; Proceedings of a Seminar held in the Centre of African Studies, University of Edinburgh*, pp. 437-52. Edinburgh: Centre for African Studies, 1977.

Peil, Margaret. "Female Roles in West African Towns." In *Changing Social Structure...*, pp. 73-90. Edited by J. Goody. 1975.

_____. "The Apprenticeship System in Accra." *Africa* XL, no. 2 (April 1970): 137-50.

_____. "Demographic Change in a Ghanaian Suburb." *Ghana Social Science Jour.* III, no. 1 (1976): 63-78.

_____. "Ghanaian University Students: The Broadening Base." *British Jour. of Sociology* XVI, no. 1 (March 1965): 19-28.

_____. "Reactions to Estate Housing: A Survey of Tema." *Ghana Jour. of Sociology* IV, no. 1 (Feb. 1968): 1-18.

Pellow, Deborah. *Women in Accra, Options for Autonomy.* Algonac, Mich.: Reference Publications Inc., 1977.

Pogucki, R. J. H. *Report on Land Tenure in Customary Law of the Non-Akan Areas of the Gold Coast Colony, Part II: Ga.* 1954. Reprint ed. Accra: Lands Dept., 1968.

Poleman, Thomas T. "The Food Economies of Urban Middle Africa: The Case of Ghana." Stanford University *Food Research Inst. Studies* II, no. 2 (May 1961): 121-74.

Pool, D. I. "Conjugal Patterns in Ghana." *Canadian Review of Sociology and Anthropology* V, no. 4 (Nov. 1968): 241-53.

_____. "Social Change and Interest in Family Planning in Ghana: An Exploratory Analysis." *Canadian Jour. of African Studies* IV, no. 2 (1970): 207-27.

_____, and McWilliams, John A. "Contraceptors in Ghana." *Ghana Jour. of Sociology* VIII, no. 2 (1974): 34-41.

Pool, Janet E. "A Cross-Comparative Study of Aspects of Conjugal Behavior Among Women of 3 West African Countries." *Canadian Jour. of African Studies* VI, no. 2 (1972): 233-59.

Quartey-Papafio, A. B. "Apprenticeship Among the Gas." *Jour. of the African Society* XIII, no. 52 (July 1914): 415-22.

_____. "The Ga Hɔmɔwɔ Festival." *Jour. of the African Society* XIX, no. 74 (Jan. 1920): 126-34. No. 75 (April 1920), 227-32.

_____. "The Law of Succession Among the Akras or the Ga Tribes Proper of the Gold Coast." *Jour. of the African Society* X, no. 37 (Oct. 1910), 64-72.

_____. "The Native Tribunals of the Akras of the Gold Coast." *Jour. of the African Society* X, no. 39 (April 1911): 320-30; no. 40 (July 1911): 434-46. XI, no. 41 (Oct. 1911): 75-94.

_____. "The Use of Names Among the Gas or Accra People of the Gold Coast." *Jour. of the African Society* XIII, no. 50 (Jan. 1914): 167-82.

Quaye, Irene. "The Ga and Their Neighbours 1600-1742." Ph.D dissertation, University of Ghana, 1972.

Reindorf, Carl C. *The History of the Gold Coast And Asante.* Ca. 1890. Reprint ed. Accra: Ghana Universities Press, 1966.

Reusse, Eberhard, and Lawson, Rowena M. "The Effect of Economic Development on Metropolitan Food Marketing: A Case Study of Food Retail Trade in Accra." *East African Jour. of Rural Development* II, no. 1 (1969): 35-55.

Robertson, Claire C. "Change in the Organization of the Fish Trade in Twentieth Century Accra." *African Urban Notes* II, no. 2 (Spring 1976): 43-58.

_____. "The Death of Makola and Other Tragedies: Male Strategies Against a Female-Dominated Distribution Network." Paper presented at Canadian Association for African Studies Meetings, Toronto, May 1982.

_____. "Economic Woman in Africa: Profit-Making Techniques of Accra Market Women." *Jour. of Modern African Studies* XII, no. 4 (Dec. 1974), 657-65.

_____. "The Nature and Effects of Differential Access to Education in Ga Society." *Africa* XLVII, no. 2 (1977): 208-19.

_____. "Post-Proclamation Slavery in Accra: A Female Affair?" In *Women and Slavery in Africa.* Edited by C. Robertson and M. Klein. Madison: University of Wisconsin Press, 1983.

_____. "Social and Economic Change in Twentieth Century Accra: Ga Women." Ph.D. dissertation, University of Wisconsin, 1974.

_____. "Socioeconomic Change in Accra: Ga Women." In *Women in Africa*, pp. 111-33. Edited by N. Hafkin and E. Bay. Stanford University Press, 1976.

_____. "Women and Change in Marketing Conditions in the Accra Area." *Rural Africana*, no. 29 (Winter 1975-76), pp. 157-71.

Sai, Florence A. "The Market Woman in the Economy of Ghana." Master's thesis, Cornell University, 1971.

_____. "Women Traders." Paper for NCWD Seminar on Women and Development, Accra, July 1978.

Sandbrook, Richard, and Arn, Jack. *The Labouring Poor and Urban Class Formation: The Case of Greater Accra*. McGill University Centre for Developing Area Studies, Occasional Monograph Series No. 12. Montreal, 1977.

Sanjek, Roger. "Cognitive Maps of the Ethnic Domain in Urban Ghana: Reflections on Variability and Change." *American Ethnologist* IV, no. 4 (Nov. 1977): 603-22.

_____, and Sanjek, Lani Morioka. "Notes on Women and Work in Adabraka." *African Urban Notes* II, no. 2 (Spring 1976): 1-25.

Schildkrout, Enid. "The Fostering of Children in Urban Ghana: Problems of Ethnographic Analysis in a Multi-Cultural Context." *Urban Anthropology* II, no. 1 (Spring 1973): 49-73.

Schneider, G., Schneider, H., and Bude, U. "The Volta Region and Accra: Urbanization, Migration and Employment in Ghana." International Labour Office Urbanization and Employment Programme, Working paper. Geneva, May 1978.

Scott, David. *Epidemic Disease in Ghana 1901-1960*. London: Oxford University Press, 1965.

Seers, Dudley, and Ross, C. R. *Report on Financial and Physical Problems of Development in the Gold Coast*. Accra: Office of Government Statistician, July 1952.

Sethuraman, S. V. "Employment Promotion in the Informal Sector in Ghana." International Labour Office World Employment Programme, Working paper. Geneva, April 1977.

Simms, Ruth, and Dumor, Ernest. "Women in the Urban Economy of Ghana: Associational Activity and the Enclave Economy." *African Urban Notes* II, no. 3 (1976/77): 43-64.

Smock, Audrey C. "Ghana: From Autonomy to Subordination." In *Women, Roles and Status...*, pp. 173-216. Edited by J. A. Giele and A. Smock. 1977.

Stanley, Henry M. *Coomassie and Magdala*. London: Sampson Low, Marston, Low, and Searle, 1874.

Steel, W. F. "Female and Small-Scale Employment Under Modernization in Ghana." Paper, Sept. 1979.

_____. *Small-Scale Employment and Production in Developing Countries,
Evidence from Ghana.* N.Y.: Praeger Publishers, 1977.

_____, and Campbell, Claudia. "Women's Employment and Development:
A Conceptual Framework Applied to Ghana." Paper, April 1979.

Steuer, Max D. "After the Crisis--Long-Term Prospects for the Economy of Ghana." Inaugural Lecture. Accra: Ghana Universities Press, 1973.

Szereszewski, R. "Patterns of Consumption." In *A Study of Contemporary Ghana,*
I: 106-17. Edited by W. Birmingham et al. 1966.

_____. *Structural Changes in the Economy of Ghana 1891-1911.* London:
Weidenfeld and Nicholson, 1965.

van Apeldoorn, G. J. "Markets in Ghana, A Census and Some Comments." ISSER
Technical Publications Series No. 17, 1972.

Van Landewijk, J. E. J. M. "What Was the Original Aggrey Bead?" *Ghana Jour.
of Sociology* VII, no. 1 (1971): 89-99.

Vellenga, Dorothy Dee. "Arenas of Judgment--An Analysis of Matrimonial Cases
Brought Before Different Types of Courts in Akwapim and the Eastern Region in the 1930s and 1960s." Paper presented at University of Ghana Institute of African Studies, Legon, Feb. 1971.

_____. "Attempts to Change the Marriage Laws in Ghana and the Ivory
Coast." In *Ghana and the Ivory Coast: Perspectives on Modernization,* pp.
125-50. Edited by A. R. Zolberg and P. Foster. Chicago: University of
Chicago Press, 1971.

_____. "Differentiation Among Women Farmers in Two Rural Areas in
Ghana." *Labour and Society* II, no. 2 (April 1977): 197-208.

_____. "Non-Formal Education of Ghanaian Women into Economic
Roles." Paper presented at African Studies Association Conference, Boston,
1976.

Vyas, Nilu, and Leith, J. Clark. "Labour Force Participation of Women in Ghana." *Economic Bull. of Ghana* IV, no. 3/4 (1974): 53-60.

Weinberg, S. Kirson. "Juvenile Delinquency in Ghana: A Comparative Analysis of
Delinquents and Non-Delinquents." *Jour. of Criminal Law, Criminology and
Police Science* LV (1964): 471-81.

_____. "Urbanization and Male Delinquency in Ghana." *Jour. of
Research on Crime and Delinquency* II, no. 2 (July 1965): 85-94.

Weis, Lois. "Women and Education in Ghana: Some Problems of Assessing
Change." *International Jour. of Women's Studies* III, no. 5 (Sept./Oct.
1980): 431-53.

Wilks, Ivor. "Akwamu and Otublohum: An Eighteenth Century Akan Marriage Arrangement." *Africa* XXIX (1959): 391-404.

Wolfson, Freda, ed. *Pageant of Ghana.* London: Oxford University Press, 1958.

Woodman, Gordon R. "The Rights of Wives, Sons and Daughters in the Estates of Their Deceased Husbands and Fathers." Paper presented at University of Ghana Institute of African Studies Family Seminar, Legon, Feb. 1971.

_____. "Some Realism About Customary Law--The West African Experience." *Wisconsin Law Review,* no. 1 (1961), pp. 128-52.

Yannoulis, Y., and Bostock, M. "Urban Household Income and Expenditure Patterns in Ghana." *Economic Bull. of Ghana* VII, no. 3 (1963): 12-18.

General and Comparative Works

Acker, Joan. "Women and Social Stratification: A Case of Intellectual Sexism." *American Jour. of Sociology* LXXVIII, no. 4 (Jan. 1973), 936-45.

_____. "Women and Stratification: A Review of Recent Literature." *Contemporary Sociology* IX (Jan. 1980): 25-35.

Adelman, Irma, and Morris, Cynthia Taft. *Society, Politics and Economic Development.* Baltimore: Johns Hopkins Press, 1967.

African Historical Demography: Proceeedings of a Seminar held at the Centre of African Studies, University of Edinburgh. Edinburgh: Centre of African Studies, 1977.

Amin, Samir. *Neo-Colonialism in West Africa.* N.Y.: Monthly Review Press, 1974.

Ardener, Shirley, ed. *Perceiving Women.* London: Malaby Press, 1975.

_____. "Sexual Insult and Female Militancy." In *Perceiving Women,* pp. 29-53. Ed. S. Ardener. 1975.

Arizpe, Lourdes. "Women's Dependency on the Informal Labour Market in Mexico City: A Case of Unemployment or Voluntary Choice?" Paper presented at Conference on Women and Development, Wellesley College, Wellesley, Mass. June 1976.

Armstrong, W. R., and McGee, T. G. "Revolutionary Change and the Third World City: A Theory of Urban Involution." *Civilisations* XVIII, no. 3 (1968): 353-78.

Aronson, Dan R. "Ijebu Yoruba Urban-Rural Relationships and Class Formation." *Canadian Jour. of African Studies* V, no. 3 (1971): 263-79.

Banton, Michael. "Role Congruence and Social Differentiation Under Urban Conditions." In *Social Structure, Stratification, and Mobility,* pp. 177-200. Edited by A. Leeds. Washington, D.C.: Pan American Union, 1967.

_____, ed. *The Social Anthropology of Complex Societies.* ASA Monograph 4. London: Tavistock Publications, 1966.

_____. "Urbanisation and Role Analysis." In *Urban Anthropology*, pp. 43-70. Edited by A. W. Southall. 1973.

Barnes, J. A. "Measures of Divorce Frequency in Simple Societies." *Jour. of The Royal Anthropological Institute of Great Britain* LXXIX, Part 1 (1949): 37-62.

Barrett, Michèle. *Women's Oppression Today: Problems in Marxist Feminist Analysis.* London: Verso, 1980.

Bascom, William R. "The Esusu: A Credit Institution of the Yoruba." *Jour. of the Royal Anthropological Institute of Great Britain* LXXXII, Part 1 (1952): 63-69.

_____. "Some Aspects of Yoruba Urbanism." *American Anthropologist* LXIV, no. 4 (Aug. 1962): 699-709.

_____. "Urbanism as a Traditional African Pattern." *Sociological Review* VII, new series, no. 1 (1959): 29-43.

Bay, Edna, ed. *Women and Work in Africa.* Boulder: Westview Press, 1982.

Beaver, Stephen. *Demographic Transition Theory Reinterpreted.* Lexington, Mass.: Lexington Books, 1975.

Belasco, Bernard. *The Entrepreneur as Culture Hero, Pre-adaptations in Nigerian Economic Development.* N.Y.: J. F. Bergin, 1980.

Berg, Elliot J. "Real Income Trends in West Africa." In *Economic Transition...*, pp. 199-238. Edited by M. J. Herskovits and M. Harwitz. 1964.

Berry, J. W., and Dasen, P. R., eds. *Culture and Cognition: Readings in Cross-Cultural Psychology.* London: Methuen and Co., Ltd., 1974.

Bloch, Maurice, ed. *Marxist Analysis and Social Anthropology.* London: Malaby Press, 1975.

Blumberg, Rae Lesser. "Fairy Tales and Facts: Economy, Family, Fertility, and the Female." In *Women...*, pp. 12-21. Edited by M. B. Bramsen and I. Tinker. 1976.

Bohannan, Paul. "An Alternate Residence Classification." In *Marriage, Family, and Residence*, pp. 317-23. Edited by P. Bohannan and J. Middleton. 1968.

_____. *Social Anthropology.* New York: Holt, Rinehart and Winston, 1965.

_____, and Dalton, George, eds. *Markets in Africa.* Evanston: Northwestern University Press, 1962.

_____, and Middleton, John, eds. *Marriage, Family, and Residence.* Garden City, N.Y.: American Museum of Natural History Press, 1968.

Bohmer, Carol. "Modernization, Divorce and the Status of Woman: Le Tribunal Coutumier in Bobodioulasso." *African Studies Review* XXIII, no. 2 (Sept. 1980): 81-91.

Bongaarts, John. "Does Malnutrition Affect Fecundity? A Summary of Evidence." *Science*, no. 208 (May 9, 1980), pp. 564-69.

Boserup, Ester. *Woman's Role in Economic Development.* London: George Allen and Unwin Ltd., 1970.

Bosman, William. *A New and Accurate Description of the Coast of Guinea.* 1704. Reprint ed. London: Frank Cass and Co., 1967.

Bossen, Laurel. "Women in Modernizing Societies." *American Ethnologist* II, no. 4 (1975): 587-601.

Bramsen, M. B., and Tinker, I., eds. *Women and World Development.* American Association for the Advancement of Science: Overseas Development Council, 1976.

Brass W., et al., eds. *The Demography of Tropical Africa.* Princeton: Princeton University Press, 1968.

Bryceson, D. F., and Mbilinyi, M. "The Changing Role of Tanzanian Women in Production: From Peasants to Proletarians." Paper, 1978.

Bryson, Judy C. "Women and Economic Development in Cameroon." USAID Report, Jan. 10, 1979.

Bujra, Janet M. "Introductory: Female Solidarity and the Sexual Division of Labour." In *Women United...*, pp. 13-45. Edited by P. Caplan and J. Bujra. 1979.

_____. "Production, Property, Prostitution, 'Sexual Politics' in Atu." *Cahiers d'Etudes Africaines* 65, XVII, no. 1 (1977): 13-39.

_____. "Women 'Entrepreneurs' of Early Nairobi." *Canadian Jour. of African Studies* IX, no. 2 (1975): 213-34.

Burkett, Elinor C. "In Dubious Sisterhood: Class and Sex in Spanish Colonial South America." *Latin American Perspectives* IV, nos. 1-2 (Winter/Spring 1977): 18-26.

Buvinic, Mayra, and Youssef, Nadia H. "Women-Headed Households: the Ignored Factor in Development." USAID paper, 1979.

Caldwell, John C. "A Theory of Fertility: From High Plateau to Destabilization." *Population and Development Review* IV, no. 4 (Dec. 1978): 553-77.

_____. "Toward a Restatement of Demograhic Transition Theory." *Population and Development Review* II, nos. 3-4 (Sept./Dec. 1976): 321-66.

_____, and Okonjo, Chukuka, eds. *The Population of Tropical Africa.* London: Longman's, Green and Co. Ltd., 1968.

Caplan, Patricia, and Bujra, Janet M., eds. *Women United, Women Divided.* Bloomington: Indiana University Press, 1979.

Chodorow, Nancy. "Mothering, Male Dominance and Capitalism." In *Capitalist Patriarchy...,* pp. 83-106. Edited by Z. Eisenstein. 1979.

Chuta, Enyinna. "The Economics of the Gara (Tie-Dye) Cloth Industry in Sierra Leone." Michigan State University African Rural Economy Program, Working Paper No. 25, Feb. 1978.

_____, and Liedholm, C. "The Role of Small-Scale Industry in Employment Generation and Rural Development: Initial Research Results from Sierra Leone." Michigan State University African Rural Employment Research Network, African Rural Employment Paper No. 11, 1975.

Clignet, Remi. *Many Wives, Many Powers.* Evanston: Northwestern University Press, 1970.

_____. "Quelques remarques sur le rôle des femmes africaines en milieu urbain: Le cas de Cameroun." *Canadian Jour. of African Studies* VI, no. 2 (1972): 303-15.

_____, and Sween, Joyce. "Social Change and Type of Marriage." *American Jour. of Sociology* LXXV (1969): 123-45.

Cohen, Robin. "From Peasants to Workers in Africa." In *The Political Economy...,* pp. 155-68. Edited by P. C. W. Gutkind and I. Wallerstein. 1976.

_____, Gutkind, P. C. W., and Brazier, Phyllis, eds. *Peasants and Proletarians, The Struggles of Third World Workers.* N.Y.; Monthly Review Press, 1979.

Cook, Scott. "The Obsolete 'Anti-Market' Mentality: A Critique of the Substantive Approach to Economic Anthropology." *American Anthropologist* LXVIII (1966): 323-45.

Coquery-Vidrovitch, Catherine. "The Political Economy of the African Peasantry and Modes of Production." In *The Political Economy...,* pp. 90-111. Edited by P. C. W. Gutkind and I. Wallerstein. 1976.

Dalton, George, ed. *Tribal and Peasant Economies.* Garden City, N.Y.: Natural History Press, 1967.

_____. *Economic Anthropology and Development.* New York: Basic Books, 1971.

D'Andrade, Roy G. "Sex Differences and Cultural Institutions." In *The Development of Sex Differences,* pp. 174-204. Edited by Eleanor E. Maccoby. Stanford: Stanford University Press, 1966.

David, A. S., Laing, E., and Addo, N. O., eds. *Interdisciplinary Approaches to Population Studies.* Ghana Population Studies No. 4, 1975 (Proceedings of the West African Seminar on Population Studies, Legon, Nov./Dec. 1972).

DeLancey, Virginia. "The Relationship Between Female Labor Force Participation and Fertility: Compatibility of Roles on a Cameroon Plantation." Paper presented at African Studies Association Conference, Baltimore, Nov. 1978.

Delaney, Janice, Lupton, Mary Jane, and Toth, Emily. *The Curse: A Cultural History of Menstruation.* N.Y.: E. P. Dutton and Co., Inc., 1976.

Dobert, M., and Shields, N. "Africa's Women: Security in Tradition, Challenge in Change." *Africa Report* XVII (July/Aug. 1972): 14-20.

D'Onofrio-Flores, P. M. "Technology, Development, and Division of Labour by Sex." In *Scientific-Technological Change and the Role of Women in Development*, pp. 13-28. Edited by P. M. D'Onofrio-Flores and S. M. Pfafflin. Boulder: Westview Press, 1982.

Dorjahn, Vernon R. "The Factor of Polygyny in African Demography." In *Continuity and Change in African Cultures*, pp. 87-112. Edited by W. R. Bascom and M. J. Herskovits. Chicago: University of Chicago Press, 1958.

Due, Jean M., and Summary, Rebecca. "Constraints to Women and Development in Africa." Paper presented at African Studies Association Conference, Los Angeles, Oct. 31-Nov. 3, 1979.

Dumont, René. *False Start in Africa.* N.Y.: Frederick A. Praeger, 1969.

Dunbar, Roxanne. "Female Liberation as the Basis for Social Revolution." In *Voices of the New Feminism*, pp. 44-58. Edited by M. L. Thompson. 1970. Reprint ed. Boston: Beacon Press, 1975.

Eames, E., and Goode, J. G. *Urban Poverty in a Cross-Cultural Context.* N.Y.: Free Press, 1973.

Ehrensaft, Philip. "The Rise of a Proto-Bourgeoisie in Yorubaland." In *African Social Studies...*, pp. 116-24. Edited by P. C. W. Gutkind and P. Waterman. 1977.

Eisenstein, Zillah R., ed. *Capitalist Patriarchy and the Case for Socialist Feminism.* N.Y.: Monthly Review Press, 1979.

Elu de Leñero, Maria del Carmen. "Women's Work and Fertility." In *Sex and Class...*, pp. 46-68. Edited by J. Nash and H. Safa. 1976.

Epstein, A. L. "Urban Communities in Africa." In *Closed Systems...*, pp. 83-102. Edited by M. Gluckman. 1964.

——————. "Urbanization and Social Change in Africa." *Current Anthropology* VIII, no. 3 (Oct. 1967): 275-95.

Etienne, Mona. "Women and Men, Cloth and Colonization: The Transformation of Production-Distribution Relations Among the Baule (Ivory Coast)." In *Women...*, pp. 214-38. Edited by M. Etienne and E. Leacock. 1980.

——————, and Leacock, Eleanor, eds. *Women and Colonization, Anthropological Perspectives.* Brooklyn, N.Y.: J. F. Bergin Publishers, 1980.

Firth, Raymond. "Bilateral Descent Groups." In *Studies in Kinship and Marriage*, pp. 22-37. Edited by J. Schapera. Royal Anthropological Institute Occasional Paper No. 16, 1963.

_____. *Elements of Social Organization*. Boston: Beacon Press, 1961.

_____, ed. *Themes in Economic Anthropology*. ASA Monograph 6. London: Tavistock Publications Ltd., 1967.

_____, and Yamey, B. S., eds. *Capital, Saving and Credit in Peasant Societies*. Chicago: Aldine Publishing Co., 1964.

Fox, Robin. *Kinship and Marriage*. London: Penguin Books, 1967.

Furtado, Celso. *Development and Underdevelopment*. Los Angeles: University of California Press, 1971.

Gardiner, Jean. "Women's Domestic Labor." In *Capitalist Patriarchy...*, pp. 173-89. Edited by Z. Eisenstein. 1979.

_____. "Women in the Labour Process and Class Structure." In *Class and Class Structure*, pp. 155-64. Edited by A. Hunt. London: Lawrence and Wishart, 1977.

Geertz, Clifford. "Social Change and Economic Modernization in Two Indonesian Towns: A Case in Point." In *Tribal and Peasant Economies*, pp. 366-94. Edited by G. Dalton. 1967.

Giele, Janet A., and Smock, Audrey C., eds. *Women, Roles and Status in Eight Countries*. N.Y.: John Wiley and Sons, 1977.

Gluckman, Max, ed. *Closed Systems and Open Minds: The Limits of Naivety in Social Anthropology*. Chicago: Aldine Publishing Co., 1964.

Godelier, Maurice. "Objet et méthodes de l'anthropologie économique." *L'Homme, Revue Française d'Anthropologie* V, no. 2 (April/June 1965): 32-91.

Goode, William J. *World Revolution and Family Patterns*. N.Y.: Free Press of Glencoe, 1963.

Goodenough, Ward H. "Residence Rules." In *Marriage...*, pp. 297-316. Edited by P. Bohannan and J. Middleton. 1962.

Goody, Jack, ed. *Changing Social Structure in Ghana*. London: International African Institute, 1975.

_____, ed. *The Character of Kinship*. Cambridge: Cambridge University Press, 1973.

_____, ed. *The Developmental Cycle in Domestic Groups*. Cambridge: Cambridge University Press, 1962.

_____. *Literacy in Traditional Societies*. Cambridge: Cambridge University Press, 1968.

_____. "Polygyny, Economy and the Role of Women." In *The Charac-
ter...*, pp. 175-90. Ed. J. Goody. 1973.

_____. "Population, Economy and Inheritance in Africa." In *The Popula-
tion Factor...*, pp. 163-70. Edited by R. P. Moss and P. J. A. R. Rathbone.
1975.

_____. *Production and Reproduction, A Comparative Study of the Domes-
tic Domain.* Cambridge Studies in Social Anthropology No. 17. London:
Cambridge University Press, 1976.

_____, and Buckley, Joan. "Inheritance and Women's Labour in Africa."
Africa XLIII, no. 2 (April 1973): 108-21.

Gugler, Josef. "The Second Sex in Town." *Canadian Jour. of African Studies* VI,
no. 2 (1972): 289-301.

_____. "Unbalanced Urban Sex Ratios: An Exploration." *African Urban
Notes* VI, no. 1 (1971): 15-18.

_____, and Flanagan, William G. *Urbanization and Social Change in West
Africa.* Cambridge: Cambridge University Press, 1978.

Gutkind, Peter C. W. "African Urban Family Life." *Cahiers d'Etudes Africaines*
III, no. 10 (1962): 149-217.

_____. "African Urban Family Life and the Urban System." *Jour. of
Asian and African Studies* I, no. 1 (Jan. 1962): 35-42.

_____. *The Emergent African Proletariat.* McGill University Centre for
Developing Area Studies, Occasional Paper Series No. 8. 1974.

_____. "The Energy of Despair: Social Organisation of the Unemployed
in Two African Cities: Lagos and Nairobi." *Civilisations* XVII (1967): 186-
211.

_____. *Urban Anthropology.* Assen, Netherlands: Van Gorcum and Co.,
1974.

_____, and Wallerstein, I., eds. *The Political Economy of Contemporary
Africa.* Beverly Hills: Sage Publications, 1976.

_____, and Waterman, Peter, eds. *African Social Studies, A Radical
Reader.* London: Heineman, 1977.

Guyer, Jane I. "Female Farming and the Evolution of Food Production Patterns
Amongst the Beti of South-Central Cameroon." *Africa* L, no. 4 (1980):
341-55.

_____. "Household Budgets and Women's Incomes." Boston University
African Studies Center, Working Paper No. 28. 1980.

_____. "Woman's Work in the Food Economy of the Cocoa Belt: A Com-
parison." Boston University African Studies Center, Working Paper No. 7.
1978.

Hafkin, N., and Bay, E., eds. *Women in Africa, Studies in Social and Economic Change*. Stanford: Stanford University Press, 1976.

Hance, William A. *Population, Migration, and Urbanization in Africa*. N.Y.: Columbia University Press, 1970.

Hanna, William J., and Hanna, J. L. *Urban Dynamics and Black Africa*. Chicago/N.Y.: Aldine/Atherton, 1971.

Hansen, Karen Tranberg. "Married Women and Work: Explorations from an Urban Case Study." *African Social Research*, no. 20 (Dec. 1975), pp. 777-99.

_____. "When Sex becomes a Critical Variable: Married Women and Extradomestic Work in Lusaka, Zambia." Paper presented at African Studies Association Conference, Los Angeles, Oct. 31-Nov. 3, 1979.

Harkness, S., and Super, Charles M. "Why African Children Are So Hard to Test." In *Issues in Cross-Cultural Research*. Edited by L. L. Adler. *Annals of the N.Y. Academy of Sciences* 285:326-31. N.Y.: N.Y. Academy of Sciences, 1977.

Harris, Olivia. "Households as Natural Units." In *Of Marriage and the Market*, pp. 49-68. Edited by K. Young et al. London: CSE Books, 1981.

Heer, David H. "Educational Advance and Fertility Change." *International Population Conference Proceedings*, no. 3 (1969), pp. 1903-15.

Hendrickse, R. G. "Some Observations on the Social Background to Malnutrition in Tropical Africa." *African Affairs* LXV, no. 261 (Oct. 1966), 341-49.

Herskovits, M. J. *Economic Anthropology*. N.Y.: Alfred A. Knopf, 1952.

_____, and Harwitz, M., eds. *Economic Transition in Africa*. Evanston: Northwestern University Press, 1964.

Hill, Polly. "Some Characteristics of Indigenous West African Economic Enterprise." *Economic Bull. of Ghana* VI, no. 1 (1962): 3-14.

_____. "The West African Farming Household." In *Changing Social Structure...*, pp. 119-36. Edited by J. Goody. 1975.

Horton, Robin. "From Fishing-Village to City-State: A Social History of New Calabar." In *Man in Africa*, pp. 37-58. Edited by M. Douglas and P. M. Kaberry. London: Tavistock Publications, 1969.

Hughes, Arnold, and Cohen, Robin. "An Emerging Nigerian Working Class: The Lagos Experience, 1897-1939." In *African Labor History*, pp. 31-55. Edited by P. C. W. Gutkind, R. Cohen and J. Copans. Beverly Hills: Sage Publications, 1978.

Hutchison, Thomas W., ed. *Africa and the Law*. Madison: University of Wisconsin Press, 1968.

Hutton, Caroline, and Cohen, Robin. "African Peasants and Resistance to Change: A Reconsideration of Sociological Approaches." In *Beyond the Sociology of Development*, pp. 105-30. Edited by J. Oxaal, T. Barnett, and D. Booth. Boston: Routledge and Kegan Paul, 1975.

Ifeka-Moller, Caroline. "Female Militancy and Colonial Revolt." In *Perceiving Women*, pp. 127-57. Edited by S. Ardener. 1975.

Jewsiewicki, Bogumil. "Lineage Mode of Production: Social Inequalities in Equatorial Central Africa." In *Modes of Production in Africa, The Precolonial Era*, pp. 92-113. Edited by D. Crummey and C. C. Stewart. Beverly Hills: Sage Publications, 1981.

Jones, William O. "Economic Man in Africa." Stanford University *Food Research Institute Studies* I, no. 1 (Feb. 1960): 107-34.

Jules-Rosette, B., ed. *The New Religions of Africa*. Norwood, N.J.: Ablex, 1979.

Katz, Stephen. *Marxism, Africa and Social Class: A Critique of Relevant Theories*. McGill University Centre for Developing Area Studies Occasional Monograph Series No. 14. Montreal, 1980.

Katzin, Margaret. "The Role of the Small Entrepreneur." In *Economic Transition...*, pp. 179-98. Edited by M. J. Herskovits and M. Harwitz. 1964.

Kilby, Peter. *African Enterprise: The Nigerian Bread Industry*. Hoover Institution Studies No. 8. Stanford: Stanford University Press, 1965.

Kisekka, Mere Nakateregga. "Polygyny and the Status of African Women." *African Urban Notes* II, no. 3 (1976-77): 21-42.

Kitching, Gavin. *Class and Economic Change in Kenya, The Making of an African Petite Bourgeoisie 1905-1970*. New Haven: Yale University Press, 1980.

Krapf-Askari, Eva. *Yoruba Towns and Cities*. London: Oxford University Press, 1969.

Kuczynski, R. R. *Demographic Survey of the British Colonial Empire. West Africa*. Vol. I. London: Oxford University Press, 1948.

Kuhn, A., and Wolpe, A., eds. *Feminism and Materialism*. London: Routledge and Kegan Paul, 1978.

Leach, Edmund. "Complementary Filiation and Bilateral Kinship." In *The Character...*, pp. 53-58. Edited by J. Goody. 1973.

_____. *Rethinking Anthropology*. New York: Humanities Press, 1966.

Leacock, Eleanor. "Class, Commodity, and the Status of Women." In *Women Cross-Culturally*, pp. 601-16. Edited by R. Rohrlich-Leavitt. 1975.

_____. *Myths of Male Dominance*. N.Y.: Monthly Review Press, 1981.

_____. "Women, Development, and Anthropological Facts and Fictions." *Latin American Perspectives* IV, nos. 1 and 2 (Winter/Spring 1977): 8-17.

LeClair, E. E., and Schneider, H. K., eds. *Economic Anthropology.* N.Y.: Holt, Rinehart and Winston, 1968.

Leeds, Anthony, ed. *Social Structure, Stratification and Mobility.* Washington, D.C.: Pan American Union, 1967.

_____. "Some Problems in the Analysis of Class and the Social Order." In *Social Structure...*, pp. 327-61. Edited by A. Leeds. 1967.

Leith-Ross, Sylvia. *African Women.* 1939. Reprint ed. N.Y.: Frederick A. Praeger, 1965.

Lewis, Barbara C. "Economic Activity and Marriage Among Ivoirian Urban Women." In *Sexual Stratification*, pp. 161-91. Edited by A. Schlegel. 1977.

_____. "Female Strategies and Public Goods: Market Women in the Ivory Coast." Paper presented at Conference on Women and Development, Wellesley College, Wellesley, Mass. June 1976.

Lewis, I. M., ed. *History and Social Anthropology.* London: Tavistock Publications, 1968.

Lewis, Oscar. *Anthropological Essays.* New York: Random House, 1970.

Lewis, W. Arthur. *Aspects of Tropical Trade, 1883-1963.* Stockholm: Almquist and Wiksell, 1969.

_____. *Some Aspects of Economic Development.* Accra: Ghana Publishing Corp., 1969.

_____, ed. *Tropical Development 1880-1913.* London: George Allen and Unwin, 1970.

Leys, Colin. "Capital Accumulation, Class Formation and Dependency--The Significance of the Kenyan Case." In *Socialist Register 1978*, pp. 241-66. Edited by R. Miliband and J. Saville.

Liedholm, Carl, and Chuta, Enyinna. "The Economics of Rural and Urban Small-Scale Industries in Sierra Leone." Michigan State University African Rural Economy Program Paper No. 14. 1976.

Little, Kenneth. *African Women in Towns.* Cambridge: Cambridge University Press, 1973.

_____. "Some Urban Patterns of Marriage and Domesticity in West Africa." *Sociological Review* VII, new series, no. 1 (1959): 65-82.

_____. *West African Urbanisation.* Cambridge: Cambridge University Press, 1965.

Llewelyn-Davis, Melissa. "Two Contexts of Solidarity Among Pastoral Maasai Women." In *Women United...*, pp. 206-37. Edited by P. Caplan and J. Bujra. 1979.

Lloyd, Barbara B. "Education and Family Life in the Development of Class Identification Among the Yoruba." In *The New Elites...*, pp. 163-81. Edited by P. C. Lloyd. 1966.

Lloyd, Peter C. "Divorce Among the Yoruba." *American Anthropologist* LXX, no. 1 (Feb. 1968): 67-81.

_____. "Elite or Social Class?" In *The New Elites...*, pp. 49-62. Edited by P. C. Lloyd. 1966.

_____, ed. *The New Elites of Tropical Africa.* London: Oxford University Press/International African Institute, 1966.

Mabawonku, Adewale F. "An Economic Evaluation of Apprenticeship Training in Western Nigerian Small-Scale Industries." Michigan State University African Rural Economy Program Paper No. 17. 1979.

Mabogunje, Akin L. "A Typology of Population Pressure on Resources in West Africa." In *Geography in a Crowding World*, pp. 114-28. Edited by W. Zelinsky et al. N.Y.: Oxford University Press, 1970.

_____. "Urbanization in Nigeria--A Constraint on Economic Development." *Economic Development and Cultural Change* XIII (July 1965): 413-38.

Magubane, Bernard. "The Evolution of the Class Structure in Africa." In *The Political Economy...*, pp. 169-97. Edited by P. C. W. Gutkind and I. Wallerstein. 1976.

Mangin, William, ed. *Peasants in Cities: Readings in The Anthropology of Urbanization.* Boston: Houghton Mifflin, 1970.

Marris, Peter. *Family and Social Change in an African City.* Evanston: Northwestern University Press, 1962.

_____, and Somerset, Anthony. *The African Entrepreneur.* N.Y.: Africana Publishing Corporation, 1972.

McCaffrey, Kathleen M. *Images of Women in the Literature of Selected Developing Countries.* Pacific Consultants, 1978.

McGee, T. G. *The Urbanization Process in the Third World.* London: G. Bell and Sons, 1976.

Meillassoux, Claude, ed. *The Development of Indigenous Trade and Markets in West Africa.* London: Oxford University Press/International African Institute, 1971.

Miner, Horace, ed. *The City in Modern Africa.* N.Y.: Frederick A. Praeger, 1967.

Mintz, Sidney W. "The Employment of Capital by Market Women in Haiti." In *Capital, Saving and Credit...*, pp. 256-86. Edited by R. Firth and B. S. Yamey. 1964.

_____. "Men, Women and Trade." *Comparative Studies in Society and History* XIII (1971): 247-69.

_____. "Peasant Market Places and Economic Development in Latin America." Vanderbilt University Graduate Center for Latin American Studies, Occasional Paper No. 4. July 1964.

Miracle, M. P., and Fetter, Bruce. "Backward-Sloping Labor-Supply Functions and African Economic Behavior." *Economic Development and Cultural Change* XVIII, no. 2 (Jan. 1970): 240-51.

_____, Miracle, D. S., and Cohen, Laurie. "Informal Savings Mobilization in Africa." *Economic Development and Cultural Change* XXVIII, no. 4 (July 1980), 701-24.

Mitchell, J. C. "Social Change and the Stability of African Marriage in Northern Rhodesia." In *Social Change...*, pp. 316-29. Edited by A. W. Southall. 1961.

_____. "Theoretical Orientations in African Urban Studies." In *The Social Anthropology...*, pp. 37-68. Edited by M. Banton. 1966.

Monteiro, Ramiro. "From Extended to Residual Family: Aspects of Social Change in the Musseques of Luanda." In *Social Change in Angola*, pp. 211-34. Edited by F. W. Heimer. Munich: Weltforum Verlag, 1973.

Morgan, W. B. "Food Imports and Nutrition Problems in West Africa." In *The Population...*, pp. 208-25. Edited by R. P. Moss and R. J. A. R. Rathbone. 1975.

Moses, Yolanda T. "Female Status, The Family, and Male Dominance in a West Indian Community." In *Women and National Development...*, pp. 142-53. Edited by Wellesley Editorial Committee. 1977.

Morton-Williams, P. "Social Consequences of Industrialism Among the S. W. Yoruba--A Comparative Study." In *West African Institute of Social and Economic Research Conference Proceedings*, pp. 21-30. Ibadan: University Press, 1953.

Moss, R. P., and Rathbone, R. J. A. R., eds. *The Population Factor in African Studies.* London: University of London Press, 1975.

Nash, June. "Aztec Women: The Transition from Status to Class in Empire and Colony." In *Women and Colonization...*, pp. 134-48. Edited by M. Etienne and E. Leacock. 1980.

_____, and Safa, H. I., eds. *Sex and Class in Latin America.* N.Y.: Praeger, 1976.

Needham, Rodney, ed. *Rethinking Kinship and Marriage.* London: Tavistock Publications, 1971.

Nelson, Nici. "'Women Must Help Each Other': The Operation of Personal Networks Among Buzaa Beer Brewers in Mathare Valley, Kenya." In *Women United...*, pp. 77-98. Edited by P. Caplan and J. Bujra. 1979.

_____, ed. *Women in the Development Process.* London: Frank Cass and Co., 1981.

O'Barr, Jean, ed. *Third World Women: Factors in Their Changing Status*. Duke University Center for International Studies, Occasional Paper No. 2. Durham, N.C. 1976.

Obbo, Christine. *African Women, Their Struggle for Economic Independence*. London: Zed Press, 1980.

_____. "Women's Careers in Low Income Areas as Indicators of Country and Town Dynamics." In *Town...*, pp. 288-93. Edited by D. J. Parkin. 1975.

Ominde, S. H., and Ejiogu, C. N., eds. *Population Growth and Economic Development in Africa*. London: Heineman, 1972.

Pala, Achola, and Seidman, Ann. "A Proposed Model of the Status of Women in Africa." Paper presented at the Conference on Women and Development. Wellesley College, Wellesley, Mass. June 1976.

Parkin, David J. *Neighbors and Nationals in an African City Ward*. London: Routledge and Kegan Paul, 1969.

_____, ed. *Town and Country in Central and Eastern Africa*. Studies presented at the 12th International African Seminar. London: International African Institute/Oxford University Press, 1975.

_____. "Types of Urban African Marriage in Kampala." *Africa* XXXVI, no. 3 (1966): 269-85.

Pateman, Carole. "Hierarchical Organizations and Democratic Participation: The Problem of Sex." *Resources for Feminist Research* VII, no. 1 (March 1979): 19-22.

Peace, Adrian. "The Lagos Proletariat: Labour Aristocrats or Populist Militants." In *The Development of an African Working Class*, pp. 281-302. Edited by R. Sandbrook and R. Cohen. London: Longman, 1975.

Phillips, Arthur, ed. *Survey of African Marriage and Family Life*. London: Oxford University Press, 1953.

Piault, Colette. "Contribution à l'étude de la vie quotidienne de la femme maouri." *Etudes Nigériennes*, no. 10 (Jan. 1965).

Raymond, G. Alison. "Woman in Africa: Her Baby Off Her Back." *Jour. of Human Relations* VIII, nos. 3 and 4 (1960), 700-08.

Reiter, Rayna R., ed. *Toward an Anthropology of Women*. N.Y.: Monthly Review Press, 1975.

Remy, Dorothy. "Underdevelopment and the Experience of Women: A Nigerian Case Study." In *Toward an Anthropology...*, pp. 358-71. Edited by R. Reiter. 1975.

Rey, P.-P. "The Lineage Mode of Production." *Critique of Anthropology* I, no. 3 (Spring 1975): 27-80.

Robertson, Claire C., and Klein, Martin A., eds. *Women and Slavery in Africa.* Madison: University of Wisconsin Press, 1983.

Rogers. Susan G. "Anti-Colonial Protest in Africa: A Female Strategy Reconsidered." *Heresies* III, no. 1 (1980): 22-25.

Rohrlich-Leavitt, Ruby, ed. *Women Cross-Culturally.* Paris: Mouton, 1975.

Rosaldo, M. Z., and Lamphere, Louise, eds. *Woman, Culture and Society.* Stanford: Stanford University Press, 1974.

Rousseau, Ida Faye. "African Women: Identity Crises? Some Observations on Education and the Changing Role of Women in Sierra Leone and Zaïre." In *Women...,* pp. 41-52. Edited by R. Rohrlich-Leavitt. 1975.

Rubbo, Anna. "The Spread of Capitalism in Rural Colombia: Effects on Poor Women." In *Toward an Anthropology...,* pp. 333-57. Edited by R. Reiter. 1975.

Sacks, Karen. *Sisters and Wives. The Past and Future of Sexual Equality.* Westport, Conn.: Greenwood Press, 1979.

Saffioti, Heleith. *Women in Class Society.* Translated by Michael Vale. N.Y.: Monthly Review Press, 1978.

_____. "Women, Mode of Production, and Social Formations." *Latin American Perspectives* IV, nos. 1 and 2 (Winter/Spring 1977): 27-37.

Safilios-Rothschild, Constantina. "The Study of Family Power Structure: A Review 1960-1969." *Jour. of Marriage and the Family* XXXII, no. 4 (Nov. 1970): 539-52.

Sanjek, Roger. "New Perspectives on West African Women." *Reviews in Anthropology* III, no. 2 (1976): 115-34.

Saunders, Margaret O. "Women's Divorce Strategies in Mirria County, Niger Republic: Cases from the Tribunal de Premier Instance." Paper presented at African Studies Association Conference, Los Angeles. Oct. 31-Nov. 3, 1979.

Schiavo-Campo, Salvatore, and Singer, Hans W. *Perspectives of Economic Development.* Boston: Houghton-Mifflin Company, 1970.

Schildkrout, Enid. "Age and Gender in Hausa Society: Socio-Economic Roles of Children in Urban Kano." In *Sex and Age as Principles of Social Differentiation,* pp. 109-37. Edited by J. S. LaFontaine. N.Y.: Academic Press, 1978.

Schlegel, Alice, ed. *Sexual Stratification, A Cross-Cultural View.* N.Y.: Columbia University Press, 1977.

Schnaiberg, A., and Reed, D. "Risk, Uncertainty and Family Formation: The Social Context of Poverty Groups." *Population Studies* XXVIII, no. 3 (1974): 513-33.

Schumacher, E. F. *Small is Beautiful, Economics as if People Mattered.* N.Y.: Harper Colophon Books, 1973.

Schuster, Ilsa. "Marginal Lives: Conflict and Contradiction in the Position of Female Traders in Lusaka, Zambia." Paper presented at Women and Work in Africa Conference, University of Illinois, Urbana, Ill., April 29-May 1, 1979.

——————. *New Women of Lusaka.* Palo Alto: Mayfield Publishing Co., 1979.

Scribner, S., and Cole, M. "Cognitive Consequences of Formal and Informal Education." *Science,* no. 182 (Nov. 1973): 553-59.

Simon, Julian L. *The Effects of Income on Fertility.* Carolina Population Center Monograph No. 19. Chapel Hill: University of North Carolina, 1974.

Smith, Paul. "Domestic Labour and Marx's Theory of Value." In *Feminism...,* pp. 198-219. Edited by A. Kuhn and A. Wolpe. 1978.

Smith, Raymond T. "The Matrifocal Family." In *The Character...,* pp 121-44. Edited by J. Goody. 1973.

——————. *The Negro Family in British Guiana.* London: Routledge and Kegan Paul, 1956.

Smock, Audrey Chapman. "Conclusion: Determinants of Women's Roles and Status." In *Women...,* pp. 383-421. Edited by J. A. Giele and A. Smock. 1977.

Southall, A. W., ed. *Social Change in Modern Africa.* London: Oxford University Press/International African Institute, 1961.

——————. "Stratification in Africa." In *Essays in Comparative Social Stratification,* pp. 231-72. Edited by L. Plotnicov and and A. Tuden. Pittsburgh: University of Pittsburgh Press, 1970.

——————, ed. *Urban Anthropology: Cross-Cultural Studies of Urbanization.* London: Oxford University Press, 1973.

——————. "Urban Migration and the Residence of Children in Kampala." In *Peasants...,* pp. 170-92. Edited by W. Mangin. 1970.

Staudt, Kathleen. "Agricultural Productivity Gaps: A Case Study of Male Preference in Government Policy Implementation." *Development and Change* IX (1978): 439-57.

——————. "Class and Sex in the Politics of Women Farmers." *Jour. of Politics* IV, no. 2 (1979): 492-512.

Steel, William F. "The Small-Scale Sector's Role in Growth, Income Distribution and Employment of Women." Paper presented at joint African Studies Association/Latin American Studies Association Meeting, Houston, Nov. 2-5, 1977.

——————. "Toward Functional Definition of Firm Size: Alternatives to the 'Informal' Sector." Paper. Feb. 1979.

Strobel, Margaret. *Muslim Women in Mombasa 1890-1975*. New Haven: Yale University Press, 1979.

Sudarkasa, Niara. *Where Women Work: A Study of Yoruba Women in the Market-place and in the Home*. University of Michigan Museum of Anthropology, Anthropological Papers No. 53. Ann Arbor: Univeristy of Michigan Press, 1973.

Sutton, Constance, Makiesky, S., Dwyer, D. and Klein, L. "Women, Knowledge and Power." In *Women...*, pp. 581-600. Edited by R. Rohrlich-Leavitt. 1975.

Tadesse, Zenebworke. "Women and Technology in Peripheral Countries: An Overview." In *Scientific-Technological Change and the Role of Women in Development*, pp. 77-111. Edited by P. M. D'Onofrio-Flores and S. M. Pfafflin. Boulder: Westview Press, 1982.

Tiffany, Sharon W. "Models and the Social Anthropology of Women." *Man* XIII, no. 1 (March 1978): 34-51.

Trager, Lillian. "Urban Market Women: Hoarders, Hagglers, Economic Heroines?" Paper presented at African Studies Association Conference, Los Angeles, Oct. 31-Nov. 3, 1979.

Urdang, Stephanie. *Fighting Two Colonialisms, Women in Guinea-Bissau*. N.Y.: Monthly Review Press, 1979.

Uyanga, Joseph. "Family Size and the Participation of Women in the Labor Force: A Nigerian Case Study." *African Urban Notes* II, no. 2 (Spring 1976): 59-72.

Van De Walle, Etienne. "Marriage in African Censuses and Inquiries." In *The Demography...*, pp. 183-238. Edited by W. Brass et al. 1968.

Vaughan, Mary K. "Women, Class, and Education in Mexico, 1880-1928." *Latin American Perspectives* IV, nos. 1 and 2 (Winter/Spring 1977): 135-52.

Vidal, Claudine. "Guerre des sexes à Abidjan, Masculin, Féminin, CFA." *Cahiers d'Etudes Africaines* 65, XVII, no. 1 (1977): 121-53.

Wallerstein, Immanuel. "Class and Status in Contemporary Africa." In *African Social Studies...*, pp. 277-83. Edited by P. C. W. Gutkind and P. Waterman. 1977.

_____. "The Three Stages of African Involvement in the World Economy." In *The Political Economy...*, pp. 30-57. Edited by P. C. W. Gutkind and I. Wallerstein. 1976.

Weeks, J. "Employment and the Growth of Towns." In *The Population...*, pp. 146-56. Edited by R. P. Moss and R. J. A. R. Rathbone. 1975.

_____. "Wage Policy and the Colonial Legacy--A Comparative Study." *Jour. of Modern African Studies* IX, no. 3 (1971): 361-87.

Wellesley Editorial Committee. *Women and National Development: The Complexities of Change*. Chicago: University of Chicago Press, 1977.

Whetham, E. H., and Currie, J. I., eds. *Readings in the Applied Economics of Africa.* Vol. II. Cambridge: Cambridge University Press, 1967.

White, Frances. "Creole Women Traders in the Nineteenth Century." Boston University African Studies Center, Working Paper No. 27. 1980.

Whyte, Martin King. *The Status of Women in Preindustrial Societies.* Princeton, N.J.: Princeton University Press, 1978.

Wilson, Francille. "Reinventing the Past and Circumscribing the Future: *Authenticité* and the Negative Image of Women's Work in Zaïre." In *Women and Work in Africa,* pp. 153-70. Edited by E. Bay. Boulder: Westview Press, 1982.

Wise, Colin G. *A History of Education in British West Africa.* N.Y.: Longmans, Green and Co., 1956.

The Woman Question, Selections from the Writings of Marx, Engels, Lenin and Stalin. N.Y.: International Publishers, 1951.

Wright, E. O., and L. Perrone. "Marxist Class Categories and Income Inequality." *American Sociological Review* XLII (1977): 32-55.

Young, Kate. "Modes of Appropriation and the Sexual Division of Labour: A Case Study from Oaxaca, Mexico." In *Feminism...,* pp. 124-54. Edited by A. Kuhn and A. Wolpe. 1978.

_____, et al., eds. *Of Marriage and the Market.* London: CSE Books, 1981.

Youssef, Nadia H. "Women in Development: Urban Life and Labor." In *Women...,* pp. 70-77. Edited by M. B. Bramsen and I. Tinker. 1976.

Documents (no authors listed)

Ga National Archives.
     Ga Maŋtsɛ's Civil Court Record. 1922-24.
     Ga Maŋtsɛ's Court of Appeals, *Record Book.* 1919-24.
     Ga Maŋtsɛ's Court Proceedings. 1922-24.
     Ga Maŋtsɛ's Criminal Court Records. 1923-26.
     James Town Maŋtsɛ's Court Proceedings. 1919-36.

Ghana. Accra City Council.
     Accra City Handbook. 1977.

Ghana/Gold Coast. Census Office.
     Census of Population, 1891, 1901, 1911, 1921, 1931, 1948.
     Population Census of Ghana, 1960.

Ghana. Central Bureau of Statistics.
     Annual Report of the Labour Department. 1962-63.
     Economic Survey, 1961-64, 1965-68, 1969-71, 1972-74.
     Education Statistics, 1955-59, 1962-63, 1968-69.
     Population Census of Ghana, 1970.
     Statistical Handbook of the Republic of Ghana, 1969.

Statistical Yearbook of Ghana, 1961, 1963, 1965-66.

Ghana. Commission on University Education.
   Report on the Commission on University Education, Dec. 1960-Jan. 1961.

Ghana/Gold Coast.
   The Gold Coast Handbook, 1937.

Ghana/Gold Coast. Department of Social Welfare and Community Development.
   Groupwork, Welfare Manual No. 3, 1973.
   Welfare and Mass Education in the Gold Coast 1946-51.

Ghana. Ministry of Agriculture.
   Fisheries Research Report, 1962.

Ghana. Ministry of Education.
   *Digest of Education Statistics (Pre-University) 1976-77. Accra: Ghana Pub-
   lishing Corporation, 1978.*
   "The New Structure and Content of Education for Ghana." Feb. 1974.
   Reports, 1958-62.

Ghana. Ministry of Housing.
   Accra, A Plan for the Town. Accra: Government Printer, 1958.

Ghana/Gold Coast. Ministry of Labour.
   Report of the Gold Coast Ministry of Labour, 1953-54.
   Republic of Ghana Labour Statistics, 1964.

Ghana. National Archives.
   Basel Mission Papers. EC 7/19.
   District Commissioner's Court Records.
         Civil Court, Accra, 1875-1960. SCT 17/4/2-105.
         Criminal Court, Accra, 1875-1960. SCT 17/5/1-280.
   Gold Coast Administrative Papers. Secretary for Native Affairs.
         SNA and ADM Series.
   High Court Judgment Books.

Ghana. National Council on Women and Development (NCWD).
   "A Declaration on Women's Seminar held in Accra, June 7-8, 1975, on the
   Occasion of the International Woman's Year."

Ghana/Gold Coast. Office of the Secretary and Executive Officer.
   Town and Country Planning in the Gold Coast. Bulletin No. 2, [1950?].

Ghana/Gold Coast. Reports.
   Report of the Accra Earthquake Rehousing Committee, Gold Coast. 1940.
   ADM 5/3/37.
   Report of the Commission of Enquiry into Trade Malpractices in Ghana,
   1965.
   Report of the Education Committee, 1937-41. ADM 5/3/40.
   Report of Enquiry into Rentals, 1951. ADM 5/3/75.

Ghana. University of Ghana. Institute of Statistical, Social, and Economic
   Research (ISSER).
   "Economics of Operation of Outboard Motors in Ghana's Canoe Fisheries."
   1977.
   Survey of Ghana Middle Schools, 1967.

Great Britain. Colonial Office.

Annual Reports.

Great Britain. Public Record Office.
Papers of the Secretary of State for the Colonies.
Report Presented by the Secretary of State for the Colonies to Parliament, May 1941. Orde-Browne, Maj. G. St. J. *Labour Conditions in West Africa.*

United Nations Economic and Social Council.
Statistical Yearbook, 1950, 1963, 1968, 1970, 1972, 1975, 1978, 1982.

United Nations Economic and Social Council. Economic Commission for Africa.
Report of the Workshop on Urban Problems: The Role of Women in Urban Development. Sixth Session, Addis Ababa, Feb. 19-March 3, 1964. E/CN. 14/241.

United Nations. Food and Agriculture Organization.
The Economic Value of Breast-Feeding. Rome: 1979.
Management Training for Agricultural and Food Marketing. Rome: 1978.
Market Women in West Africa. Rome: 1977.
Training in Agricultural and Food Marketing at the Middle Level. Rome: 1974.
Training in Agricultural and Food Marketing at the University Level in Africa. Rome: 1976.
Women in Food Production, Food Handling and Nutrition, with Special Emphasis on Africa. Rome: 1979.

United States. American University Foreign Area Studies.
Area Handbook for Ghana. Washington, D.C.: U.S. Printing Office, 1971.

United States. Agency for International Development. Office of Women in Development.
"Report on Women in Development." Aug. 1978.
Women in Development Conference Report. 1975.

United States. Department of Commerce.
Country Demographic Profiles: Ghana. No. 2, ISP-30. Nov. 1973.

Newspapers, Periodicals

Accra Mirror (Accra).
Africa News.
Africa Report.
Africa Woman (Accra).
African Women (University of London Institute of Education).
Daily Graphic (Accra).
Famille et développement (Dakar).
Ghanaian Times (Accra).
Gold Coast Chronicle (Accra).
Gold Coast Echo (Accra).
Ideal Woman (Teiko Publications, New Times Corporation, Accra).
Small Industry Development Network Newsletter (Georgia Institute of Technology Office of International Programs).
Wall Street Journal (New York).
Western Echo (Cape Coast).

INDEX

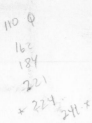